COMING
of AGE

COMING
of AGE

Teaching and Learning
Popular Music in Academia

EDITED BY

CARLOS XAVIER RODRIGUEZ

Maize Books

Published in the United States of America by Michigan Publishing
Manufactured in the United States of America

DOI: http://dx.doi.org/10.3998/mpub.9470277

ISBN 978-1-60785-383-1 (paper)
ISBN 978-1-60785-384-8 (e-book)

An imprint of Michigan Publishing, Maize Books serves the publishing needs of
the University of Michigan community by making high-quality scholarship widely
available in print and online. It represents a new model for authors seeking to
share their work within and beyond the academy, offering streamlined selection,
production, and distribution processes. Maize Books is intended as a complement to
more formal modes of publication in a wide range of disciplinary areas.

http://www.maizebooks.org

Contents

Acknowledgments

The purpose of Ann Arbor Symposium IV: Teaching and Learning Popular Music, held at the University of Michigan, November 18–21, 2015, was to represent the formidable presence of popular music research, scholarship, and teaching in colleges and universities. This book comprises essays from selected symposium presentations, which are intended to further promote the status of popular music in the curriculum. Contributions from the perspectives of music education, music theory, and musicology preserve the interdisciplinary purview of the symposium and reflect the essence of popular music at its finest—innovative, layered, and culturally rich human practice.

It has been my pleasure to edit this collection, and I would like to acknowledge the sources of support, inspiration, and expertise that made it all possible. First and foremost, I would like to thank University of Michigan School of Music, Theatre & Dance former dean Christopher Kendall, who provided initial funding for the symposium, and current dean Aaron Dworkin, who has so significantly championed the future role of popular music in the curriculum; the School of Music, Theatre & Dance and the University of Michigan Office of Research, contributors of additional funding toward the publication subvention for this book; the team of chapter reviewers who provided wisdom and guidance to authors—Patrick Hernly, Jere Humphreys, Jody Kerchner, Adam Kruse, Ed Sarath, Gareth Dylan Smith, and Dan Zanutto; Jason Coleman, director of Michigan publishing services, and Amanda Karby, digital publishing coordinator, for extended guidance through the production phase; and finally, the esteemed chapter authors who represent so well the breadth and integrity of popular music scholarship in higher education.

—Carlos Xavier Rodriguez

PART I

Discourses of Popular Music in Education

CHAPTER 1

The Politics of and in Teaching Popular Music

A RANCIÈRIAN VIEW

LAURI VÄKEVÄ
SIBELIUS ACADEMY OF THE UNIVERSITY OF THE ARTS

INTRODUCTION

This chapter[1] is a philosophical effort to understand the conditions of politics in teaching popular music. Even if I view the topic through lenses borrowed from Jacques Rancière, my approach can best be characterized as a variety of critical pragmatism. From a critical pragmatist perspective, popular music gains political meaning both from its inner workings and from its transformative potential. Thus I do not subscribe to a negative dialectical view of popular music that sees it simply as part of ideological machinery fine-tuned to prevent intellectual emancipation of its consumers (see Adorno 2002, chapter 3; Adorno and Horkheimer 2002 [1944], 94ff.). Rather, my guiding idea is that emancipation is as possible in popular music pedagogy as in any other field of education. Moreover, I am not at all sure that the success of popular music education should be only judged on the basis of intellectual emancipation. There might be a variety of pedagogical functions for popular music and they all might have different emancipatory potentials. I believe that critical pragmatism, when informed by Rancière's political and aesthetic philosophies, can offer us tools to understand these functions.

▎RANCIÈRE ON POLITICS, AESTHETICS, AND EDUCATION

Politics

A common dictionary definition sees politics as management or governing of public affairs. In academic textbooks, politics is often characterized as involving a public interest to reach consensus (Berndtson 2008). Deviating radically from such views, Rancière suggests that we see politics (*la politique*) as an outcome of disagreement between those whose voices are heard and those who are silenced in a society. Politics marks a "conflict over what is meant by 'to speak' and 'to understand'"; it is a dispute over "the horizons of perception that distinguish the audible from the inaudible, the comprehensible from the incomprehensible, the visible from the invisible" (Rancière 2006, 88). Such dispute emerges when someone claims a right to speak, understand, or be visible equal to those who already get themselves heard, understood, or seen. Thus politics is a subversive activity that will "make heard a discourse where once there was only place for noise; it makes understood as discourse what was once only heard as noise" (Rancière 1999, 30). Moreover, "politics only exists in intermittent acts of implementation that lack any overall principle or law" (Rancière 2006, 95). In other words, one cannot plan for politics to take place—only wait for it to happen. Such efforts are always exceptions, unpredicted ruptures in the social fabric.

Aesthetics

Whereas many philosophers place aesthetics and politics in different categories, Rancière makes a connection between them. For him, aesthetics (*l'esthétique*) covers more than appreciation of the arts or philosophical study of sense perception; it incorporates the "horizons of perception"— that is, the diverse ways in which we make distinctions in the sensible realm of everyday life. More specifically, "aesthetics" marks a "distribution of the sensible that determines a mode of articulation between forms of action, production, perception, and thought." This distribution also delineates "the conceptual coordinates and modes of visibility operative in the political domain" (86). What is at stake in politics, then, is precisely the distribution of the sensible, or "the system of self-evident facts of sense perception that simultaneously discloses the existence of something in common and the delimitations that define the respective parts and positions within it" (7).

Education

The primary function of social institutions is to maintain modes of articulation in the sensible realm as basis of social differentiation. This also applies to educational institutions. For Rancière, the primary function of schools is to sustain the "police order" (*l'ordre policier*) of the society by establishing an epistemic power structure that controls the distribution of the sensible. In his idiosyncratic terminology, "police order" refers to "a system of coordinates defining modes of being, doing, making, and communicating that establishes the borders between the visible and the invisible, the audible and the inaudible, the sayable and the unsayable" (93). Rancière observes school as a specific "model of an inequality which identifies itself with the visible difference between those who know and those who do not know and which devotes itself, visibly, to the task of teaching those who are ignorant that which they do not know . . . thus reducing such inequality" (Rancière 2010, 8).

Rancière (1991) highlights the significance of the critique of educational "policing" for understanding how politics finds its way into public life (see also Bingham and Biesta 2010; Chambers 2012). In *Le maître ignorant* (*The Ignorant Schoolmaster*), he suggests that political acts can also emerge inside the police order of the school, as long as the "schoolmasters" abandon their roles as "explicators" and "stultifiers" and accept that learning is not dependent on pedagogical structures but rather on each learner's ability and will to learn (Rancière 1991). Even if the teacher can influence the students' wills to learn, the students' abilities to learn are innate in the sense that they can learn practically anything in the same way they have learned their mother tongue—by gradually building the required competencies in informal transactions with other people and cultural products and by grasping the meanings of things by using them in everyday life (Dewey 2008b [1916], 19).[2]

For Rancière, this presupposition of each individual's potential to learn—what he calls the "axiom" of equal intelligence—provides an analogue for understanding democracy, for democracy is based on its own "axiom" of equality that assumes that everyone can partake in the "communal distribution of the sensible" (Rockhill 2006, xiii). Democracy is "an act of political subjectivization that disturbs the police order by polemically calling into question the aesthetic coordinates of perception, thought, and action." It is thus "an act of contention that implements various forms of dissensus" (Rancière 2006, 87). In Rancière's scheme, political agency emerges as a function of the emancipatory process of learning, or of finding oneself as a subject with a voice in a democratic community. Learning is at the heart of politics—and so is aesthetics.

While there might be a possibility for emancipatory learning in school, from Rancière's standpoint, such learning does not take place in the way that critical educationalists proclaim—that is, the students are not emancipated by the kinds of teachers who make it their mission to open their students' eyes to the ideologically masked social realities (see Bingham and Biesta 2010, 23–24). For Rancière, the teacher's task is not to close the epistemological gap between him or herself and his or her students by explicating how things are and why they are as they are. Rather, teachers should feed the spark of learning and help each student find his or her own learning trajectories, to use Wenger's term (Wenger 1998). This necessitates that teachers are able and willing to make a distinction between two logics—namely, the logic of "the act of intellectual emancipation" and the logic of "the institution of the people's instruction"—and critically look for ways they can support the former in the conditions established by the latter (Rancière 2010, 9).

Emancipatory pedagogies, when successful, can help students empower themselves as political subjects, bringing forth new "identities that were not part of and did not exist in the existing order" (Bingham and Biesta 2010, 35). Consequently, becoming a political subject is as much a matter of learning how to be oneself as a matter of social adjustment. At the heart of emancipation is what Rancière calls "subjectification": "the production through a series of actions of a body and a capacity for enunciation not previously identifiable within a given field of experience, whose identification is thus part of the reconfiguration of the field of experience" (Rancière 1999, 35). Becoming oneself, politically speaking, is a poietic act in the sense that it generates new agencies. Such production of agencies is also the core process of democracy. Instead of seeing democracy merely as "a form of government" or "a system of social life" that adjusts the interests of disparate parties, Rancière sees it as "random process that redistributes the system of sensible coordinates without being able to guarantee the absolute elimination of the social inequalities inherent in the police order" (Rockhill 2006, xiv–xv). Like John Dewey, Rancière conceives democracy as a continuous project, but more so than Dewey, he emphasizes the uniqueness of its constitutive political acts.

Let us sum up at this point: From the Rancièreian perspective, politics is based on dissident impulses that stem from the attempts of individuals to operate along with the axiom of equality. The potential of such dissident impulses is realized in political acts—that is, in particular "sensible events" that redistribute the aesthetic realm, restaging our relationships to each other and to the things around us (Rancière 2006, xi; Holmboe 2014). As such, political acts are productive, and what they produce are new sensible orders—new configurations of the aesthetic. In Rancière's (2006) own words, there is "an 'aesthetics' at the core of politics," and vice versa (8). Any intervention that has the power to disrupt the distribution of the sensible can be seen as a political act, even if it would not lead into major improvements in society. Such interventions are also possible in school, the prototypical police order of the modern society.

One interesting consequence of Rancière's view is that power emerges from politics rather than producing it. While power is invested in politics, what precedes the emergence of both politics and power is the police order, the organized distribution of the sensible. Here we can observe a disparity between Rancière and Michel Foucault. Whereas Foucault (1990) understands power as a condition of political action and claims that all resistance is based on power (95), for Rancière (1999), "nothing is political . . . merely because power relationships are at work in it." Still, "anything may become political" as far as it "gives rise to a meeting of . . . two logics"—namely, the logic of the police order and the logic of politics proper (32). If this is true, popular music can become political as well, and its political significance does not have to have anything to do with advocating a commitment—that is, music can gain political significance without making an explicit statement.

▎ WHAT MAKES ART POLITICAL?

Even if Rancière accepts that politics can take place in any realm of social life, he takes a special interest in art as a scene where such acts are staged. In his view, the aesthetic practices characteristic of art can point at radically new possibilities of reconfiguring the social order, or new ways to define "what is common to the community" (Rancière 2006, 8). Thus art provides important study object for understanding how aesthetics is tangled in politics and the other way around. (Note that Rancière talks about "art" in singular rather than in plural; why this is so, I will discuss shortly.)

Again, actualization of the political potential of art does not necessitate that artworks have to transmit explicit ideological messages. While there are "politics of art that are perfectly identifiable" (58), Rancière claims that "political art cannot work in the simple form of a meaningful spectacle that would lead to an awareness' of the state of the world" (59). In short, art does not have to preach in order to teach. An artist does not have to open the eyes of his or her audience to social realities in order to realize the political potential of his or her work. Rancière even claims that political "commitment" is not "a category of art" (56). In the same way that politics incorporates its own aesthetics that are not dependent on artistic commitment, art implicates its own politics that instead of making us aware of "the state of the world" (59) defines new "forms of community laid out by the very regime of identification in which we perceive art" (56). In Rancière's point of view, this political function of art is primary to any overt political messages it might transmit.

Instead of conveying its political message directly, then, art can display its political significance in the interlaced fields of the primary aesthetics of the distribution of the sensible and the secondary aesthetics of art-specific expression. This makes analysis of political art much more complex issue than decoding politically intended messages. As Rancière puts it, there is not one way to define a "criterion for establishing a correspondence between aesthetic virtue and political virtue"; a work of art that can be judged as having important political value in certain context can be criticized as kitsch in another (57). We have to understand artistic-political acts against their historical, social, and cultural contexts.

In terms of Rancière's political theory, artistic practices can be charged with political potential to a degree that they can help us locate fundamental injustices in how the sensible realm is distributed in the society—that is, on the level of the primary aesthetics (Rancière 1999). An added bonus is that such practices can suggest ways to adjust society's "wrongs," but this is not necessary for their political potential to actualize. Nevertheless, this possibility provides art a twofold nature that reflects Rancière's nominalist belief that "the political universal only takes effect in singularized form" (48). Or, to put the same idea in the somewhat cryptic words of Slavoj Žižek (2007), art can demonstrate how "the Singular" appears "as a stand-in for the Universal, destabilizing the 'natural' functional order of relations in the social body" (183). According to Rancière (2006), the power of the singular to stand in for the universal is accountable for the power of art to produce "a double effect" that is based, on the one hand, on "the readability of a political signification" and, on the other hand, on "a sensible or perceptual shock caused . . . by the uncanny, by that which rests signification" (59). Note how this reflects the duality of the two logics of politics discussed previously. Art, when actualizing its political potential, introduces something novel into the sensible realm, shaking the aesthetic order. This possibility is the origin of artistic creativity, and it is also the source of art's impact as political force.

POPULAR MUSIC AS ART AND POLITICAL FORCE

I would next like to try to elaborate the argument that popular music can be seen as a political force in the double sense discussed in the previous section. My claim is that there can be politics *of* popular music as well as politics *in* popular music. Moreover, I suggest that it would be good for music educators to be aware of both these modes of politics and to detect their particular manifestations as individual acts of expression. In order to back up these ideas, it is useful to delve deeper into Rancière's philosophy of art.

Note the thrice-repeated disclaimer in what I just wrote. Such caution is needed because, as Rancière remarks, even if art and politics find a mutual point of reference in the primary aesthetic realm of the sensible, they are still "contingent notions," which means that it is not easy to identify their points of intersection (Rancière 2006). In the same way that the fact that "there are always forms of power does not mean that there is always such a thing as politics," the fact that "there is [for instance] music . . . in a society does not mean that art is [yet] constituted as an independent category" (47). There is more in this claim than the modest observation that art (including music) might not be understood in the same way in every society. Rancière actually argues that "art," in singular, is a specific product of historical processes that redefine the relationship between "arts," in plural, or "ways of doing and making" (17), and thus, the political significance of what is done and made.

The Aesthetic Regime of Art

The realization of the historical singularity of art emerges from what Rancière (2013) calls "the aesthetic regime of art": "a form of specific experience" that "has only existed in the West since the end of the eighteenth century" (ix, xii). This claim is based on an observation that it is possible to discern three historically distinct but culturally overlapping "regimes of identification" "with regard to what we call *art*" (Rancière 2006, 16).

First, "the ethical regime of images" did not yet recognize art as such but "subsumed it under the question of images." This question asked where different ways of doing and making come from and what they are for. The fundamental distinction between arts proper (as imitations of the truth) and arts as appearance (as imitations of imitations) was based on this twofold question. Plato famously made this distinction, arguing that the only arts really worth practicing are those that imitate actions that have precise ends. Such actions are also pedagogically significant, as they indicate the respective positions in the community for different social groups, thus maintaining harmony in the city-state. Virtually launching the Western philosophical discourse over the pedagogical value of the arts, Plato claimed that only such productive actions that imitate what is true, good, and beautiful have ethical value and are suitable for liberal education. According to Rancière, this ethical judgment of the value of the arts established a lasting hierarchy in the poietic realm that made it impossible to think about art "as such" for a long time (16).

Second, ethical regime of images replaced the "poetic—or representative—regime of the arts." This regime identified the substance of the arts on the basis of the dual principle of mimesis/poiesis. Drawing inspiration from Aristotle, the poetic regime of the arts isolated each way of doing or making to its own productive domain on the basis of what kinds of imitations it produced. The principle regulating this compartmentalization also became a "normative principle of inclusion," as it defined the conditions on which certain ways of doing and making can be identified as artistic. Furthermore, it defined the value of artistic products in terms of how "good or bad, adequate or inadequate" they are based on the criteria relevant to each domain. The principle of poiesis thus demarcated artistic genres, whereas the principle of mimesis offered guideposts for assessing the respective worth of their outcomes.

The poetic regime also established a new "regime of visibility" that defined the conditions of who could be counted as an artist. This differentiation of the social role of artists eventually rendered "the arts autonomous" and linked their autonomy to a more "general order of occupations and ways of doing and making." Thus, the poetic regime of the arts established a new distribution of the sensible in Western societies, introducing a new police order in the aesthetic realm. Rancière argues that this order was based on a "logic of representation," which entered "into a relationship . . . with an overall hierarchy of political and social occupations," defining a "fully hierarchical vision of the community" (17).

Finally, with the emergence of the "aesthetic regime," the "identification [of art] no longer occur[red] via a division within ways of doing and making." Rather, identification of art was now "based on distinguishing a sensible mode of being specific to artistic products" (18). This new regime broke with three principles of judgment characteristic of the poetic regime: (1) the "hierarchy of high and low subjects and genres," (2) the "Aristotelian superiority of action over life," and (3) the "traditional scheme of rationality" that was defined "in terms of ends and means, causes and effects" (Rancière 2005, 14). Liberating art "from any specific rule . . . hierarchy . . . subject matter, and genre," the aesthetic regime also destroyed "the mimetic barrier that distinguished ways of doing and making affiliated with art from other ways of doing and making" (Rancière 2006, 19). Thus art became to be seen as a general qualifier applicable to any creative act that has the potential to transform the conditions of our "sensory apprehension" (Rancière 2009, 29).

This redefinition of art as particular acts of creation of new aesthetic order made it a heteronomous matter. Aesthetic quality could now be claimed by any work that fits itself into "a specific sensorium," finding itself "a mode of being" where it could be perceived as art (ibid.). Connected to this, art lost its specific place in the social order and became nomadic. The "artification" of common objects and events in contemporary art can be taken as archetypal form of such nomadic being, or rather becoming (Erjavec 2012). In the aesthetic regime of art, any ready-made object—a soap box, a cauliflower, a urinal, or ambient or industrial noise—can become an artwork or a part of an artwork, and it is not the artist's technical skill but his or her vision that defines the aesthetic status of such works. Rancière's notion of "art as life" (Rancière 2009, 51) grasps this heteronomy of artistic expression well: rather than just "made," art is "lived through," or "experienced," as Dewey would say (Dewey 2008d [1934], 10; see also Shusterman 1992).

Again, Rancière makes a distinction between two coexisting "politics of aesthetics" that define the coordinates of art within the aesthetic regime: (1) the politics of the "becoming-life of art" and (2) the politics of the "resistant form" (Rancière 2009, 44). As described by Berrebi (2008), in the first instance, "the aesthetic experience . . . tends to dissolve into other forms of life"; art becomes life, life becomes art. In the second kind of politics, "the political potential of the aesthetic experience derives from the separation of art from other forms of activity and its resistance to any transformation into a form of life" (2). Hence the very aloofness of art as cultural determinant provides it political significance. As nomads, artists can point at—and inhabit—new places and positions in the sensible reality, transforming our common ways of perceiving.

Moreover, "in the aesthetic regime of art, the future of art, its separation from . . . non-art, incessantly restages the past" (Rancière 2006, 20). Thus the aesthetic regime is not defined by modernist appeal to autonomy, uniqueness, and authenticity of the artist's vision "that links the conquests of artistic innovation to the victories of emancipation" (4). Rather, Rancière uses the concept of the aesthetic regime to criticize discourses of modernism, claiming that both modern and postmodern theories of art are but "imaginary stories about artistic 'modernity'" that inform "vain debates over the autonomy of art or its submission to politics" (13). For Rancière, "artistic modernity" itself is an "incoherent label" for historical changes in artistic practices, unable to grasp the complexity of the phenomena that can be best discussed under the notion of the aesthetic regime of art (19).

Justifying Popular Music as Art in the Classroom
At this point, two questions emerge: (1) What are the conditions for understanding popular music as art in the aesthetic regime? and (2) What are the conditions of understanding politics in connection to popular music in this regime?

Perhaps for some readers, to question the artistic value of popular music might seem anachronistic, a distant echo of the cultural wars of the 1960s and 1970s, put to rest by postmodern cultural critics who toward the end of the last millennium brought down the walls between high and popular culture (e.g., Shusterman 1992; McRobbie 1994; Gracyk 1996). There have been also music and music education scholars who have questioned the feasibility of judging music in aesthetic terms. Some of these scholars have pointed at the practical nature of music in general, arguing that it is pointless to try to find music a common nominator from aesthetic theories that are based on the idea of autonomy of the artwork (e.g., Alperson 1991; Elliott 1995; Regelski 1996, 2000; Bowman 2000). Yet it is still not uncommon to find philosophers, critics, and teachers who object to the inclusion of popular music in education on the basis of aesthetic criteria (e.g., Scruton 1999; Bayles 2004; Walker 2007). While I am not sympathetic toward such views, I do suggest that the issue of legitimation is important for music educators to deal with. After all, all of us eventually find ourselves in a position where we have to make value judgments about what we teach and justify such choices for our students, the powers that be, and ourselves. To paraphrase Rancière, such selection is part and parcel of the policing function of educational institutions, and it is impossible to avoid it when working within such contexts.

The issue of curricular justification of popular music is made even more complex when one observes that there are differences in educational cultures regarding what is taken as appropriate repertoire for musical classrooms. For instance, while rock music is accepted as classroom repertoire in many countries (including my own), in many other countries (such as the United States), it is still uncommon to find rock songs rehearsed during school music lessons (although the situation seems to be changing rapidly with the emergence of such initiatives as Little Kids Rock). Even in more lenient educational systems, there are popular genres and styles that teachers are not willing to accept as part of classroom repertoire. For instance, in a recent study, Alexis Kallio (2015) found that in order to avoid conflicts, Finnish music teachers often feel the need to navigate "the school censorship frame"—that is, the "broad and specific social narratives that draw associations between particular musics or songs and socially constructed notions of deviance" (ii). Such navigation is especially needed in situations where teachers have to decide whether to censure popular songs that imply such themes as overt nationalism, religion, sexuality, and ethnicity. While it can be argued that these decisions are part of every teacher's work as cultural gatekeepers, they can also be seen as problematic if they give the student the message that "your music is not welcome in school" (i). Kallio suggests that through "recognizing, reflecting upon, and engaging with the political processes of legitimation and exclusion in popular repertoire selection . . . teachers and students may learn beyond bias and assumption, engage in collaborative critical inquiry, and interrogate who music education serves, when, why, how and to what ends" (ii). From this standpoint, to constantly reflect on the selection criteria of the repertoire is important in order to maintain critical distance to what is taught and learned in musical classrooms.

Even if censuring of popular music in classrooms does not have to mean that it is not accepted as art outside the school walls, it is still interesting to focus on the reasons at least some forms of popular music are disregarded in music education and to reflect on the possible philosophical ramifications of such patterns of exclusion. In what follows, I will present critical pragmatism as a possible philosophical point of departure for judging popular music as pedagogically legitimate study content. I will also apply critical pragmatism as a tool to reexamine Rancière's notions of how, why, and when art-in-singular becomes a political category through the more specific questions of how, why, and when popular music suggests political potential.

CRITICAL PRAGMATISM AND THE POLITICAL
POTENTIAL OF POPULAR MUSIC AS ART

The variety of critical pragmatism I am interested in this context can be traced, on the one hand, to John Dewey's middle and later works and, on the other hand, to the critical educational approaches based on the ideas developed by the social theorist of the first Frankfurt school. I will next provide an aerial view of how I understand these two sets of ideas before continuing to more specific questions.

John Dewey's Naturalist Pragmatism on
Experience, Education, and Art
Naturalist Pragmatism

In his middle and later works, Dewey established a complex system of philosophical ideas that later commentators have labeled "pragmatist naturalism" or "naturalist pragmatism," depending on the emphasis (e.g., Väkevä 2003, 2004; Aikin 2006).[3] Here I will examine this system of ideas from the pedagogical standpoint. After all, while Dewey was once titled "leading living philosopher of America" (Russell 2013 [1946], 646), most people today identify him as pioneer of contemporary pedagogical thought and as a key architect of the progressive education movement. Pedagogical perspective also helps us focus on the relationship between Deweyan naturalist pragmatism and critical theory.

From the pedagogical standpoint, the term *naturalism* simply reminds us that learning is based on natural processes of interaction between an organism and its environment. The more evolved the organism is, the more complex such processes become, and the more efficient tools the organism can develop for coping with its habitat. Culture can be understood as a set of habits that help human organisms effectively adapt to their living environment. Preservation of the human species is dependent on both natural and cultural adaptation, meaning that we cannot understand human development and growth without paying attention to both of these levels.

Dewey's insistent use of the word *experience* to refer to complex systems of organic adaptation confused many empirically inclined contemporaries, who had been accustomed to using the term to refer to amassed sense perception. The word *pragmatism* reminds us that Dewey looked at human life from a holistic viewpoint, where adaptive systems of action make experience a unity. To the degree that such adaptive systems are based on symbolically mediated social interactions, experience can be shared and understood. What makes Dewey's holistic view of experience "pragmatist" is the recognition of the functional nature of physical, cognitive, and sociocultural adaptations, and thus all learning, development, and growth. We learn in order to learn more, and the value of what we learn is judged in terms of how successfully we can act in future situations. As Alison Kadlec (2007) puts it, we learn "to improve our individual and shared capacity to tap into the critical potential of lived experience in a world that is unalterably characterized by flux and change" (7).

Art as Inquiry

One upshot of this naturalist pragmatist view is that learning is always both situational and contextual. This means that one learns when one aims to solve problems encountered in the specific circumstances of one's daily life. Such "problems" are not merely cognitive; they permeate human experience, and we encounter them on all three "plateaus" of our lives: physical, psychological, and cultural (Dewey 2008c [1925], 208). To solve problems is to commit "inquiry," which Dewey uses as generic name for all processes that help us cope with the world more effectively and fruitfully (Dewey 2008e [1938], 12). "Art" can also be understood as a mode of inquiry. In turn, what we identify as "the arts," music included, can be understood as more or less systematic attempts to solve problems that emerge from our interactions with nature and culture. Whereas Rancière connects art-in-singular with the aesthetic regime, Dewey does not make a historical distinction between the arts as ways of doing and making and art as an aesthetic discipline. Based on the naturalist background of his mature philosophy, he sees all artistic endeavors as deriving from the same root, sharing characteristics that define their value as specifically human pursuits to understand and enjoy life. In Dewey's analysis, even the most "ethereal" things that art critics elevate above everyday experience can be seen as outcomes of culturally coordinated natural processes of adaptation (Dewey 2008d [1934]). This naturalist premise explains Dewey's claim that in order to understand the aesthetic moments of life, we must inspect experience "in the raw," observing how enjoyment can be found from absorption in everyday activities (10).

Among other arts, music can be understood as a culturally differentiated practice based on our tendency to inquire what is valuable in life. Because music can elevate experience high above the "threshold of perception," it can also make us enjoy our everyday activities (63). There is no a priori difference among genres, styles, or idioms of music that would make some of these forms more valuable than others. While Dewey does grant a place for "classics" in his aesthetics, he highlights their practical value: a "work of art no matter how old and classic is actually, not just potentially, a work of art only when it lives in some individualized experience" (113). Moreover, Dewey does not endorse a hard distinction between highbrow and lowbrow taste: all human beings have a propensity to enjoy aesthetic phenomena in the arts in the same way that all human beings are able to enjoy aesthetic phenomena in nature. It is only because of certain contingent socioeconomic conditions—conditions that Rancière would identify with the police order of the society—that some modes of aesthetic experience are placed above others. For Dewey, understanding art as inquiry is a powerful way to contest such hierarchies.

Art as Consummatory Experience

To say that art is a mode of inquiry is to highlight its poietic, or creative, character. In a book called *Pragmatism and Social Theory*, Hans Joas (1993) presents a characterization of pragmatism as philosophy of creative action. Instead of judging pragmatist philosophy as mere doctrine of natural adjustment, Joas highlights its notion of "situated freedom," arguing that, for the pragmatists, meaningfulness of action is as important as adaptation to environing conditions (4). Such a view clearly characterizes Dewey's later writings, where he often routes his discussion of the naturalist function of inquiry through aesthetics, highlighting the importance of "esthetic" experiences as meaningful "consummations" of human life (Dewey 2008c [1925], 2008d [1934]).

In Deweyan reading, "esthetic experience" is a function of our immediate relationship with qualities of life. Art is born directly out of this relationship: it offers us ways to inquire into the meaning-potential of immediate experience in a sharable medium. A painting, statue, or symphony does not epitomize the work of art for Dewey; rather, the artwork is what these "art products" (or artistic performances) do "with and in experience" (2008d [1934], 9). For Dewey, the most important function of art is to help us encounter and enjoy the qualities of life as they come by in everyday experience. Every now and then, experiences are rounded out by a singular aesthetic quality that binds them together into a single unit. The result is a specific phenomenological state, an experience, in which one can feel unity with the world and perceive a strong emotional sense of belonging to it. Whenever such moments occur, the aesthetic potential of experience-as-art has been consummated.

Art as Communication
For Dewey, art is also communication—but not merely in the sense that it conveys messages. Rather, to communicate in art is to share an experience with others. Such communication can be a momentary encounter between two persons, or it can leave its imprint on a whole society. In a similar vein, Rancière (2006) locates the appearance of art-in-singular as marking a special moment when "people, a society, an age" are "taken at a certain moment in the development of its collective life," introducing a new relationship between "the artist's personality and the shared world that gives rise to it and that it expresses" (14). Again, Rancière's understanding of artistic communication is histori-cally more focused than Dewey's. For Dewey, in any artistic communi-cation, an aesthetic realm is made common, producing the conditions of what can be called "aesthetic community" (Pappas 2008, 299). Instead of merely establishing a relationship between the artist and his or her audience, Dewey suggests that art can enhance commu-nity life by providing possibilities to share consummatory experiences. Again, there is no a priori reason popular music could not provide such possibilities.

Critical Theory and Popular Music Education
Dewey's educational ideas are well known in the pedagogical academic discourse, and there is no need to scrutinize them further here. I have

reviewed Dewey's naturalist pragmatism in order to pay attention to the ideas underlying his mature educational thought and his egalitarian views that grant aesthetic potential for any artistic expression. More important than examining the naturalist pragmatist underpinnings of Dewey's philosophy in this connection is exploring how his ideas have been contested by the critical pedagogical theories and what kinds of implications such encounters can have to our main problem—that of locating politics in popular music education.

Culture Criticism as a Basis for Judging the Pedagogical Value of Popular Music

In Dewey (2008b [1916], 9), the most important function of education is to provide tools for enriching community life by expanding the scope of our meaningful interactions with nature and culture. Like all education, art education should be student centered in the sense that students' experiences (that are partially shared) provide a laboratory for inquiring the pedagogical relevance of the subject matter (see also Dewey 2008a [1899], 1). The cultural milieu of students is an important point of reference for judging the significance of what is learned. To close students' everyday experiences out of the selection of the subject matter would be to neglect the situationality and contextuality of learning.

Deweyan naturalist pragmatism encourages teachers to select educational content that is relevant for their students' lives. From this standpoint, it would be hard to argue against including popular music in education. As Dewey wrote in 1934, aesthetic consummations can be found from daily encounters with such popular forms as "the movie, jazzed music [sic], the comic strip," as well as from contemplation of classical masterpieces (Dewey 2008c [1934], 11). While Dewey was critical to the most industrialized forms of creativity (e.g., "newspaper accounts of love-nests, murders, and exploits of bandits" [11–12]), he obviously had different view of the aesthetic and educational value of popular culture than many of his contemporaries.

In this respect, there is a particularly striking contrast between Dewey and the first Frankfurt school theorists. The latter saw popular culture as an outcome of an entertainment industry of standardized products that are distributed in mass media to sustain the ignorant oblivion of common people, anaesthetizing their political sensibilities (see Adorno and Horkheimer 2002 [1944]). Such a view leaves little room for discussing the political significance of popular music, except in the negative sense that it offers examples of ideological oppression.

One can understand critical theory as a system of ideas that aims to empower and emancipate people from ideologically controlled domination of social systems of government. Such systems aim to maintain the economic conditions introduced by modern capitalism. In contemporary educational discourse, critical theory reminds us of the need to emancipate students from the disenfranchising effects of the neoliberal economy that are reflected in the epistemological regime that drives public education. In its most productive form, such emancipation takes place with the help of theory-driven scrutiny of the social conditions of learning. The task of the critical educator is to lead his or her students to recognize links between their individual learning experiences and the social-cultural context in which such experiences become meaningful. Critical consciousness is openly political: it attempts to make sense of ideational structures that discipline our minds, aiming at social transformation through open confrontation with the ideologically obscured conditions of oppression.

Famously, Paulo Freire (1970) called such open confrontation of the forces of oppression "praxis," drawing a link between his "pedagogy of the oppressed" and the Marxist idea of theory-driven action as a vehicle of transformation. This ideal of transformation has also characterized critical music education philosophy in association with views that do not settle for pointing at music's universal practical nature but demand political consciousness from the music teachers in the form of developing an ability to reflect on musical practices and products in terms of their possible harmful societal outcomes (Regelski 2005, 2013). In this reading, "praxis" indicates "those actions that bring about right results qualified with regard to situated variables and criteria of success" (Regelski 2005, 21). What the "right results" and "criteria of success" are is a contextual matter. Still, critically oriented music educators should be able to find normative criteria that help them make a distinction between emancipatory pedagogy and stultification (to use Rancière's terms). However, such judgment is a highly complex matter. To educate toward critical consciousness necessitates negotiating over what (and whose) theories are most suitable in explaining the cultural context of learning and how they are best applied to the concrete situations of social life.

One realm where such negotiations seem to be inevitable is the selection of teaching content. This takes us back to the question of how to judge popular music as classroom repertoire. Whereas Dewey's educational philosophy can be criticized for making the child's immature experience an unquestionable point of departure for pedagogy, in *Democracy and Education*, he argued that it is the duty of the educator to distinguish between pedagogically valuable and invaluable subject matter (Dewey 2008b [1916]; see also *Experience and Education*, Dewey 2008e [1938], 1–62). The teacher has to weed "out what is undesirable" and expand the student's semiotic reach in ways that reveal the social significance of what he or she is about to learn (Dewey 2008b [1916], 24).

Dewey's call for weeding out what is undesirable in education can be interpreted through many different lenses, but it seems likely that he meant that the subject matter should be selected by paying attention to the more extensive social needs of the democratic community. This selection process can be associated with cultural criticism in the sense that the latter requires consciousness of the ideological and political underpinnings of the curricular choices. What critical pedagogy adds to this is that selection of the teaching content necessarily involves conflict—or at least tension— between individual needs of subjectification and society's need to subject its members. As both Ira Shor (1992, 13) and Michael Apple (1995, 142) argue, what we choose to teach in our classrooms is a political decision, and any selection of teaching content is always a complex and contested issue. To apply Shor's and Apple's wisdom to our case, we can question the pedagogical relevance of popular music even when its selection would be based on our students' preferences (compare with Green 2009). However, we should also challenge views that see popular music categorically as aesthetically inferior subject matter. Any musical genre, style, idiom, work, or piece of music can be educationally relevant if dealt with in the proper context, and to find out how, we should be open to the metalevel of criticism that informs our attempts to judge the pedagogical value of cultural forms. While it might be true that not all music is appropriate for all educational contexts, the worst we can do is close out the possibility of negotiating over the selection criteria.

Indeed, if we follow Rancière, any artistic expression in the sonic domain can be seen as a potentially political act. Elsewhere, I have suggested that digital music culture offers creative possibilities beyond conventional ways of organizing the sonic space, as exemplified by the work of sound artists and digital musicians that cross aesthetic domains fluently, recycling cultural artifacts in freewheeling manner (Väkevä 2010, 2012, 2013; see also Mullane 2010; Moreino and Stegno 2012). To a degree that music educators can tap into such possibilities, they can convert the policed spaces of music classrooms into political places where sonic landscapes can be transformed in ways that herald new sensibilities and, perhaps, more democratic aesthetic orders (see also Kanellopoulos 2015; Väkevä, Westerlund, and Juntunen 2015). While it should be recognized that the aesthetic spaces of digital artistry are conditioned by global economic interests, we might also celebrate the fact that digital commodification of music offers new possibilities for creativity (Burnard 2012).

Digital production, reproduction, and dissemination of music also offer ways to explore what Rancière seems to take as self-evident—namely, the fact that in the aesthetic regime of art, there are no clear-cut boundaries between "police order" and "politics." Politics materializes in cultural fields that are already aesthetically structured by the police order. To search for authentic expressions that avoid heteronomies that such structuring processes produce would be to fall into the modernist error of thinking that there should be something pure or original about an artist's work. From Rancière's standpoint, heteronomy requires autonomy and vice versa. This observation has reverberations to the discussion about singularity and universality I touched upon previously. It is only against the aesthetic regime framed by expectations of what an artwork can achieve in society that we can witness the full political impact of art. In music education, this suggests that we should be able to look at both sides of the double bind between music as teaching repertoire and as political action. On the one hand, we should recognize the politics of music based on "the readability of a political signification" in musical repertoire. On the other hand, we should understand politics in music as that "which rests signification," thus providing new possibilities of subjectification and political agency.

CONCLUSION

From the aforementioned standpoint, the most important task of the music educator is to coordinate specific learning situations in ways that transform the students' experiences toward more critically informed ways to participate in social-cultural life. This is also where naturalist pragmatists and critical theorists seem to find a common terrain. Indeed, in recent decades, several educationalists have worked on conceptual frames that mix cultural criticism and pragmatist perspectives (e.g., Giroux and McLaren 1994; Apple 1995). According to these writers, there is always tension between the freedom of an individual to construct new cultural reality in symbolic practices and the ideologically framed symbolic order that delimits such efforts—or, in Rancièrian terms, politics and police order. What critically prepared music educators can do in such conditions is help their students determine how the current symbolic orders afford reconstruction of meaning by looking for new critical possibilities in musical-cultural texts and processes. Rancière can be useful in understanding this pursuit, as he shows that political resistance is conditioned by existing distribution of the sensible that can be contested by specific acts of expression that can help us claim new discursive spaces. Such reclaiming of discursive space can take place as well in the classroom as outside the school walls, and it does not have to lead to major improvements in society. Yet all social improvement begins from particular attempts to redistribute the sensible; in this sense, all instances of redistribution of the sensible carry political potential, including those that are characteristic of popular culture.

Rancière's philosophy suggests that there cannot be a universal rationale for understanding how politics figures in popular music. Likewise, politics of (and in) popular music education is as multifaceted and unexpected as politics in other realms of shared experience. The most music educators can do is help their students find themselves in situations that allow for political acts to emerge as artistic expressions. In my critical pragmatist reading, this means that however politics finds its way into music education, its appearance is based as much on the personal needs of the students to find new meanings in the sonic-cultural space as on their more general level need to transgress received perceptual orders. Hence, if popular music education wants to build on Rancièrian notions, music educators need to accept that their work is more than enculturation or socialization of their students to existing musical practices (or praxes). The task of a critically astute music educator is to empower his or her students to seek new niches for expressive acts in musical cultures that in one way or another can rearrange the distribution of the sensible in the realm of both primary and secondary aesthetics—that is, the realm of the sensible writ large and the specific realm of artistic expression. I will finish this chapter by suggesting one way in which music educators can rationalize such projects.

While most critical theorists following the teachings of the first Frankfurt school mistrusted the emancipatory value of popular culture, there was one interesting exception in their ranks. Whereas Adorno saw popular arts as providing a false illusion of freedom, denying the aesthetic potential of all mass-mediated cultural expressions, Walter Benjamin (2008 [1936]) defended the aesthetic value of art based on "mechanical reproduction." Benjamin's argument was based on the premise that even if art loses its authenticity (or "aura") in the age of mechanical reproduction, and even if such auraless art offers itself easily to commodification, the very possibility of mechanical reproduction also "frees the work of art . . . from its existence as a parasite upon ritual" providing new possibilities of subjectification. In such conditions, Benjamin argues, art begins to be based on politics (sec. IV). This is because "mechanical reproduction . . . changes the reaction of the masses toward art" by transforming the sheer "quantity" of the available cultural products to new "quality" of perception (sec. XII, XV). Through constant exposure to reproductive art, "the masses" can learn to utilize their newly cumulated critical power and, in this way, build a new participatory culture where "the distinction between author and public is about to lose its basic character" (sec. X). With such development, the distinction between production and consumption becomes indistinct, providing everyone means of partaking in conjoint projects that transform the prevalent ways of cultural production. One way to make this happen is to liberate cultural objects from their original context of production by recombining and juxtaposing "the leftover cultural fragments," thus creating new demands for aesthetic enjoyment

(Moore 2012). In this way, the means of cultural production can be social-ized, and everyone can become an artist.

While Rancière sympathizes with Benjamin's attempt to show that mechanical reproduction is not a deathblow to people's ability to subject art under cultural criticism, he opposes Benjamin's attempt to deduce "the aesthetic and political properties of a form of art from its technical properties" (Rancière 2006, 27). Rancière suggests that we turn "things the other way around" and acknowledge that "in order for the mechani-cal arts to be able to confer visibility on the masses . . . they first need to be recognized as [art]" (28). Such recognition can only take place if "mechanical arts" are situated in the aesthetic regime, which presupposes a new way of thinking that can provide the conditions for identifying art-in-singular-as-political-act (27). In the case of popular music, we could then argue that we need to relate the technical modes of its production and reproduction to the general conditions of the aesthetic regime of art, making visible (and audible) its political potential.

How can this be achieved in music classrooms? Following Benja-min and Rancière, I suggest that music educators focus on how politics emerges in popular music specifically in two areas: (1) redistribution of musical sound in the digital culture and (2) integration of music with other arts, especially those that use sound as a central expressive device. These two areas best exemplify how contemporary technical modes of production and reproduction meet the political potential of the aes-thetic regime of art in the domain of musical expression, expanding the latter across the borders of the traditional artistic disciplines. As Ran-cière (2011) eloquently puts it, "It is where the vast poem of yesterday's music and sounds runs up against that of the needle that scratches and the amplifier that crackles, the synthesizer that creates and the computer that invents, that the fusion of the two contradictory powers comes about: that of the grand Schopenhauerian background . . . of the 'ocean of sound', whence all images emerge like specters, only to disappear once again; and that of the Schlegelian 'poem of the poem'—of meta-morphicity, collage and indefinite recreation produced in the basis of the great storehouse of images, ultimately identical to the life of the storehouse itself" (128).

Guided by a pragmatist confidence in the transformative meaning potential of all sonic expressions, combined with critical alertness to how the policed power conditions artistic expressions in contemporary media environment, we can perhaps best benefit from recognition of these contradictory powers. At present, digital music culture seems to offer the best opportunity to cash in such recognition in music education.

NOTES

1. The chapter is based on my keynote presentation at Ann Arbor Symposium IV: Teaching and Learning Popular Music, held at the University of Michigan, November 18–21, 2015. This research has been undertaken as part of the ArtsEqual project funded by the Academy of Finland's Strategic Research Council from its Equality in Society program (project no. 293199).
2. While from the standpoint of intellectual development such learning could be called accretion, understood in the rudimentary sense of "accumulation of data and facts that the memory system has available for organization or reorganization" (Sternberg and Berg 1992, 283), both Dewey and Rancière seem to also have in mind the more extensive process of enculturation, where one becomes socialized to the norms of one's culture (Herskovits 1948, 39). Obviously both Dewey and Rancière see such learning as a basis for political room for maneuver.
3. Dewey ([1938] 2008f, 28) himself preferred the term "cultural naturalism."

REFERENCES

Adorno, Theodor W. 2002. *Essays on Music.* Berkeley: University of California Press.
Adorno, Theodor W., and Max Horkheimer. (1994) 2002. *Dialectic of Enlightenment: Philosophical Fragments.* Stanford: Stanford University Press.
Aikin, Scott F. 2006. "Pragmatism, Naturalism, and Phenomenology." *Human Studies* 29 (3): 317–40. doi: 10.1007/s10746-006-9026-5.
Alperson, Philip. 1991. "What Should One Expect from a Philosophy of Music Education?" *Journal of Aesthetic Education* 25 (3): 215–42.
Apple, Michael W. 1995. *Education and Power.* New York: Routledge.
Bayles, Martha. 2004. "None So Deaf: Toward a New Pedagogy of Popular Music." In *Bridging the Gap: Popular Music and Music Education,* edited by Carlos Xavier Rodriguez, 71–88. Lanham, MD: Rowman & Littlefield.
Benjamin, Walter. (1936) 2008. *The Work of Art in the Age of Mechanical Reproduction.* London: Penguin.
Berndtson, Erik. 1996. *Politiikka tieteenä: Johdatus valtio-opilliseen ajatteluun (Politics as Science: Introduction to Political Thinking).* Helsinki: Hallinnon kehittämiskeskus.

Berrebi, Sophie. 2008. "Jacques Rancière: Aesthetics Is Politics." *Art & Research* 2 (1). Accessed August 4, 2016. http://dare.uva.nl/document/2/66892.

Bingham, Charles, and Gert Biesta. 2010. *Jacques Rancière: Education, Truth, Emancipation.* London: Continuum.

Bowman, Wayne. 2000. "Discernment, Responsibility, and the Goods of Philosophical Praxis." *Finnish Journal of Music Education* 5 (1–2): 96–119.

Burnard, Pamela. 2012. *Musical Creativities in Practice.* Oxford: Oxford University Press.

Chambers, Samuel A. 2012. *The Lessons of Rancière.* Oxford: Oxford University Press.

Dewey, John. (1899) 2008a. *The School and Society.* Vol. 1 of *The Middle Works of John Dewey, 1899–1924.* Carbondale: Southern Illinois University Press.

———. (1916) 2008b. *Democracy and Education.* Vol. 9 of *The Middle Works of John Dewey, 1899–1924.* Carbondale: Southern Illinois University Press.

———. (1925) 2008c. *Experience and Nature.* Vol. 1 of *The Later Works of John Dewey, 1925–1953.* Carbondale: Southern Illinois University Press.

———. (1934) 2008d. *Art as Experience.* Vol. 10 of *The Later Works of John Dewey, 1925–1953.* Carbondale: Southern Illinois University Press.

———. (1938) 2008e. *Experience and Education.* Vol. 13 of *The Later Works of John Dewey, 1925–1953.* Carbondale: Southern Illinois University Press.

———. (1938) 2008f. *Logic: The Theory of Inquiry.* Vol. 12 of *The Later Works of John Dewey, 1925–1953.* Carbondale: Southern Illinois University Press.

Elliott, David J. 1995. *Music Matters.* New York: Oxford University Press.

Erjavec, Aleš. 2012. "Artification and the Aesthetic Regime of Art." *Contemporary Aesthetics* 4. Accessed August 4, 2016. http://www.contempaesthetics.org/newvolume/pages/article.php?articleID=636.

Foucault, Michel. 1990. *The History of Sexuality.* Vol. 1. New York: Vintage.

Freire, Paolo. 1970. *Pedagogy of the Oppressed.* New York: Continuum.

Giroux, Henry, and Peter McLaren, eds. 1994. *Between Borders: Pedagogy and the Politics of Cultural Studies.* New York: Routledge.

Gracyk, Theodore. 1996. *Rhythm and Noise: An Aesthetics of Rock.* New York: I. B. Tauris.

Green, Lucy. 2009. *Music, Informal Learning and the School: A New Classroom Pedagogy.* Aldershot: Ashgate.

Herskovits, Melville J. 1948. *Man and His Works: The Science of Cultural Anthropology.* New York: A. A. Knopf.

Holmboe, Rye D. 2014. "Interview with Jacques Rancière." *The White Review* (10). Accessed August 4, 2016. http://www.thewhitereview.org/interviews/interview-with-jacques-ranciere/.

Joas, Hans. 1993. *Pragmatism and Social Theory.* Chicago: University of Chicago Press.

Kadlec, Alison. 2007. *Dewey's Critical Pragmatism.* Latham, MD: Lexington Books.

Kallio, Alexis. 2015. *Navigating (Un)popular Music in the Classroom: Censure and Censorship in an Inclusive, Democratic Music Education.* Helsinki: Sibelius Academy of the University of the Arts.

Kanellopoulos, Panagiotis. 2015. "Musical Creativity and 'The Police.'" In *The Oxford Handbook of Social Justice in Music Education*, edited by Cathy Benedict, Patrick

Schmidt, Gary Spruce, and Paul Woodford, 319–39. New York: Oxford University Press.

McRobbie, Angela. 1994. *Postmodernism and Popular Culture*. London: Routledge.

Mullane, M. 2010. "The Aesthetic Ear: Sound Art, Jacques Rancière and the Politics of Listening." *Journal of Aesthetics & Culture* 2. Accessed August 4, 2016. http://www .socioaffectiveneuroscipsychol.net/index.php/jac/article/viewArticle/4895.

Moore, Ryan. 2012. "Digital Reproducibility and the Culture Industry: Popular Music and the Adorno-Benjamin Debate." *Fast Capitalism* 9 (1). Accessed August 8, 2016. https://www.uta.edu/huma/agger/fastcapitalism/9_1/moore9_1.html.

Pappas, Gregory F. 2008. *John Dewey's Ethics: Democracy as Experience*. Bloomington: Indiana University Press.

Rancière, Jacques. 1991. *The Ignorant Schoolmaster: Five Lessons in Intellectual Emancipation*. Palo Alto: Stanford University Press.

———. 1999. *Disagreement: Politics and Philosophy*. Minneapolis: University of Minnesota Press.

———. 2005. "From Politics to Aesthetics?" *Paragraph* 28 (1): 13–25.

———. 2006. *The Politics of Aesthetics*. London: Bloomsbury.

———. 2009. *The Emancipated Spectator*. London: Verso.

———. 2010. "On Ignorant Schoolmasters." In *Jacques Rancière: Education, Truth, Emancipation*, edited by Charles Bingham and Gert Biesta, 1–24. London: Continuum.

———. 2011. "Metamorphosis of the Muses." In *Sounds: Documents of Contemporary Art*, edited by Caleb Kelly, 124–29. London: Whitechapel Gallery; Cambridge, MA: MIT Press.

———. 2013. *Aisthesis: Scenes from the Aesthetic Regime of Art*. London: Verso.

Regelski, Thomas A. 1996. "Prolegomenon to a Praxial Philosophy of Music and Music Education." *Finnish Journal of Music Education* 1 (1): 23–39.

———. 2000. "Accounting for All Praxis: An Essay Critique of David Elliott's 'Music Matters.'" *Bulletin of the Council for Research in Music Education* 144: 61–88.

———. 2005. "Critical Theory as a Foundation for Critical Thinking in Music Education." *Visions of Research in Music Education* 6: 1–25.

———. 2013. "Re-setting Music Education's 'Default Settings.'" *Action, Criticism, and Theory for Music Education* 12 (1): 7–23.

Rockhill, Gabriel. 2006. "Editor's Introduction." In *The Politics of Aesthetics*, by Jacques Rancière, edited by Gabriel Rockhill, xii–xvii. London: Bloomsbury.

Russell, Bertrand. (1946) 2013. *History of Western Philosophy: Collector's Edition*. London: Routledge.

Scruton, Richard. 1999. *The Aesthetics of Music*. Oxford: Oxford University Press.

Shor, Ira. 1992. *Culture Wars: School and Society in the Conservative Restoration*. Chicago: University of Chicago Press.

Shusterman, Richard. 1992. *Pragmatist Aesthetics: Living Beauty, Rethinking Art*. Oxford: Blackwell.

Sternberg, Robert J., and Cynthia A. Berg. 1992. *Intellectual Development*. Cambridge: Cambridge University Press.

Väkevä, Lauri. 2003. "Music Education as Critical Practice: A Naturalist View." *Philosophy of Music Education Review* 11 (2): 141–56.

———. 2004. *Kasvatuksen taide ja taidekasvatus: estetiikan ja taidekasvatuksen merkitys John Deweyn naturalistisessa pragmatismissa* (*Art of Education and Art Education: The Significance of Aesthetics and Art Education in John Dewey's Naturalist Pragmatism*). Academic dissertation, University of Oulu. Accessed August 4, 2016. http://jultika .oulu.fi/files/isbn9514273109.pdf.

———. 2010. "Garage Band or GarageBand®? Remixing Musical Futures." *British Journal of Music Education* 27 (1): 59–70.

———. 2012. "Digital Artistry and Mediation: (Re)mixing Music Education." *Yearbook of the National Society for the Study of Education* 111 (1): 177–95.

———. 2013. "Digital Musicianship in the Late Modern Culture of Mediation: Theorizing a New Praxis for Music Education from a Pragmatist Viewpoint." *Journal of Pedagogy and Psychology "Signum Temporis"* 6 (1): 38–47.

Väkevä, Lauri, Heidi Westerlund, and Marja-Leena Juntunen. 2015. "Teacher as Ignorant Music Master: Some Rancièrian Musings on Instrumental Pedagogy." In *Knowledge Formation in and through Music—Festschrift in Honor of Cecilia K. Hultberg*, edited by Jan-Olof Gullö and Per-Henrik Holgersson, 233–42. Stockholm: Royal College of Music.

Walker, Robert. 2007. *Music Education: Cultural Values, Social Change and Innovation.* Springfield, IL: Charles C Thomas.

Wenger, Etienne. 1998. *Communities of Practice: Learning, Meaning, and Identity.* Cambridge: Cambridge University Press.

Žižek, Slavoj. 2007. *The Universal Exception.* New York: Continuum.

CHAPTER 2

The Long Revolution and Popular Music Education

OR, CAN POPULAR MUSIC EDUCATION CHANGE SOCIETY?

RUTH WRIGHT

WESTERN UNIVERSITY

I n this chapter, I consider some of the issues presented by the learn-ing and teaching of popular music from a sociological perspective. As the title indicates, the main concern of the chapter will be with the relationship between popular music education and social change. It should be emphasized from the beginning, however, that I do not believe that popular music education is only useful in an instrumental sense—that is, to facilitate societal change. Indeed, I hold passion-ately to the belief that all young people have a right to participate in music education that allows them to engage with contemporary popu-lar music for its own sake and its own intrinsic rewards. Alongside this belief is a commitment to social justice and working toward chang-ing long-established and accelerating societal patterns of injustice and inequity. From these commitments emanates my interest in examining how one part of the sociological picture—in this case, the interactions of young people with popular music in education—might influence the bigger one, the behemoth we call society.

Sociology concerns "the science of society, social institutions, and social relationships; specifically: the systematic study of the devel-opment, structure, interaction, and collective behavior of organized groups of human beings" (Merriam-Webster, n.d.). As a sociologist of music education, it follows that my work involves the study of music education in relation to society—its institutions and social relationships—and I have a particular interest in the study of popular music in these respects. The sociological approach is particularly useful in this regard in its provision of robust theoretical frameworks forming a series of lenses through which issues, events, actions, and interactions can be scrutinized. The same can be said of several other disciplinary perspectives, such as philosophy and psychology; however, one of the particular strengths of sociology is its foundations in the integration of insights from both its own field and other fields—something I have previously described as "a sociology of integration" (Wright, 2014b). For instance, the works of sociologists such as Bourdieu and Bernstein have variously combined thoughts of previous sociologists such as Marx, Durkheim, and Weber with those of philosophers such as Wittgenstein, Althusser, and Foucault; linguists such as Saussure; and psychologists such as Luria while adding their own unique insights to their fields. This makes the sociological perspective particularly capable of finely nuanced description and analysis of phenomena as multifaceted, socially situated, and constructed as popular music and music education.

This chapter is framed as a response to one of the big questions of sociologists of education throughout history; indeed, it has probably been asked by philosophers since the dawn of civilization, and it is the question asked by renowned critical pedagogue Michael Apple in the title of his 2013 book *Can Education Change Society?* The question is problematic on many levels, as Apple acknowledges. In a later article, he discusses this in the following way: "It is important to realize that education is a part of society. It is not something alien, something that stands outside. Indeed, it is a key set of institutions and a key set of social, economic, political, and personal relations" (Apple, 2015, p. 305). Furthermore, Apple continues to outline the role of schools as sites of labor relations stratified in terms of class, race, and gender. As sites of paid work, they are "**integral parts** of the economy," increasingly subject to commodification and marketing (p. 306; emphasis in original). They have been sites of resistance to and reproduction of racial and other inequities. Moreover, they are key sites of identity production. Beyond these roles, schools also play a part in the definition and reproduction of legitimate knowledge, or as Apple asserts, "They are key mechanisms in determining what is socially valued as 'legitimate knowledge' and what is seen as merely 'popular'" (p. 307). This is an important point I shall discuss in relation to sociological theory later in the chapter. Apple continues: "In their role in defining a large part of what is considered to be legitimate knowledge, they also participate in the process through which particular groups are granted status and which groups remain unrecognized or minimized" (p. 307). Yet despite these entanglements with society itself, Apple asserts that it is possible to answer the question of whether education can change society in the affirmative—so long as we look beyond only countering class-related economic inequity. He suggests that previous Marxist and neo-Marxist analysis has been limited by viewing change in this respect as the only change that matters. While crucial, this overlooks the potential of other changes that might be made possible through education. Apple suggests such transformation might occur through the interaction of various projects, originating from several different points of departure, all concerned with countering injustice that meet and coalesce in what Apple terms "decentred unities" (p. 302). In this sense, Apple suggests, they become important aspects of Williams's (1961) *Long Revolution*, which we shall consider in more detail in the following sections, and in this sense, perhaps we can argue that education might change society.

A modification is required to Apple's question to bring it more specifically into alignment with the topic of this chapter. Refining and slightly redirecting Apple's original query, the question is rephrased to ask whether popular music education can change society.

Perhaps the first thing to be clarified is why social change is necessary. There is no doubt, in my opinion, that we live in an era of encroaching global capitalism and increasingly universal neoliberal governmental policies that give rise to ever increasing inequalities. As the distance between the rich and the poor continues to grow, it becomes increasingly important that society steps in to redress the balance in terms of support for those at the lower end of the economic scale, for whom necessities such as work, food, housing, and medical care are becoming less and less obtainable. Moreover, as Thomas Piketty (2014) has shown in his influential book *Capital in the Twenty-First Century*, this is a situation that will worsen unless radical societal intervention occurs. Analyzing data from more than twenty countries and dating back to the eighteenth century, Piketty has discovered many important economic and social patterns that lead to ever increasing inequity. Rooted in the fact that the rate of return on investment constantly outstrips that of economic growth, Piketty predicts that unless checked by political intervention, this pattern of economic inequity will continue and will produce extreme inequality and social unrest in the future. The situation, as we have seen only too clearly in the 2016 US presidential election campaign and election results, is further exacerbated in countries where the neoliberal agenda is in control and by policies gaining increasing popular support involving the demolition of social programs for the poor, causing rising hunger and homelessness (affecting an ever younger population); growing work, pension, and health care insecurity; and the recurrence of xenophobia, homophobia, racism, and violence toward minorities. There are serious problems with the current social organization in many countries, when viewed from the perspective of social justice. My own conceptualization of social justice follows that of Rawls (1971, 1999), expressed in his seminal work *A Theory of Justice*. Reisch (2002) suggests that, for Rawls, the justice of a system should be assessed "on how fundamental rights and duties are assigned and on the economic opportunities and social conditions in the various sectors of society" (p. 346; Rawls, 2001). Reisch (2002) goes on to state that Rawls's self-termed maximin theory is founded on two principles:

1. "Each person has an equal right to the most extensive system of personal liberty compatible with a system of total liberty for all."
2. "Social and economic inequality are to be arranged so that they are both (a) to the greatest benefit to the least advantaged in society and (b) attached to positions open to all under conditions of fair equality of opportunity." (p. 346)

In addition to this, the concept of social justice operative in this chapter is underpinned by a belief in a robust link between social justice and social responsibility as expressed in a commitment to identifying and countering inequity, oppression, and domination wherever they occur throughout society.

For education, the effects of global neoliberalism have also failed to contribute to an educational system that encourages *Bildung* in its original sense. *Bildung* is a German word for education that nurtures autonomy and individuality and focuses on personal responsibility for constant development of the whole person, or a striving toward perfection, as Prange (2004, p. 503) describes. Instead of this, however, the educational trend appears to be an ever increasing concentration on employability and more rigidly defined pathways through education that lead to distinct career outcomes—an interpretation to which the term *Bildung* has interestingly, although erroneously, also been applied (Prange 2004). This comes at the expense of any underlying philosophy of *Bildung* in its original sense. Against a reminder of "the fact that liberty is at risk in ways that may be different, but which nevertheless require a constant reminder of what is lost when we [educators] are treated as mere functionaries of the status quo" (p. 509), Prange suggests that the remnant of the original notion of *Bildung* serves a useful function in considerations of education, as it "serves as the critical ferment, not so much by way of public protest, rather by its very existence as a living memory of our potential to give a meaning to what we do and experience" (p. 509).

British sociologist Basil Bernstein (1996, 2000) also identified risks inherent in education as the state moved to increasing control of the content of education, a move that, although beginning earlier than the 1970s in the United Kingdom, was given critical impetus by the Thatcher government. As decentralization of institutions' management was accompanied by centralization of school monitoring and funding, the culture of education changed to one in which teachers and their professional and subject bodies had less autonomy and voice in the control and direction of education. This permitted increased state regulation of the content of education and a shift toward curricula Bernstein defines as embodying a generic performance mode. A simplified description of this mode is that it embodies a generic set of skills (e.g., transferable skills) that underlie a specific set of performances by students (i.e., completion of tasks in a range of subjects) by which achievement is judged. He further indicates that these generic modes and the tasks to which they give rise are instrumental to the economy and to the formation of the sort of flexible workforce the market foresees as necessary to future economic competitiveness. He considered this education policy to be based on a new conceptualization of "work" and "life"—one he named "short-termism" (p. 59). Short-termism projects an employment future that is in constant flux, where positions are constantly changing, shifting, and disappearing and where the individual can have no expectation of employment stability. All this is underpinned by a pedagogic concept Bernstein termed "trainability," or the ability to train and retrain—to be able "to profit from continuous pedagogic re-formations and so cope with the new requirements of 'work' and 'life'" (p. 59). Bernstein expressed his concerns that in this employment future, the actor was required to possess, without any means of developing, a capacity to create his or her own coherent identity, normally constructed "through relations which the identity enters into with other identities of reciprocal recognition, support, mutual legitimisation and finally through a negotiated collective purpose" (p. 59). In the trainable future, however, the actor would appear to be unlikely to find other identities to which to relate in these ways, and for these reasons, Bernstein thought the concept of trainability was "socially empty" (p. 59). The institutionalization of the concept of trainability was of concern to Bernstein, as it removed the imaginary world of "work" and "life" produced by the educational institution from the power relations that gave rise to it in real life, making it difficult to engage with it as a topic of debate and critique.

In this conception of education, the arts, including music, have become increasingly marginalized at both the compulsory schooling and the post-secondary education levels. They are marginalized or in some cases eliminated in favor of concentration in curriculum and in research funding on the somewhat repellently titled science, technology, engineering, and mathematics (STEM) subjects, deemed by governments to be most important to national competitiveness in the ever-changing global labor economy. The STEM acronym unfortunately conveys a conceptualization of knowledge as composed of a stem or core group of important or essential subjects (science, technology, engineering, and math) that support the leaves, or nonessential/less important forms of knowledge, such as the arts and humanities.

Alongside this has been the reversal of progressive music curricula that were moving toward closer connections among the popular music–based sound worlds of adolescents outside the school and those experienced in their music education; now we see retrospective conservative curriculum models that resonate with the neoconservative government ideology of preserving tradition and reconfirming elite culture. Attendant upon such curricular reversals are likely to be the societal effects of their accompanying hegemonic actions, reinforcing middle-class, Eurocentric, elite culture and alienating vast numbers of students from music in schools. It is not surprising, therefore, that some music educators, particularly those advocating for the role of popular music in education with a keen eye to social justice, might feel that the time is ripe for a reconsideration of how popular music education might disrupt patterns of social exclusion and inequity.

As we have seen previously, however, Apple (2015) points out that there are problems if we conceptualize the question of education's potential to effect social change in terms only of its impact on society's economic relations. The same might be true of considerations of popular music education and its effect on social change, and we will be considering this in more detail in the following sections. Demanding of education that it, acting alone, change patterns of global, national, or local wealth distribution or decrease the distance between the rich and poor (Apple, 2013, 2015) is to miss other important aspects of the matter. So, perhaps, is gauging the effectiveness of education with respect to social change solely by its impact on these relations. Many scholars do just this, however, and Apple (2015) indicates as much in his paper in a volume of the journal *Educational Theory*. By these criteria, the only change that can be valued, or indeed looked for, says Apple, as a result of education will involve change in the economy and in class relations. Viewed in this way, the answer to the question of whether education can change society is, as agreed by many scholars, very emphatically, no!

It is perhaps a little peremptory, however, to dismiss the question quite so abruptly. Let us consider, as Apple does, if restricting our thinking to whether education can interrupt economic inequities and resulting class positions is rather one-dimensional in the interconnected and complex world of contemporary human societies and relationships. Apple suggests that such a reading fails to recognize the many complex inter-relations of power at work in society and the ways in which they affect each other. Moreover, he says it prevents activists from forming important alliances—or "decentered unities," as he terms them—that he says are "absolutely essential" to progress toward social justice (Apple, 2013, p. 31). He suggests that a more fruitful way to approach this question might be to ask, "Can schools play a role in making a more just society possible? If not, why not? If so, what can they do?" (Apple, 2015, p. 300).

In our case, the question then becomes, Can popular music education in schools play a role in making a more just society possible? If not, why not? If so, what can they do? This is obviously still an ambitious question and covers an enormous scope, encompassing many types of educational inequity and social injustice in each area of which there is a growing body of specialist literature to which one cannot possibly do justice in a single chapter. If, however, the reader will bear with me in pursuing this as an interesting macro-level question, it might offer a good five-thousand-foot-high perspective from which to examine issues of popular music educa-tion and society, and it is a variation on a question Apple believes has potential to yield useful answers.

I am equally aware that the field of what I am calling popular music is at least as vast—if not vaster—than that of social justice, as, for example, the Every Noise at Once project (McDonald, n.d.) is demonstrating. This mapping project is using big data obtained from the digital music service Spotify to attempt "an algorithmically-generated, readability-adjusted scatter-plot of the musical genre-space, based on data tracked and analyzed for 1460 genres by Spotify" (McDonald, n.p.). Admittedly, not all 1,460 genres could be classified as popular music, but there is a predominant amount of popular music of very diverse nature and ori-gin represented on this map. This leads to the admission that describing these musics by one term, "popular," is also a vast oversimplification. As Middleton (2002, 1990) demonstrates, defining popular music is tre-mendously difficult: "The danger is of over-rigid definition, usually built on a failure to recognize the framework of assumptions underlying every distinction" (p. 7). Middleton, after rejecting six definitions of the term, advocates locating musical categories "topographically" (p. 7)—"on the ground on which the transformations are worked" (Hall, 1981, p. 228).

This makes the Every Noise project, with its particular topographical mapping, appear particularly apposite. Again, it is hoped that you will bear with this oversimplification for the purposes of examining this very big-picture issue from a macroperspective.

What is Apple (2013) thinking of when he asks whether school can contribute to a more just society? First is a vision of "an education that responds to all of us, one that embodies a vision of the common good that says it needs constant criticism and revision to keep it alive" (p. 21).

It is here, I suggest, that the potential of popular music education to effect change toward a more just society lies. In concentrating on the socially reproductive effects of music education to perpetuate injustice, we might have overlooked the corresponding power and influence of culture to act as an agent of positive social change. Our hopes of successfully countering the effects of educational policies in contributing to a more unjust society might rest, as Apple (2013) suggests, precisely on acknowledging the socially transformative power of culture. And in this chapter, this is conceptualized in terms of the power of popular culture to effect individual growth and change in music education. I join with Apple in believing that cultural work is required alongside activism in the economy and politics and that this can contribute to social change, or what Raymond Williams (1961) termed "the long revolution."

In his seminal work in the field of cultural studies, *The Long Revolution*, Williams (1961), credited as one of the founders of the sociology of culture, envisaged history since the industrial era as a series of revolutions—political, industrial, and cultural. These interlinked revolutions, he believed, engendered and would continue to engender gradually increasing popular control over society—hence the title, *The Long Revolution*: "It seems to me that we are living through a long revolution, which our best descriptions only in part interpret. It is a genuine revolution, transforming men and institutions; continually extended and deepened by the actions of millions, continually and variously opposed by explicit reaction and by the pressure of habitual forms and ideas" (p. x).

Williams observed, however, that this revolution was elusive to definition, uneven in action and occurring over such a protracted timespan that observation was problematic and the observer capable of becoming lost in complexity. First, Williams discussed the democratic revolution he identified occurring in the first sixty years of the twentieth century. He saw a rising determination of peoples to govern themselves and to own the political decision-making process. He also observed resistance to this movement by violence, deceit, and custom and suggested that, in terms of the maxim that people should have the right to govern themselves, the democratic revolution was at a very early stage.

Williams then turned to the industrial revolution, the aims of which, he asserted, had been almost universally accepted. He was uncertain what sort of correlation this bore to the development of democracy, both affording and constraining democratic rights and organization of the workforce.

Of particular interest to our concerns here is a third revolution Williams observed. He suggested that this was the most difficult of all to interpret—a cultural revolution. He described it thus: "We must see the aspiration to extend the active process of learning, with the skills of literacy and other advanced communication, to all people rather than to limited groups, as comparable in importance to the growth of democracy and the rise of scientific industry" (p. xi).

This revolution was also at a very early stage, however. Williams thought that we could not understand the process of change in society as a whole if we thought of these three revolutions separately. This longer quotation is essential to grasping the interrelationship of the three revolutions in Williams's eyes:

> Our whole way of life, from the shape of our communities to the organization and content of education, and from the structure of the family to the status of art and entertainment, is being profoundly affected by the progress and interaction of democracy and industry, and by the extension of communications. This deeper cultural revolution is a large part of our most significant living experience, and is being interpreted and indeed fought out, in very complex ways, in the world of art and ideas. It is when we try to correlate change of this kind with the changes covered by the disciplines of politics, economics and communications that we discover some of the most human questions. (pp. xi–xii)

The long revolution is, therefore, an ongoing popular quest for freedom advanced through interlinked social movements within which, importantly, the power of culture is acknowledged alongside politics and economics. It is here I believe that popular music education conceived of as both an educational and a social movement might have an important role to play in the journey toward a more just society.

In keeping with post-Weberian sociological thought, in which culture and society exist in complex interrelationship, with conditions in one affecting the other, Gramsci (1977) developed an explanation of the mechanism by which some of the less overt opposition to circumstances such as this ongoing popular quest took place. Gramsci (1977) asserted that bourgeois society was maintained by cultural as well as material constraints. He termed this cultural hegemony—the control of society's intellectual values by cultural means. Through the imposition on society of the cultural preferences and values of the most powerful social group, reproduction of the status quo was assured. This involves a process whereby the views and tastes of the powerful become so ingrained that they are perceived and accepted as common sense. We can see this in postsecondary music education when the entrance requirements for further study in music are rigidly defined to include piano skills, understanding of Eurocentric art music theory, and harmony and performance skills on an orchestral instrument. For many years—although in some places, it is changing now—these gatekeepers were seen as inviolable, as common sense, as the "legitimate knowledge" with which any music education should be concerned. How could one even begin to access the music curriculum at university/conservatoire if one did not possess them? How could one contribute to the ensembles? Mere attempts to discuss broadening them or changing them to include other notations, histories, or theories beyond those of Eurocentric art music could bring faculty meetings to a halt, let alone suggesting candidates be allowed to audition on popular music instruments such as electric guitar. The common-sense understandings of those in elite positions in postsecondary music education were shaken to the core by such suggestions. This was not what music education was. The tastes, values, and corresponding skills and knowledge requisites of Eurocentric art music were deeply ingrained in many music academics' worldviews. One might argue, therefore, that the long revolution has been even longer in influencing music education.

Although Williams observed these conjoint revolutions to be at a very early stage in 1961, he suggested that we could not possibly understand social development if we conceived of the three revolutions separately. For Williams (1961, pp. xi–xii), the profound cultural revolution occurring in the sixties formed a great part of the contemporary human experience. Williams, perhaps overly optimistic, saw even the industrial and democratic revolutions of the time as examples of humanity's creative influence—humanity changing the world and insisting we all took power to direct our own lives. While some would question the extent to which industrial and democratic developments in the intervening years have lived up to Williams's aspirations, it is interesting to consider events such as the Arab Spring and other recent popular interventions by the people of nation states in the affairs of their countries in this light.

Of course, the key question, asked by Williams in the sixties and still asked by scholars today, is whether the new opportunities thus created are used for human growth or as means of perpetuating existing systems of social organization with their attendant inequities—or indeed of generating new oppressive forms of social organization. Sadly, the aftermaths of some recent popular political interventions have demonstrated the ability of new forms of inequity to arise from moments of potential freedom. One wonders if the same might not be true or in danger of becoming true regarding the introduction of popular music into education. I shall come back to this point a little later in considering the thought of Richard Day.

I see very clear connections between Williams's rather abstract theorization of the role of culture in society and the more concrete theoretical work of the French sociologist Pierre Bourdieu in his theory of practice (1977 [1972]).

Bourdieu developed this theory as a means of understanding a puzzling situation he observed in his fieldwork in rural France and in Algiers. He could not find a satisfactory way to explain social practice—basically, behavior. In his fieldwork, he noticed that social actions such as marriage, for example, did not happen solely by obeying a set of rules agreed on by the society. Instead he observed that something more akin to a game of strategy appeared to be going on.

There are three main concepts around which Bourdieu's theory is centered. The first is the concept of habitus, the second is that of field, and the third is that of capital. These concepts have independent meanings but function together. The first concept, habitus, is "a way of being, a habitual state (especially of the body) and in particular a predisposition, tendency, propensity or inclination" (Bourdieu, 1977, p. 214). It goes a long way toward explaining why we behave as we do. The habitus acts retrospectively in that it is formed by past experiences, of which those within the family are particularly important. It also has a forward-facing element, as it tends to direct how we act both now and in the future by keeping our behavior consistent with our previous experiences and the values they dictate.

This is not the totality of the actions and effects of habitus, however, because it also connects and reacts to another element, the field. This was how Bourdieu described the arena in which the action takes place. Returning to the game analogy, Bourdieu likened the field to a football field. The social field, like that in football, has designated positions for players and has limits formed by boundaries. It has rules that over time become implicit, but new players must learn the rules of the game.

The social game is also competitive—there are winners and losers. The actors use various strategies, such as marrying advantageously, to try to improve their position on the field. There are numerous fields, but the strongest one is the field of power. Position is determined by the third of Bourdieu's concepts, capital. He discerned four types of capital: economic (wealth), cultural (knowledge of art, music, literature, etc.), social (networks and connections), and symbolic (a signifier of possession of one of the other forms, such as a degree or a mansion). The object of the game of life, therefore, was to accumulate these forms of capital.

Bourdieu summarized the relationship among the three concepts in the equation "[(habitus)(capital)] + field = practice" (Bourdieu, 1984, p. 101).

A way of expressing this in words is to say that our practice, or behavior, in everyday life is the product of the relationship between our dispositions (habitus) and our field position, which is in turn determined by how much capital we hold in the field.

Let's see now how these concepts might work to help answer my question: Can popular music education in schools play a role in making a more just society possible? If not, why not? If so, what can it do? I would argue that one of the things popular music education might do to further a more just society would happen at the level of the individual habitus. When popular music is used as curriculum content in which learning and teaching embrace pedagogies and technologies authentic to the musics being studied, such as informal learning (Green, 2008), the results permit student autonomy and ownership of the learning and teaching process. I have suggested (Wright, 2015a, 2015b) that positive changes to habitus can occur. My colleagues Carol Beynon, Betty Anne Younker, Leslie Linton, and Jennifer Lang and I conducted a study over two academic years with two groups of Canadian elementary and secondary school students using the informal learning model that came to attention through Lucy Green's work in the UK Musical Futures project (Wright et al., 2012; Wright, 2016). While this is not by any means the only pedagogical model that may be used to work with popular music in authentic pedagogical ways, it is one with which I had some experience and was interested to trial in Canada. In case there are readers who have not heard of informal learning, I recommend Lucy Green's (2001, 2008, 2014) work.

The original form of this pedagogy was trialed with high school students in the United Kingdom as part of the Musical Futures project (https://www.musicalfutures.org). In this model, which Green (2014) has since called HELP (hear, listen, play), students choose music they want to learn and then do so by listening to recordings, copying, and teaching each other with support from their teacher as needed. Green (2014) has since expanded this pedagogy to incorporate strategies for use of a similar approach with students in individual instrumental lessons and has identified a pedagogy based on the model for large ensembles. Musical Futures projects based on this and other nonformal music teaching approaches are now thriving in many countries around the world.

In our Canadian pilot project, we found that students developed an increased sense of their own musical capabilities that confounded many of their previous expectations concerning what they would be able to achieve when presented with "real" pop music instruments. They also developed a different relationship with their teacher, who adopted the role of a coach and colearner, and they gained increasing confidence in themselves as both learners and teachers.

I have developed this thesis with illustrations from the data elsewhere (Wright, 2015a, 2015b, 2016). I have suggested that within the music learning situation, two distinct forms of cultural capital might be identified, which I have called "pedagogical" and "musical capital." While I am not the first to use these terms, I believe I define them differently than previous authors. Livingstone (2007), in discussing pedagogical capital, describes it as "a quality that some students possess that enables them to arrive at the academic table better positioned to take advantage of our educational offerings." Hayes (2011) describes pedagogic capital as an attribute of teacher practices. My interpretation of this term is based on a more agentic view of students as peer and self-teachers; it comprises "skills, knowledge, and understanding related to learning and teaching, moreover it concerns ownership of pedagogical decision-making" (Wright, 2015a, 2015b). I feel this is in keeping with the new sociology of childhood (Corsaro, 2011), which positions children as active agents involved in interpretation and reproduction of their own culture and ultimately their own childhoods. Coulson (2010) defines musical capital as "a useful shorthand for the interconnected cultural, social and symbolic assets that musicians acquire and turn to economic advantage in the music field" (p. 257). My own definition emphasizes emotions and perceptions rather than economic concerns and involves "skills in and knowledge and understanding of music affecting self-perceptions of musicality and musical potential" (Wright, 2015a, p. 95).

Just as Bourdieu plotted positions within the dominant field of power against axes of economic and cultural capital, I think we could plot positions within informal music learning classrooms against axes of musical and pedagogical capital. Many of the students involved in our informal learning project with popular music appeared to have made significant gains in their accumulation of these capitals; this altered individual habitus, and in turn, for a significant number, improved their position within the field of power. It is possible that if such pedagogic models were to be allowed to expand and challenge other dominating models of music education, the nature of common sense—or, in Apple's terms, "legitimate knowledge"—in music education might gradually be changed. It is possible that such work using popular music and pedagogies such as informal learning in education might form part of the cultural element of Williams's long revolution.

This might be said to be an example of counterhegemony, and it is along these lines that I have previously been thinking and writing. Gramsci (1977) argued that one of the tasks of a truly counterhegemonic education was not to throw out "elite knowledge" but to reconstruct its form and content so that it served genuinely progressive social needs (p. 42).

So far, so good. It is, however, fairly inescapable that previous efforts to engender larger social change through concerted efforts in education, and through music education, have not been universally successful. All too often, dominant societal forces manage to pervert the course of such movements from their original egalitarian goals. Canadian sociologist, political scientist, and activist Richard Day has suggested that our previous conception of counterhegemony might be the problem in this respect. He has proposed that we learn lessons from some of the newest social movements in approaching social change from what he calls the logic of affinity rather than that of hegemony. The next section of this chapter examines popular music education from this perspective. It is a challenging perspective but one that I think presents some ideas that might be useful to think with.

Day (2004) has noted that several contemporary social movements have departed from "the universalizing conception of social change that is characteristic of the logic of hegemony as it has developed within (post) Marxism and (neo) liberalism" (p. 717). Replacing this *logic of hegemony* is a *logic of affinity* drawn from anarchist social movements and accompanied, according to Day, by a focus on direct action (Day, 2004, p. 717). Such movements resist what he terms "the hegemony of hegemony" (p. 717). The hegemony of hegemony represents the understanding that change in society, or indeed order therein, requires "universalizing hierarchical forms" (p. 717). In other words, discriminatory macrostructures are essential to social order and social change.

It is here that we must be careful when we attempt to advance notions of popular music education as a means of social justice. There is, advises Day, the possibility that in attempting to counter hegemony by working for macro-level social change, radical new forms of activism or, in our case, of popular music education might become engulfed by dominant societal forces and turned into new "universalizing hierarchical forms" that lack the reformative power of their original initiative. Indeed, one does not have to think for too long to identify instances of this within music education. It is how neoliberalism works—engulfing and assimilating the radical and transforming it for its own ends.

Day continues to show, however, not only that creating new universal hierarchical forms might be unnecessary to achieving social change but also that some very important examples of twenty-first-century social activism (e.g., alternative media and antiglobalization) challenge this premise, following on from a long tradition of "affinity-based direct action" that he claims "has been submerged under (neo)liberal and (post) Marxist theory and practice" (p. 717).

He therefore discusses the potential of alternative nonhegemonic modes of action that might achieve radical social change. This he claims as a provisional definition of the logic of affinity: "It is that which always already undermines hegemony" (Day, 2004, p. 717).

And now we come back to culture, referring to Williams among other authors he acknowledges—those cultural scholars who have considered the possibilities of what Day calls "different logics of struggle" (p. 717). He acknowledges Williams (1973) and Hall (1983), who like Bourdieu, were insistent that "culture involves struggle, not only over meaning and identity, but also over political and economic power" (pp. 717–718).

He analyzes the successes of some of the newest social movements in achieving "a shift from a counter-hegemonic politics of demand to a non-hegemonic politics of the act" (p. 719). And it is here that I think we need to pay particular attention if we really intend popular music education to help us advance the long revolution—that is, to move toward a more just and inclusive society. Day describes as fantasy what he calls a previous politics of demand—one I believe we have engaged with in music education, myself included.

As Day opines, "Clearly, the fundamental fantasy of the politics of demand is that the currently hegemonic formation will recognize the validity of the claim presented to it, and respond in a way that produces an event of emancipation. Most of the time, however, it does not; instead it defers, dissuades or provides a partial solution to one problem that exacerbates several others" (p. 734). In other words, one expects that by representing the social injustice presented by, for example, hegemonic forms of music education to the dominant institution or group, they will realize the injustice being brought to their attention and accept the validity of the claim for change. This will subsequently respond, one hopes, in a manner that engenders a more just situation. However, this does not happen in most cases. Instead, procrastination occurs or counterarguments are presented or partial acquiescence is achieved that results in further problems. I would also add that there might appear to be prima facie gains made that result long term in engulfment, perversion, and submergence of previously radical ideas to the agenda of the dominant social form.

Day explains that a method more likely to achieve the desired ends is to "cross the fantasy" to an approach that does not "reproduce the conditions of its own emergence" (p. 733). This involves abandoning the anticipation of "a nondominating response from structures of domination"; it involves surprise both to oneself and to the structure "by inventing a response that precludes the necessity of the demand and thereby breaks out of the loop of the endless perpetuation of desire for emancipation" (p. 733). This involves an abandonment of attempts to change state power by advocating or activating for macro-level changes and instead giving increased recognition to the fact that the state itself is composed of interpersonal relationships and that it is at this level that fruitful change may take place.

Day provides examples of twenty-first-century social movements, such as the antiglobalization movement, that recognize the dangers of the logic of hegemony and respond to them by taking active measures at their deepest organizational and operational levels to prevent creating a new power around a hegemonic center; rather, activists seek to "challenge, disrupt and disorient the processes of global hegemony, to refuse, rather than rearticulate those forces that are tending towards the universalization of the liberal-capitalist ecumene" (p. 729).

They do so, according to Day, not by pursuing a sudden and complete departure from dominant structures but by embracing the strategy of structural renewal proposed by Landauer, among others, which embraces a willingness to coexist alongside one's "enemies" while one puts in place alternatives that will render these enemies redundant. In this way, Day suggests that "it does not provide positive energy to existing structures and processes in the hope of their amelioration. Rather, it aims to reduce their efficacy and reach by rendering them redundant" (p. 739).

At this point, I should be clear that I am not proposing that forms of music education other than those involving popular music are the "enemy" or that they should be rendered redundant. What I *am* in favor of eliminating, however, are elitist hegemonic attitudes and practices that reify musics, thereby placing Western art music and its attendant skills, knowledges, and understandings in a position of dominance and excluding so many young people from a rewarding engagement and conceivable future in music education. It is these attitudes and practices that I wish to see become redundant.

What might movements based on the logic of affinity look like in popular music education? How might the long revolution, the ongoing popular quest for freedom, be played out in twenty-first-century popular music education contexts? What might these new forms of popular music education look like? Some initial guiding thoughts inspired by Day are that they will do the following:

- Deliberately refute the "logic of hegemony" by protecting themselves from developing universalizing power centers that position themselves above the groups that constitute them.
- Recognize that because social structures such as capitalism and socialism are ways of coexisting as humans, changing such macro-structures is, in large part, a matter of changing microrelations and that culture and its effects on habitus formation play key roles in this.
- Acknowledge that new forms "become reality only in the act of being realized" (Landauer, 1911/1978, p. 138 in Day, 2004). The enactment of change, of providing ourselves and our communities with new realities alongside other forms of the self and other communities, is, as Day says, "intersubjective and deeply ethical" (p. 740).
- Embrace the "logic of affinity" that arises out of a rejection of hegemony in "its dual (Gramscian) form" (p. 740). For Day, this requires looking for alternatives to "state and corporate forms of organization" (p. 741). It means rejecting the view of society as constructed by domination over others by government or big business. It also involves a rejection of large-scale persuasion or advocacy attempts. Instead, it will proceed with action, producing

alternative forms of music education practice that work alongside current practices.

- Advance through "disengagement and reconstruction rather than by reform or revolution"—the goal being not to produce a "new knowable totality (counter-hegemony)" (p. 740) but to enable experiments and the rise of new ways of being musically, pedagogically, and socially.
- Investigate the relationships among these newly formed actors in the hope of creating new types of musical community (p. 740).

Perhaps such modes of popular music education will produce for us what Day terms a new "uncommon" sense.

As he observes of independent media centers, "this is precisely what is being done through the use of tactics that not only prefigure non-hegemonic alternatives to state and corporate forms, but also create them here and now" (p. 731). Are there now, or might there be in the future, popular music education equivalents? If so, what are or might they be? Is Musical Futures one such example? What about Little Kids Rock?

▌CONCLUSION

I began this chapter by reframing Michael Apple's question, "Can education change society?" as "Can popular music education play a role in making a more just society possible? If not, why not? If so, what can it do?" I hope that I have explored some of the issues these questions present from a sociology of music education perspective. I have discussed the challenges posed by viewing education's potential for social change only from a macroeconomic perspective and the opportunities presented, as identified by Apple, in adopting Williams's view of social change as a long revolution in which politics, economics, and culture play equally important roles. I have briefly presented some thoughts on how a micro-perspective, utilizing Bourdieu's theory of practice and the formation and change of habitus through popular music education, might play a positive role in such a revolution.

Finally, I have suggested that we approach these issues from the perspective Day provides, in which the hegemony of hegemony is challenged by approaching social change from a logic of affinity drawn from the anarchist tradition of social movements. This would involve developing and adopting multiple approaches to popular music education that consider the precepts on which contemporary social movements have achieved success. Such approaches undermine hegemony. I do not see Day's thoughts as running contrary to those of Bourdieu. In fact, I think that Bourdieu presents exactly the sort of analytical tools required to conduct analysis of the effects of the changes in practice that Day advocates.

At the least, I hope that I have provided a provocation for future discussion and a consideration of how the long revolution might advance through popular music education, not via counterhegemony, but via affinity. I'll let Michael Apple have the last word: "Changing the world, rewriting it would require a combination of economic work, political work and cultural work. The task is to continue the work in each sphere" (Apple, 2013, p. 651).

Let us continue.

▌ REFERENCES

Apple, M. W. (2013). *Can education change society?* New York: Routledge.

Apple, M. W. (2015). Reframing the question of whether education can change society. *Educational Theory, 65*(3), 299–315.

Bernstein, B. (1996, 2000). *Pedagogy, symbolic control and identity.* Lanham, MD: Rowman & Littlefield.

Bourdieu. (1972, 1977). *Outline of a theory of practice (Esquisse d'une theorie de la pratique: Precede de trois etudes d'ethnologie kabyle* [Geneva: Droz]). (Nice, Trans.) Cambridge, UK: Cambridge University Press.

Corsaro, W. (2011). *The sociology of childhood* (3rd ed.). London: Sage.

Coulson, S. (2010). Getting "capital" in the music world: Musicians' learning experiences and working lives. *British Journal of Music Education, 27*(3), 255–270.

Day, R. (2005). *Gramsci is dead: Anarchist currents in the newest social movements.* London: Pluto Press.

Day, R. J. (2004). From hegemony to affinity: The political logic of the newest social movements. *Cultural Studies, 18*(5), 716–748.

Gramsci, A. (1977). *Selections from the political writings (1910–1920).* New York: International.

Green, L. (2001). *How popular musicians learn.* Farnham, UK: Ashgate.

Green, L. (2008). *Music, informal learning and the school: A new classroom pedagogy.* Farnham, UK: Ashgate.

Green, L. (2014). *Hear listen play.* Oxford: Oxford University Press.

Hall, S. (1981). Popular culture, politics and history. *Popular Culture Bulletin, 3.*

Hall, S. (1983). The problem of ideology? Marxism without guarantees. In B. Matthews (Ed.), *Marx a Hundred Years On* (57–85). New York: Humanities Press.

Hayes, D. (2011). How teachers create valuable learning opportunities (pedagogical capital) by making knowledge the means and not just the ends in classrooms. In J. Sefton-Green, P. Thomson, K. Jones, & L. Bresler (Eds.), *The Routledge international handbook of creative learning.* London: Routledge.

Landauer, G. (1911, 1978). *For socialism.* St. Louis: Telos Press.

Livingstone, C. (2007). The privilege of pedagogic capital: A framework for understanding scholastic success in mathematics. *Philosophy of Mathematics Education Journal, 20*(1).

McDonald, G. (n.d.). *Every noise at once.* Retrieved from http://everynoise.com/engenremap.html.

Merriam-Webster. (n.d.). *Merriam-Webster online dictionary.* Retrieved June 2, 2016, from the Merriam Webster online dictionary. http://www.merriam-webster.com/dictionary/sociology.

Middleton, R. (1990, 2002). *Studying popular music.* Buckingham, UK: Open University Press.

Piketty, T. (2014). *Capital in the twenty-first century.* (A. Goldhammer, Trans.). Harvard, MA: Harvard University Press.

Prange, K. (2004). Bildung: A paradigm regained? *European Educational Research Journal, 3*(2), 501–509.

Rawls, J. (1971, 1999). *A theory of justice.* Cambridge, MA: Harvard University Press.

Rawls, J. (2001). *Justice as fairness: A restatement.* Cambridge, MA: Belknap Press of Harvard University Press.

Reisch, M. (2002). Defining social justice in a socially unjust world. *Families in Society, 83*(4), 343–354.

Williams, R. (1961). *The long revolution.* London: Chatto and Windus.

Williams, R. (1973). *The country and the city.* Oxford: Oxford University Press.

Wright, R. (2014a). Debunking the myths of Musical Futures. *The Recorder, 56(2).*

Wright, R. (2014b). The fourth sociology and music education: Towards a sociology of integration. In P. Dyndahl, S. Karlsen, & R. Wright (Eds.), *Action, Criticism and Theory, 13*(1), n.p.

Wright, R. (2015a). Bourdieu and music education: Habitus, field and capital in Canadian music education. In P. H.-T. Burnard & J. Soderman (Eds.), *Bourdieu and the sociology of music education* (79–98). Farnham, UK: Ashgate.

Wright, R. (2015b). Music education and social reproduction: Breaking the cycle. In C. Benedict, P. Schmidt, G. Spruce, & P. Woodford (Eds.), *The Oxford handbook of social justice and music education* (340–356). New York: Oxford University Press.

Wright, R. (2016). Informal learning in general music education. In C. Abril & B. Gault (Eds.), *Oxford approaches to teaching general music* (209–240). New York: Oxford University Press.

Wright, R., Younker, B. A., Hutchison, J., Linton, L., Beynon, S., Davidson, B., & Duarte, N. (2012, July). Tuning into the future: Sharing initial insights about the 2012 Musical Futures pilot project in Ontario. *Canadian Music Educators Magazine, 53*(4).

CHAPTER 3

Popular Music Education as Educational Policy

PATRICK SCHMIDT

WESTERN UNIVERSITY

INTRODUCTION

T his chapter is a provocation to thought and action led by the following question: Can popular music education impact music
education policy in the next decade? Conceptualizing culture and theorizing policy together is what McRobbie (1996) has called "the missing
agenda"—one that is largely absent in the field of music education.
Culturally led economic models have recently sprung to notoriety, hail-
ing the rise of the creative class (Florida, 2003) or the growth of creative
industries. Not surprisingly, when culture is viewed as one of "those
industries that have their origin in individual creativity, skills and talent [that show] a potential for wealth and job creation through the
generation and exploitation of intellectual property" (DCMS, 2001, p.
4), policy actions ensue that can lead to social polarization, charges of
gentrification, ethnic and gendered segregation or displacement, and the
marketization of communal heritages.

The challenges brought by intersecting culture and policy thought is
wide and unwieldy, particularly if one is to consider that "causal arrows
among civic and cultural involvement, reciprocity, honesty and social trust
are as tangled as well tossed spaghetti" (Putnam & Feldestein, 2003, p. 38).
Approximating these larger challenges to the field of music education

might begin through actions led by questions such as how the music education field can address challenges among cultural and educational policy that aims at excellence and those that aim at cultural renewal or social justice. What are the meeting spaces, if they are available, among strong organizations, individual entrepreneurship, and schooling? Or between welfare-oriented educational policy and culture-as-economic-driver initiatives? To what extent should such questions be more forcefully inserted in teacher/musician preparation as well as programmatic practices?

The role of popular musics and, more specifically, popular music education (PME) in all these questions and issues is wide and potentially significant. Yet in North America, no systematic engagement with popular music education as a conduit for the implementation of a broad range of cultural and educational policy has been attempted in schools, contrary to decades-long experiences in Britain, Sweden, and Australia. Regardless of its pervasiveness and potential as a tool for educative policies aimed at cultural relevancy, equity of opportunity, and creative entrepreneurship, popular music (and its cultural ideals of self-directed learning, democratic disposition, syncretic aesthetics, sampling and borrowing, and production rather than reproduction) remains largely at the periphery of music education endeavors in North America.

In this chapter, I present a case for policy thinking and policy learning as significant contributors to any lasting and systemic change to the discipline of music education, particularly change prompted by PME. I invite the reader to consider that PME's success within American schools can only be materialized alongside a change in emphasis of music education's aims in schools. Challenging as this task may be, one can take solace in the fact that such a mandate is aligned with, and has been propped by, a long line of progressive traditions stemming from Dewey to constructivism to critical pedagogy. The wide implementation of PME, I suggest, would imply and necessitate policy action predicated on a rebalance among heterogeneity of styles and musics and a unified cannon, democratized instruction and taste formation, multimodal learning and skill/content acquisition, and finally, a culture of production and sharing and one directed toward performance outcomes.

| MANY CONTEXTS, MULTIPLE FRONTS

It is clear from the significant extant literature that popular music and PME has been approached, historically, from a cultural studies standpoint. In Britain, the Centre for Contemporary Cultural Studies (CCCS) at the University of Birmingham (Cloonan, 2005) is an important marker. In American higher education, popular music is predominantly linked to sojourns into the political economies of mass culture production and its industries, as well as wide-range classes on, for example, the Beatles (Middleton, 1992). While popular music has been part of university studies since the seventies, it really gained ground in the eighties, establishing itself as part of popular music *studies*—often within or in linkage to cultural studies. In the nineties, popular music secured a space as an undergraduate programmatic opportunity; in Britain, this is especially propelled by the Further and Higher Education Act of 1992, which moved polytechnic and community schools up to university status and brought with it the academization of a skill-based, vocational educational structure. Contrary to the United Kingdom's mix of broader access and credentialism, in the United States, popular music programs today seem to be on their way to match the high hopes of all other university programs—namely, selectivity and differentiation. Programs perceived to be of high quality are in high demand. For example, the dean of the school of music at the University of Southern California (USC) recently announced that USC's popular music program is one of the most selective in the entire university.[1] Acceptance in the popular music program at USC is as competitive as admission to an Ivy League university!

In music education proper (music teacher education and music in schools), we can look back to Keith Swanwick, who in 1968 published *Popular Music and the Teacher*, a conceptual precursor to the sociologically oriented work Lucy Green developed in the nineties—a work that in the 2000s was redirected toward empirically based pedagogical practice, subsequently proselytized as method, and packaged as curricular opportunity through Musical Futures. In the United States, Patricia Shehan Campbell published perhaps the first piece on garage bands in 1995. Randall Allsup finished his dissertation on the same subject in 2002 and published on "mutual learning" in 2003. In 2004, Carlos Rodriguez set the pace with

Bridging the Gap, an edited book focusing on bringing the discussion of the role of popular music in music education to the mainstream. (In 2012, Rodriguez also edited a special issue of ACT, with many articles revolving around popular music.) In practice, however, popular music has faced an uphill battle within public schools (the main stage for music education in North America), no doubt a representation of the cultural wars enacted on behalf of a *sequential* and *quality* music education, read Western classic or its band derivatives; twelve years later, Rodriguez's gap has not been bridged. While it is hard to deny the current growth in the number of school districts using *informal* learning approaches, it is as easy to notice how it is often used as a proxy, attending to *traditional* needs and skills of music education.[2]

Regardless, the markers of an expansionist period are clear. Ten years of curricular experience in the United Kingdom and twenty years of practice in Scandinavia have provided some level of legitimacy to popular music in education. Further, and more recently, PME advocates established an "interest group" for research within the National Association for Music Education (NAfME) and the International Society for Music Education (ISME), the Association for Popular Music Education was created (ASPME; see http://www.popularmusiceducation.org), and in 2016, the *Journal for Popular Music Education* was published—the first of its kind. On the ground, particularly through "modern band" efforts, PME has seen significant momentum in the United States, which has been largely financed by Little Kids Rock (LKR; http://www.littlekidsrock.org).

Regardless of developments and growth in the last decade that have made popular music (albeit not in its etymological heterodoxy) a significant stream of education in and through music, popular music discourse and discussions are still rather marked by a Kulturkampf disposition. While PME has experienced institutionalization, and its discourse is growingly present in daily decision-making challenges (from admissions to higher education music programs to school principal's curricular priorities, for example), the cultural tensions that remain embedded and insidious to this area—particularly in the United States—are rarely addressed in policy terms. Moreover, the lack of directed and clear policy investigation in this area could be read as an indication of the extent to which ideological lines still mark and exclude popular music engagements within music education as a discipline.

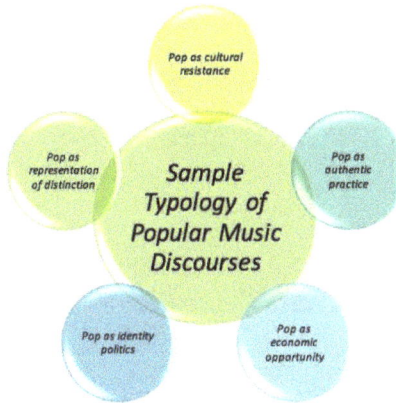

Pop as cultural
resistance

Pop as
representation
of distinction

Sample
Typology of
Popular Music
Discourses

Pop as
authentic
practice

Pop as identity
politics

Pop as
economic
opportunity

FIGURE 1. Typology of discourses.

The multiple discourses surrounding and promoting versions of PME (broadly construed) are certainly a challenge, particularly as one might attempt to establish a policy approach to the issue. For example, there are multiple standpoints heralding the value of cultural practices and cultural spaces, helping us resist institutionalized learning even when, contradictorily, we hope to facilitate the insertion of these practices into schools (pop as cultural resistance). From another standpoint, Green (2002) speaks of the unschooled way peer learning takes place and how it is linked to an "ideology of authenticity" that supposedly permeates the naturalized world of popular music, read rock (pop as authentic practice). Soderman (2013) is one among many to highlight hip hop's outsider status. He presents the conundrum of constructing a renegade identity and pigeonholing it to the structuring structures (with a nod to Bourdieu) that are a clear and unmistakable part of life within institutions of learning (pop as identity politics). The economic imperatives of credentialism is another discourse, whereby record numbers of applicants hoping for the *privilege* to learn how to become a popular musician enroll in higher education at the tune of fifty-five thousand dollars a year in tuition (pop as economic opportunity). Further still, ideology is clearly present, for example, (1) in the way the vast majority of music programs in the United States still keep "popular musicians" at bay by segregated or narrow audition protocols (pop as representation of distinction) or (2) in the way principals hire noneducation professionals to address pop music in schools (pop as labor stratification). Figure 1 presents a noncomprehensive typology of what amounts to a very complex network of discourses at play, with consequent implications to policy considerations.

This is just the tip of the iceberg. The nature of our problem is complex, and its political economy plays in different ways globally. Its presence, however, is deep and ecumenical. To exemplify this depth, one needs only to read the myriad critiques (from Bruno Nettl to Christopher Small) of the conservatoire apparatus.[3] Conservatoires are neither evil incarnate nor the source of all our problems. What they are is a representation of larger social stratification and differentiation struggles, as Bourdieu has explored (1984). The ideal of the conservatoire, then, continues to play a key role in the music education policy environs. They are successful (regardless of all the economic challenges and the many eulogies to classical music) precisely because they are embedded in a large cultural policy discourse that is taken by many (individuals, organizations, and governments alike) to be vital. Conservatoires are foundational to support the cultural policies currently in place; consider, for example, the huge impact of soft policies that still support repertoire as the marker for and equivalent of learning despite the growing hard-policy parameters established by accrediting agencies and governments (program learning objectives, anyone?). Thus change in conservatoires, as well as other institutions that are still linked to them or emulate their ideological norms, would require substantial change in the whole of the policy environs—that is, in the discursive, practical, and political ways in which cultural production is constructed and supported.[4]

To understand the force of our persisting and still prevailing cultural/ educational policy environs, we can use both Mantie (2012) and Tagg (1998). Mantie provides insight into the historical recontextualization of bands from community to school and the subsequent meso- and microcodification (at the level of district and school) of bands as the pedagogical drive for school music. Tagg, on the other hand, provides insight into the astonishing example of Sweden, articulating how a cultural environment (mirrored by an aligning policy environment) created the space for initially soft policies to take place facilitating popular musics in schools (subsequently fomented by "harder" educational policy action). The explanation of the environmental cultural reasons popular music surged early in that country helps us consider the challenges ahead, particularly in terms of changing popular music as music education within American institutions. He states:

> [Sweden lacks the] high cultural historical ballast in relation to other nations. Put simply, Swedes did not have to contend with legacies of the likes of Bach, Bacon, Beethoven, Descartes, Debussy, Dante, Gallilei, Goethe, Haydn, Hegel, Mozart, Pascal, Purcell, Sartre, Schiller or Shakespeare . . . there were no big historical names of high culture on which to focus bourgeois national identity and that the institutionalization of high culture was therefore less substantial and less powerful than elsewhere. . . . Sweden's history of class conflict also differs radically from the UK or Central Europe and the nation experienced a much later and faster process of industrialization. . . . all these factors and others . . . contributed to the establishment of a political climate in which [popular music education] was able to materialize and flourish earlier. (Tagg, 1998, pp. 220–221)

Regardless of the problem of if and how popular music education can establish itself as a systemically significant element in the music education landscape, another, perhaps more substantial challenge is whether popular music education can *substantially alter* the nature of the current music education landscape, its purposes and priorities? The answer is clearly not simple and not at hand. In policy terms, the potential benefits of a more systematic investment in PME (as a curricular/programmatic proposition and as a socially oriented learning endeavor) are rather compelling: PME could create a cleavage for socially just practices in the field; it could lead to the professionalization of a more diverse cadre of teachers (in terms of race, ethnicity, and social class); it could drive in and educate a larger subset of the school population than the currently reached; it could facilitate stronger cross-disciplinary and politically oriented curricular development; it could facilitate vocational educational development and technical training; or it could aid music teaching to address/meet the pervasive critical and creative mandates of educational policy discourse today. I am not presenting PME as a "policy solution" (Wildavsky, 1988), nor am I dismissive of significant critiques of popular music programs—for instance, how they can emphasize heteronormativity and sustain problematic gendered norms (Smith, 2013) or how social justice and access issues have often been peripheral considerations to the milieu (Koza, 1996). What I am saying is that in the absence of a reconfigured cultural and educational policy environment—developed within the field and communicated from the music education field outward—popular music will likely remain marginal in schools and linked to the realities such as those at USC, becoming, as it happened to jazz in the 1970s, just another way of sustaining higher education programmatic and enrolment needs.

It is critical to ask, then, if the political climate today would allow the materialization and the flourishing of PME as a systemic and structural element in our educational environment. As this analysis is rather broad, I will address only a segment of it in this chapter. In what follows, I argue that the abovementioned materialization and flourishing demands that we pay greater attention to the role of policy, policy thinking, and policy learning as pertinent elements in the popular music education puzzle.

POPULAR MUSIC AND CULTURAL POLICY

The unoriginal stance from which I start is that the global work developed on behalf of informality and popular music education as important avenues for learning represents a set of compelling opportunities for students. The not-argued portion of this stance is that to be effective and impactful, this work must also be thought of and framed within a policy perspective using policy tools. A full description of the latter is beyond the scope of this chapter. The chapter focuses, therefore, on the first because it can present a larger strategic element to PME efforts. Essential to these efforts is a layered work that functions concomitantly on macroconceptual and strategic discourse and on micro-, curricular-pedagogical efforts—a dual front approach needed for any policy design—from its conceptualization to implementation (Howlett, 2011).

The center of the argument here is that, at the policy level, popular music must be placed as appropriate culture work on behalf of a thoughtful educational strategy. This means emphasizing culture in the traditional sense—that is, as *the* arts and heritage for which popular music studies as cultural studies have provided plenty of rhetoric and evidentiary ammunition. It also means presenting popular music as an indisputable element in the political economy of culture—an element to which higher education has latched on but from which K–12 schools continue to be insulated, at least in the United States. In near simplistic, almost instrumental terms, "the simple fact is that those who engage with cultural experiences when young are more likely to engage with it later." This is traditional policy at its best, and it has everything to do with public education. If we "expand the range of experiences that are offered, the demand for them will rise" (Hewison, 2014, p. 229).

In more complex and specific terms, there are two other key layers to be addressed. First, the macrodiscourse ought to propose and evidence how popular music as an educational avenue can facilitate important ways of making meaning, helping youth understand that both "politics and the arts [key features of popular music, historically] have a common interest in shaping a society's wider culture" and fostering an opportunity to see culture "not just as a way of life, but as a way of organizing life" (Hewison, 2014, p. 3). Britain has understood this potential, and its rather active policy sphere in music education has led to an implementation of this macrostrategy. The policy learning experienced by music education in England, particularly in the 1990s and early 2000s, was generated by a clos(er) relationship between the field and government and is an interesting example.[5] It allowed/generated a policy disposition that sees popular music as a way to amplify cultural opportunities (social justice as access), not simply in a social studies kind of way, but in an artistic, creative, and yes, functional way. The intellectual argument is rather old; Simon Frith (1978) articulated that popular music functions to produce rather than reproduce culture. But its policy translation has been slow and arduous. Nevertheless, the notion of developing opportunities for critical thinking, listening, creating, and composing via popular music is accepted educational and cultural policy today.

The dispersed, federalist nature of political decision making in the United States has limited such gains, but as I write, the new Every Student Succeeds Act (ESSA) provisions suggest a shift toward local decision making and might move us away from the marked narrowing of the curriculum institutionalized during the 2000s (Beveridge, 2009; Gerrity, 2009). As the United States moves from struggles over major federal policies to multiple and perhaps more influential spaces at the local and state levels, states and local school districts will likely reestablish education polices on curricula, assessment, teacher education, and all the accompanying nuts and bolts of providing a *well-rounded* education for all students.[6] The extent of these changes is difficult to predict, but devolution might allow for practices focused on local needs and for constituencies to gain traction again. A regular effect of localization is heightened implementation irregularity and/or dissimilarity, which might create space for local yet coordinated efforts to implement PME initiatives. All this could prove an opportune moment for PME and its curricula in American public schools.

The second area of a larger cultural policy from which PME can benefit and to which it could contribute is the growing integration among three areas of cultural production that today live in tension. First, one has an *official culture* that provides "the supply of certain forms of cultural production" and is often supported by gatekeepers who "fund people and institutions to create them [cultural products] at the risk—or even in the expectation—that there will be a financial loss" (Hewison, 2014, p. 221). Second (these are not hierarchical), one has a *commercial culture* that is led by gatekeepers investing in what they hope will make a profit. Both are long and well-established traditions. The last generation, however, has seen the rise of a *homemade culture* that is "self-starting and self-funded, and depends of a self-appointed network of peers to share enthusiasm and approval for whatever is produced" (p. 221). The latter has been amplified by digital environs and fostered by "digital artistries," as Väkevä (2012) has clearly explained.

Addressing these three areas within curricular and pedagogical forms is a key educational challenge for schools and universities today. At the same time, popular music practices and dispositions are, arguably, at an advantage to explore how to synergize these three cultural realms and how to use that synergy to engage youth as producers, creators, and consumers. This would be apt and helpful policy framing (Schmidt, 2017) and would reenergize music as a way of learning the world (a Freirean challenge). Being in the world while within schools, which can be alienating, and thus approximating education to the realm of the daily can aid in the enormous but valuable challenge of fostering *deliberative democracy* and, by consequence (potentially), social justice within schools (Gaztambide-Fernandez, 2011).

Here, then, a policy approach—which at first glance might be read as instrumentalist—in fact helps capture Dewey's procedural ideals for what education could do for and should be in people's lives.

What Dewey did not anticipate but what a policy outlook on popular music must contend with is the nature of homemade culture, particularly in that much of what is constructed there "might involve great skill, but can also be done without much difficulty," with the decision about "quality of what is produced now lying in the hands of those who see, hear, or taste the finished article" (Holden, 2008, p. 11). Central to the policy argument to be made is that participatory culture (Jenkins, 2008) or deliberative democracy (Gutmann & Thompson, 2004) are not and should not function at the periphery of schooled environments; rather, particular practices such as music can have an important function in infusing schooling with these dispositions, approximating individual interest to institutional needs and providing institutional support to diversified pursuits. Schooling, particularly the public kind, remains a pertinent space not because of the teacher but because technology and homemade culture have an underbelly where access is not widely available (economics) and participatory claims can be transient and provide limited impact.[7]

The disposition that PME could help facilitate within the school setting is one that is often missing not only within music but also in the overdetermined reality of today's schools—that is, that education is to be developed *with* and not *for*. There is a clear link here to the homemade culture concept. As Charles Leadbeater (2009) points out, "If the culture that the web is creating were to be reduced to a single, simple design principle it would be the principle of *With*. The web invites us to think and act *with* people, rather than for them, on their behalf or even doing things to them" (p. 5).

A cultural policy for PME should be based on the notion that a school is defined as an assemblage of voices. As a field, music education has a long tradition of doing things *to* students and a long cultural history of doing things on *behalf* of populations (while commonly disregarding minorities or "peripheral" populations, such as those in urban centers or rural areas). Policy thinking aligned with the challenges and opportunities placed by the conflation of the three cultural domains I mentioned previously can provide both a more integrated curricular experience and a renewal for action within the field. A cultural policy for PME would create the vision for schools to act as cultural organizations whose mission is to "mediate between the intrinsic purposes of culture and the instrumental outcomes that follow," fostering and generating social capital, and thus supporting social justice work on multiple levels and for multiple (and diverse) populations (Hewison, 2014, p. 228). This needs not be the sole or focused aim of schools, but it can become at least a partial mission—a mission that can be delivered aptly and ethically through music.

PME, then, is not simply about more music and more diverse music; it is not just about pedagogical diversity; it is not about sociologizing the classroom. As articulated here, PME is presented as itself (curricular action) but also as something beyond itself (a proxy for policy strategy). Thus it becomes a policy orientation, a tool to help music education provide a serious and encompassing pathway for cultural capital production, recentering an antiquated and hierarchical model (band/Western classical) to provide a more expansive and democratic vision that is ethical and pragmatic.

▎AFTER THE VISION, THE (HARD) WORK OF POLICY

Going beyond the Traditional Policy Cycle

Policy analysis can be defined as an "applied social science discipline which uses multiple methods of inquiry and arguments to produce and transform policy-relevant information that may be utilized in political settings to resolve policy problems" (Dunn, 1981, p. 35). Dunn's balanced approach of "inquiry and argumentation" remains an important reminder that policy thinking requires both information and conceptualization. As a discipline, policy dates to the postwar and arguably was established by Lasswell and Lerner in their landmark book *The Policy Orientation* (1951). There Lasswell funds the notion of the "policy sciences" and the development of a cadre of experts capable of bringing the necessary knowledge to the decision-making table. Lasswell's vision focused (importantly) on both better understanding the policymaking process and providing the intelligence needs of the policymaker.

Over the years, the policy-analytic enterprise followed a much more constricted path of evolution. As Fischer (2003) asserts, "Policy inquiry as it is known today, particularly what we call policy analysis emerged in the 1960s and 1970s and took a narrower technocratic form geared more to managerial practices than to the facilitation of democratic government" (p. 4). Stone (2011) has called this the "rationality project," where policy thinking was not multidisciplinary and methodologically rich as envisioned by Lasswell but rather shaped by a neopositivist/empiricist outlook, which formed the efficiency and effectiveness discourses that were catastrophically applied by governments in attempts to *solve* complex issues; for instance, the war on poverty (sixties and seventies), housing problems (throughout the eighties and beyond), and educational ills (starting with A National at Risk all the way to the accountability projects of No Child Left Behind and Race to the Top). This view of policy portrayed and constructed the decision maker as a *satisficer*—someone who seeks only "satisfactory" information that will "suffice." Out of this, evaluative research thrived, featuring precise and impartial empirical measurement of program impacts and establishing itself as the sine qua non of policy work (Fischer, 2003, p. 8).

Many of the large-scale historic policy experiments have shown us, however, that not only "a heavy emphasis on quantitative analysis neglected [the challenges of] critical social and political variables" but, as DeLeon (1988) clarifies, "the putatively 'objective' nature of [empiricist policy] modeling exercises and their computational opaqueness, concealed the reality that their underlying and usually unspoken political and social assumptions were what actually drove their results" (p. 70). Enter Majone and Wildavsky (1979), who developed an evolutionary theory that established policy issues as evolving processes and placed policy construction in relation to changing group interests. Alongside this, we saw the emergence and the trials of the politics of implementation, where the challenge became how to reconcile policy directives and the implementation differentiation presented by distinct contexts and dissenting constituencies. My point—finally—is that the naïve but resistant notion that better information leads to better solutions has historically been proven incorrect, showing that empirical capability is always in service of normative framing, and thus that the latter matters as much, if not more, than the first.

All this is to say that policy, certainly in music education, needs to be conceived differently. I am not suggesting a postempiricist era, as data-driven information can be illuminating (e.g., Elpus, 2014). Rather, I want to focus on the idea that policy thinking taken on broader terms can be an important tool for change. For example, knowing how to conceptualize ideas and enterprises in terms of policy framework can help us approximate social and political challenges (in education and/or culture) while constructively managing and influencing them. A policy stance, or framing (Schmidt, 2013), helps us keep in mind that meanings and discourses that circulate around groups (say, music educators) are often not fully their own—that is, not fully individually owned (in the sense of individuals having full autonomy over their views) but are at least partially communally and discursively constructed. The point here is to consider that an opposition to popular music in schools is not simply a position individuals may take but a position of the current systemic policy environs, which in turn reinforces individual dispositions, even when those individuals don't openly voice them. Adding to the challenge is the idea that "even when social groups succeed in loosening the hold of a particular social meaning, they do it by embracing a different one" (Fischer, 2003, p. 13).

This politics of representation (another way of seen policy action) is key to understanding the possible entrée of PME as a substantial and impactful pathway for curricular delivery and renewed programmatic construction within public schools in the United States. Unless compelling analytical reasons for embracing PME are made (focused on policy directives based on cultural shift and pragmatic outcomes), a systemic modification of allegiances is unlikely.

Symbolism and Strategic Change

What I argued in the previous section—that is, that policy is equal measures data framing/collecting and symbolic politics—is nearly taken for granted in policy studies. To reiterate, my central claim is that PME can be a way to manifestly change the role of school in positively and pertinently impacting cultural policy today. This is the kind of ideational prism that is constitutive of how policy thinking conceptualizes notions, garners actionable support, and traces feasible implementation strategies— the definition of symbolic politics. Wildavsky (1988) made this point already, arguing that under conditions of uncertainty, ideas serve as guides to behavior. Claims to realpolitik are often established by citing Weber (1948), as he argues that "not ideas, but material and ideal interests, directly govern men's conduct." While the dictum has run the world, the caveat that follows it is often, and conveniently, omitted: "Yet very frequently the 'world images' that have been created by 'ideas' have, like switchmen, determined the tracks along which action has been pushed by the dynamic of interest" (p. 280). Thoughtful policy thinking is necessary if we hope for impactful policy change.

In North America, any policy thinking and action directed at PME requires attention to the impact and influence LKR has today. This is perhaps the central example of how a dynamic of interest is creating the space in which a global image of popular music (unfortunately, not fully PME) is generating political and policy traction. Historically, we might be witnessing a similar policy/political event to the institutionalization of wind bands, which was fomented by a conflating set of dynamic interests, as Roger Mantie (2012) articulates in convincing terms. Mantie argues that *band* remains perhaps the most unique signifier of school music. While concurring, I posit that this is not because of well-crafted policy work. What is true is that the world image of band found economic and ideational track (based on cultural value that emulated but extended the Westernized notions of value) that enabled successful implementation by generating buy-in. Material and ideal interests, via LKR, are having significant influence in the music education landscape today. That energy can be harvested and multiplied, but only appropriate policy framing can guarantee the same scale and impact in today's complex and challenging educational and cultural environments.

Policy action toward PME is significant because there is no such a thing as the institution of PME in the United States (unlike the institution of band). Without an inclination to act and think in policy terms, such institutionalization will be necessarily delayed, and even a cohesive PME discourse (which doesn't exist yet) will be less likely to break through the general institution of schooling. In other words, policy can make an institution out of PME. This is meaningful because although institutions do not affect political action, their discursive practices shape the behaviors of actors that do. This is explained by Fischer (2003) and is worth citing at length:

Supplying [individuals] with regularized behavioral rules, standards of assessment, and emotive commitments, institutions influence political actors by structuring or shaping the political and social interpretations of the problems they have to deal with and by limiting the choice of policy solutions that might be implemented. The interests of actors are still there [for instance, to provide quality music education or to constitute musical skill] but they are influenced by the institutional structures, norms, and rules through which they are pursued. Such structural relationships give shape to both social and political expectations and the possibility of realizing them. Indeed . . . it is often the opportunities and barriers of such institutions that determine people's preferences, rather than the other way around, as more commonly assumed. (p. 28)

Important here is to note that the institution of PME via policy thinking and policy learning is necessary for it to penetrate school music discourses, but this same institution (that must also be represented within and by multiple concrete institutions/organizations/bodies) will also be necessary so that individuals, enmeshed in a traditional understanding of what is valid practice in music education, can think differently about their milieu. This institution of PME is necessary so that teachers can see themselves migrating to it. Once their own self-interest and the potential of PME as institution become significant enough, change can be rapidly paradigmatic.

Modeling Policy Thinking

My own research (Schmidt, 2014; Schmidt, 2012; Laes & Schmidt, 2016) suggests that the merger of three key practices—policy thinking, framing disposition, and activism—can help us address today's market-compelled environment of accountability and push back at it while creating the wherewithal to engage in the necessary changes in our fields. These practices can become leading dispositions toward more diverse models of interaction with music learning, making, and performing that are "out in the world"—PME certainly has a role here.

While these ideas are delineated in further detail elsewhere (Schmidt & Colwell, 2017), it is important to outline some of these notions. First, I would argue that music educators interested in an environmental change where PME becomes a constitutional element of the cultural/educational experience that schools must provide to the well-rounded education of children and youth should see themselves as contributors to and consumers of policy thinking and analysis; they would benefit from becoming more broadly conceptualized as agents within cultural policies and its study and practice. Then, to achieve greater engagement with policy, individuals and organizations must focus on how to develop a framing disposition— that is, the individual or organizational wherewithal to generate opportunities and put innovative projects to practice. Engaging with and developing a framing disposition—where voice and creative agency are built from an informed understanding of contextual complexities—is thus a professional right as well an ethical responsibility, one that can lead to the "demand for a rights approach as a central component of policy action" in education (Barton & Armstrong, 2007, p. 6). Elsewhere, I talk about a framing disposition (Schmidt, 2013) as a "disposition toward unusual connections and a facility to engage with unconventional concepts" (p. 24), proposing that this is an essential consciousness for educators of all stripes—particularly to those in the arts. Change is dependent on these skills/requisites/dispositions, and so a framing disposition becomes an important identity formation element to individuals interested in PME. Finally, I suggest that, as it comes together, this scenario delineates an activist disposition for music educators in the twenty-first century (Laes & Schmidt, 2016), which in the words of Stuart Cunningham (1992), works to "avoid a politics of status quo—a sophomoric version of civics" precisely by focusing on the "well-springs of engagements with policy" (p. 9). This is crucial in sustaining and expanding nonnormative spaces where music education can flourish, providing an education in and through music that is equally concerned with aesthetics and equity, sound and interaction, skill and participant voice.

I argue then that policy thinking might be an important way to foster what Angela McRobbie (1996) calls a program for change, which attempts to systematically operationalize the disposition toward practice critique and change that already exist within those committed to enacting PME. Policy engagement can be presented as both a disposition and another strategic way of thinking the field. My argument for policy engagement, then, is predicated on the idea that "once we introduce notions of policy

[they] assists us in excavating the structures that push cultures in certain directions" (Lewis & Miller, 2003, p. 19), leading us to acknowledge our own role in it, be it passive or active. As I see it, this leads to an awareness of policy as a field of action and provides a better understanding of how policy discourses can be influential, often working "to privilege certain ideas and topics and speakers and exclude others" (Ball, 2009, p. 5).

In rather practical terms, our field—and particularly those advocating for PME—must become familiar with policy frameworks and know how to apply them in their work (as an organizational leader, researcher, practitioner). Could we, for instance, be more apt at using the notion of policy gap to insert PME as an apt pathway to address cultural learnings thus far unaddressed by schools? Could we use the language of agenda setting and learn from its vast literature? Could we benefit from the work of Kingdon (1995) and become better prepared to identify and use policy windows? Could we address program development using these and multiple other guides and the conceptual richness that comes with them? Could we better interact with general educators and administration, let alone legislators, by doing so? Might those have useful and constructive effects? As you guessed, my answer is yes.

▌ POLICY LEARNING, POLICY THINKING, POLICY CHANGE

What the following diagram describes is a representation of the process of policy change as I propose in this chapter. It suggests that policy learning and thinking are required to exert influence and consequently change policy environs (see Figure 2). The model purposively avoids a "center" and clearly delineates the boarders of two policy environs as neither clearly marked nor amorphous but rather as fluid and changing. It is important to articulate that the model is not a fixed entity or a goal; it is simply a snapshot of a sequence of moments. The idea is one of a strategic map that could be used by a policy analyst; for instance, as he or she prepares to communicate with a community, using it as a way to gauge and explain the work done and to be done. One of the goals is to avoid notions of policy cycle, where clean and clear structures of problem-narrowing or finding, conceptualization, enactment/implementation, and evaluation (then repeat) are the norm. This is significant, as this "analytical" tactic is limited (although at times useful) and often leads to detached thinking and contextually disconnected efforts, contributing to possible policy failure. My model suggests that establishing a PME in a systemic and far-reaching manner within American schools will require more than advocacy and curricular campaigning. Learning about policy and developing policy thinking capacity are also necessary.

To this end, the model points to the fact that if policy issues evolve—and they do—the evolution process is more cellular than teleological. Growth and change happen as agents act within an environment. As they do so, they simultaneously affect and are affected by it, providing both opportunity for change as well as understanding resistance, which needs to be strategically addressed. This elastic understanding of change is particularly apt when addressing complex issues such as education and are also appropriate when evaluating the landscape of the issue at hand, the status and potential for popular music education.

Policy learning (PL) as first explained by Heclo (1974) represents a "relatively enduring alteration in behavior that results from experience" (p. 306). Perhaps more significant here, the concept of PL captures the efforts "to reduce the gap between what is expected from a program and what governments [but also organizations, agencies, institutions, or groups of individuals] are doing" (Rose, 1993, p. 50). This change from experience, which is channeled through a conceptual idea that helps one focus on specific strategic objectives (reducing the gap between PME reality today and the manner in which it can seriously become a part of curricular policy in schools), is critical to policy change and the construction of a new policy. For this reason, PL is characterized by a traced line in the policy change model. The line cuts across the whole of the policy environ, both in its current and in its expanded (or envisioned) form. It is neither uniform nor unidirectional; it forms a terrain, drawing from multiple spaces, opportunities, and environments. It certainly impacts/informs and is redirected by policy thinking as well.

Policy thinking as articulated previously is a more focused and directed kind of effort that benefits from policy learning but also functions independently. Thus policy learning is the effect and outcome of efforts by a larger community or sets of communities. Indeed, at times, it is what happens to participants in a network just by the fact that individuals are working and acting within said network. Policy thinking, on the other hand, is the directed action of a specific, well-delineated group as they follow or trace a particular policy agenda or strategy. Both policy learning and thinking are significant. Each work in distinct ways.

Using a notion of change that is not linear (although certainly has lines of pressure and motion), the diagram presents policy learning and policy thinking as critical and in fact integral to both temporary shifts and more sedimentary changes in policy environs (the latter depending on a series of the first). At the macro level, as I articulated previously, it seems critical to provide a policy vision for PME as a significant contribution to the formation of schools as a space for cultural production—that is, a space where culture is created/generated, consumed/reproduced, and critiqued. In some ways, these are the basic criteria guiding the new (2014) National Standards, established on the basis of Create, Perform, Respond (see http://www.nafme.org/my-classroom/standards). And this is significant, as there is an important policy environment that has been created by the standards (and their relation to Common Core efforts) and should not be undervalued or dismissed. Unfortunately, and in many ways as a reaction to the larger US educational policy today, the standards take these elements (create, perform, respond) not as formational to one's engagement with cultural production but rather as functional ways to "evaluate students' progress" while encountering cultural products—often of a

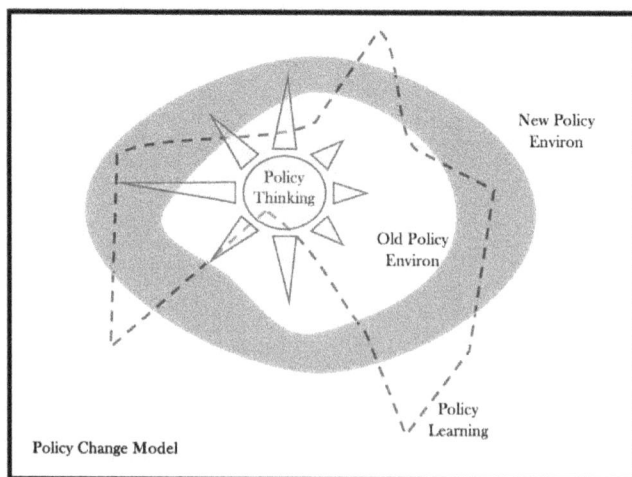

FIGURE 2. Policy change model.

very limited kind. Mostly locked within traditional music formats (band, choir, orchestra), where creation is nominally and marginally engaged, the standards began as a reaction to current policy norms; thus, they fail to contribute and influence it. Given the programmatic homogeneity within K–12 settings (not their contexts, which can be very diverse, but the structure of programs, which are rather undiverse), it is also unsurprising that, historically, the standards catered to and enforced the maintenance of these established policy environs.

This is one reason the establishment of PME is not and cannot simply be a matter of curricular-pedagogical efforts or an issue for traditional advocacy campaigns. Naturally, both are important and necessary, but in my view, a systemic and impactful shift will necessitate a larger cultural impact–based argumentation. And this argument will need to be constructed into a new, or at least ampler, policy environment. This will require new discourse as well as the cooptation of current discourses— from the formation of teachers to the education of principals, from diverse and contextual curricular development to thoughtfully conceptualized white-papers, from organizational campaigning and lobbying to empirical policy analysis.

One practical action would be for PME actors to become students of the work on policy coalitions approaches (PCAs) by Sabatier and Jenkins-Smith, which concentrates on subsystems and policy learning (1993). This work emphasizes the impact of policy ideas and analysis in the policy process. This is not the same as the formation of "networks" generated by assembling individuals or groups that already interact with each other regularly. Coalitions focus on wider ties than their own (without neglecting those, naturally), always paying attention to how communication is key in capacity formation. PCAs help frame political questions and programmatic solutions, whereby the manner in which issues are presented (e.g., here, a cultural production vision supported by a wide coalition and carried by serious academic/research backing) can affect policy decision making in both direct and indirect ways. This in turn can increase the space for change and alter the policy environs. Sabatier (1993) offers three ways to consider how individuals tend to organize their lifeworld and how that can be useful in terms of policy change. These three categories are "a deep core of fundamental normative and ontological axioms that define a person's underlying political philosophy, a near (policy) core on basic strategies and policy positions for achieving deep core beliefs in the policy area or subsystem in question [e.g., PME], and a set of secondary aspects comprising a multitude of instrumental decisions and information searches necessary to implement the policy core in the specific policy area" (p. 30).

While these can be seen as a bit manipulative, they delineate the complex and challenging work to be done if policy change is desired. Hopefully they also serve as an entry point to understanding how policy thinking and learning should be carefully considered within our field.

▍THE (RATHER SIMPLE) TAKEAWAY

The question that opened this chapter is, Can popular music education impact music education policy in the next decade? What I hope to have made clear is that the answer is yes. My central claim is that PME can be a way to manifestly change the role of school in positively and pertinently impacting cultural policy today. I also argued, however, that in order for a vision of PME to take place within a timely manner (a decade), proponents of PME need to better understand and develop their own policy thinking, facilitating policy learning as part of what informs the field and its actions.

The outcome of successful work in these areas could be PME being placed as appropriate culture work on behalf of a thoughtful educational strategy. As I articulated in the previous sections, a cultural policy for PME could create the vision for schools to *also* act as cultural organizations whose mission is to "mediate between the intrinsic purposes of culture and the instrumental outcomes that follow," fostering and generating social capital and thus supporting social justice work on multiple levels and for multiple (and diverse) populations (Hewison, 2014, p. 228).

It is important to highlight that what I am proposing is not akin to replacement but the expansion and the leveraging of wider policy change through PME efforts. PME is well positioned to aid a broadening of the discourse that, if helped by the development of policy efforts, can effect change. However, this shift will necessarily involve other and well-established constituencies. The replacement of canons is not in anyone's interest (well . . . some people's interest) and will not effect the sort of significant change that I am suggesting here (it has not in Sweden or in England). Thus PME's success within American schools will require a rebalance of the de facto and stated aims of music education, from skill/content acquisition and taste formation to cultural production and sharing. Most significantly, PME, predicated on heterogeneity of styles and musics, democratized instruction, multimodal learning, and a culture of production and sharing—not reproduction and performance—is a key venue for a shift in the current music education policy environment. This does not mean, by any stretch of imagination, a manifested destiny as some proselytize. It simply means that the payoff, a significant amplification (pun intended) of and change in music education's role in schools, is certainly worth the effort.

| NOTES

1. Robert Cutietta, dean of USC's Thornton School of Music, made this comment in his remarks at the College Music Society Summit on the Undergraduate Curriculum, which took place on June 2016 at the University of South Carolina. According to him, admission in 2016 was given to only 7% of applicants.
2. This instrumentalist approach is clear on NAfME's website and how it portraits popular music. See http://www.nafme.org/tag/pop-music/.
3. Patrick Jones provides an important critique and extensive background on this issue, with detailed citations on a series of critiques of the conservatoire and its problematics in relation to policy. See Jones, 2017, pp. 242–251.
4. Economics is the other meaningful factor, but it is only a political shift—that is, a different, ampler cultural policy paradigm can be sufficient a catalyst.
5. Policy learning is a term of art that is widely available in the policy studies literature. Peter May's article "Policy Learning and Failure" is an early and important example. I explore policy learning further later in this chapter.
6. For detailed information on the legislation and the definition of "well-rounded," see the National Association for Music Education, "Full Legislative Analysis of All Key Music and Arts Provisions of the Every Student Succeeds Act (ESSA) [S. 1177]," 2015, http://www.nafme.org/wp-content/files/2015/11/NAfME-ESSA-Comprehensive-Analysis-2015.pdf.
7. As Hewison (2014) argues, "A study for the Arts Council in 2010 [in Britain] concluded that there was little evidence that digital technology offered a way to engage people who had little or no current interest in arts and culture. The problems of education, access and exclusion have not been resolved" (222).

▌REFERENCES

Allsup, R. E. (2002). *Crossing over: Mutual learning and democratic action in instrumental music education.* (Unpublished dissertation). Teachers College Columbia University.

Allsup, R. E. (2003). Mutual learning and democratic action in instrumental music education. *Journal of Research in Music Education, 51*(1), 24–37.

Allsup, R. E. (2008). Creating an educational framework for popular music in public schools: Anticipating the second-wave. Presentation at the American Education Research Association Conference, New York City, NY.

Ball, S. J. (2009). *The education debate.* Bristol, UK: Policy Press.

Barton, L., & Armstrong, F. (2007). Disability, education and inclusion: Cross-cultural issues and dilemmas. In G. Albrecht, K. Seelman, & M. Bury (Eds.), *The handbook of disability studies* (34–67). London: Sage.

Beveridge, T. (2009). No child left behind and fine arts classes. *Arts Education Policy Review, 111*(1), 4–7.

Bourdieu, P. (1984). Distinction: A social critique of the judgement of taste (R. Nice, Trans.). Cambridge, MA: Harvard University Press.

Bourdieu, P. (2002). Habitus. In J. Hillier & E. Rooksby (Eds.), *Habitus: A sense of place.* Aldershot, UK: Ashgate.

Campbell, P. S. (1995). Of garage bands and song-getting: The musical development of young rock musicians. *Research Studies in Music Education, 4.*

Cloonan, M. (2005). What is popular music studies? Some observations. *British Journal of Music Education, 22*(1), 1–17.

Cunningham, S. (1992). *Framing culture: Criticism and policy in Australia.* Sydney: Allen and Unwin.

DeLeon, P. (1988). *Advise and consent: The development of policy sciences.* New York: Russell Sage Foundations.

Dunn, W. N. (1981). *Public policy analysis.* Englewood Cliffs, NJ: Prentice-Hall.

Elpus, K. (2014). Evaluating the effect of No Child Left Behind on U.S. music course enrollments. *Journal of Research in Music Education, 62*(3), 215–233.

Fischer, F. (2003). *Reframing public policy: Discursive politics and deliberative practices.* New York: Oxford University Press.

Florida, R. (2003). *The rise of the creative class.* New York: Basic Books.

Frith, S. (1978) *The sociology of rock.* London: Constable.

Gaztambide-Fernández, R. (2011). Musicking in the city: Reconceptualizing urban music education as cultural practice. *Action, Theory and Criticism in Music Education, 10*(1), 1–23.

Gerrity, K. (2009). No child left behind: Determining the impact of policy on music education in Ohio. *Bulletin of the Council for Research in Music Education, 179,* 79–93.

Green, L. (1999). Research in the sociology of music education: Some introductory concepts. *Music Education Research, 1*(2), 159–170.

Green, L. (2002). *How popular musicians learn: A way ahead for music education.* Aldershot, UK: Ashgate.

Green, L. (2008). *Music, informal learning and the school: A new classroom pedagogy.* Aldershot, UK: Ashgate.

Gutmann, A., & Thompson, D. (2004). *Why deliberative democracy?* Princeton, NJ: Princeton University Press.

Heclo, H. (1974). *Modern social politics in Britain and Sweden.* New Haven, CT: Yale University Press.

Hewison, R. (2014). *Cultural capital: The rise and fall of creative Britain.* London: Verso.

Holden, J. (2008). *Democratic culture: Opening up the arts to everyone.* London: Demos.

Howlett, M. (2011). *Designing public policies: Principles and instruments.* London: Routledge.

Jones, P. (2017). Policy and higher education. In P. Schmidt & R. Colwell (Eds.), *Policy and the political life of music education* (242–251). New York: Oxford University Press.

Kingdon, J. W. (1995). *Agendas, alternatives, and public policies* (2nd ed.). Boston: Little, Brown & Company.

Laes, T., & Schmidt, P. (2016). Activism in music education: Working towards inclusion, policy, and teacher activism in the Finnish music school context. *British Journal of Music Education, 33*(1), 5–23.

Lasswell, H. D. (1951). The policy orientation. In H. Laswell & D. Lerner (Eds.), *The policy sciences.* Stanford: Stanford University Press.

Leadbeater, C. (2009). *The art of with: An original essay for Cornerhouse, Manchester.* Published under Creative Commons license.

Lewis, J., & Miller, T. (Eds.). (2003). *Critical cultural policy studies: A reader.* Malden, MA: Blackwell.

Majone, G., & Wildavsky, A. (1979). Implementation as evolution. In J. Pressman & A. Wildavsky (Eds.), *Implementation.* Berkeley: University of California Press.

Mantie, R. (2012). Bands and/as music education: Antinomies and the struggle for legitimacy. *Philosophy of Music Education Review, 20*(1), 63–81.

May, P. (1992). Policy learning and failure. *Journal of Public Policy, 12*(4), 331–354.

McRobbie, A. (1996). All the world's a stage, screen or magazine: When culture is the logic of late capitalism. *Media, Culture and Society, 18*(3), 335–342.

Middleton, R. (1992). *Studying popular music* (2nd ed.). Buckingham and Bristol: Open University Press.

Nettl, B. (1995). *Heartland excursions: Ethnomusicological reflections on schools of music.* Urbana: University of Illinois Press.

Putnam, R. D., & Feldstein, L. (2003). *Better together: Restoring American community.* New York: Simon & Schuster.

Rodriguez, C. (Ed.). (2004). *Bridging the gap: Popular music and education.* Reston, VA: MENC.

Rodriguez, C. (Ed.). (2012). Ethics in music education. *Action, Criticism and Theory in Music Education, 11*(1), 1–6.

Rose, R. (1993). *Lesson-drawing in public policy: A guide to learning across time and space.* Chatham, NJ: Chatham House.

Sabatier, P. A. (1993). Policy change over a decade or more. In P. A. Sabatier & H. Jenkins-Smith (Eds.), *Policy change and learning: An advocacy coalition approach.* Boulder, CO: Westview Press.

Sabatier, P., & Jenkins-Smith, H. (Eds.). (1993). *Policy change and learning: An advocacy coalition approach*. Boulder, CO: Westview Press.

Schmidt, P. (2012). Critical leadership and music educational practice. *Theory Into Practice, 51*(3), 221–228.

Schmidt, P. (2013). Creativity as a complex practice: Developing a framing capacity in higher music education. In P. Burnard (Ed.), *Developing creativities in higher music education: International perspectives and practices* (23–36). London: Routledge.

Schmidt, P. (2014). NGOs as a framework for an education in and through music: Is the Third Sector viable? *International Journal of Music Education, 32*(1), 31–52.

Schmidt, P. (2017). Why policy matters: Developing a policy vocabulary within music education. In P. Schmidt & R. Colwell (Eds.), *Policy and the political life of music education*. New York: Oxford University Press.

Schmidt, P., & Colwell, R. (Eds.). (2017). *Policy and the political life of music education*. New York: Oxford University Press.

Small, C. (1977). *Music, education, society*. Hanover, NH: Wesleyan University Press.

Smith, G. (2013). Seeking "success" in popular music. *Music Education Research International, 6*, 26–37.

Soderman, J. (2013). The formation of "Hip Hop Academicus": How American scholars talk about the academisation of hip hop. *British Journal of Music Education, 30*(3).

Stone, D. (2011). *Policy paradox: The art of political decision making*. New York: W. W. Norton.

Swanwick, K. (1968). *Popular music and the teacher*. London: Pergamon Press.

Tagg, P. (1998). The Göteborg connection. *Popular Music, 17*(2), 219–242.

Väkevä, L. (2012). Digital artistry and mediation: (Re)mixing music education. In C. Benedict & P. Schmidt (Eds.), *The Place of music in the 21st century: A global view*. National Society for the Study of Education, *111*(1), 177–195. Teachers College Press.

Weber, M. (1948). *The social psychology of the world religions*. Reprinted in H. H. Gerth & C. Wright Mills (Eds.), *From Max Weber*. London: Routledge.

Wildavsky, A. (1988). *Speaking truth to power: The art and craft of policy analysis*. New Brunswick, NJ: Transaction Publishers.

PART II

Performance Analyses

CHAPTER 4

Multimodal Analysis of Popular Music Video

GENRE, DISCOURSE, AND NARRATIVE IN STEVEN WILSON'S "DRIVE HOME"

LORI BURNS

UNIVERSITY OF OTTAWA

P opular music videos communicate narratives through dynamic interrelationships of words, music, and images. This chapter presents and
illustrates a method for analyzing the discursive construction of meaning
in music videos, with the aim of studying how music videos rely on the
workings of genre, discourse, and narrative in order to be both intelligible
and meaningful.[1]

The proposed interpretive method is influenced by three theoretical perspectives—genre theory, critical discourse theory, and narrative
theory—each of which is concerned with the expression of social and
cultural meanings in and through texts. Figure 1 offers a summary of
these perspectives. Genre theorists explore the ways in which social
groups express cultural norms and values, create shared realities, and

1. Earlier versions of this chapter were presented at the Art of Record Production conference in Philadelphia (November 2015) and the Ann Arbor Symposium (November
2015). The research was supported by the Social Sciences and Humanities Research
Council of Canada.

shape understandings of the world.[2] Critical discourse analysts aim to lay bare the discursive determinants that drive texts and, in doing so, examine how texts do the persuasive work that they do.[3] More specifically, critical discourse analysts are concerned with how relations of power, dominance, and inequality are inscribed in texts; how such relations are enacted; and ultimately how these acts are grounded in underlying ideologies.[4] Narrative theorists are concerned with how stories are told, what stories are told, and who is doing the telling.[5] In his definition of the elements of narrative, literary theorist David Herman invokes the concept of "worldmaking" practices, suggesting the potential impact of storytelling on social understanding.[6] By putting these theoretical approaches into dialogue with one another, I mean to illustrate a significant common ground for these methods of understanding texts. Taking music videos as multimodal texts, the proposed framework is designed to facilitate systematic thinking about how the individual domains of words, music, and images work together—in mutually reinforcing ways—to be culturally productive and constitutive of the social realm.

GENRE THEORY
- how genres express cultural norms and values
- how genres create shared realities
- how genres shape understandings of the world

---

2. Stuart Borthwick and Ron Moy, *Popular Music Genres: An Introduction* (Edinburgh: Edinburgh University Press, 2004); David Brackett, "Popular Music Genres: Aesthetics, Commerce and Identity," in *The SAGE Handbook of Popular Music*, ed. Andy Bennett and Steve Waksman (London: SAGE, 2015), 189–206; Franco Fabbri, "A Theory of Musical Genres: Two Applications," in *Popular Music: Perspectives*, ed. D. Horn and P. Tagg (Götebord: International Association of the Study of Popular Music, 1982), 52–81; John Frow, *Genre*, reprint ed. (London: Routledge, 2010); Fabian Holt, *Genre in Popular Music* (Chicago: University of Chicago Press, 2007).

3. Norman Fairclough, *Analysing Discourse: Textual Analysis for Social Research* (New York: Routledge, 2003); David Machin and Andrea Mayr, *How to Do Critical Discourse Analysis: A Multimodal Introduction* (London: SAGE, 2012); Ken Hyland and Brian Paltridge, *Continuum Companion to Discourse Analysis* (London: Bloomsbury, 2011); Teun Van Dijk, "Aims of Critical Discourse Analysis," *Japanese Discourse* 1 (1995): 17–27.

4. Van Dijk, "Aims of Critical Discourse Analysis."

5. Mieke Bal, *Travelling Concepts in the Humanities: A Rough Guide* (Toronto: University of Toronto Press, 2009); David Herman, *Basic Elements of Narrative* (West Sussex: Wiley-Blackwell, 2009).

6. Herman, *Basic Elements*, 9.

CRITICAL DISCOURSE ANALYSIS (CDA)
- how to identify the discursive determinants that drive texts
- how texts do persuasive work
- how power relations are enacted through texts

NARRATIVE THEORY
- how stories are told
- what stories and whose stories
- impact of storytelling on social understanding

FIGURE 1. Summary of theoretical perspectives borrowed from genre theory, critical discourse analysis, and narrative theory.

This chapter applies these theoretical perspectives to the video treatment of Steven Wilson's "Drive Home." As I examine the video, I will consider *how* the artist shapes his cultural commentary in and through the intersection of words, music, and images; how the song and music video are culturally productive; and how these materials shape representations—in other words, how these texts carry out persuasive work. More specifically, the theoretical framework will be mobilized to reveal how these artists present *narratives* that are grounded in the *discursive contexts* and *genres* in which they work.

ANALYTIC FRAMEWORK

In order to analyze the multimodal content of a music video, the proposed framework offers a method for distinguishing the expressive and structural content in the domains of words, music, and images according to five interpretive parameters: norms and values, storyworld and plot, space and time, subjectivity and address, and gesture and activity (see Figure 2).[7]

---

7. This framework expands on a number of cross-domain analytic models that I have developed in several publications, beginning with one in Burns, Lafrance, and Hawley (2008), which was designed only for the analysis of lyrics and music. Subsequently, in developing models for videos and live concert film, I have developed cross-domain models for lyrics, music, and images (Watson and Burns, "Subjective Perspectives"; Burns and Lafrance, "Gender, Sexuality and the Politics of Looking") and for lyrics, music, staging, and film mediation (Burns and Watson, "Spectacle and Intimacy"). Although the crosscutting parameters are subject to change depending on the objectives of a given analysis, what remains constant in these studies is an

As I discuss each of these parameters, I will identify specific connections to genre, discourse, and narrative theories, relying on leading authors in those fields of inquiry. In order to constrain what could be an extensive interdisciplinary task, I turn primarily to literary theorist John Frow's work on *Genre* (2010), critical discourse analysts David Machin and Andrea Mayr's work on *How to Do Critical Discourse Analysis* (2012), and narrative theorist David Herman's work on *The Basic Elements of Narrative* (2009). Illustrating the common ground to these approaches, I suggest ways to transfer the analytic and interpretive concepts to the realm of the music video. As Mieke Bal has explored in *Travelling Concepts in the Humanities* (2002), the task of applying theoretical concepts from one domain to another is not scientific or absolute but rather open to creative interpretation while the analyst reflects on what aspects of the theoretical construct are appropriate to the new domain. To be sure, a qualitative and interpretive approach is a crucial aspect of multimodal analysis as scholars work toward analytic methods for the interpretation of texts that rely on language, music, and images to communicate meanings.[8]

To begin, the parameter of *norms and values* is of foundational importance to the interpretive process. I would go so far as to suggest that this parameter lies at the very heart of any interpretation of genre, discourse, or narrative, for it asks us to reflect on the ideologies that underlie a particular text and to discern what Michel Foucault would refer to as the "regime of truth" that is suggested by the text.[9] Machin and Mayr express this concern

interest in understanding how the expressive content in individual domains (e.g., word-music-image) intersects across those domains to create multimodal meanings. See Lori Burns, Marc Lafrance, and Laura Hawley, "Embodied Subjectivities in the Lyrical and Musical Expression of PJ Harvey and Björk," *Music Theory Online* 14, no. 4 (2008); Lori Burns and Jada Watson, "Subjective Perspectives through Word, Image and Sound," *Journal of Music Sound and the Moving Image* 4, no. 1 (2010): 3–37; Lori Burns and Jada Watson, "Spectacle and Intimacy in Live Concert Video: Lyrics, Music, Staging and Film Mediation in P!nk's *Funhouse Tour* (2009)," *Journal of Music, Sound and the Moving Image* 7, no. 2 (2013): 108; Lori Burns and Marc Lafrance, "Gender, Sexuality and the Politics of Looking in Beyoncé's 'Video Phone' (Featuring Lady Gaga)," in *The Routledge Handbook to Gender and Sexuality in Popular Music*, ed. Stan Hawkins (New York: Routledge, 2017), 102–16.

8. See David Machin, *Introduction to Multimodal Analysis* (New York: Bloomsbury, 2016); Carey Jewitt, *The Routledge Handbook of Multimodal Analysis* (New York: Routledge, 2013); G. Gunther Kress and Theo van Leeuwen, *Multimodal Discourse: The Modes and Media of Contemporary Communication* (London: Arnold, 2001).

9. Michel Foucault, *Discipline and Punish: The Birth of the Prison*, trans. Alan Sheridan (New York: Pantheon, 1977); Clare O'Farrell, "What Is a 'Regime of Truth'?" *Foucault*

as follows: "Texts will use linguistics and visual strategies that appear normal or neutral on the surface, but which may in fact be ideological and seek to shape the representation of events and persons for particular ends."[10] The concept of meaning that resides beneath the surface is also addressed by Frow to explain how genre-based texts operate to shape cultural understanding. In this regard, he defines "inferences" as "the interpretive actualization of textual implications."[11] Asserting the importance of the interpretive act for genre study, he declares, "This is where the real complexity of texts lies; if we are to read well, we cannot but attend to those embedded assumptions and understandings which are structured by the frameworks of genre and from which we work inferentially to the full range of textual meaning."[12]

FRAMEWORK	WORDS	MUSIC	IMAGES
Norms and values	• assumptions • "truth"	• genre and style • production	• genre and style • costumes and props

Storyworld and plot	• event
	  sequence
	• situation
	  ("state of
	  affairs")
		• form
		• structure
			• image sequence
			• visual composition
			  and design

Space and time	• space • time • place	• arrangement • sonic space • temporal features	• setting • lighting • framing, editing
Subjectivity and address	• identities • relations • stance	• quality • dynamics • intensity	• staging • focus • gaze/address
Gesture and activity	• utterances • actions	• musical patterns • interactions	• movement • choreography

FIGURE 2. Analytic framework for words, music, and images.

News, October 31, 2013, https://foucaultnews.com/2013/10/31/what-is-a-regime-of-truth-2013/.

10. Machin and Mayr, *Critical Discourse Analysis*, 9.

11. Frow, *Genre*, 81.

12. Ibid., 101.

It is important to acknowledge that the reader's (or listener's) social and ideological orientation has an impact on his or her awareness of embedded belief systems. For instance, Herman understands such orientations to yield sensitive and nuanced interpretive insights: "Worldmaking practices are of central importance to narrative scholars of all sorts, from feminist narratologists exploring how representations of male and female characters pertain to dominant stereotypes about gender roles, to rhetorical theorists hypothesizing about the kinds of assumptions, beliefs and attitudes that must be adopted by readers if they are to participate in the multiple audience positions required to engage fully with fictional worlds."[13]

In the analytic model presented here, the parameter of norms and values asks the interpreter to unearth the assumptions that underpin the text—that is, the social and cultural ideologies—and the suppositions of "truth." For musical analysis, this perspective would emerge when considering the concepts of genre, style, and production values, specifically as these elements have the potential to invoke social and cultural contexts. In the visual domain, the analyst could reflect on elements of style, including costumes and props, which have the potential to communicate social contexts and cultural assumptions. The suggested applications for analysis and interpretation are not meant to be fixed, nor are they limited. In applying this model to a chosen example, the analyst would be free to extend and elaborate the details of the analytic process.

The parameter of *storyworld and plot* invites the analyst to reflect on the specific situations, social contexts, and events that shape a given story. In the field of narrative theory, Herman treats the storyworld as a "global mental model of the situations and events being recounted" and understands narrative artifacts (a text, film, song, etc.) to "provide blueprints for the creation and modification of such mentally configured storyworlds."[14] Connecting his idea of storyworld to an understanding of genre, he indicates that "part of the meaning of 'genre' consists of distinctive protocols for worldmaking."[15] I interpret Herman's comments to mean that individual genres can be distinguished based on their unique strategies for

---

13. Herman, *Basic Elements*, 106.
14. Ibid., 197n13.
15. Ibid., 112.

storyworld creation. This notion is supported in genre theory when Frow identifies thematic content as an important dimension of genre, defining thematic content as "the shaped human experience that a genre invests with significance and interest."[16] This theoretical understanding supports the view that creators within a given genre will invest in those human experiences that pertain to the worldview of the cultural group from which the genre has arisen. In the proposed model, the parameter of storyworld and plot transfers quite coherently from the events and situations—the "state of affairs"—conveyed by the lyrics to the musical form and structure and to the sequence of images as well as the visual composition and design.

The parameter of *space and time* owes a debt to literary theorist Mikhail Bakhtin's notion of the chronotope, a concept that is used to explore the interrelationships of time, space, and place in a text.[17] We see Bakhtin's influence in Frow's inclusion of formal features (comprising time, space, and enunciative position) as one of three parameters that contribute to the expression of genre.[18] In the context of narrative theory, the model that Herman proposes might be understood to distinguish the concepts of space and time, as he discusses spatial dimensions in relation to storyworld building and temporal dimensions in relation to event sequencing.[19] In the domain of critical discourse analysis, Machin and Mayr examine how space is discursively created and expressed in order to signify values, identities, and actions.[20] With these theoretical concepts in mind, Figure 2 elaborates how, for each expressive domain (words, music, and images), the analytic parameter of space and time might be applied. With respect to the lyrics of the song, we would look for references to space, time, and place. In order to transfer these concepts to the domain of music, we could consider the textural arrangement and sonic space of the music as well as the temporal features of the song. Finally, as we would apply this

16. Frow, *Genre*, 75.
17. Mikhail Bakhtin, *The Dialogic Imagination: Four Essays*, ed. Michael Holquist, trans. Caryl Emerson and Michael Holquist (Austin: University of Texas Press, 1981).
18. Frow, *Genre*, 74.
19. Herman, *Basic Elements*, 75, 131.
20. Machin and Mayr, *Critical Discourse Analysis*, 52.

parameter to the video images, we might examine the setting and lighting as well as the framing and editing of the visual images.

The parameter of *subjectivity and address* allows for analytic reflection on the narrative subject and the subject's expressive stance. In Frow's framework for genre theory, this parameter is evident in both the "position of enunciation" that is indicated within the formal features of a text as well as the rhetorical structure of the text.[21] In the context of narrative theory, Herman identifies situatedness as his first basic element of narrative, by which he means the discursive context or occasion for telling the story.[22] This element allows us to reflect on the perspective of the storyteller and also on the subject who is featured in the story. In the domain of critical discourse analysis, interpreters would discern a speaker's attitude by examining how his or her discourse is shaped, how his or her gaze or attention is directed and structured, and how he or she adopts a pose.[23] Figure 2 suggests how the parameter of subjectivity and address might be applied to the domains of words, music, and images. Beginning with the domain of words, the analyst might invoke the notion of identities, relations, and stance in the lyrics. In the music, this parameter transfers nicely to the quality, dynamics, and intensity of the voice and instruments in the recording.[24] With respect to the images, we could analyze the staging and focus of the subjects and the invocation of the subject's gaze toward the camera as well as toward others.[25]

---

21. Frow, *Genre*, 63, 74–75.
22. Herman, *Basic Elements*, 9.
23. Machin and Mayr, *Critical Discourse Analysis*, 70–75.
24. In the field of popular music studies, this parameter connects to writings on persona and on musical voice. See Lori Burns, "Vocal Authority and Listener Engagement: Musical and Narrative Expressive Strategies in the Songs of Female Pop-Rock Artists, 1993–95," in *Sounding Out Pop*, ed. John Covach and Mark Spicer (Ann Arbor: University of Michigan Press, 2010), 154–92; Allan Moore, "The Persona-Environment Relation in Recorded Song," *Music Theory Online* 11, no. 4 (2005); Eric Clarke, *Ways of Listening: An Ecological Approach to the Perception of Musical Meaning* (Oxford: Oxford University Press, 2005); Simon Frith, *Performing Rites: On the Value of Popular Music* (Cambridge: Harvard University Press, 1998); and Philip Auslander, "Musical Persona: The Physical Performance of Popular Music," in *The Ashgate Companion to Popular Musicology*, ed. Derek Scott (Abingdon: Ashgate, 2009), 303–16.
25. In the field of visual studies, it is important to mention here the work of Laura Mulvey, "Visual Pleasure and Narrative Cinema," *Screen* 16, no. 3 (1975): 6–18; bell hooks, "The Oppositional Gaze: Black Female Spectators," in *Black Looks: Race and*

Finally, the parameter of *gesture and activity* allows for consideration of a subject's actions and behaviors. In Herman's conception of narrative, gestures would be considered marked events in the timeline, with some of these events disrupting the storyworld, since Herman understands event disruption to be an essential component of narrative.[26] Taking a critical discourse analysis perspective, Machin and Mayr would examine gestures to determine how the actions are represented, especially as these actions might situate one subject in a controlling or powerful role in relation to another subject.[27] For discourse analysis, every gesture is significant for our understanding of social relations. Similarly, within the field of genre theory, gesture and activity would be interpreted as actions with potential rhetorical power and social significance. Frow, for instance, understands an action within a text to have a specific rhetorical purpose, such as a questioning or assertive function.[28] These understandings of gesture and action are highly suggestive for the analysis of words, music, and images. Figure 2 proposes how the analyst might apply the parameter of gesture and activity to the three domains: the actions and gestures that emerge from the lyrical content, the musical patterns (gestures) and interactions between and among the performers, and the movement and choreography portrayed in the images.

The five analytic parameters can be applied as crosscutting axes of intersection for the domains of words, music, and images, allowing us to observe the textual strategies within an individual domain and across domains. With this framework in hand, we can gather data that will allow us to distinguish the content of the music video in each of its multimodal domains (words, music, images) and to reflect on how that content intersects to constitute meaning. As Machin and Mayr might suggest, we are concerned with *how* the text in question—in this case, the music video—creates meaning, how it does its cultural work, and how the resources of a discourse are used.

Representation (Boston: South End, 1992), 115–31; and Marita Sturken and Lisa Cartwright, *Practices of Looking: An Introduction to Visual Culture*, 2nd ed. (New York: Oxford University Press, 2009).

26. Herman, *Basic Elements*, 133.
27. Machin and Mayr, *Critical Discourse Analysis*, 104–5.
28. Frow, *Genre*, 74–75.

STEVEN WILSON'S "DRIVE HOME," *THE RAVEN THAT REFUSED TO SING (AND OTHER STORIES)*, 2013 (KSCOPE 240)

Steven Wilson released *The Raven That Refused to Sing (and Other Stories)* in February 2013 on Kscope. The album features live-band members Nick Beggs (bass), Marco Minnemann (drums), Guthrie Govan (guitar), Adam Holzman (keyboards), and Theo Travis (winds), with whom he recorded the six tracks in so many days. He describes his goals for the album as a series of live takes with analog recording and minimal digital editing, aiming to achieve a sense of logic and storytelling.[29]

Wilson considered the writing to be inspired by the ghost stories of nineteenth-century authors Poe and Dickens, which he valued for their use of the supernatural elements, not for their own sake, but as a dramatic device to amplify emotional stories.[30] The concept album is tied to multidimensional materials, including the artwork of Hajo Mueller and video treatments for two of the tracks by stop-motion animation videographer Jess Cope of Owl House Studios. The album and its materials have been well received by the critical press, with a celebration of the musicianship, the conceptual compositional work, the integration of songwriting and production, and the organic long-form approach reminiscent of the '70s.[31]

---

29. Joe Bosso, "Steven Wilson Talks *The Raven That Refused to Sing (and Other Stories)*," *Musicradar*, February 7, 2013, http://www.musicradar.com, February 7, 2013, http://www.musicradar.com/news/guitars/steven-wilson-talks-the-raven-that-refused-to-sing-and-other-stories-570809.

30. Anil Prasad, "Steven Wilson: Past Presence," *Music without Borders Innerviews*, 2013, http://www.innerviews.org/inner/wilson2.html.

31. See UG Team, "*The Raven That Refused to Sing (and Other Stories)*," *UltimateGuitar*, March 6, 2013, https://www.ultimate-guitar.com/reviews/compact_discs/steven_wilson/the_raven_that_refused_to_sing_and_other_stories/index.html; "20 Best Metal Albums of 2013," *Rolling Stone*, December 11, 2013, http://www.rollingstone.com/music/lists/20-best-metal-albums-of-2013-20131211/steven-wilson-the-raven-refused-to-sing-and-other-stories-19691231; Bosso, "Steven Wilson Talks *The Raven That Refused to Sing*"; Dom Lawson, "Steven Wilson: *The Raven That Refused to Sing*—Review," *The Guardian*, February 21, 2013, https://www.theguardian.com/music/2013/feb/21/steven-wilson-raven-refused-review; Thom Jurek, "Steven Wilson: *The Raven That Refused to Sing (and Other Stories)*—Review," *AllMusic.com*, accessed April 12, 2015, http://www.allmusic.com/album/the-raven-that-refused-to-sing-and-other-stories-mw0002475916; Jean-Frederic Vachon, "An Interview with Steven Wilson on His New Album, Success and Conceptual Rock," *Diary of a Music Addict*, June 22,

The music video for the second track of the album, "Drive Home," is remarkable for its seamless musical production and its smooth visual flow. The stop-motion animation delivers a powerful representation of human emotion, psychological development, and physical movement that knits together the lyrical story and the musical narrative. The song lyrics tell a story that Wilson describes as follows: "The idea is about a couple driving along in a car at night, very much in love; the guy is driving, and his partner is in the passenger seat, and the next minute she is gone. . . . The song is basically about missing time; it's the idea of blocking out time because of something so traumatic that you literally remove it from your mind."[32]

My application of the analytic framework begins with the song lyrics (Figure 3), which establish the *norms and values* to be revealing the truth of a terrible accident and the subject's struggle with his feelings of guilt (e.g., "bear the blame" and "face the truth"). The parameter of *storyworld and plot* points us to a story of loss that opens with an upturned car in a storm. The lyrics do not offer an event-driven plot sequence but rather convey the pain of the experience and a psychological progression toward a release from suffering. With respect to *space and time*, there is a sense of disruption and suspense caused by the upside-down car (e.g., "wait on in vain" and "a pause without end"). The lyrics also convey the cyclic nature of time (e.g., "the darkness always ends") and ongoing action ("drive home"). A sense of distance is evident in the *subjectivity and address* of the lyrics, as the story is told through an alternation between second-person (e.g., "*you're* still alone" and "release all *your* guilt") and third-person voice (e.g., "a car upturned in the rain"), offering imperatives and observations rather than first-person reflections. Following the accident, the *gestures and activity* emerge through verb choices that carry emotional weight. The acts of waiting in vain, bearing blame, dealing with pain, facing the truth, and making amends all connote burdensome tasks that require psychological effort until the final passage of the second

---

2015, http://musicaddict.ca/2015/06/an-interview-with-steven-wilson-on-his-new-album-success-and-conceptual-rock/.

32. See Bosso, "Steven Wilson Talks *The Raven That Refused to Sing*."

FRAMEWORK	LYRICS
Norms and values	• external forces lead to accident • struggle with truth and guilt
Storyworld and plot	• story of loss and pain, leading toward a release from suffering
Space and time	• disconnection (time and space) • loss and reestablishment of memory
Subjectivity and address	• third person (distance) • imperatives ("you need to . . .")
Gesture and activity	• accident • burdensome acts (wait, bear, deal, grieve, etc.)

FIGURE 3. Analytic framework for the lyrics of "Drive Home." Lyrics available here: https://genius.com/Steven-wilson-drive-home-lyrics.

verse, which features more positive actions: releasing guilt, giving up pain, holding up your head.

Let us now consider how these analytic parameters apply to the domain of music (Figure 4). To begin with the musical *norms and values*, the genre in which Steven Wilson works is received as "progressive" rock, owing much of its style and form to '70s-era progressive rock. Wilson prefers the term "conceptual" rock; nevertheless, his work is certainly classified by many reviewers as progressive.[33] His choice to work with engineer Alan Parsons led to an atmospheric and crisply detailed style of production. His aim was to work with analog recording and digital editing and limit the number of takes in the live-performance capture.[34]

The *storyworld and plot* parameter leads us to consider the form and structure of the recorded track. Example 1 provides a summary of the form, aligned with the amplitude wave and peak-frequency spectrograph yielded by the Sonic Visualiser program.[35] The spectrograph

---

33. Vachon, "An Interview with Steven Wilson."
34. Bosso, "Steven Wilson Talks *The Raven That Refused to Sing*."
35. Chris Cannam, Christian Landone, and Mark Sandler, "Sonic Visualiser" (computer software, version 2.4.1., 2013), accessed October 28, 2016, http://www.sonicvisualiser.org/. The peak frequency settings in the program track the musical

Multimodal Analysis of Popular Music Video • 93

FRAMEWORK	MUSIC
Norms and values	• "conceptual" rock genre • atmospheric arrangement (Alan Parsons, producer) • analog recording with digital edit • single-take guitar solo
Storyworld and plot	• developmental form with instrumental sections, end with guitar solo • distinctive sonic values for each section convey story
Space and time	• arrangement: acoustic guitar, lead guitar (Sustainiac), sax, flute, kit, bass, keyboards • breadth and depth to sonic field: warm, dark, anthemic • wide dynamic range
Subjectivity and address	• filtered versus clear vocals • layering of textures • guitar solo "speaks"
Gesture and activity	• melancholy melodic lines in contrapuntal relationships • irregular metric structure • Sustainiac: glissandi, sustain, shred, registral shifts

FIGURE 4. Analytic framework for music, "Drive Home."

reveals clearly how each section of the song is characterized by distinctive sonic values and how these distinct sections create a strong degree of dynamic contrast over the course of the track. The song articulates a well-executed and developmental form, beginning conventionally (intro–verse 1–link–chorus [with refrain]–verse 2–link–chorus [with extended refrain]), while the second half of the song departs from the verse-chorus structure with a return to the material from the instrumental introduction, followed by a bridge and an extensive guitar solo that leads to a final vibrant and densely textured presentation of the refrain.

---

layers that emerge with the greatest intensity. Lower intensity is represented by green and yellow, while red represents the greatest levels of intensity. The individual layers are set out in logarithmic order so that space opens up easily between registral layers. As a tool, it is valuable for demonstrating the overall registral narrative of the song as well as the levels of intensity on individual lines within the texture.

EXAMPLE 1: FORMAL CHART ALIGNED WITH SPECTRAL AND WAVE GRAPHS: "DRIVE HOME"

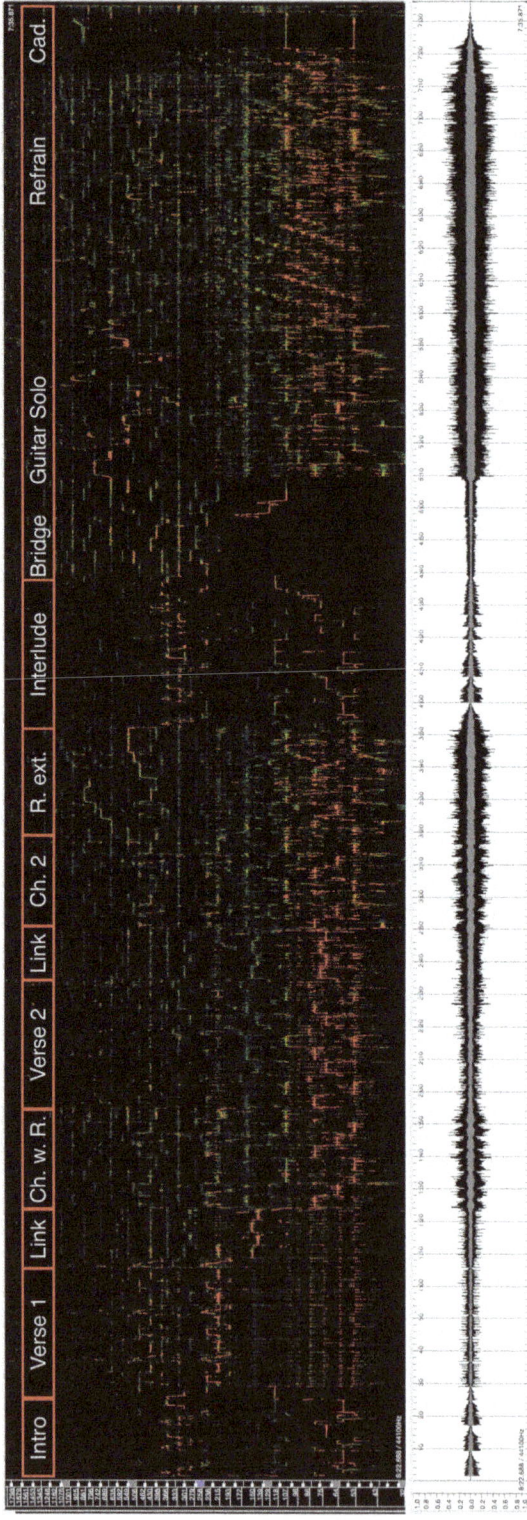

| Intro | Verse 1 | Link | Ch. w. R. | Verse 2 | Link | Ch. 2 | R. ext. | Interlude | Bridge | Guitar Solo | Refrain | Cad. |

The track is characterized by a sensitive treatment of *spatial and temporal* factors. The richly varied arrangement offers a breadth and depth of sonic field in which individual layers are clearly placed as well as a wide dynamic range.[36] In a more detailed analysis that follows, I will illustrate some of the unique aspects of the instrumental texture and arrangement, which includes acoustic guitar, electric guitar, flute, sax, keyboards, bass, and kit.[37]

The song varies in the levels of *subjectivity and address*—for instance, the vocal is treated to masking and filtering that indicate an internal rather than external process of communication, and individual voice tracks and instrumental lines are layered to create complex effects. The guitar solo passages have the effect of "speaking," or voicing, the narrative.

A consideration of the musical *gestures and activity* reveals that melancholy melodic lines and delicate arpeggiation patterns predominate, with the exception of the soaring lines of the electric guitar solo. I will explore these summary claims about the musical content in greater detail in the sections that follow. But first, I will provide a few comments about the visual world that was created for the video.

Example 2 applies the analytic framework to the images of the music video and includes several stills in order to illustrate the video treatment for "Drive Home." Videographer Jess Cope of Owl House Studios worked with the drawings of illustrator Hajo Mueller to create a vulnerable subject in a unique setting.[38] The *norms and values* of the visual world point

---

36. The track has a dynamic range factor of fourteen, which is considered to offer a good level of contrast. Dynamic range is discussed in William Campbell, Rob Toulson, and Justin Paterson, "The Effect of Dynamic Range Compression on the Psychoacoustic Quality and Loudness of Commercial Music" (paper presented at the Internoise 2010 Conference, June 13–16, 2010, Lisbon, Portugal), http://repository.uwl.ac.uk/2068/1/IN2010%20The%20effect%20of%20dynamic%20range%20compression%20on%20the%20psychoacoustic%20quality%20and%20loudness%20of%20commercial%20music.pdf.
37. Wilson describes the specific guitar equipment in an interview with James Rotondi, "Steven Wilson—of Ravens, Revenants, and Creeping Things," *Premier Guitar*, April 15, 2013, http://www.premierguitar.com/authors/560-james-rotondi.
38. The drawings are available in a 128-page, limited-edition hardback book that was released as part of the box set, deluxe edition. For more information on the release history of the album and the details of the box set (Kscope240), please visit https://www.discogs.com/Steven-Wilson-The-Raven-That-Refused-To-Sing-And-Other

us toward the visual style and genre as well as the costumes and props that convey the social contexts. The stop-motion animation genre takes the viewer into a materially fabricated world. Cope created the simple puppet design and the world in which he lives from torn-up paper. All the materials—with the exception of some special personal objects (glasses, hairbrush, necklace, typewriter)—are papered over with newsprint. This aesthetic effect is a material manifestation of the endless composition of letters to the lost loved one (02:12). Color and light are used to convey the emotional states, distinguish the stages of the narrative, and mark the supernatural effects: sepia tones color the postaccident timeline, during which the subject does not recall the events; shades of blue are used for the activities in the car and near the water's edge; and red is used for the accident sequence once the subject experiences his memory recovery.

The *storyworld and plot* of the video give shape to the traumatic story of the accident, the loss of memory, and the progress toward recovery. The storyworld conveys the psychological journey of the subject as he experiences the accident (01:47) and then lives on in an injured state, unable to recall the events. A series of supernatural occurrences (e.g., 04:01) ultimately lead to a cathartic second accident—a fall into the water (05:10)—triggering the return of his memory (05:30).

The *spatial and temporal* elements are designed to communicate important aspects of the psychological journey of the subject; more specifically, the two-dimensional scenes represent the events in the past, and the three-dimensional scenes convey the present timeline. Adding further to this strategic use of spatial effects, the supernatural experiences in the present timeline feature transparent, two-dimensional "ghost" figures. The 2-D scenes of the video (e.g., 01:02, 01:11) were made from cutout puppets that were animated on a glass plane. Backlighting creates a perception of depth in the background. Some of the lighting and water effects were done in postproduction—for instance, when the light hits the subject's eyes (01:02), leading to the accident. The story unfolds in a number of external

---

-Stories/release/4318160. Jess Cope describes her process of video composition in a behind-the-scenes video. See Owl House Studios, "Making Drive Home with Jess Cope," Vimeo video, 11:41, posted by Owl House Studios, 2014, https://vimeo.com/80079268.

EXAMPLE 2: ANALYTIC FRAMEWORK: IMAGES, "DRIVE HOME"

	Images (timecodes)	Notes
Norms & Values	[02:12] [02:20] [03:24] [04:42] [05:39]	• Stop-motion puppet • World papered over • Symbolic use of color and light
Storyworld & Plot	[01:47] [04:01] [05:10] [05:30]	• Accident leads to memory loss • Supernatural effects and a second accident aids recovery of memory
Space & Time	[01:02] [01:11] [03:16] [06:17]	• Symbolic use of 2D/3D, dark/light, external/internal spaces • Rupture of linear time
Subjectivity & Address	[00:55] [01:09] [04:01] [04:38] [04:50] [06:01]	• Subject's gaze at Lucy leads to accident • "Tries to see": reflection in glasses • Finally "sees" himself and truth
Gesture & Activity	[01:30] [01:58] [04:38] [04:38] [05:08] [05:39]	• Driving leads to accident that causes his own injury and memory loss • Repetitive action of typing letters to Lucy • Follows "ghost" figure to water • Falls into water triggering memory sequence; recalls failed attempt to rescue Lucy

and internal physical spaces: the car on the road, the pier at the water's edge, the inside of the subject's home, and—ultimately—under water.

Our first consideration of *subjectivity and address* in the music video must be given to the characteristics and communicative capacity that Cope has attributed to her puppet. The puppet's oval head, which is disproportionately large in relation to his small body, is endowed with glasses and ears on which the glasses rest. The size of and focus on the subject's head is a manifestation of the psychological emphasis that is accorded to this story. Although he has no eyes, Cope has managed to create the effect of a powerful and thoughtful gaze. Tragically, it is when he gazes at Lucy (00:55) that the accident occurs. The reflection of the shadow figure (01:09) and the fire of the accident in his glasses (06:01) signal to the viewer what he is seeing and experiencing. When he finally "sees" himself on the pier and realizes the truth (04:38), this moment launches the sequence of memory recovery.

The *gestures and activities* of the video communicate a story of accident, injury, stasis, a second accident, and memory recovery. The repetitive and insistent action of typing letters to Lucy represents the severity of his memory loss: he does not know what happened to her. A visit to the water's edge in his wheelchair leads him to find Lucy's hairbrush in the water (02:54), and this material object then triggers a series of supernatural confrontations that lead him back to the water's edge (04:38). His fall into the water (05:08) is the action that induces the memory recall.

With this summary review of the individual domains (lyrics, music, video images) in place, I now turn to a more detailed analysis of the song in order to integrate the domain-based analysis into a multimodal interpretation. Following the temporal order of the track and video according to the formal song sections, the following analysis is intended to illuminate how the model facilitates the interpretation of the word-music-image *intersections*. Example 3 summarizes the detailed analysis and clarifies the content that describes the music and the images; in addition, Example 3 reproduces transcriptions of selected passages.[39] The reader is strongly

---

39. I would like to thank Craig Visser for his careful transcription of the guitar content of the song and Joshua Wynnyk for his thoughtful comments about the kit activities throughout the song.

encouraged to watch the video clip, section by section, as the analysis follows. Ideally, each section should be watched twice—first to attend to the musical content and second to consider the connections between that musical content and the images.

INTRO (00:00–00:29). The song opens with a delicate texture featuring a guitar melody supported by piano chords; the third and final phrase of the intro closes with a gently falling and rising arpeggiation gesture (00:17–00:29). The warm jazzy tone of the LaRose classic jazz guitar is dry and forward as if in a small space, while the piano is further back (as if in a larger space) and supported by quiet bass tones. The depth of textural space in the music—forward guitar and distant piano—maps onto the depth of the visual space in the opening water sequence, followed by the car sequence. Jess Cope used multiplaning animation to create foreground, middleground, and background layers to suggest a 3-D texture. (We saw this visual layering in the video stills of the *subjectivity and address* parameter in Example 2: images 00:55 and 01:09.) During this introductory sequence, the necklace is attributed a 3-D design, giving it a particularly vibrant visual appeal. As we consider the intersections between image and sound in this passage, the warm guitar at the very front of the texture seems to trace the fall of the necklace to the water's surface and then to convey us to the scene in which the subject and Lucy are driving in the car.

VERSE 1 AND LINK (00:30–01:23). The intro leads into the first verse, in which the third-person narrator describes the upturned car of the accident and then delivers a second-person imperative to deal with the trauma and start anew. The music features a bright, sparkling Octavian acoustic guitar, which is doubled by the electric guitar to give depth to the sound. The guitar, accompanied by piano and a stripped-down kit, support a filtered vocal. The voice is very dry and forward, while the guitar and kit occupy their own clear positions in the texture. At the vocal cadence (01:10), a brief instrumental link expands the texture with the toms and a bell-like keyboard sound overdubbing a guitar arpeggiation pattern. Wilson's filtered vocal maps onto the 2-D visual presentation of the subject driving his car. The opening up of the musical texture and the motion of the guitar arpeggiation during the link supports the intensification of the subject's emotion—he sees a shadowy figure at the water's edge and the empty seat beside him where Lucy had been sitting—while his thoughts race to understand what has happened, and the car continues to move forward.

CHORUS 1 (01:24–01:55). The chorus ushers in a lush, broad texture, featuring a counterline in the upper strings and deep round bass tones. The kit has a more prominent role, with quarter accents on the ride cymbal and tom fills to mark the phrase endings. The voice is no longer filtered but has a clearer sound with a lush reverb. It is doubled at the upper octave, with the main vocal centered and the overdubbed layer sounding above and behind. In the video, this vocal conveys omnipresence, as the subject is encouraged to "face the truth." Falling from the vehicle and calling for Lucy, the perspective broadens to consider the ominous water's edge.

VERSE 2 AND LINK (01:56–02:49). The second verse features a heavier filter effect on the vocal with modulation, or phasing, of both pitch and time. Each phrase adds another layer of vocal harmony, such that the third phrase features three layers. Whereas the first verse was very transparent, the texture here is heavier and denser with the entrance of the strings and the greater intensity on kit and bass. In the video of this passage, now with the 3-D representation of the subject in a wheelchair typing his letters, we are evidently in a postaccident timeline, and we can now understand the previous 2-D sequence to have been a representation of the past. The filtered vocals suggest once again the perspective of the subject's inner thoughts, but in a much more layered and complex orientation, potentially signaling his repeated efforts to remember the events of the accident. During the brief link (02:36–02:49), the enhanced guitar arpeggiation pattern with bell-like tones returns to represent his racing mind and his effort to understand what happened.

CHORUS 2 (02:50–03:20). The second chorus is marked by an even clearer and brighter vocal articulation, signaling sonically that the earlier chorus statement featured some masking or darkening of the upper frequencies. A slight left-to-right delay in the splitting of the vocal creates the effect of depth and layering. Against this more pointed and intense vocal presentation, the images emphasize the subject's ability to "see." The subject, now in 3-D representation and in a wheelchair, retrieves Lucy's hairbrush at the water's edge and is later awoken to the apparition of Lucy, a transparent 2-D figure.

CHORUS EXTENSION (03:21–03:51). The chorus is extended with a passage featuring a soaring line on the LaRose guitar, fitted with a Sustainiac sustainer circuit (pick-up), supported by added fills and crashes in the kit, a driving eighth pulse on the ride with quarters on the hat, and a very active bass. The voice repeats the chorus refrain, "drive home." During the chorus extension, Lucy brushes her hair as the subject gazes at her. Reflecting on what he has experienced, he is visited by the shadowy figure. The slowly rising but intense line is bound to the image of Lucy reaching for the brush and combing her hair. When the light disappears and she is gone, the subject himself picks up the brush and holds it to his chest as the Sustainiac guitar line continues to climb. In this scene, the guitar solo marks Lucy's gesture and the significance of a personal object to aid in the recovery of his memory.

INTERLUDE (03:52–04:38). Following the suggestive moment of memory and its sonic attachment to the Sustainiac line, the texture falls back to the sparse and transparent introductory material; however, there is more depth and layering than before. The guitar melody is joined by the sax in counterpoint, and here the spatial effects suggest three layers: the reverberant guitar; the sax, which is further back; and the piano, which is very distant in the mix. A sweep-arpeggio melody in the guitar traces the subject's movement back to the water's edge, where he now succeeds in encountering the figure.

BRIDGE (04:39–05:08). The bridge is a remarkable moment for the intersection of sound and images, opening with a transparent section in which arpeggiation patterns in the acoustic guitar present the harmonic progression of the chorus (Em-CM7-A-AM7). The texture is brighter and lighter, with no bass or kit in the first four bars of the section. As the bass enters against a rising flute line, the space opens up for the solo guitar to enter. The image sequence from this opening phrase of the bridge suggests a kind of suspended moment in time, the lightness and transparency of the texture allowing the subject to "see" that he is himself the shadowy figure. Shocked by his realization, he stumbles at the end of the pier and begins to fall—a second accident that will prove to be cathartic in the release of his memory.

GUITAR SOLO (05:09). The guitar solo that ensues is characterized by intensity and breadth of field. The Sustainiac provides a florid, legato, and blended sound without the characteristic decay and transients of the guitar. String bends and glissandi further contribute to the smoothness of the line. The eighth-note triplets and long-held notes create an open and soaring quality. The kit reenters with a cymbal roll into the first bar of the solo (05:09): we hear the strong kick on 1, the syncopated kick on 3, and a powerful reverberant backbeat snare that is right on the beat. In the video, the subject's fall is timed very carefully with these musical gestures: the rising glissando emerges over the acoustic guitar, suspending our sense of time; the kick drum and guitar accentuate the downbeat when he strikes the water; and the powerful backbeat snare articulates the resulting splash. As the memory sequence begins, the Sustainiac gestures are timed to the images of the moments leading up to the accident.

The fourth phrase of the guitar solo (05:56–06:12) features another rise from the high E to G—this time in a deliberate stepwise pattern. In this passage, the string-bend approach is more heavily weighted and slower; faster pull-offs give a light, agile feel to the syncopated figure in bar 2; and a very dense passage (featuring what guitarists would refer to as "shredding," which involves highly virtuosic fast playing) concludes the phrase, with muted strumming at the end adding to the cacophonous texture. The phrase begins by marking beats but progresses toward syncopation and more complex rhythms. The rising bass line (starting at 06:00) is prominent against the active guitar. Central to the memory sequence, this is the moment when the subject falls after trying to pull Lucy from the burning vehicle. Holding the necklace, he watches helplessly as the car is engulfed in flames. As the guitar moves into the shred passage, we return to the image of him falling through the water, where he has experienced the memory recall.

The guitar solo delivers a total of eight phrases that track the subject's memory recovery of the traumatic accident while he falls into the water. Landing on the riverbed during the sixth phrase, he finds Lucy's necklace and then recalls throwing it into the water the night of the accident. In the final phrase of the solo, now layered with the chorus refrain ("drive home"), he rises again to the surface with the necklace in hand. A final three-bar phrase, delivered on open, detuned guitar strings, creates the effect of unwinding after the intensity of the story's climax. Our subject sits on the dock and holds the necklace to his heart as the final note of the guitar slowly bends and fades away.

▌CONCLUSIONS

My aim with this chapter has been to examine the aesthetic materials of "Drive Home" in order to understand how these are structured and designed to create meaning, communicate cultural messages, and shape a particular worldview. Figure 5 summarizes the analytic findings from the earlier examples (Figures 3 and 4 and Example 2), facilitating the interpretation of the multimodal materials. In this consolidated form, the analyst can reflect on the data in each crosscutting parameter to understand the conceptual transfer and multimodal integrations achieved by the artistic work. Using a cross-domain analytic methodology that is grounded in domain-specific content, the analyst is provided with coherent content from which to draw interpretive conclusions. In other words, by this stage of the analysis, each claim in the framework can be backed up by detailed analytic observations from the foregoing effort. I emphasize this aspect of the analytic process in order to illuminate the pedagogical potential of this method. Analysts can succeed in the rigorous gathering of domain-specific content, according to clearly defined crosscutting parameters, before attempting to assemble an explication of meaning. It can be challenging to identify appropriate content for each parameter in each domain, but the process of making analytic decisions by distinguishing content is vital to one's understanding of how the expressive materials function and

EXAMPLE 3: SUMMARY OF ANALYSIS

Intro Clips 1 & 2	• Warm jazzy guitar tone with dry, forward sound (small space) • Distant piano (larger space) supported by quiet bass tones • Rising and falling arpeggiation gesture closes section

	• Dimensions of space in water and outside of the car • Multiplaning: foreground, mid-, and background layers to create 3D effect
Verse 1, link Clips 3 & 4	• Bright sparkling acoustic guitar doubled by electric guitar, accompanied by piano chords, stripped down kit • Dry filtered vocal • Link: enhanced guitar arpeggiation, distant toms at very end of phrase
	• 2D image of subject complements filtered vocal • Enhanced guitar arpeggiation marks moment of "seeing" shadowy figure and realizing Lucy is gone
Chorus 1 Clips 5 & 6	• Lush, broad texture with counter line in upper strings and deep round bass tones • Quarter notes added on ride and simple tom fills mark phrases • Clearer vocal, lush reverb; doubled at upper 8ve
	• Omnipresent lush, layered vocal encourages subject to "face the truth" • Perspective returns to ominous water
Verse 2, link Clips 7 & 8	• Heavier vocal filter effect • Three layers of vocal harmony • Entrance of strings and greater intensity of kit and bass
	• 3D subject linked to filtered and layered vocal • enhanced guitar arpeggiation links to effort to understand
Chorus 2 Clips 9 & 10	• Voice clearer, brighter (articulation of upper partials), closer, more intense • Slight L to R delay in splitting of vocal
	• 3D subject's actions of retrieving and contemplating the brush • Awoken from sleep by bright light and apparition of Lucy (transparent and 2D figure)
Chorus Extension Clips 11 & 12	• Lead guitar (with sustainiac) rises while added fills and crashes boost intensity • Driving 8th pulse on ride with quarters on hat and active bass

	• During rising sustainiac line, Lucy tentatively reaches for brush and combs hair • When light disappears, subject holds brush while sustainiac guitar rises

EXAMPLE 3: SUMMARY OF ANALYSIS (*CONTINUED*)

Interlude Clips 13 & 14	• 3 layers: reverberant guitar; sax further back; more distant piano with ride cymbal hits on chord changes • Sweep arpeggio melody in guitar leads to cadence

	• Subject sees shadowy figure, returns to water; succeeds in encountering the figure

Bridge, Opening Clips 15 & 16	• Transparent arpeggiation in acoustic G • Harmonic progression from CH (Em-Cm7-A-Am7) • Brighter, lighter: no bass, kit • Bass enters + leads down while rising flute line opens space for sustainiac to enter

	• Light and transparent musical texture offers suspense and space of opening as subject begins to "see" self • Discovery leads him to stumble at the end of the pier

Guitar solo, phrase 1 Clips 17 & 18	• Intensity of sound; breadth of field • Sustainiac: florid, legato sound; string bends + glissandi; open, soaring quality • Strong kick and powerful reverberant backbeat snare

	• The fall is synced with music: rising gliss during fall; kick drum and guitar chord as he hits water; snare as water splashes • Memory sequence is enhanced by sustainiac gestures

Guitar solo, phrase 4 Clips 19 & 20	• String bend approach is more heavily weighted and slower while faster pull-offs give a light agile feel to the sync figure in the second bar • Very dense shred passage concludes phrase with muted strumming • Prominent rising bass line

	• With necklace in hand, subject helplessly watches the scene • During guitar shred passage, his fall into the water continues and memories return during descent

interrelate. Avoiding the rush to interpretation, this method looks first to the material content and secondarily to interpretive claims.

NORMS AND VALUES. At a foundational level, the "Drive Home" music video communicates a powerful message about a subject's personal experience and feelings of responsibility for the loss of a human life. This profound struggle of consciousness is set musically within the genre of "conceptual" rock, allowing for an atmospheric and detailed arrangement. Visually, the vulnerable subject is placed within an animated and surreal world that allows for a representation of his harsh reality and his inner battle. The intensity of color and light, as well as the prominence of personal material objects, draw us into a dreamlike world in which his psychological development is the focus.

STORYWORLD AND PLOT. The narrative of loss leading toward release has a goal-oriented design that is crafted carefully in the developmental form and expansive guitar solo. The video images ground this narrative in the psychological consequences of the accident, the subject's experience of loss, and his own stasis in the denial of that loss. The supernatural effects lead him to a second accident that serves as a cathartic moment of memory recovery.

SPACE AND TIME. The disruption of physical space and linear time in the story are important bearers of meaning. It is this disruption that allows us to understand the subject's psychological struggle, including his traumatic loss of memory. To convey this musically, Wilson creates a lush, detailed, and dynamic sonic space that allows for a full range of emotional expression and subjective reflection. Visually, the disruption is conveyed in the treatment of perspective and temporality. The viewer experiences the disruption of the temporal sequence in keeping with the subject's conscious experience.

VOICE AND ADDRESS. The distant address creates the sense of a narrator who has the power to observe and comment on the subject's situation. The voice is treated musically to a number of production effects: in the verses, the voice is filtered and phased to create a thin sound that is texturally distinct from the supporting instruments. This sonic separation

FRAMEWORK	WORDS	MUSIC	IMAGES
Norms and values	• external forces lead to accident • struggle with truth and guilt	• "conceptual" rock • atmospheric, detailed arrangement	• vulnerable subject • animated, surreal world
Storyworld and plot	• story of loss leading toward release of pain	• developmental form with dynamic instrumental sections (guitar solo) • distinctive sonic values for each section	• accident memory loss • supernatural effects lead to recovery
Space and time	• disconnection (time and space) • memory loss	• breadth and depth to sonic field • multilayered • wide dynamic range • irregularities in metric structure	• 2-D/3-D dimensions • perspective • rupture of temporality
Subjectivity and address	• distance from self (second- and third-person address)	• filtered versus clear vocal • layering of texture • guitar solo "speaks"	• tries to see • eventually sees self/truth
Gesture and activity	• emotional actions (wait, bear, deal, grieve)	• melancholy melodic lines on contrapuntal relationships • virtuosic guitar solo	• accident, fire, failed rescue • waiting, immobile, writing letters

FIGURE 5. Complete framework of words, music, and images.

of the voice connotes distance, which can be connected to the temporal distance of the present time and the events of the past. Although the voice-over delivery suggests a distance between the narrator and the subject, it is when the guitar "speaks" that the subject makes connections and comes to an understanding of his past experience. The intense guitar solo is strongly connected to the recovery of memory. Visually, the guitar solo is tied to images that invoke the concept of seeing or gazing; the subject is always preoccupied with looking—at Lucy in the car, at the image of the accident, at the shadowy figure who appears to send a message, at the water—to learn what happened.

Ultimately, he sees himself in the shadowy image and then begins to see the truth.

GESTURE AND ACTIVITY. The weighty emotional actions of the lyrics are conveyed musically as melancholy lines and guitar arpeggiations that work visually with the long period of reflection and stasis following the traumatic car accident. In contrast, the soaring guitar (Sustainiac) lines seem to drive the subject into awareness and full memory recovery. The accident itself is revealed during the guitar solo, with Guthrie Govan garnering his incredible range of virtuosic expression to the purpose of conveying the tragedy. For this sequence, Jess Cope casts the angular movements of the car in an intense bath of red as it moves out of control, carrying the viewer to the peak of visual intensity as a pictorial realization of the accident.

Textual choices not only represent the world but also constitute it. In other words, cultural texts—including musical texts and visual texts—produce meanings that shape social understanding. Strategies of artistic expression are always grounded in ideologies and assumptions of truth about the world, and words, music, and images have individual affordances and attributes with the potential to connote meaning. By exploring this approach to cultural texts, we understand better the social world that is constituted by a given text and how the strategies and choices capture a worldview. Transferring the concepts of genre theory, discourse analysis, and narrative theory to the multimodal content of a music video, the interpretive goal is to reveal how expressive materials work together to communicate social values and tell powerful human stories.

BIBLIOGRAPHY

Auslander, Philip. "Musical Persona: The Physical Performance of Popular Music." In *The Ashgate Research Companion to Popular Musicology*, edited by Derek Scott, 303–16. Abingdon: Ashgate, 2009.

Bal, Mieke. *Travelling Concepts in the Humanities: A Rough Guide*. Toronto: University of Toronto Press, 2002.

Borthwick, Stuart, and Ron Moy. *Popular Music Genres: An Introduction*. Edinburgh: University of Edinburgh Press, 2004.

Bosso, Joe. "Steven Wilson Talks *The Raven That Refused to Sing (and Other Stories)*." *Musicradar*, February 7. http://www.musicradar.com/news/guitars/steven-wilson-talks-the-raven-that-refused-to-sing-and-other-stories-570809.

Brackett, David. "Popular Music Genres: Aesthetics, Commerce and Identity." In *The SAGE Handbook of Popular Music*, edited by Andy Bennett and Steve Waksman, 189–206. London: Sage, 2015.

Burns, Lori. "Vocal Authority and Listener Engagement: Musical and Narrative Expressive Strategies in the Songs of Female Pop-Rock Artists, 1993–95." In *Sounding Out Pop*, edited by John Covach and Mark Spicer, 154–92. Ann Arbor: University of Michigan Press, 2010.

Burns, Lori, and Marc Lafrance. "Gender, Sexuality and the Politics of Looking in Beyoncé's 'Video Phone' (Featuring Lady Gaga)." In *The Routledge Handbook to Gender and Sexuality in Popular Music*, edited by Stan Hawkins, 102–16. New York: Routledge, 2017.

Burns, Lori, Marc Lafrance, and Laura Hawley. "Embodied Subjectivities in the Lyrical and Musical Expression of PJ Harvey and Björk." *Music Theory Online* 14, no. 4 (2008). http://www.mtosmt.org/issues/mto.08.14.4/mto.08.14.4.burns_lafrance_hawley.html.

Burns, Lori, and Jada Watson. "Spectacle and Intimacy in Live Concert Video: Lyrics, Music, Staging and Film Mediation in P!nk's *Funhouse Tour* (2009)." *Music, Sound and the Moving Image* 7, no. 2 (2013): 103–40.

———. "Subjective Perspectives through Word, Image and Sound." *Journal of Music Sound and the Moving Image* 4, no. 1 (2010): 3–37.

Campbell, William, Rob Toulson, and Justin Paterson. "The Effect of Dynamic Range Compression on the Psychoacoustic Quality and Loudness of Commercial Music." Paper presented at Internoise, Lisbon, Portugal, June 13–16, 2010. http://repository.uwl.ac.uk/2068/1/IN2010%20The%20effect%20of%20dynamic%20range%20compression%20on%20the%20psychoacoustic%20quality%20and%20loudness%20of%20commercial%20music.pdf.

Clarke, Eric. *Ways of Listening: An Ecological Approach to the Perception of Musical Meaning*. Oxford: Oxford University Press, 2005.

Fabbri, Franco. "A Theory of Musical Genres: Two Applications." In *Popular Music: Perspectives*, edited by D. Horn and P. Tagg, 52–81. Göteberg and Exeter: International Association of the Study of Popular Music, 1982.

Fairclough, Norman. *Analysing Discourse: Textual Analysis for Social Research*. New York: Routledge, 2003.

Foucault, Michel. *Discipline and Punish: The Birth of the Prison*. Translated by Alan Sheridan. New York: Pantheon Books, 1977.

Frith, Simon. *Performing Rites: On the Value of Popular Music*. Cambridge: Harvard University Press, 1998.

Frow, John. *Genre*. Reprint ed. London: Routledge, 2010.

Herman, David. *Basic Elements of Narrative*. West Sussex: Wiley-Blackwell, 2009.

Holt, Fabian. *Genre in Popular Music*. Chicago: University of Chicago Press, 2007.

hooks, bell. *Black Looks: Race and Representation*. Boston, MA: South End, 1992.

Hyland, Ken, and Brian Paltridge. *Continuum Companion to Discourse Analysis*. London: Bloomsbury, 2011.

Jewitt, Carey. *The Routledge Handbook of Mulitmodal Analysis*. New York: Routledge, 2013.

Jurek, Thom. Review of *The Raven That Refused to Sing (and Other Stories)*, by Steven Wilson. *AllMusic*. Accessed April 12, 2015. http://www.allmusic.com/album/the-raven -that-refused-to-sing-and-other-stories-mw0002475916.

Kress, Gunther, and Theo van Leeuwen. *Multimodal Discourse: The Modes and Media of Contemporary Communication*. London: Arnold Publishing, 2001.

Lawson, Dom. Review of *The Raven That Refused to Sing*, by Steven Wilson. *The Guardian*, February 21, 2013. https://www.theguardian.com/music/2013/feb/21/steven-wilson -raven-refused-review.

Machin, David. *Analysing Popular Music: Image, Sound and Text*. London: Sage, 2010.

———. *Introduction to Multimodal Analysis*. New York: Bloomsbury, 2016.

Machin, David, and Andrea Mayr. *How to Do Critical Discourse Analysis: A Multimodal Introduction*. London: Sage, 2012.

"Making Drive Home with Jess Cope." *Owl House Studios*. Vimeo video, 11:41. Posted November 22, 2013. https://vimeo.com/80079268.

Moore, Allan. "The Persona-Environment Relation in Recorded Song." *Music Theory Online* 11, no. 4 (2005).

Mulvey, Laura. "Visual Pleasure and Narrative Cinema." *Screen* 16, no. 3 (1975): 6–18.

O'Farrell, Clare. "What Is a 'Regime of Truth'?" *Foucault News*, October 31, 2013. https:// foucaultnews.com/2013/10/31/what-is-a-regime-of-truth-2013/.

Prasad, Anil. "Steven Wilson: Past Presence." *Music without Borders Innerviews*, 2013. http://www.innerviews.org/inner/wilson2.html.

Rotondi, James. "Steven Wilson—of Ravens, Revenants, and Creeping Things." *Premier Guitar*, April 15, 2013. http://www.premierguitar.com/authors/560-james-rotondi.

Sturken, Marita, and Lisa Cartwright. *Practices of Looking: An Introduction to Visual Culture*. 2nd ed. Oxford: Oxford University Press, 2009.

"20 Best Metal Albums of 2013." *Rolling Stone*, December 11, 2013. http://www .rollingstone.com/music/lists/20-best-metal-albums-of-2013-20131211/steven-wilson -the-raven-refused-to-sing-and-other-stories-19691231.

UG Team. Review of *The Raven That Refused to Sings (and Other Stories)*, by Steven Wilson. *UltimateGuitar*, March 6, 2013. https://www.ultimate-guitar.com/reviews/ compact_discs/steven_wilson/the_raven_that_refused_to_sing_and_other_stories/ index.html.

Vachon, Jean-Frederic. "An Interview with Steven Wilson on His New Album, Success and Conceptual Rock." *Diary of a Music Addict*, June 22, 2015. http://musicaddict.ca/2015/ 06/an-interview-with-steven-wilson-on-his-new-album-success-and-conceptual-rock/.

Van Dijk, Teun. "Aims of Critical Discourse Analysis." *Japanese Discourse* 1 (1995): 17–27.

Discography

Wilson, Steven. *The Raven That Refused to Sing (and Other Stories)*. Kscope. KSCOPE240, 2013, compact disc.

CHAPTER 5

Intertextual Apparitions

HAUNTING ADAM LAMBERT'S "FEELING GOOD"

ELIZABETH GOULD

UNIVERSITY OF TORONTO

F amous for unexpectedly losing the eighth season of *American Idol*, during which he neither confirmed nor denied his homosexuality, Adam Lambert became instantly notorious six months later when he performed his first single, "For Your Entertainment," on the American Music Awards. After kissing a male musician on the mouth, he positioned himself as guitarist Mark Ronson and "took Bowie's pose of fellatio one step further by getting rid of [Ronson's] intervening guitar" (Peraino 2012, 183n56). Lambert's acting on the song's lyrics was shocking to the extent that it shattered his *Idol*-manufactured straight glam rock persona, but it was also predictable in the context of his *Idol* performances, particularly the only performance all season that landed him in the bottom three: his cover of "Feeling Good." Using Philip Auslander's (2004) approach, which begins with the performer while also examining "socio-cultural norms and conventions" (11) of musical performance and music genre, my analysis here is inflected by Alan Stanbridge's (2004) expansive concept of musical intertextuality that both historicizes the "complex interrelation of texts and contexts" and insists on the contingency of any reading (83). I argue that Lambert's 2009 studio recording of "Feeling Good," haunted by his *Idol* on-air performance, covers Nina Simone's 1965 "Feeling Good," activating it as an intertextual strategy asserting queer subjectivities as lives worth living.

Both Simone and Lambert deploy intertextuality to produce resolutely embodied subjectivities: Simone's black, in which "thinking and feeling are as inseparable as politics and aesthetics" (Gaines 2013, 257); Lambert's queer, in which thinking is politics and feeling is aesthetics. Situated within disparate emancipatory projects occurring at distinct historical moments in the United States, both musicians' artistic expressions function as cultural critique in an effort to bring about sociopolitical change. While Simone's critique as continuity confronts entrenched and enduring historical racial and gender oppression, enacting potentialities for action toward future black revolution (Gaines 2013), Lambert's critique as citation addresses the violence of coercive and compulsory gender norms, enacting potentialities for action within a current and ongoing iterated catachresis.[1]

Judith Butler (1993) argues in her theory of performativity that gender functions as a gestural speech act in which the gendered subject is produced as an effect of iterative performances of gender/sexuality that are compelled by pervasive norms that "precede, constrain, and exceed" the subject (234). Displacing, "resignifying, and sometimes quite emphatically breaking . . . citational chains" of these heterosexual norms enacts queer subjectivities in the present as a rejection of hierarchical kinship relations that can neither acknowledge nor account for past or present queer identifications and affiliations (Butler 2015, 64). Inasmuch as heterosexual familial inheritance effectively disappears queers (and queerness) epistemologically as well as ontologically (Gould 2012), queer is also "an effect of how we do politics" (Ahmed 2006, 177). It is performative in the Butlerian (2004) sense of producing livable lives materially embodied as lives that matter, that are grievable—literally, lives worth living. That music is integral to queer world-making is a function of long-standing historical affinities and associations of both (Brett 2004). To the extent that it expresses and produces "queer bodies, subjectivities, desires and social relations . . . in aggressively heteronormative landscapes"

---

1. "Catachrestic acts of speech . . . fail to refer or refer in the wrong way" (Butler 1993, 217).

(Taylor 2012, 49) and in other ways and contexts—to the extent that it expresses and produces black bodies, subjectivities, desires, and social relations in virulently racist landscapes—music is intertextually mobilized by both Lambert and Simone as a "tactic of survival" in the now of queer catachresis and the future of black revolution.

COVER SONGS

Cover songs are ubiquitous in popular music, whether performed as tribute, theft, or rejection. As rereadings of cultural texts, they are already intertextual musically and lyrically. The act of "covering" may be thought of as queer—a "temporal drag" act (Freeman 2000). Elizabeth Freeman's concept of temporal drag refers specifically to how "the lesbian" functions as "the big drag" in queer theory, pulling—in a way that, as Sue-Ellen Case observed in 1997, "wasn't funny anymore" (210)—hip queer politics back to a disavowed 1970s second-wave feminist past theorized in terms of "essentialized bodies, normative visions of women's sexuality, and single-issue identity politics" (Freeman 2000, 728). Rather than conceiving the past as an obstacle to so-called progressive ways of theorizing and acting, temporal drag productively invokes, in the "movement time of collective political life" (729), a past that is not quite gone in a present that is not quite here. Covering is queer when the performer does not simply resing the original or blend into it but instead enacts a "cross-historical" practice that involves "inhabiting [the earlier] persona or body or voice . . . while self-consciously registering the performance" (Halberstam 2007, 53). This has the effect of mobilizing the cover in an iterative "complex structure of queer reproduction" (52)—what I theorize here as *haunting*[2] of and by intertextual apparitions.

Judged on how well they used their voices to cover so-called canonic American popular songs, *American Idol* contestants relied—many might say overrelied—on vocal improvisation or "melismatic variation" to make

---

2. Freeman (2000) observes that "the theoretical work of 'queer performativity' sometimes (though not always) undermines not just the essentialized body that *haunts* lesbian and gay identity politics, but political history—the expending of actual physical energy in less spectacular or theatrical forms of activist labor done in response to historically specific crises" (728–29; emphasis added).

their covers unique without deviating too far from the original or standard version. Vocal improvisation signals virtuosity outside textuality, and similar to men singing in falsetto, is associated with gendered African American singing practices. Both practices, individually as well as when taken together, operate intertextually as "a vocal, and thus embodied, symbol of blackness" (Meizel 2011, 63), making audible the racialization, genderization and sexualization of American popular music, particularly in terms of tensions associated with them.

▌ *THE ROAR OF THE GREASEPAINT, THE SMELL OF THE CROWD*

Written in British music hall style, the 1964 class-based allegorical musical *The Roar of the Greasepaint, the Smell of the Crowd*[3] features two main characters, privileged "Sir" and downtrodden "Cocky." Together they continuously play "The Game" of life. Sir always wins and keeps changing the rules to ensure his victory. "The Negro," even more abject than Cocky, enters the game late and unexpectedly wins, singing "Feeling Good" as an expression of "emancipation" from how badly Cocky had treated him. Apparently inspired by The Negro's success, Cocky presses his challenge of Sir until the two forge an alliance based on mutual interdependence.

Greasepaint's score remarkably produced six songs that became standards, notably "Feeling Good" and "Who Can I Turn To?" (Marshall 2016).[4] The show quickly flopped in England, however, in August 1964, which was mostly attributed to miscasting Norman Wisdom (because he was not Anthony Newley) as Cocky. Casting West Indian performer Cy Grant[5] as The Negro also might have been a problem, given that it was only a year after the West Indian community in Bristol,

---

3. Bricusse and Newley (1964), licensing rights owned by Tams-Witmark Music Library Inc., http://www.tamswitmark.com/shows/roar-of-greasepaint-smell-of-crowd/.
4. The other four songs are "On a Wonderful Day like Today," "Where Would You Be Without Me?," "The Joker," and "Nothing Can Stop Me Now."
5. Grant also appeared in the 1964 British documentary *Freedom Road: Songs of Negro Protest*, directed by Robert Fleming and Mike McKenzie, singing "Trouble" and "Hallelujah, I'm a-Travelling"; the soundtrack was released in 1964 as *Freedom Road: Songs of Negro Protest*, Fontana L5208, LP.

England—inspired by nonviolent civil rights activism in the United States[6]—led a bus boycott that forced the local Transport and General Workers Union to hire people of color (Kelly 2013). In addition, England's economic decline during the 1960s might have kept audiences away, or at least made them unwilling to examine class-based inequity that benefited them. Regardless, US producer David Merrick saw potential in *Greasepaint* as a struggle between individuals and agreed to take it to Broadway—on the condition that popular musical theatre performer Anthony Newley play Cocky and well-known crooner Tony Bennett record "Who Can I Turn To?" for immediate release in the United States.[7] With African American singer Gilbert Price cast as The Negro, Merrick also took the unusual step of recording the Broadway cast album early, releasing it two months before the show's May 16 opening. Intended to build audience interest during *Greasepaint*'s financially successful three-month US national tour, the album landed in stores and on radio[8] in the midst of widespread racial turmoil inspired by the US civil rights movement and just four days after what would come to be known in the United States as "Bloody Sunday."

During the morning of March 7, 1965, six hundred peaceful demonstrators set out to march from Selma to Montgomery, the Alabama state capital, to assert their long-denied voting rights. While crossing the Edmund Pettus Bridge, they were brutally attacked by Alabama state troopers using clubs, tear gas, and horses. Shocking news footage of the attack broadcast the same night on national television sparked outrage across the country. Within days, President Lyndon Johnson sent voting rights legislation to Congress, and on March 21, protected by a federal court order and hundreds of federalized troops of the Alabama National Guard, more than three thousand marchers departed on the four-day journey initially led by Martin Luther King Jr. Several prominent African American singers performed along the way, including Lena Horne, Harry

---

6. The West Indian activists were specifically inspired by the 1955 Montgomery, Alabama, bus boycott and Martin Luther King Jr.'s insistence on nonviolence (Kelly 2013).
7. It charted ten weeks on the Billboard Top 100 during late fall 1964.
8. It charted thirty-four weeks on the Billboard 200, beginning April 10, 1965, and peaking at fifty-four on July 31.

Belafonte, and Nina Simone.[9] Her cover of "Feeling Good," recorded in January, would be released in June.

"Feeling Good"

Because no recording exists of the 1964 English production of *Greasepaint*, Price's "Feeling Good" on the Broadway cast album serves as the original.[10] He performs a musical theatre ballad as an African American spiritual, a singing style and music genre that was immediately identifiable to both black and white audiences in the United States as well as in England (Ward 2014). Conveying profound emotion, Price sings powerfully and with great intensity.[11] His robust baritone voice exactly exemplifies stage-based African American singing practices of the first half of the twentieth century, recalling Paul Robeson's expansive bass voice singing "Ol' Man River" nearly thirty years earlier in the 1936 movie *Show Boat*. Halfway through the bridge of "Feeling Good," Price is accompanied by a choir of angels (*Greasepaint*'s young "Urchins"), leading into his triumphant exclamations, "And this old world is a new world and a bold world for me," and later in the third verse, "I know how I feel." He sings the final two-word refrain, "Feeling good!" in full voice, a cappella and extended out of time. Price's phrasing, subtle use of rubato, timbral shading, and melodic embellishments express the yearning, hope, and sorrow that was—and still is—heard as a performative effect of freedom. Implications of this were underscored in August 1965, when an altercation in the Watts neighborhood of Los Angeles between three African American family members and LA police officers escalated into six days of rebellion—five days after Johnson had signed national voting rights legislation.[12]

---

9. See "Nina Simone: Mississippi Goddam," YouTube video, 1:10, posted by "Nina Simone," February 6, 2013, https://www.youtube.com/watch?v=1eaxFES2YXA, for an excerpt of her singing "Mississippi Goddam" during the 1965 Selma to Montgomery march, accompanied by guitarist Al Schackman. She is incongruously dressed in a sweater-vest over a white blouse and plaid skirt.

10. Responding directly to the nation's tortured and tumultuous mood, Price's *Greasepaint* stage performances of "Feeling Good" were described as "electrifying."

11. For the Broadway cast recording, see "16 Feeling Good: The Roar of the Greasepaint, the Smell of the Crowd," YouTube video, posted by "PuissantAlgernon," October 6, 2011, https://www.youtube.com/watch?v=pulEa0cfNcw.

12. In June 2013, the US Supreme Court struck down key provisions of this act, enabling Alabama, eight other states, and numerous other counties and

In addition to Simone, several performers covered "Feeling Good" in 1965, including Cy Grant, Sammy Davis Jr., and even John Coltrane. All are stylistic departures from the original. Grant's and Davis's vocal recordings exude a spare 1960s cool jazz vibe, while Simone's is much more in the style of 1950s and '60s recordings by female African American jazz singers, such as Ella Fitzgerald and Sarah Vaughan, who were backed by string-heavy orchestras and typically given little, if any, space in which to improvise. In this case, however, the singer is *pianist* Nina Simone. The seventh track on her second album with Phillips, *I Put a Spell on You,* Simone's "Feeling Good" was recorded in the midst of her fierce commitment to composing songs and singing in support of black revolution. Referenced by almost every cover released since then, including Muse's 2001 popular version, Simone's recording serves as the standard, and to the extent that it so completely re-places without ever completely effacing Grant's original, her cover is "irredeemably queer" (Halberstam 2011).

▎ NINA SIMONE

First there was Eunice Waymon playing gospel music and committing her life to classical. Then there was racism. And then there was Nina Simone.

—A. Loudermilk

Contra to Thomas Jones (writing as A. Loudermilk 2013), I would suggest that *first* there was racism. *Then* there was Eunice Waymon, born 1933 in Tryon, North Carolina, of mixed indigenous, African, and white ancestry.[13] She played gospel from the day she climbed onto the bench of her family's pedal organ—just before her third birthday—and played the hymn "God Be With You 'til We Meet Again" completely through, without mistakes. *Then* there was Eunice Waymon's *experience* of racism in relationship to her piano playing. She was eleven years old when she refused to begin playing a public concert for community members

---

municipalities to enact and enforce punitive changes to their election laws without prior federal approval.

13. My biographical discussion is based on Simone's impressionistic autobiography, *I Put a Spell on You: The Autobiography of Nina Simone,* coauthored by Stephen Cleary and first published in 1991.

(African American and white) who were funding her private classical piano lessons until her parents were returned to the front-row seats they had vacated for a white family. A decade later, she auditioned at the Curtis Institute of Music in Philadelphia and was denied admission. *Then* there was "Nina Simone."

Preparing virtually every day of her life to fulfill her dream of becoming "the first black classical pianist," Eunice Waymon created the stage name "Nina Simone" so her mother, a devout Methodist minister for whom young Eunice had played church services and revival meetings,[14] would not know that she was performing in a bar in Atlantic City to finance piano lessons with Curtis professor Vladimir Sokhaloff. He confirmed that she should have been admitted and encouraged her to audition again. Hearing later from "white people who knew" that Curtis turned her down because she was a "very poor unknown black girl," Simone still wondered if she had played well enough because, she observes, people never admit to racism (Simone and Cleary [1991] 2003, 42). "So you feel the shame, humiliation and anger at being just another victim of prejudice and at the same time there's the nagging worry that maybe it isn't that at all, maybe it's because you're just no good" (42–43). Within the next ten years, Simone became a rich, well-known African American artist performing a mix of mostly popular music styles—until 1963, when members of the Ku Klux Klan threw dynamite into the Birmingham, Alabama, Sixteenth Street Baptist Church, killing adolescent girls Denise McNair, Cynthia Wesley, Carole Robertson, and Addie Mae Collins. And *then* there was Nina Simone: "I suddenly realized what it was to be black in America in 1963, but it wasn't an intellectual connection of the type Lorraine [Hansberry] had been repeating to me over and over—it came as a rush of fury, hatred and determination. In church language, the Truth entered into me and I 'came through.' . . . [F]or the next seven years I was driven by civil rights and the hope of black revolution. . . . My music was dedicated to a purpose more important than classical music's pursuit of excellence; it was dedicated to the fight for freedom and the historical destiny of my

---

14. Simone insists that she learned to improvise by playing gospel music, which taught her "how to shape music in response to an audience and then how to shape the mood of the audience in response to my music" (Simone and Cleary 2003/1991, 19).

people" (89, 91). Everything about performing music changed for Simone that day, including her relationship with popular music audiences who adored her but as she later observes were "too easily pleased, and [only] interested in . . . the delivery of the lyrics" (91). About eighteen months after the bombing, she recorded "Feeling Good."

Nina Simone's "Feeling Good"

Simone does not cover songs so much as she deconstructs them; with "Feeling Good,"[15] she destructs a show tune and constructs a freedom song that quickly became a jazz standard. The verses are accompanied by a distinctive four-measure, chaconne-like bass line that descends stepwise, walking the time forward in four-beat compound meter stressing beats 1 and 3. Over this, the orchestra, featuring brass and strings, plays 1960s jazz-inflected chords while Simone lightly plays closely voiced chords in even triplets in the piano's far upper range. As she completes singing the second verse, the piano continues with steady triplets while strings swing eighth notes during a four-measure instrumental transition to the bridge, which is distinctly different in character. Without brass or incessant rhythmic drive, strings play long notes over light percussion and string bass. It is here that Simone's voice and piano function intertextually on her terms, the best means for expressing what she knows musically and politically. Playing (again discretely) a sophisticated, introspective high right-hand melodic piano improvisation that frames and complements the lyrics,[16] she connects the piano line to her epistemological interjections, "don't you know," "you know," finally telling, "Sleep in peace when day is done: that's what I mean"—but the day she means is one of black revolution. Ontologically, the world has changed from "old" to "new" and, for Simone, "bold." Percussion signals the brass entrance and the shift back to the descending bass line and piano triplets.

Simone performs the last verse in the sure knowledge of how she is in the world—how she feels and what she is certain is coming. Emphatically

---

15. For a recording from the album, see "Nina Simone Feeling Good," YouTube video, posted by "Cancano Cancano," October 20, 2012, https://www.youtube.com/watch?v=D5Y11hwjMNs.

16. The bass line, piano triplets, and gestures from this improvisation define subsequent covers.

singing in full voice "Oh, freedom is mine," she cuts off the last word and then asserts her embodied subjectivity: "And I know how I feel." Gesturing to cultural continuity, she sings that it is not only a "new dawn" and a "new day" but "a new long life," expressing a future for her—and for black revolution. With the last words of the verse, "for me," time stops, and Simone immediately initiates the revolution with a vocal improvisation while the orchestra holds an altered subdominant jazz chord rather than the expected tonic, eventually moving through four sustained chords that traverse the signature descending bass line.

Simone's wordless improvisation not only provides the final word, articulating her determination to sing a future revolution, but also reveals that her cover is not jazz at all. Singing deeply personal pitched utterances outside of language as well as textuality, this is not "scatting" associated with jazz, although it is deeply implicated in historical and current African American musical practices. More than simply made up on the spot, jazz scatting serves rhythmic, melodic, and harmonic functions in relation to the original tune. It creatively "follows," or plays off and with what is pregiven, often humorously citing other tunes. Simone defined jazz in terms of black men: "To me 'jazz' meant a way of thinking, a way of being, and the black man in America was jazz in everything he did—in the way he walked, talked, thought and acted" and rejected categorization of herself as a jazz singer (68–69). She explained, "I didn't like to be put in a box with other jazz singers because my musicianship was totally different, and in its own way superior. Calling me a jazz singer was a way of ignoring my musical background because I didn't fit into white ideas of what a black performer should be. It was a racist thing: 'If she's black she must be a jazz singer.' It diminished me" (69). In addition to diminishing Simone, this interpellation obscures the *intra*textuality of her improvisation.

In her improvisation, using mostly open *a* and long *e* vowel sounds, syllables beginning with the plosive *d* soon give way to alternating nasal *m* and *n* on pitches that anticipate and set up the harmony, Simone is leading—not following—the orchestra, which is exactly why the chord changes sound inevitable. She neither scats nor interjects but sings her improvisation as interpellation, and what is at stake here is who or what is interpellated. Speaking to and with her community, Simone emerges from this *extra*textuality, again in full voice—"Oh, I'm feelin' good!"—holding the last pitch without vibrato until the fade-out as the orchestra, minus piano, picks up the groove and bass line for the outro.

But what you hear first in Simone's "Feeling Good" is her voice, materialized as all texture and depth. Starting her cover a cappella and without introduction, Simone performs the first verse freely, out of time, pausing too long at the end of each line. You hear her thinking, feeling her way through something profoundly significant: future black revolution of racial equality in the United States. As a "private and subjective response to political events" (Berman 2004, 180), Simone's presentation of interiority signals that her singing is not about aesthetics or beauty, although it is undeniably artistic and riveting. Almost ruminating, but with palpable anticipation, she repeats the last line, "It's a new dawn, it's a new day, it's a new life for me"—extended with a short descending melisma—and moves smoothly into what is for her after every verse a four-word refrain: "And I'm feelin' good" instead of the two-word declarative "feeling good" of the original that Price sings and both Grant and Davis cover. Simone's embodiment of the lyric functions as an "implicit criticism" (Berman 2004) of Bricusse and Newley, moving it from English verse to African American voice, and from (operatic) Broadway stage singing to African American lived experience, the latter underscored by her dropping Price's clearly enunciated *g* of the *-ing* suffix.

Long before you register the move, however, you realize the abrasive insistence of her voice that grabs and holds you. Suddenly internalized, her performance carries an immediacy and intimacy that can only be felt viscerally. Once you have heard Simone's deeply and darkly expressive voice, relentless and defiant, you can never unhear it, which is to say you can never not hear it. You can never silence it or turn away from it—from the "yearning in her voice [that] sometimes . . . sounds like mourning and sometimes rapture" (Dobie 1997, 235).

ADAM LAMBERT

He's like Marc Bolan meets Bowie, with a touch of Freddie Mercury and the sexiness of Prince.

—Simon Fuller (in Grigoriadis 2009)

American Idol quickly established a reputation for meanness toward contestants, despite its marketing as family entertainment. Host Ryan Seacrest's and judge Simon Cowell's recurring homophobic onscreen exchanges challenging each other's heterosexuality certainly contributed to the impression that *Idol* "reserved . . . a special sort of meanness" for contestants who presented on "the queer end of the spectrum" (Votta 2016). While *Idol* purportedly avoided exploiting sexuality "for its audience potential" (Meizel 2012), it nonetheless emerged in the first season.[17] Even Lambert, who was widely regarded as having been "basically out" during season 8, waited until after the season ended to confirm his being gay in a June 2009 *Rolling Stone* cover story. It would be five years after Lambert's runner-up finish before the first openly "LGBT contestant," lesbian MK Nobilette, competed into the Top 10 during season 13 in 2014—when a straight white cisgender man won. Overall, cisgender straight white men won nine of *Idol*'s fifteen seasons, including seasons 5, 7 through 11, and 13 through 15, demonstrating the show's inability to move beyond a regressive past of its own making that isolated it from progressive social and musical scenes, ultimately rendering it irrelevant (Votta 2016).

Unable to create a compelling backstory about Lambert's Southern California hometown or the fact that he was Jewish, the show constructed a narrative about him as a glam rocker (Meizel 2012). Not only was it plausible, given his background performing in musicals, it was also expeditious. To the extent that signifiers of glam rock, such as "flamboyant poses and aggressive sexuality" are often associated with and stereotypical of gay men, *Idol* producers might have hoped audiences would conflate glam with gay, enabling the show to "exploit [Lambert's] gayness without

---

17. *Idol* allegedly forced gay first-season contestant Jim Verraros to delete his online journal, in which he was out, because his sexuality would provide him "an unfair advantage." This was *Idol* before social media, where they could tightly control the media leaked out about contestants. Any story outside the *Idol* narrative was verboten" (Votta 2016).

naming it" (Draper 2012, 207).[18] Indeed, show producer Simon Fuller took up the glam narrative directly only after the season was over. Undermining that narrative, however, is that the vast majority of glam rockers were heterosexual white men who "posed" ambiguously in a variety of ways. All the glam rockers Fuller names—Bolan, who fathered a son; Bowie, who in 1983 repudiated his (false) 1970s claim of homosexuality; and even Mercury, widely understood now as gay, but who concealed that he was HIV positive and later died of AIDS—maintained long-standing relationships with women. Moreover, none of these performers, or other glam rockers in the 1970s and '80s, contributed politically or personally to queer causes. Auditioning for *Idol* first with Queen's "Bohemian Rhapsody" and later with Cher's "Believe," Lambert took up the glam rock persona enthusiastically even as he intensified its conventions and interrupted its narratives.[19]

For the Top 5 competition week, "Rat Pack Standards," Lambert was required to sing a song made famous by a group of American actors and singers known in the 1950s and '60s as the "rat pack." Instead of rat-pack member Sammy Davis Jr.'s version of "Feeling Good," however, Lambert covered the popular—arguably glam—version recorded in 2001 by the English progressive hard (space) rock band Muse. While Muse's version shares some affinity with Simone's standard, it is mechanistic (Matthew Bellamy sings the second verse through a megaphone while moving robotically) and densely scored, representing a naïvely hopeful futuristic vision where people might begin a new life (MuseWiki 2014).

Adam Lambert's "Feeling Good"

Lambert's on-air cover of "Feeling Good" practically mirrors Muse's cover in terms of accompaniment, form, and harmony and might be easily heard as a

---

18. This assertion is underscored by singer Ryan Cassata's experience with *American Idol.* Cassata, "who just happens to be transgender," claimed in a YouTube video open letter that *Idol* casting directors, after rejecting him for season fourteen because he wasn't "contemporary enough" and "being transgender wasn't such a hot issue in the media like it is now," reached out to him to audition for season fifteen in an effort to "boost their ratings." See "American Idol: Turn Down 4 What?," YouTube video, posted by "Ryan Cassata," July 20, 2015, https://www.youtube.com/watch?v=bOWFjLd-kf8.

19. See Gould (2017) for a more extensive and detailed Deleuzian analysis of twelve of Lambert's performances on *American Idol.*

tribute.[20] In addition to beginning with a Liberace-like keyboard gesture, the intro for both versions foregrounds keyboard playing repeated triplets. Both play the distinctive single-note walking bass line during verse 1, and both use stop time after "feelin'" in the first iteration of the refrain. Both full ensembles enter powerfully on "good," eliding the transition to the next verse; both play nearly identical transitions to the bridge, and both efface the root of the coda's first chord to stabilize the pitch that both Bellamy and Lambert sing. Their improvisations move through the same pitches—the former untexted, the latter on the words "I'm feelin'." Further, both singers use falsetto in the bridge, begin their falsetto improvisations in the coda on high D, and eventually move to the F above.

Perhaps most importantly, though, Lambert takes up Bellamy's small but significant last verse lyric change, replacing Simone's (and Grant's) assertion of embodied subjectivity, "Freedom is mine, and *I* know how I feel," with "Freedom is mine, and *you* know how I feel." For Bellamy, depending on how you read Muse's "Feeling Good" official video,[21] this generalized *you* is a faceless or deformed, anonymous audience of the future. For Lambert, the generalized *you* is queer community produced as an effect of the performative arc he traversed through his performances on *Idol*. Using *Idol*'s misnomer glam rock to "interrupt" and "re-sound" the faux homosexuality of the former (glam) and hegemonic masculinity of the latter (rock),[22] Lambert's song and performance choices articulate ontological potentialities of queer desire—in and for the present.

His on-air "Feeling Good" presentation is nonintuitive and fairly ridiculous. Festooned in white shoes and an ill-fitting gangster-inspired white satin suit and tie over a black shirt, Lambert stands about midway

---

20. For Lambert's on-air *American Idol* performance of "Feeling Good," see "Adam Lambert Feeling Good Performance HQ," YouTube video, posted by "mrslilianaadamjonas's channel," January 15, 2010, https://www.youtube.com/watch?v=D5Y11hwjMNs.

21. See "Muse—Feeling Good (Official Music Video)," YouTube video, posted by "Across The Museiverse," December 1, 2009, https://www.youtube.com/watch?v=KOEZMjuoIEY.

22. Daphne Brooks (2011) similarly argues that as an "intervention in rock masculinist narratives," Simone's 1984 cover of "The Alabama Song" "interrupts the hedonistic boys-are-back-in-town versions of the song and instead choreographs a guerilla action that re-sounds, re-centers, that surrogates black female voices buried at the bottom of the bottom of the rock and roll archive" (193).

on a tall staircase and sings the first verse tenderly, slowly, and freely. Coinciding with the last word of the refrain ("good"), he begins to lurch down the staircase awkwardly and out of time while the band, alternating splashy cymbals with brass, pounds out the descending bass line. The cumulative effect of this self-contained botched iteration of masculinity in the context of the band's overplayed accompaniment is heterosexual drag. To the extent that "there is no original or primary gender that drag imitates . . . heterosexuality is always in the process of imitating and approximating its own phantasmatic idealization of itself—*and failing*" (Butler 1991, 21; original emphasis). Exposing the precariousness of heterosexuality's infinitely repeating imitative structure, Lambert's heterosexual drag materializes in his live performance as poignant in the first verse and emphatic in the last (the only verses he sings). In the coda, it verges on overwrought as his ascending vocal melodic sequence, like Bellamy's, follows rather than leads the band through the four sustained chords. He holds the top pitch D powerfully for easily nine seconds and then descends an octave smoothly and precisely, outlining the dominant seventh. Time stops, and he quietly finishes the lyric "good" with the band lightly vamping, finally ending his excruciating live cover performance with a surprisingly subtle jazz chord sustained by guitar.

INTERTEXTUAL STRATEGIES

Forced to abandon her classical music aspirations, Simone directed her intertextual strategies toward a future black revolution situated in relationship to gender. She performed across and mixed musical genres, including classical, gospel, folk, popular, blues, jazz, cabaret, and show tunes, engaging this "combinatory textual approach" to transgress and conjoin styles compulsively and continuously (Gaines 2013). Accomplished "in a variety of musical aesthetics, genres, and traditions, black and white," Simone claimed to prefer no particular style, creating concoctions that were simultaneously surprising and musically brilliant (Heard 2012, 1060). Indeed, Simone's musical choices so thoroughly resisted genre and style classification that marketing her recordings and reviewing her performances was nearly impossible.

In her remarkable 1962 live studio amalgam of the "existential love song" (Gaines 2013) "For All We Know"[23]—composed in 1934 by Tin Pan Alley, songwriter J. Fred Coots, and lyricist Sam M. Lewis and recorded by African American singers such as Dinah Washington, Abbey Lincoln, and Billie Holliday[24]—Simone plays a Bach-like invention while singing the lyrics slowly, out of time and melody, without affect. Infused by guitarist Al Schackman's equally remarkable improvised guitar counterpoint, this performance—even more so than the 1960 recorded version (without Schackman) on the album *Nina Simone and Her Friends*—is unquestionably one of the most poignant and profoundly artistic examples of her combinatorial gifts. She wears a sleeveless flower-print dress and a tiny tiara in straight hair, appearing youthful yet composed and wise. The interplay of piano and guitar carries all the emotion, her voice enveloped as part of the music's texture: "For all we know, this may only be a dream." Certainly the most famous of her shocking juxtapositions, however, is the jaunty show tune piano accompaniment she created for her wildly provocative and antagonistic civil rights protest song "Mississippi Goddam."

In the aftermath of the September 1963 "bombing of the little girls in Alabama and the [June 1963] murder of Medgar Evers . . . shot to death on the steps of his [Jackson, Mississippi] home," Simone, in a self-described murderous rage, composed in just one hour the astounding "Mississippi Goddam" (Simone and Cleary [1991] 2003, 89, 88).[25] This

---

23. For an excerpt of the studio-recorded version broadcast August 13, 1961, on the CBS show *Camera Three*, see "For all we know—Live!," YouTube video, posted by "berta berta," September 3, 2008, https://www.youtube.com/watch?v=6proYaAfwtM. For information about the recording session, see "The Nina Simone Database," http://boscarol.com/ninasimone/pages/php/show_session.php?id=nyc61A.

24. "The lyric's suggestion that 'tomorrow may never come,' resonates with the tragic story of Holliday, who innovated an original African American woman's voice, but who was physically defeated by the circumstances of which she was an object," notes Gaines (2013, 262), connecting Simone's performance to Billie Holliday's 1958 version recorded on *Lady in Satin*, the last album released before Holliday's death.

25. With "her propulsive [Carnegie Hall] performance, Simone brings her listeners close(r) to the voice and obstinacy coursing through her song; she delivers the sonic equivalent of AfricanAmericans' [*sic*] utter discontent living under quotidian Jim Crow subjugation—dodging and countenancing hound dogs, imprisonment, and police brutality. At the same time, it is precisely this musical testimony of a visceral open wound that Simone seeks to expose, to articulate, to sing into contestation here" (Brooks 2011, 184). See "Nina Simone: Mississippi Goddam (Live in New York/

stunningly redefined 1960s freedom song, completely unlike anything performed by other activists such as Fannie Lou Hamer or the Student Nonviolent Coordinating Committee Freedom Singers, "teem[s] with a penetrating rage and sadness" even as it manages to invoke humor (Heard 2012, 1062).[26] Although most obviously associated with the piano's parody of show tunes supporting "darkly candid lyrics" (Brooks 2011, 187)—"Oh but this whole country is full of lies / You're all gonna die, and die like flies!"—delivered with a "Vaudevillian . . . quick and witty pitter-patter" (Gaines 2013, 253), "the actual poetics of the tune reveals deeply comic structures which play with understatement, parody, and the sharp incongruities of quotidian experiences of American life" that Simone knew firsthand only too well (Heard 2012, 1062).

She was renowned for mesmerizingly brilliant and typically unpredictable live performances during which she changed or interpolated lyrics and rearranged or mispronounced words, inventing new stresses and variations while improvising introductions, "bridges, codas, and reprises" (Gaines 2013). Underscoring this, Danielle Heard (2012) argues that her music and performances are resonant with free jazz but "even more 'far out' than the free jazz cats [in that] her unique theater of invisibility distinguishes itself from any one artistic movement" (1060).[27] In the end, however, Simone's virtuosic pianism challenged, but could not completely dislodge, the assumed masculinity of the African American jazz soloist that Simone articulated (Feldstein 2005; Monson 1995). While it might be accurate that both "jazz and masculinity—lose their shape as a result of Simone's . . . intertextual strategy" (Gaines 2013, 264), "free jazz cats" such as Dizzy Gillespie were characterized as "unorthodox geniuses," while Simone—(dis)reputed to be temperamental, rude, and arrogant—"was

Mono)," YouTube video, posted by "Gordon Paul II," December 15, 2014, https:// www.youtube.com/watch?v=scGVEwaUsdg.
26. Simone's parodic adaptation of Alex Comfort's "Go Limp" is an example of her ironic use of distinctly bawdy humor (Feldstein 2005). For a compelling discussion of "an economy of laughter" and Simone's uses of comic figures of speech in "Mississippi Goddam," see Heard (2012). For a short musical analysis of "Mississippi Goddam," see Kernodle (2008).
27. For an insightful discussion of Simone's "invisibility" in subsequent accounts of civil rights music and activism of the 1960s, see Feldstein (2005).

far more likely to be depicted as 'a witch' than as an artist with high standards" (Feldstein 2005, 1359).

Singing with a usually rough-edged but always uniquely expressive voice that "seems to trigger grief, in the same way that certain sounds do—a fog horn, light rain on an empty lake" (Dobie 1997, 232), she "dar[ed] audiences to see and hear 'America' differently and on a different frequency" (Brooks 2011, 182). Indeed, the ways Simone used her voice, manipulating its distinctively fluctuating timbre, itself defying categorization, particularly in its lowest register, elides gender as well as sexuality.[28] Simone describes her voice as a "third layer, complementing the other two layers, right and left hands" of her piano (Simone and Cleary [1991] 2003, 51) in a form of intertextuality that Malik Gaines (2013) characterizes as transvocal: "Singer of diverse materials and the virtuoso soloist . . . speak[ing] complementary languages" in ways that were invariably controversial (262). The intertextual strategy that would make clear her critique talks back—not only to uncomprehending audiences, reviewers, and critics but also for a faltering future revolution.

"Don't Let Me Be Misunderstood" was composed for Simone and released in 1964 on her first album with Phillips, *Broadway, Blues, Ballads*. An effect of songwriter Horace Ott's working through a marital argument, Simone was immediately "intrigued" when Ott pitched the song to her, perhaps "transmigrating" it to beatings she regularly endured from husband and manager Andy Stroud (Cohodas 2010). The recorded version is overorchestrated with lush strings, woodwinds, percussion, and the Malcolm Dodds singers, all of which nonetheless combine to "highlight the singular edge in [Simone's] voice every time she cut through the swooning violins" as she finds "her way to the heart of the song, raw but completely without melodrama" (152, 153)—which, of course, was true of everything she sang.

---

28. This is vividly demonstrated in a 1968 live performance in which she sings the folk song "Black Is the Colour of My True Love's Hair" as a duet with guitarist Emile Lattimer. Her voice, husky and raw, scrapes the bottom reaches of her range and—but for its timbre—is virtually indistinguishable from his. For an extended discussion of this performance, see Gaines (2013) and "Nina Simone: Black Is the Color of My True Love's Hair," YouTube video, posted by "lukeslark," March 15, 2011, https://www.youtube.com/watch?v=NWmCbEbMmeU.

Simone performed "Don't Let Me Be Misunderstood" live in London for the 1968 British television special *Sound of Soul*.[29] Wearing an African-like tunic and matching kerchief covering her hair, Simone's performance voices a metadialogue of her critique as continuity—not a plea for reconciliation but an imperative to the studio and viewing audiences and a challenge for an agonizingly vanishing black revolution. Of the lyrics, she sings only the first verse and hook:

Baby, you understand me now if sometimes you see that I'm mad
No one can always be an angel; when everything goes wrong, you see some bad
I'm just a soul whose intentions are good; oh lord, please don't let me be
  misunderstood

The band vamps as she continues to play and sing, freely improvising the melody and rhythm:

Don't let me be misunderstood; don't let me be misunderstood
'Cause if I'm misunderstood all my life would have been in vain
And lord knows I don't want to come here again, so don't let me be
  misunderstood
Give me a clear mind
Give me the words to say what I mean, no, no, no, no
Don't let me be misunderstood

Signaling the final chord, she looks up and lifts her hands from the keyboard, turns away from the band, and looks down. Her face is fully visible to the camera, her mouth slightly open as if in midsentence. The band abruptly stops, and the studio is instantly silent. Surprised, the audience

---

29. Smiling slightly while vamping the immediately recognizable introduction, Simone introduces "Don't Let Me Be Misunderstood" by intoning, "We're doing the requests now. We're doing the things that we think will please you the most, at least for the next four minutes." Furious that the Animals' cover, released just a few months after her original in 1964, enjoyed so much airplay that it came to be mistaken as the original, she ironically adds, "As you know, the Animals had a hit with this tune. In England." See "Nina Simone: Don't Let Me Be Misunderstood," dailymotion video, posted by "Nina Simone," n.d., https://www.dailymotion.com/video/x13ul6o_nina-simone-don-t-let-me-be-misunderstood_music.

responds with scattered applause that starts to build. Simone turns quickly back to the keyboard, cutting off the applause as she vamps the introduction to the next song, assuring, "Thank you very much. I love you too."

By contrast, Lambert's intertextual strategies on *American Idol* do not combine musical styles but interrupt and re-sound them toward materializing queer subjectivities in the present. With his heartbreaking performance of the Bee Gees' "If I Can't Have You,"[30] he interrupts an up-tempo disco tune and re-sounds it as a starkly personal ballad. Dressed conservatively in a gray suit and dark tie over a white shirt, he never leaves his spot on the stage, leaning slightly as he sings, persistently standing up to disco-associated homophobia. Moving seamlessly from a fully embodied high tenor voice into falsetto and back again, his delivery—unyielding in its intensity, emotion, and intimacy—refutes so-called disco diva vocal stereotypes with subtle rubatos and restrained melismas. His despair reads in the context of gay bashing ("no chance for me," "my life would end," "am I strong enough to see it through"), as he omits the second prechorus lyric, "to dreams that never will come true," and produces imperatives of queer desire, without which ("I don't want nobody") there is no desire.

Similarly, Lambert interrupts Steppenwolf's ponderously serious rock anthem "Born to Be Wild,"[31] synonymous with hard rock and masculinist biker culture, and re-sounds it as a wild gay-boy play-full romp. Performed at a frenetic (by comparison) tempo, Lambert, wearing tennis shoes, skips downstage to an introduction haunted by disco, as it highlights drums instead of electric guitar. The delayed entrance of guitars and overdetermined backbeat produce a ridiculously exuberant and campy rock performance that queers the original by affectionately overplaying it without ever letting it go. Lambert's camp rock persona juxtaposes glam guyliner with biker fingerless gloves and "tak[es] the world" in a queer "love embrace." The specter of disco appears again when he interpellates homophobia associated

---

30. For Lambert's on-air *American Idol* performance, see "Adam Lambert If I Can't Have You Performance," YouTube video, posted by "mrslilianaadamjonas's channel," September 27, 2010, https://www.youtube.com/watch?v=6UZ8I_jk88k.

31. For Lambert's on-air *American Idol* performance, see "Adam Lambert: Born to Be Wild (HQ)," YouTube video, posted by "Club Lambert," May 23, 2009, https://www.youtube.com/watch?v=JYlNoCynlSU.

with both the music genre[32] and the place where it was played[33] by changing "never *wanna* die" in the lyrics of "Born to Be Wild" to "never *gonna* die" from the lyrics of "Play That Funky Music" (which he covered earlier in the season). Deciding to "disco down," the "boogie singer" is exhorted to "lay down the boogie and play that funky music till you die." In this context, the firing "guns" of "Born to Be Wild" read more political than phallic,[34] rendering queer the rockers born to be wild.

APPARITIONAL "FEELING GOOD"

Simone's "Feeling Good" is everywhere yet nowhere. It appears—dismembered and disembodied—as the opening soundtrack to the trailer for the documentary *What Happened, Miss Simone?* (2015), directed by Liz Garbus, only to disappear, silent in this film aspiring to answer its title question first posed by Maya Angelou (1970) to the vividly opaque Nina Simone.[35] Never released as a single and a song Simone almost certainly never performed live, "Feeling Good" echoes endlessly—"her voice vibrates, a rich, deep thrumming under the cracked surface, . . . a motor running, running" unseen, but never unheard (Dobie 1997, 232). Perhaps "Feeling Good" is too amorphous for the exquisite excavations Simone enacted in her relentlessly improvisatory live performances. Perhaps it is too intimate, conjuring the phantom future black revolution that she dreamed but never realized with her beloved friend, African American

---

32. Homophobia associated with disco music was perhaps most evident in the "Disco Demolition Night," staged in 1979 at Comiskey Park, the Chicago White Sox baseball stadium, where thousands of disco records were literally blown up during the break between a doubleheader while tens of thousands of baseball fans cheered and chanted, "Discos sucks!"

33. Homophobia associated with discos is demonstrated in the June 2016 mass killing of revelers at the Orlando, Florida, nightclub Pulse.

34. As performed in the soundtrack of the movie *Easy Rider*, the "Born to Be Wild" lyric is "Fire all of your guns at once and / explode into space." See "Steppenwolf: Born to Be Wild," YouTube video, posted by "Max Shkiv," August 8, 2007, https://www.youtube.com/watch?v=rMbATaj7Il8.

35. In her poetic meditation about and with Simone, Angelou (1970) suggests that Simone's answer about "what happened" was her prodigious talent for the piano, lessons and practicing that isolated her from her family and other children, as well as performances that separated her from her only true love, a young Cherokee man back in Tryon.

playwright, activist, and lesbian Lorraine Hansberry, who died of cancer at thirty-four within days of Simone recording "Feeling Good." It would be four years later in 1969, and just months after her interpellative "Don't Let Me Be Misunderstood," that she composed—with help on the lyrics from her musical director, Weldon Irvine—"To Be Young, Gifted and Black," inspired by and dedicated to Hansberry, about whom Simone comments, "I really think that she gave it to me."[36] An "anthem of black pride" (Feldstein, 1995), it was released as a single and became one of her biggest hits, reaching the top ten on the R&B charts.

"Feeling Good" haunts Simone's performance of "To Be Young, Gifted and Black" in a 1969 concert with her band in a gymnasium at Martin Luther King Jr.'s alma mater, Morehouse College in Atlanta, Georgia. Two members of the band sing the lyrics with her. During the second verse, she simultaneously summons Lorraine and interpellates Nina (3:01):

You are young, gifted and black
We must begin to tell our young
There's a world [little girl] waiting for you
Yours is the quest that's just begun
So when you're feelin' [depressed, alienated, and] real low
There's a great truth that you should know
To be young, gifted and black
Your soul's intact [don't you forget it!] your soul's intact

The band vamps in an improvisatory section immediately after the final line, and Simone exclaims, "Oh! I'm feelin' good now." Continuing to play during the vamp, she muses, "Yes, yes, yes, yes" and then calls Langston Hughes and Billie Holliday, adding, "Now, of course, Lorraine is gone." Gathering herself, she intones, "Enough, enough, enough, Nina. I feel so good!" and sways, dancing at the piano with her upper body in the rhythm, perhaps, of black revolution materializing—some forty years hence. She and the band sing one last verse:

---

36. For a video of the interview in which Simone expresses this (preceding her performance of "To Be Young, Gifted and Black"), see "Nina Simone: To Be Young, Gifted and Black," YouTube video, 1:52, posted by "Nina Simone," February 21, 2013, https://www.youtube.com/watch?v=_hdVFiANBTk.

To be young, gifted and black
Oh, how I long to know the truth
There are times when I look back
And I am haunted by my youth
But my joy of today
Is that we can all be proud to say
To be young, gifted and black
Hey! Is where it's at!
Is where it's at! Is where it's at!

Simone jumps up to ecstatic applause, and the band continues playing as she turns and rapidly walks away from the piano, her hands up in the performative gesture of "Don't shoot," now associated with Black Lives Matter.

Haunted by the phantasm of his on-air performance of failed hetero-sexuality, Lambert's studio version of "Feeling Good," with its references to both disco music and queerness, is not a tribute to Muse's popular version but an anticover of both the music and message. It immediately disrupts the impersonal sophistication of Muse's progressive rock by starting with keyboard bass holding D. The song's dominant pitch begs the ensuing G minor Liberace-like flourish, followed by the keyboard triplets of the intro emphatically stomping beats 1 and 3. Further, Lambert's studio version replaces Muse's discrete fade at the end, with guitar holding pitches G and D, decaying in an excruciatingly slow wah-wah vibrato. Perhaps the most overt reference to disco, however, is Lambert's complex vocal improvisation during the coda, featuring not only his versatile falsetto but the striking beauty and expressivity of his voice across its entire range.

Heard as false and artificial, falsetto signified 1970s disco and all that allegedly was wrong with it—"excessive, synthetic, overproduced, orna-mental" (François 1995, 443). In its hauntingly intimate immateriality, however, falsetto functions as both "the voice of exception, crisis, and interruption, if not intervention [and] a rhetorical deployment of differ-ence, a staging of an otherness imposed from without by oppressive . . . gender-based structures" (François 1995, 445). Traversing an exceptionally wide range, Lambert intensifies Simone's lyric in his solo, repeating, "I'm feelin', I'm feelin', I'm feelin'" on an ascending sequence that begins on D above middle C and ends in falsetto an octave higher. Gliding from there up to F, he seamlessly descends through his head and middle voices, resting on "good," and then continues his intricate improvisation untexted. Lambert moves all the way down into his chest voice, holding precariously onto D below middle C, more than two octaves below his highest pitch. Singing now in the depths of Simone's haunting voice—the voice triggering grief—Lambert's fragile and rarely heard huskily embodied low tenor voice, interpellating Simone, materializes queer bodies. Singing one last "I'm feelin'," cut off by an audibly aspirated "hah," he finishes quietly with a short melisma on "good," holding not the tonic pitch but B♭, the blues minor third—a tenuous, temporary possibility for just this moment.

▎ AFTER-WORD

In the end, "Feeling Good" was pivotal to the plot of the now "famously problematic musical" (Dorsey 2016) that critics panned in 1965[37] for taking on big questions in a musical comedy form wholly inadequate to the task. Closing in early December after a modestly successful run of 231 performances and 6 Tony nominations, *Greasepaint* has never been revived on Broadway. It is, however, sporadically staged in community theatre productions, two of which improbably played at virtually the same moment in May–June 2016. The Rose Compass Theater (Annapolis, Maryland) version, accompanied only by piano, mostly delivers Bricusse and Newley's original concept with two exceptions: a young man is cast as Sir's protégé, "The Kid," instead of the "abrasive, androgynous young woman" (Marshall 2016) specified in the script,[38] and The Negro is renamed "The Foreigner." Reviewer Jack Marshall (2016) finds the former change inexplicable and the latter attributable to "timidity."

By contrast, the Norma Terris Theatre (Chester, Connecticut) version is—with Bricusse's blessing[39]—completely reimagined, including "new

---

37. For a collection of review reprints, see David Suskin (1997).
38. In a musical that features a homosocial pairing of two white, cisgender, straight men as the lead couple, scripting The Kid as a woman may have been simply a pragmatic decision to add a second woman soloist to the cast. That the woman is "androgynous" may be read as Bricusse and Newley self-consciously registering gender inequities on- and offstage.
39. Newley died in 1999.

orchestrations" performed by just six instrumentalists (Arnott 2016). It is set in a postapocalyptic dystopia in which the cast, now reduced to four characters (Sir, Cocky, The Kid/The Girl, and The Negro—renamed "The Stranger") play the game—not of life but of survival (Dorsey 2016). What is at stake here is food.[40] The Stranger's physical appearance is racially and sexually ambiguous in an effort to honor what director Don Stephenson describes as the show's original "brave" intent during the 1960s civil rights movement to "giv[e] voice to a disenfranchised, voiceless group" (quoted in Dorsey 2016). Portrayed by Gregory Treco, a self-described "light-skinned African American man" (Moore 2015), The Stranger is tall, ample, and imposing, wearing blondish straight long hair pulled back in an explicitly feminine manner and vivid makeup highlighted with splotches of blue, white, and red; a bit of glitter; and bright-red lipstick. The strange-ness this produces is heightened by The Stranger's costuming: a long slit-sleeve cloak over layers of clothing and scarves. Moving about the stage with increasing energy, turning with arms spread wide, emphasizing shoulders in readily identifiable drag queen gestures, The Stranger sings with an unmistakable (male) tenor voice. In this context of mixed gender/sexuality signifiers, The Stranger is meant to present as trans. Indeed, Stephenson refers to the North Carolina bathroom law targeting trans people (Dorsey 2016), implying equivalence between transgender rights now and African American civil rights then that is impossible in a politics of representation where ambiguity stands in for lived actuality.

Inasmuch as this purposefully deracialized/ungendered performance silences—which is to say, overcomes—Grant's and Simone's historically explicit racialized/gendered performances, Treco's cover is not temporal drag, queer, or even trans. With its signifiers evacuated of meaning, The Stranger's performance presents instead as closeted covering. Further, the production's refusal to confront entrenched and enduring historical racial oppression for action toward future black revolution delegitimates The Stranger's attempt to take up Lambert's action against coercive and compulsory gender/sexuality norms within a present iterated catachresis.

---

40. For excerpts of this performance, see "Highlights from Goodspeed's *The Roar of the Greasepaint, the Smell of the Crowd*," YouTube video, 1:10, posted by "Goodspeed Musicals," June 6, 2016, https://www.youtube.com/watch?v=ZZ7kCnT9_pY.

Misunderstanding Simone's revolutionary call, albeit with intentions claimed to be good, The Stranger floats decontextualized, cast adrift without a past and no chance to (really) win, signifying no future in an existential void of a neoliberal forever.

| REFERENCES

Ahmed, Sara. 2006. *Queer Phenomenology: Orientations, Objects, Others*. Durham, NC: Duke University Press.

Angelou, Maya. (1970) 2014. "Nina Simone: High Priestess of Soul." Reproduced in *Aaron Overfield Facebook*, May 30. Accessed July 26, 2016. https://www.facebook .com/notes/aaron-overfield/nina-simone-high-priestess-of-soul-by-maya-angelou -redbook-november-1970/10154171643955346/.

Arnott, Christopher. 2016. "Goodspeed Takes on Cult Musical, 'Roar of the Greasepaint . . .'" *Hartford Currant*, May 23. Accessed November 5. http://www.courant .com/entertainment/arts-theater/hc-preview-roar-of-the-greasepaint-goodspeed -20160523-story.html.

Auslander, Philip. 2004. "Performance Analysis and Popular Music: A Manifesto." *Contemporary Theatre Review* 14 (1): 1–13.

Berman, Russell A. 2004. "Sounds Familiar? Nina Simone's Performances of Brecht/Weill Songs." In *Sound Matters: Essays on the Acoustics of Modern German Culture*, edited by Nora A. Alter and Lutz Koepnick, 171–82. New York: Berghahn Books.

Brett, Philip. 2006. "Music, Essentialism, and the Closet." In *Queering the Pitch: The New Gay and Lesbian Musicology*, 2nd ed., edited by Philip Brett, Elizabeth Wood, and Gary C. Thomas, 9–26. New York: Routledge.

Bricusse, Leslie, and Anthony Newley. 1964. *The Roar of the Greasepaint, the Smell of the Crowd*. London: Essex Music Group.

Brooks, Daphne A. 2011. "Nina Simone's Triple Play." *Callaloo* 34 (1): 176–97.

Butler, Judith. 1991. "Imitation and Gender Insubordination." In *Inside/Out: Lesbian Theories, Gay Theories*, edited by Diana Fuss, 13–31. New York: Routledge.

———. 1993. *Bodies That Matter: On the Discursive Limits of "Sex."* New York: Routledge.

———. 2004. *Precarious Life: The Powers of Mourning and Violence*. London: Verso.

———. 2015. *Notes toward a Performative Theory of Assembly*. Cambridge: Harvard University Press.

Case, Sue-Ellen. 1997. "Toward a Butch-Feminist Retro-Future." In *Cross-Purposes: Lesbians, Feminists, and the Limits of Alliance*, edited by Dana Heller, 205–20. Bloomington: Indiana University Press.

Dobie, Kathy. 1997. "Midnight Train: A Teenage Story." In *Trouble Girls: The Rolling Stone Book of Women in Rock*, edited by Barbara O'Dair, 225–35. New York: Random House.

Dorsey, Kristina. 2016. "Team Has New Take on 'Roar of the Greasepaint' at Terris Theater." *TheDay*, A&E/Music, May 18. Accessed November 4. http://www.theday.com/ article/20160518/ENT10/160519244.

Draper, Jimmy. 2012. "Idol Speculation: Queer Identity and a Media-Imposed Lens of Detection." *Popular Communication: The International Journal of Media and Culture* 10 (3): 201–16.

Feldstein, Ruth. 2005. "'I Don't Trust You Anymore': Nina Simone, Culture, and Black Activism in the 1960s." *Journal of American History* 91 (4): 1349–79.

François, Anne-Lise. 1995. "Fakin' It/Makin' It: Falsetto's Bid for Transcendence in 1970s Disco." *Perspectives of New Music* 33 (1/2): 442–57.

Freeman, Elizabeth. 2000. "Packing History, Count(er)ing Generations." *New Literary History* 31 (4): 727–44.

Gaines, Malik. 2013. "The Quadruple-Consciousness of Nina Simone." *Women & Performance: A Journal of Feminist Theory* 23 (2): 248–67.

Gould, Elizabeth. 2017. "Queer Transversal: The Spectacle Adam Lambert." In *Musical Encounters with Deleuze and Guattari*, edited by Pirrko Moisala, Taru Leppänen, Milla Tianinen, and Hannah Vaatainen, 128–57. New York: Bloomsbury Academic.

Grigoriadis, Vanessa. 2009. "Wild Idol." *Rolling Stone*, RS1081: 50–57.

Halberstam, Judith. 2007. "Theorizing Gender, Culture, and Music: Keeping Time with Lesbians on Ecstasy." *Women & Music* 11: 51–58.

Heard, Danielle C. 2012. "'Don't Let Me Be Misunderstood': Nina Simone's Theater of Invisibility." *Callaloo* 35 (4): 1056–84.

Kelly, Jon. 2013. "What Was behind the Bristol Bus Boycott?" *BBC News*, August 27. Accessed October 18, 2016. http://www.bbc.com/news/magazine-23795655.

Kernodle, Tammy L. 2008. "'I Wish I Knew How It Would Feel to Be Free': Nina Simone and the Redefining of the Freedom Song of the 1960s." *Journal of the Society for American Music* 2 (3): 296–317.

Loudermilk, A. 2013. "Nina Simone & the Civil Rights Movement: Protest at Her Piano, Audience at Her Feet." *Journal of International Women's Studies* 14 (3): 121–36.

Marshall, Jack. 2016. Review of *The Roar of the Greasepaint—the Smell of the Crowd*, by Leslie Bricusse and Anthony Newley. DC Theatre Scene, May 9. Accessed November 4. http://dctheatrescene.com/2016/05/09/roar-greasepaint-smell-crowd-compass-rose-review/?utm_campaign=shareaholic&utm_medium=email_this&utm_source=email.

Meizel, Katherine. 2011. *Idolized: Music, Media, and Identity in "American Idol."* Bloomington: Indiana University Press.

Moore, John. 2015. "Meet the Cast Video Series: Gregory Treco." *DCPA Newscenter*, April 19. Accessed November 4, 2016. http://www.denvercenter.org/blog-posts/news-center/2015/04/19/meet-the-cast-video-series-gregory-treco.

MuseWiki. 2014. "Feeling Good." *Blog*, last modified April 20. http://www.musewiki.org/Feeling_Good_(song)#cite_note-4.

Peraino, Judith. 2012. "Plumbing the Surface of Sound and Vision: David Bowie, Andy Warhol, and the Art of Posing." *Qui Parle* 21 (1), 151–84.

Simone, Nina, with Stephen Cleary. (1991) 2003. *I Put a Spell on You: The Autobiography of Nina Simone.* Cambridge, MA: Da Capo Press.

Stanbridge, Alan. 2004. "A Question of Standards: 'My Funny Valentine' and Musical Intertextuality." *Popular Music History* 1 (1), 83–108.

Suskin, Steven. 1997. *More Opening Nights on Broadway: A Critical Quotebook of the Musical Theatre 1965–1981*. New York: Schirmer Books.

Taylor, Jodie. 2012. *Playing It Queer: Popular Music, Identity and Queer World-Making*. Bern, Switzerland: Peter Lang.

Votta, Rae. 2016. "Why LGBT Performers Never Won 'American Idol.'" *Rolling Stone*, April 4. http://www.rollingstone.com/music/news/why-lgbt-performers-never-won -american-idol-20160404.

Ward, Brian. 2014. "Music, Musical Theater, and the Imagined South in Interwar Britain." *Journal of Southern History* 80 (1), 39–72.

CHAPTER 6

Swing, Shuffle, Half-Time, Double

**BEYOND TRADITIONAL TIME SIGNATURES IN THE
CLASSIFICATION OF METER IN POP/ROCK MUSIC**

TREVOR DE CLERCQ

MIDDLE TENNESSEE STATE UNIVERSITY

▌ INTRODUCTION

For the past few decades, the field of music theory has struggled with the question of how well traditional concepts—that is, those that were developed to describe and analyze the music of Bach, Beethoven, and Brahms—can be applied to popular music, for example, Beck, Björk, and Beyoncé. For instance, it is somewhat unclear if and how the precepts of classical functional harmony are relevant to rock music.[1] On the one hand, it seems useful to employ existing terminology when talking about new styles, if only because a common language helps us communicate and connect ideas. On the other hand, categorization schemes that were developed within a centuries-old musical practice might be ill-equipped to fully describe music of the modern era. Very often, the perfect balance between these two opposing views is difficult if not impossible to achieve.

Generally speaking, scholarship to date on pop/rock music—whether implicitly or explicitly—takes the use of traditional time signatures to be

---

1. For a few different perspectives on the validity of functional harmony in rock music, see Moore (1992), Stephenson (2002), Everett (2004), and de Clercq and Temperley (2011).

an adequate classification scheme for meter in pop/rock music.[2] Recent
work focuses instead on analyses of metric dissonance, microtiming,
and complex/mixed meters in specific styles (e.g., Butler 2001; Pieslak
2007; Osborn 2010; Danielsen 2010; McCandless 2013; Osborn 2014;
Biamonte 2014), sidestepping issues of pedagogy and meter classification taken more broadly. One notable exception is Rosenberg (2011),
who discusses the use of popular music in the teaching of rhythm and
meter, but her goal is primarily to show how pop/rock songs can be
used to illustrate traditional concepts, not how pop/rock songs might
challenge them.

   In contrast to this earlier work, I argue in this chapter that traditional
time signatures are limited in their ability to fully represent the typical
metric organizations found in pop/rock music, and accordingly, it is useful to include features beyond the traditional time signature in descriptions of rhythm and meter in pop/rock music. Specifically, I posit that
two additional factors—swing and drum feel—are critical components
of meter in pop/rock music and that our classification system should
include information about these factors to adequately portray the rhythmic and metric hierarchy of a song. I thus do not deprecate traditional
time signatures; rather, I show that the combination of traditional time
signatures with various drum feels and swing rhythms engenders a robust
language to catalog the diverse landscape of normative metric configurations found in pop/rock music. My focus here will thus be on a general
scheme, and I will not address complex, additive, mixed, or irrational
meters. (Theoretical investigation into these interesting but less common
metric organizations can be found in the references cited in the previous
paragraph.)

   For some readers, the addition of categories beyond traditional time
signatures might seem like the byproduct of an overactive concern with
taxonomy. The conventional approach—by which a piece of music is
considered, at least on a basic level, to be duple or triple (whether the
beat is organized into groups of two or three) and as simple or compound

2. Similar to the approach in Covach (2009), I adopt a broad definition of "pop/rock"
   music in this chapter, using the term to encompass most Anglo-American popular
   commercial music styles aimed at a youth audience, including but not limited to rock,
   R&B, country, hip-hop/rap, blues, pop, and folk.

(whether the beat divides into two or three)—is, one might argue, an elegantly efficient categorization scheme, one that balances too much versus too little information.[3] Indeed, it is entirely feasible to categorize meter in pop/rock with this basic scheme as a starting point. But as I show below, this approach ignores many important aspects of rhythmic and metric organization in pop/rock music. In adopting a more detailed language for meter in pop/rock, therefore, I hope to attune the reader (and thus our students) to these other central features.

As a sort of epistemological background, my approach to meter in pop/rock music derives from my own teaching of meter in the classroom. In my current position, I teach music theory in the department of recording industry, which is structured primarily around popular music; classical, jazz, and art music is taught in the music department across campus. For a number of semesters, I taught meter identification exclusively through traditional time signatures. This approach was manageable, although I began to sense that using this method was often like trying to fit a square peg into a round hole. I now teach using the approach I describe in the following sections, which arose in part through research on how popular musicians think about and talk about rhythm and meter. My bibliography, for example, includes many practical "how-to" books written by professional drummers and studio musicians (e.g., Matthews 1984; Morgenstein and Mattingly 1997; Randall and Peterson 1997; Potter 2001; Mattingly 2006; Zoro 2007; Riley 2010; Williams 2012; Zoro 2013; Riley 2015). I do not purport that my method mirrors how all pop/rock musicians conceptualize meter—certainly, there are many ways to approach these issues—but I believe I have developed a flexible approach that best balances both traditional and contemporary perspectives.

Before bringing this introduction to a close, I should mention that the current chapter serves as a sequel to the paper I gave at the Ann Arbor IV symposium, which was recently published in a longer version (2016). In that paper, I argue that pop/rock songs typically exhibit a fairly moderate pacing of harmonic and melodic content and that this pacing of harmonic

---

3. I have closely paraphrased here the definition of meter categorization as presented in the *Grove Dictionary of Music* (London 2016).

and melodic content is relatively stable in terms of absolute time, despite the various rhythmic frameworks that might be implied by the drum pattern. Specifically, I argue that the optimal length for a measure is about two seconds, and so—all else being equal—we are often better guided when assessing measure lengths by this two-second ideal than by any particular drum pattern. In what follows, I consider the implications of that article for a classification system of rhythm and meter in pop/rock music. I recommend reading my 2016 article before engaging with the following discussion. That said, the current chapter does not necessarily require any familiarity with the earlier article, since I will touch on the more relevant aspects when necessary.

▌DRUM FEELS IN 4/4

As many readers are probably aware, most pop/rock songs can be categorized as having a simple quadruple meter—that is, a time signature of 4/4.[4] Given a time signature of 4/4, the drum pattern of a song will often be organized according to the model shown in Figure 1, which I refer to as the "standard," or "normal," rock beat.[5] In a normal rock beat, the kick occurs on beats 1 and 3 of a 4/4 bar, while the snare occurs on beats 2 and 4. Drum patterns in real songs often depart from this exact configuration, of course, since the drummer will typically include a great amount of variety and embellishment around this basic framework. For example, the kick pattern might include smaller note values or anticipations of the beat, as shown in Figure 2, or the hi-hat pattern might consist of eighth notes instead of quarter notes.[6] But if we strip away the ornamentation in any real drum part, the model shown in Figure 1 will often

---

4. In my 2016 article, I look at three corpora of popular music—Covach (2009), Burgoyne et al. (2011), and Temperley and de Clercq (2013)—and find that 4/4 is by far the most common meter chosen by the analysts.

5. Throughout this chapter, I will use standard drum notation, in which the kick drum is notated on the bottom space of a five-line staff, the snare on the second space from the top, and the hi-hat on the space above the top line.

6. Temperley (1999) argues that anticipations to the beat can be normalized (or "desyncopated") so as to conceptually belong to the beat that follows. Thus the kick that occurs one eighth note prior to the downbeat of measure two in Figure 2 can be considered to be a displaced version of the downbeat.

be the underlying scheme. The widespread use of the standard rock beat across all styles of popular music—including rap, blues, country, folk, electronica, and R&B—has encouraged many contemporary scholars to use it as the primary determinant of measure lengths and time signatures in popular music.[7]

Using this standard rock beat as the universal yardstick for time signatures and measure lengths turns out to be a somewhat problematic strategy, however. In this regard, consider the song "Human Nature" by Michael Jackson (1982).[8] The reader should take the opportunity now to listen to this song, and while doing so, consider where the primary beat lies and how the drums interact with this beat. In my own hearing, the primary beat of "Human Nature" occurs around 92 beats per minute (BPM). Hearing the song this way, the kick and snare pattern does not conform to the standard rock beat; rather, it operates as what professional drummers refer to as a "half-time feel" (see Figure 3), whereby the snare regularly occurs on beat 3 instead of on beats 2 or 4, and the kick occurs only on the downbeat of the measure instead of on beats 1 and 3.[9] (For reference, the reader can hear a "normal-time feel" of "Human Nature"—in which the kick and snare align with the 92 BPM primary beat—in Tarrus Riley's 2009 cover of the song.)

The fact that drummers often refer to the scenario shown in Figure 3 as a change in the drum "feel" rather than a change in the drum "pattern" relates, I believe, to the perceptual effect of shifting the metric location of the snare. When the snare is on beat 3, it "feels" as if the tempo is half as fast as if the snare were on beats 2 and 4, but for various other reasons (some of which I discuss in the following two paragraphs), the primary

---

7. For examples of how the standard rock beat is taken as a model for measure lengths and time signatures, see the discussions in Moore (2001, 42) and Stephenson (2002, 2).

8. Throughout this chapter, I will cite songs to exemplify and illustrate different meter types. I eschew transcriptions of these songs, primarily due to copyright concerns although also because a transcription can never fully capture the sound and feel of the recording. Accordingly, it is best if the reader listens to each of these songs, which is easy to do nowadays through YouTube, Spotify, or some other online source. I will always specify the tempo (in BPM), time signature, and drum feel of each song so that the reader can hear these examples in the same manner as I do.

9. This terminology can be found in a variety of publications authored by professional drummers, including Morgenstein and Mattingly (1997), Mattingly (2006), Riley (2010), and Berry and Gianni (2012).

FIGURE 1. Standard rock beat, showing a normative kick, snare, and hi-hat pattern.

FIGURE 2. Embellished version of the standard rock beat.

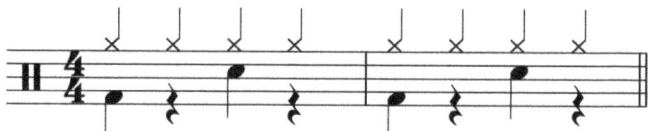

FIGURE 3. Model for a half-time drum feel.

beat level is perceived at a different rate than what is implied by the alternation of the kick and snare. Without question, the overall rhythmic "feel" of the drums involves much more than the question of what particular level the snare articulates in the metric hierarchy. That said, in this chapter—so as to remain faithful to the vernacular terminology used by professional drummers—I use the term "feel" (e.g., different "drum feels") to refer specifically to situations where the tempo implied by the drums (especially the backbeat as implied by the snare) might differ from or conflict with the primary beat level implied by the rest of the music.

I should concede that it is not impossible to hear the rate of kick and snare alternations in "Human Nature" as the primary beat itself, thereby engendering a tempo of around 46 BPM. I would speculate, however, that most listeners perceive the beat of this song as 92 BPM, if only because it is easier to dance to the song at this faster tempo.[10] As some evidence of

10. The reason for foot-tapping or head-bobbing at this particular rate relates to issues of embodiment, which are described in Iyer (2002).

this, note that the rhythmic body movements of Michael Jackson during various live performances currently available on YouTube tend to occur at the 92 BPM rate. Part of what makes 92 BPM seem more viable as the primary beat thus relates to what tempos are most ideal or lie near the center of our perceptual window. Research in music cognition, for instance, has shown that ideal tempo lies somewhere within the range of 100–125 BPM.[11] When the rate of kick and snare alternations becomes too slow, therefore, our perception of the primary beat may flip into a higher rhythmic octave to more easily entrain to a steady pulse.

One question the reader might raise here is how to determine whether a song is a "half-time feel" (the snare on beat 3) or simply a slow "normal-time feel" (the snare on beats 2 and 4). My 2016 article addresses some possible factors, such as harmonic rhythm and form, but it is impossible to offer a set of definitive guidelines. Nonetheless, I find that the disbursement of harmonic and melodic content in pop/rock songs tends to occur at a moderate rate; the drum pattern thus often creates the sense (or illusion) of slower or faster tempos, while the melody and lyrics hew to a more moderate pacing. In other words, the tempo implied by the drums might be twice or half that of the tempo implied by the harmonic and melodic content if assessed in isolation from the drums. Some examples will be clearer than others, of course. "Butterfly" by Mariah Carey (1997) and "Get Up on a Room" by R. Kelly (1998), for instance, are fairly unambiguous examples of a half-time 4/4 meter, both at a tempo of 108 BPM. "Radioactive" by Imagine Dragons (2012) is somewhat less clear, although I still hear it as a half-time 4/4 at the rate of 136 BPM. In all three of these cases, one factor that influences my choice of meter is my perception and conception of measure lengths. In "Radioactive," for example, the harmonic rhythm operates primarily at the rate of one chord per kick-snare alternation. These chords organize into groups of four, with the minor tonic starting each four-chord group. For me, this harmonic grouping delineates the

---

11. Research reported in London (2012)—such as work by Fraisse (1982), Parncutt (1994), and Semjen, Vorberg, and Schulze (1998)—suggests that ideal tempo lies around 100 BPM. More recent work by Moelants (2002), Moelants and McKinney (2004), and Levy (2011) suggests that ideal tempo lies closer to 120 or 125 BPM. As reported in my 2016 article, average tempo for pop/rock songs in 4/4 is somewhere close to 120 BPM.

four-bar phrase, which is further reinforced by the melodic structure. It would be possible, I admit, to maintain the same measure lengths and posit a 2/4 or 2/2 meter instead of a half-time 4/4. The difference is simply where one hears the primary beat: Are there only two beats per bar (i.e., a 2/4 or 2/2 meter), each of which aligns with a kick or snare hit, or are there four beats per bar (i.e., a half-time 4/4 meter), with the beats occurring at twice the rate of the kick and snare? I leave such distinctions to the individual analyst, although my own preference is to choose the half-time hearing instead of a time signature change. One central reason is that many songs go back and forth between different drum feels, and thus it seems preferable to maintain a consistent time signature while altering only the drum feel. Along these lines, consider the song "I Wish You Would" by Taylor Swift (2014), which alternates between a normal-time feel in the verse (e.g., 0:08–0:24) and a half-time feel in the chorus (e.g., 0:24–0:36).

A different though related situation can be found in the song "The Devil Went down to Georgia" by the Charlie Daniels Band (1979). Again, I urge the reader to listen to this song now, and while doing so, consider where the primary beat lies and how the drum pattern interacts with this beat. As I hear it, this song has a main tempo of around 136 BPM. The drums at the opening of the song are thus playing a "double-time feel," as shown in Figure 4. Like a half-time feel, the kick and snare in a double-time feel alternate at a different metric level than the primary beat—in this case, at a rate twice that of a normal drum beat. As before, the perception of ideal or comfortable tempos affects our hearing of this song as a double-time feel. Specifically, the rate of 272 BPM that would be required to hear the opening of "The Devil Went down to Georgia" as having a standard drum beat is simply too fast to sustain for any extended period of time; most listeners will undoubtedly choose to tap their feet instead at the slower rate of 136 BPM. The drums do eventually revert to a normal-time feel at around 1:26 in the studio recording (when the devil plays his solo with the "band of demons"). Again, the usual practice among popular musicians in such cases is to posit a drum feel change rather than a time signature change.[12]

---

12. See, for example, the chart to "Feeling's Gone" in Riley (2010, 32).

I will pause the discussion of half-time and double-time feels here. Some of the most interesting metric frameworks arise when these drum feels interact with time signatures other than 4/4 as well as different types of swing rhythms. I will thus shift to a discussion of swing and shuffle rhythms in pop/rock music, after which I will circle back to examples of these drum feels in other metric contexts.

▎ SWING AND SHUFFLE RHYTHMS VERSUS COMPOUND METER

As mentioned previously, the meter of most pop/rock songs can be (and usually is) categorized as 4/4—that is, a simple meter wherein the beat is divided (at least as implied by the time signature) into two equal parts. But in many songs that are notated in 4/4, the beat divisions heard in the sounding music are not, in fact, equally spaced. Instead, the divisions are *unequal*, such that the subdivision that occurs *on* the beat is longer than the subdivision that occurs *off* the beat. For example, consider "I Fall to Pieces" by Patsy Cline (1961). At a moderate tempo of 112 BPM in a 4/4 time signature, this song evinces what pop/rock musicians typically refer to as a "shuffle" rhythm.[13] In the prototypical shuffle rhythm, the divisions of the beat articulate a 2:1 timing relationship, which pop/rock musicians typically represent and conceptualize in one of two ways— namely, either as a notated quarter-eighth triplet within a 4/4 meter or as notated straight eighth notes that are understood to be swung in their performance as quarter-eighth triplets. For the sake of illustration, these two conceptual approaches are represented by the hi-hat part in the drum

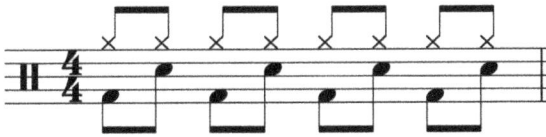

FIGURE 4. Model for a double-time drum feel.

---

13. Most of the transcriptions of this song, found with a Google image search of the words "sheet music i fall to pieces," set the song in a meter of 4/4 (accessed December 2, 2016).

notation of Figures 5 and 6, respectively.[14] Note that this drum notation is provided here for illustration purposes only; typically, all members of the ensemble will participate in the shuffle rhythm if it is present in the music.

I take Figures 5 and 6 to be essentially equivalent representations of the same rhythm, differentiated only by notational preference. It would also be possible to notate the shuffle rhythm as shown in Figure 7—that is, using a 12/8 time signature such that the quarter-eighth subdivisions align with the normative division scheme of a compound meter. Yet the notation in Figure 7 is generally deprecated among pop/rock musicians, even among those with formal academic training in music.[15] In other words, pop/rock musicians tend to prefer thinking about shuffle rhythms in a simple quadruple meter rather than in a compound quadruple meter. The difference between Figure 7 and the other two representations of the shuffle rhythm in Figures 5 and 6 might seem trivial, but I believe the preference for a 4/4 time signature is an important and meaningful shift among pop/rock musicians in terms of thinking about rhythm and meter.

One central reason that 4/4 is preferred to 12/8 might relate to the exact timing of the beat divisions. Specifically, a compound meter such as 12/8 implies three *equal* divisions of the beat. In contrast, shuffle and swing rhythms in pop/rock can be considered two *unequal* divisions of the beat.[16] That is to say, the triplets (or implied triplets) in Figures 5 and 6 serve only as approximations of the actual sounding rhythms. Although the conventional assumption for swung eighth notes is that they reflect an underlying triple pulse and should be performed in a 2:1 ratio, recent studies of jazz performances have shown that the ratio between swung eighth notes in practice will vary anywhere from 1:1 (i.e., straight eighth notes) to

14. Figure 5 models the standard notational approach to shuffle rhythms used in the pop/rock drum literature, as found in Morgenstein and Mattingly (1997, 61), Potter (2001, 7), Mattingly (2006, 39), Zoro (2007, 37), Berry and Gianni (2012, 32), Zoro (2013, 22), and Riley (2015, 33). Figure 6 models the standard notational approach to shuffle rhythms used in vocal/guitar/piano songbooks, such as Randall and Peterson (1997, 23).

15. Jim Riley has a degree in music from the University of North Texas, for example, yet in his 2015 book, he uses the notation shown in Figure 5 for swing rhythms.

16. I take the terms "swing" and "shuffle" to be essentially synonymous for the purposes of this chapter, although "shuffle" seems to usually imply a type of swing rhythm that hews closely to the 2:1 ratio (Riley 2015).

FIGURE 5. Typical drum notation for a standard shuffle beat.

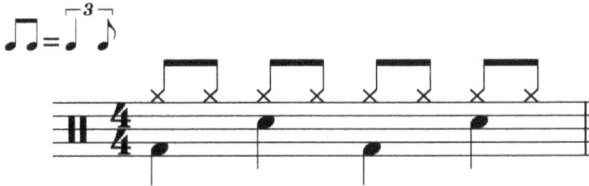

FIGURE 6. Shuffle drum pattern written with swing notation.

FIGURE 7. Shuffle drum pattern renotated in 12/8.

3.5:1 (i.e., a doubly dotted eighth note followed by a thirty-second note).[17] Butterfield elegantly sums up the situation when he writes, "Swing is not a specifiable quantity . . . nor is it a quality that is precisely quantifiable" (2011, 24).[18] We should surmise, therefore, that swing and shuffle rhythms in pop/rock music might not correspond exactly to the 2:1 configuration either.

In reality, when listening to shuffle and swing rhythms in pop/rock music, it is usually difficult to determine solely by ear the exact timing of the subdivisions. In "I Fall to Pieces," for example, I perceive the shuffle rhythm to be very close to a 2:1 ratio. But is it exactly 2:1, or is there a subtle yet pervasive timing discrepancy that is responsible for the overall

---

17. One important metastudy on swing ratios in jazz can be found in Butterfield (2011). This article surveys a variety of other research on jazz microtiming, including work by Friberg and Sundström (2002) and Benadon (2006), who find that 2:1 swing ratios are more often the exception than the norm in performance practice.

18. It may also be worth emphasizing that "swing" as a term encompasses much more than simply a timing relationship between beat divisions, which is why I refer to these as swing "rhythms," not simply as "swing."

metric quality of the song? Without loading the song into a digital audio workstation, I have no obvious way to know. Even if I looked at the song more closely using a computer, a certain amount of estimation would be required to identify the precise location of each note. I might take the clear triplet rhythm in the opening guitar part of "I Fall to Pieces" as evidence for a consistent 2:1 ratio, but a fleeting moment of evenly spaced triple subdivisions does not necessarily mean that a 2:1 ratio is maintained throughout the song. For instance, the swing ratio of the ensemble in "Girl They Won't Believe It" by Joss Stone (2007) is obviously not in a 2:1 ratio; instead, the swing occurs at something like a 3.5:1 relationship, according to my own measurements. Despite this pervasive "hard swing," the drum fill prior to the first chorus (around 0:49) switches to what sounds like evenly spaced triplets, if only briefly. It is possible, therefore, that swing ratios change during different sections of the song—or possibly, different instruments might swing at different ratios.[19] In PJ Harvey's "The Words That Maketh Murder" (2011), for example, Azevedo et al. (2015) find that the autoharp is swung while the drums articulate a straighter eighth-note pattern.

Because there is no notated score to a pop/rock song, it is thus usually unclear how the beat precisely divides in any given recording. Accordingly, I posit that there should be three ways to classify meter on the basis of the beat division: (1) as *simple*, where the beat is divided into two equal parts; (2) as *compound*, where the beat is divided into three equal parts; or (3) as *swung*, where the beat is divided into two unequal parts. When a quadruple meter is swung, it seems preferable to conceive of it in a 4/4 time signature rather than a 12/8, if only because the 12/8 time signature implies a strict division of the beat into three equal parts. To be clear, I do not mean to posit that there are never cases in which a song seems to warrant a compound quadruple meter. "Call Me" by Blondie (1980), "Everybody Wants to Rule the World" by Tears for Fears (1985), "When the Going Gets Tough, the Tough Get Going" by Billy Ocean (1985), and "I'm Your Baby Tonight" by Whitney Houston (1990) are good examples of songs in which the three-part division of the beat is

---

19. For jazz performances, Butterfield (2011) finds that soloists typically have swing ratios less than 2:1, while rhythm section players typically have swing ratios greater than 2:1.

consistent and clear throughout the song. But songs like this are much less frequently encountered in pop/rock music than those with shuffle and swing rhythms, perhaps because the binary up-down strumming pattern typically used on a guitar creates an inherent preference for duple divisions over triple divisions.

Although incontestable compound quadruple meters (12/8) might be somewhat rare in pop/rock music, compound duple meters (e.g., 6/8) are more common. One reason for this difference might derive from the way in which our perception of the primary beat is influenced by our limited window for comfortable tempos. According to conventional wisdom, for instance, it is a fundamental misunderstanding of 6/8 to hear the eighth note as the beat.[20] This explanation does not, however, coincide with the way many pop/rock musicians, including drummers, explain their own hearings of 6/8. For example, Jim Riley—the bandleader and drummer for Rascal Flatts as well as a graduate of the University of North Texas with a degree in music education—writes that 6/8 has "six beats per measure with the eighth-note pulse representing each beat" (2010, 28). Similar statements can be found in Matthews (1984, 45) and Williams (2012, 12). We could say, of course, that these professional musicians (all of whom studied music in college) are misconstruing the nature of 6/8—that they either are ignorant of or have forgotten basic tenets of their musical education. Yet these musicians are describing where they perceive the beat, and it would be somewhat unsympathetic to disregard how they report their own perception.

As a point of reference, consider the song "Nothing Else Matters" by Metallica (1991), which I consider to be a classic example of 6/8.[21] The drum pattern in this song illustrates the standard pattern of kick and snare in pop/rock music for a 6/8 meter, as shown in Figure 8. If we take the kick and snare to imply the primary beat level of the song (i.e., the traditional approach), then we would say that "Nothing Else Matters" has

---

20. See, for example, the length taken in Kostka, Payne, and Almén (2013, 30–31) to make clear to the student that 6/8 does not have six beats in the measure.
21. Most of the transcriptions of this song, found with a Google image search of the words "sheet music metallica nothing else matters," set the song in a meter of 6/8 (accessed May 17, 2016).

a tempo of around 48 BPM—near the lower limit for beat perception.[22] The reader should notice, however, that the standard 6/8 beat is more similar to a half-time 4/4 feel than a standard 4/4 feel, in that each bar has only one kick and snare instance. In other words, 6/8—like a half-time 4/4—potentially presents the listener with a conflict between two metrical levels. For example, the rate of the eighth note in this song (as articulated by the hi-hat part) is about 144 BPM—much closer to estimates of ideal tempo than the 48 BPM rate articulated by the kick and snare. I do not mean to imply here that we should necessarily abandon hearing the dotted quarter note as the beat. Rather, the dotted quarter is one level of beat, and there is a complementary level of beat that can be felt on the eighth-note level.

The ability to hear the eighth note as the beat in a 6/8 meter contrasts strongly with the typical situation in a 12/8 meter. Compare "Nothing Else Matters," for example, to the Blondie song "Call Me" mentioned previously. In both songs, the eighth-note pulse is consistently articulated in the music. But the speed of the eighth note in "Call Me" is tremendously fast—somewhere around 426 BPM if we were to take the eighth note as the beat—and thus far beyond the limits for beat perception.[23] In "Call Me," therefore, it is clear that the dotted quarter is the beat (assuming a meter of 12/8), which results in a tempo of around 142 BPM. Note that this tempo is almost exactly the same tempo as the eighth note in "Nothing Else Matters" (around 144 BPM). The 12/8 in "Call Me" and the 6/8 in "Nothing Else Matters" are thus very different types of compound meters. In "Call Me," we can hear only the dotted quarter as the beat, whereas in "Nothing Else Matters"—even though it is possible to hear the

FIGURE 8. Model for a standard 6/8 drum beat.

22. London (2012, 30) puts the floor on realistic rates of beat perception at around 30 BPM.
23. London (2012, 30) puts the ceiling on realistic rates of beat perception at around 240 BPM.

dotted quarter as the beat—our perceptual window for tempo encourages us to hear the eighth note as the beat.

For popular music, the concept of compound meter is thus well suited to describe triply divided duple meters, since the eighth note can often be heard as the beat itself; in contrast, the concept of compound meter is somewhat unnecessary for triply divided quadruple meters, since the fast subdivision can be conceptualized instead as a pervasive triplet division of a quarter note beat. Wyatt, Schroeder, and Elliott summarize this sentiment in their ear training manual for contemporary musicians, writing that "in popular music, compound meter is generally used only at slower tempos; when the tempo picks up, the triplet feeling is better defined as shuffle or swing" (2005, 77). Part of the issue is that as the tempo of a compound meter increases, the middle note of the triple division typically gets dropped; as a result, there arises an inherent ambiguity with regard to the precise division of the beat, such that it is preferable to think of the meter as 4/4 with swing instead of a strict compound quadruple.

THE INTERACTION OF DRUM FEELS AND SWING RHYTHMS IN 4/4

In the previous sections, I discussed two additional factors—drum feels and swing rhythms—that I take to be important aspects of meter in pop/rock music beyond the time signature itself. Considered in isolation, each of these factors might not seem to signal any significant shortcoming with traditional time signatures. It is when these two factors combine, however, that time signatures alone more obviously fall short of modeling the metric hierarchy of a song. In the current section, I consider the interaction of drum feels and swing rhythms in 4/4; in the next section, I look at the interaction of these two factors in other time signatures.

To my ears, one of the most aurally compelling metric organizations in pop/rock music arises from the combination of a half-time 4/4 feel with swung eighth notes, as shown in Figure 9—a groove that is typically referred to as the "half-time shuffle." The half-time shuffle has also been called the "Purdie shuffle" in honor of drummer Bernard Purdie, who plays this beat on the song "Home at Last" by Steely Dan (1977).[24] "Home at Last" is not the first instance of the half-time shuffle in history; earlier instances include the 1968 live recording of "Please Return Your Love to Me" by the Temptations and the 1972 song "Loose Booty" by Funkadelic (Zoro 2013, 12). But "Home at Last" has become an iconic instance of the half-time shuffle, perhaps because of how clearly the drum part implies a half-time feel against (or combined with) the shuffle subdivision of the primary beat. Specifically, the 126 BPM rate for the main beat lies very near ideal tempo, and so the listener is encouraged to hear the primary beat on a different level of the metric hierarchy than the kick and snare alternations.

It is important to note that the metric organization of a half-time shuffle is impossible to fully convey using only traditional time signatures. To be sure, we could notate Figure 9 as in 12/8, but doing so would not reflect the tension between the perceived primary beat and the kick and snare pattern. Alternately, we could notate Figure 9 in a duple meter so as to coincide with the kick and snare, but then there would be no way to reflect the persistent triple-based divisions of the hi-hat rhythm in the time signature itself. (Compound meters only allow for triple divisions at the level immediately below the beat.) One might argue that traditional time signatures are not meant to indicate all these aspects of rhythm and meter; I would counter that this is the exact limitation of using traditional time signatures alone with popular music. To fully capture the complete rhythm and metric organization of a song like "Home at Last" requires language that goes beyond the time signature itself.

Because a half-time shuffle relies on hearing the kick and snare as alternating at half the rate of the primary beat, most classic half-time shuffles

FIGURE 9. Prototypical drum beat for a half-time shuffle.

---

24. This is the provenance of the half-time shuffle as explained in Zoro (2013, 14).

employ speeds near the center of our perceptual window for tempo. In "Fool in the Rain" by Led Zeppelin (1979), for instance, drummer John Bonham clocks in at around 130 BPM; similarly, the half-time shuffle in "Nothing Compares 2 U" by Sinéad O'Connor (1990) has a primary beat rate of about 120 BPM. In the song "Rosanna" by Toto (1982), drummer Jeff Porcaro speeds the half-time shuffle up to around 172 BPM.[25] At this tempo, the listener might be tempted to hear the primary beat at half this rate—that is, 86 BPM—thus aligning with the kick and snare. Indeed, this faster tempo starts to push the limit of our perception of this particular groove as a half-time feel. That said, the contrasting section in the song, which first occurs at around 0:45, switches back to a normal-time feel (thus providing more evidence for hearing the fast tempo); documentary evidence from Porcaro also shows that he conceives of the tempo at the faster rate of 172 BPM.[26]

As the half-time shuffle continues to increase in tempo, it becomes easier and easier to hear the kick and the snare as aligning with the primary beat. Consider in this regard the song "Been Caught Stealing" by Jane's Addiction (1990). I encourage the reader to listen to this song now, and while doing so, think about how to best classify its metric organization. To my ears, the song sounds like a normal-time 4/4 at a moderate tempo of around 104 BPM, and I believe this hearing would be shared by most listeners. But what might not be obvious is the pervasive swing at the sixteenth-note level (assuming a 4/4 meter at 104 BPM). Swing at the sixteenth-note level in a normal-time 4/4 can be seen, arguably, as the result of the half-time shuffle speeding up even faster than the "Rosanna" example. For instance, it is not impossible to hear "Been Caught Stealing" as a half-time shuffle at a tempo of 208 BPM. But the melodic phrase structure and the harmonic rhythm, combined with our preference to hear the main pulse at a more moderate rate, encourage us to hear the

---

25. Interestingly, Jeff Porcaro was the drummer for Steely Dan prior to Bernard Purdie, even though—by Porcaro's own admission—he "stole" the beat for "Rosanna" from Bernard Purdie, as documented in "The Rosanna Half Time Shuffle by Jeff Porcaro," YouTube video, posted by "Mark S.," August 27, 2011, https://www.youtube.com/watch?v=pwyO1qr0edI.

26. In a Drummerworld video on "Rosanna," Porcaro's discussion shows that he clearly conceives of the beat as in 4/4 with triplets and the snare on beat 3 ("Rosanna Half Time Shuffle").

song as a normal-time feel at the tempo of 104 BPM, such that the six-teenth notes rather than the eighth notes are "shuffled."

Swing at the sixteenth-note level in a normal-time 4/4 can be a subtle effect, perhaps because traditional time signatures tend to encourage us to think primarily in terms of the beat level and the first level of division below this beat. In addition, the hi-hat might only articulate the straight eighth-note pulse, leaving us to infer the swung sixteenth notes from the rhythmic motives in other instruments. But once a listener becomes used to hearing half-time shuffles at moderate tempos, sixteenth-note swing should aurally evoke a similar metric hierarchy—that is, that swing is occurring on a pulse layer two levels down from the kick and snare alternations. Other examples of sixteenth-note swing in normal-time 4/4 include "Poison" by Bell Biv DeVoe (1990), "Someday" by Mariah Carey (1990), and "Love on Top" by Beyoncé (2011). The swung sixteenth in a normal-time 4/4 is particularly characteristic of the "new jack swing" movement to come out of New York City in the late 1980s and early '90s, catalyzed perhaps in large part by the ability to program a swung sixteenth note into drum sequencers of the time.

Swung sixteenth notes can also be combined with a double-time 4/4 drum feel to create yet another possible metric organization. A double-time 4/4 with swung sixteenths could also be heard as a sped-up version of a normal-time 4/4 shuffle. For example, consider the song "Redneck Woman" by Gretchen Wilson (2004). It is possible to hear the tempo of this song as around 184 BPM, with the kick and snare articulating the main beat of the song. With this hearing, the eighth-note shuffle rhythm in the rhythm guitar and drum fills should be clear. As I conceptualize the song, though, the primary beat level is around 92 BPM, such that the kick and snare are alternating at twice the rate of my foot tapping. Hearing the song at 92 BPM makes much more sense in terms of form as well, since the verse and chorus sections become twelve-bar modules that closely mirror the harmonic structure of a twelve-bar blues. The eighth-note shuffle rhythm at the 184 BPM tempo, therefore, turns into swung sixteenths at 92 BPM in this double-time hearing. Other songs, such as "Up from Below" by Edward Sharpe and the Magnetic Zeros (2009), more clearly evince this swung sixteenth, double-time 4/4 framework due to the increased tempo that further encourages us to hear the kick and snare at a metric level above the primary beat.

THE INTERACTION OF DRUM FEELS AND SWING IN 6/8 AND 3/4

In this last main section of my chapter, I consider how various types of swing rhythms and drum feels interact with time signatures other than 4/4. Specifically, I focus here on 6/8 and 3/4, in part because it is sometimes difficult to determine which of these two time signatures best describes the metric hierarchy of a song. This ambiguity, as we will see, derives from the way in which a nonnormative drum feel can blur the boundary between 6/8 and 3/4.

I will begin with a discussion of 3/4, since I have not yet described its normal drum feel. As shown in Figure 10, the standard drum pattern for a song in 3/4 involves a kick on beat 1 and a snare on beat 3; beat 2 is shown as a rest, although drummers will often play either a kick or a snare on this beat as well. The song "No Other One" by Weezer (1996) is one of the clearest examples of 3/4 in pop/rock music, due primarily to the harmonic rhythm of the song and the moderate tempo of 100 BPM.[27] Instances of 3/4 in pop/rock music are relatively rare, at least in comparison to 4/4 and 6/8, perhaps in part because of the unequal (or nonbinary) alternation of kick and snare in a simple triple meter. That is to say, in both 4/4 and 6/8, the kick and snare are consistently separated by equal intervals of time, whereas in a normal-time 3/4, the possibility to evenly space the kick and snare is thwarted (assuming the snare lands on a beat), thereby creating a somewhat lopsided sensation.

In my experience, pop/rock songs in 3/4 more often than not include swing on the eighth-note level, as approximated in Figure 11. This metric framework can be found in songs such as "I Never Love a Man (the Way I Love You)" by Aretha Franklin (1967) and "(Who Says) You Can't Have It All" by Alan Jackson (1992), both of which have a moderate tempo of

27. Rosenberg (2011) classifies "No Other One" as in 6/4, but I am not sure if she is hearing the hi-hat as the beat at a tempo of 200 BPM or measure lengths that are twice as long as in my reading. Either way, I think this is an incorrect categorization of the meter for this song.

about 90 BPM. It would be possible, of course, to notate the rhythm in Figure 11 in a time signature of 9/8. But as discussed previously, it is difficult to tell whether the timing of the hi-hat (or other percussive part, such as the rhythm guitar) is precisely in a 2:1 ratio, so 3/4 seems preferable as the primary time signature.[28]

Swing rhythms in a 6/8 time signature cannot occur at the eighth-note level (the meter would cease to be compound), but swing often occurs in 6/8 at the sixteenth-note level. Like sixteenth-note swing in 4/4, sixteenth-note swing in 6/8 can be subtle. Typically, though, the hi-hat pattern or rhythm guitar gives away the unequal lengths of the sixteenth-note subdivisions. For illustration purposes, Figure 12 depicts the triplet-based approximation of a normal 6/8 drum pattern with sixteenth-note swing, wherein the swung sixteenth note is articulated by the hi-hat on the middle eighth note of each dotted-quarter beat. The song "Trouble" by Ray LaMontagne (2004) is a good example of this metric organization, most obviously at the beginning of the song. Note that while the drummer for "Trouble" often retreats to a straight eighth-note pattern on the hi-hat, the rhythm guitar continues to articulate swung sixteenth notes, which give the song an extra lilting quality beyond the usual lilt of a 6/8.

FIGURE 10. Standard drum pattern for a 3/4 meter.

FIGURE 11. Swung eighth notes in a 3/4 meter.

28. Note that some of the songs Rosenberg (2011, 65) classifies as 3/4—for example, "Manic Depression" by Jimi Hendrix (1967) and "Miss Misery" by Elliot Smith (1997)—have swung eighth notes, yet Rosenberg does not classify these songs (rightly so, I would say) as in 9/8.

Other good examples of 6/8 meters with swung sixteenth notes include the cover of "With a Little Help from My Friends" by Joe Cocker (1969), "Breaking the Girl" by the Red Hot Chili Peppers (1991), and "Paperwork" by T.I. (2014). For those readers (or their students) that might have trouble hearing sixteenth-note swing in 6/8, I recommend trying to hear the eighth note as the beat, since it is usually easiest to hear swing at the metric level just below the main pulse.

Different types of drum feels can also occur in 3/4 and 6/8, with or without the addition of swing rhythms. As in 4/4, these drum feels result in a shifting of the kick and snare alternations up or down a level in the metric hierarchy as compared to their normal-time versions. Variations in drum feels with time signatures of 3/4 or 6/8 are admittedly not common metric organizations due to the relative rarity of 3/4 and 6/8 time signatures overall (at least in comparison to 4/4). But this rarity only makes the instances found in real songs that much more fascinating. Consider, for example, the song "Synchronicity" by the Police (1983). Most if not all transcriptions of this song cast it in a time signature of 6/4, which is problematic for at least two reasons.[29] First, a 6/4 time signature would imply—at least in its usual understanding—a compound duple meter (with the dotted half note getting the beat), which obviously does not

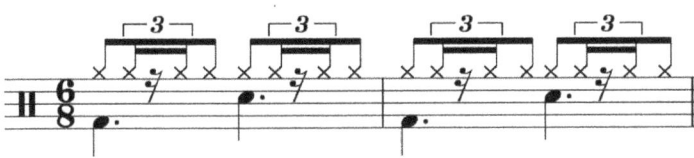

FIGURE 12. Swung sixteenth notes in 6/8.

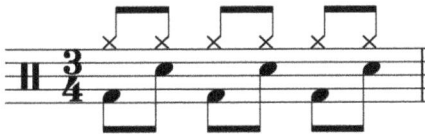

FIGURE 13. Double-time drum feel in 3/4.

29. Specifically, a Google image search of "synchronicity police sheet music" shows all versions to be in 6/4 (accessed May 19, 2016).

match the metric organization of the song.[30] Second, if we are to understand the 6/4 time signature as an extended bar of 4/4, then this implies a tempo of around 200 BPM, which although possible, lies at about twice the value for ideal tempo. As I hear it, "Synchronicity" is a double-time 3/4 at the more moderate tempo of 100 BPM, as modeled in Figure 13.[31] Some evidence for this hearing is provided by the lead singer, Sting, who counts off the song in concert as "one, two, three" at a moderate tempo.[32] Note that a double-time 3/4 hearing maintains the same measure lengths as the 6/4 hearing, so the phrase structure of the song is unaffected. But rather than employing (somewhat awkwardly) a nonstandard time signature such as 6/4, we can understand the metric organization of the song as a combination of standard metric parameters.

In addition to a double-time feel, 3/4 can also be organized as a half-time feel, as shown in Figure 14. In a half-time 3/4, the kick occurs on the downbeat of every other measure instead of every measure—that is, half as often. The song "Dig a Pony" by the Beatles (1970)—which includes a "one, two, three" count off at the beginning of the studio recording and has been analyzed as occurring in triple meter by various authors, including Fujita et al. (1989, 194), Pollack (1993), and Everett (2009, 305)—provides a good example of a half-time 3/4. Note that "Dig a Pony" also includes swing on the eighth notes. In fact, all instances of half-time drum feels in 3/4 that I have encountered include swung eighth notes, including "Still Crazy after All These Years" by Paul Simon (1975), "If It's Over" by Mariah Carey (1991), and "Sometimes I Cry" by Chris Stapleton (2015).

It is worth noting that a half-time 3/4 could be heard as a normal-time 6/8, with the quarter note in 3/4 equaling the eighth note in 6/8.

30. The idea that 6/4 is typically a notational variant of 6/8 can be found in various music theory textbooks and rhythm readers—for example, Kostka, Payne, Almén (2013, 30) and chapter 15 of Hall (2005).
31. The pattern in Figure 13 could be called a triple-time 3/4 in that the kick and snare are alternating at three times the normal-time rate. But since the kick and snare imply a tempo that is only twice the primary beat and double-time is the standard term used in 4/4, I prefer to refer to this pattern as a double-time 3/4.
32. See the various live videos available on YouTube of their November 3, 1983, concert in Atlanta, Georgia, at the Omni Coliseum. For example, "The Police—'Synchronicity I' Live," YouTube video, posted by "SenseiSlaughter666," August 30, 2011, http://www.youtube.com/watch?v=FMmCJ6-uu3M.

Similarly, a double-time 6/8, as shown in Figure 15, might alternatively be heard as a normal-time 3/4, with the eighth note in 6/8 equaling the quarter note in 3/4. The difference can sometimes be ambiguous, especially if one is acclimated to hearing the eighth note as the pulse in 6/8. In this regard, consider the song "Take It to the Limit" by the Eagles (1975). Based on the drum pattern at the beginning of the song, we might initially posit a normal-time 6/8 with swung sixteenths at a tempo of 30 BPM for the dotted quarter note. With this hearing, the change in the drum pattern at 1:12 (just prior to the chorus) would be considered a double-time 6/8 with swung sixteenths. Alternatively, we could posit that the opening of the song is a half-time 3/4 with swung eighths at a tempo of 90 BPM, after which the drums shift to a normal-time feel at 1:12.[33] Ultimately, our choice of which reading is best affects the measure lengths we posit for this song and thus its overall form (the 6/8 reading will have half as many measures as the 3/4 reading). As the reader might have guessed, I believe the 3/4 reading is highly preferable in this case, since it creates measure lengths of exactly two seconds. (The tempo of 30 BPM also lies

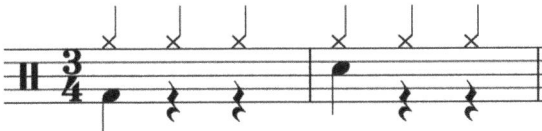

FIGURE 14. Half-time drum feel in 3/4.

FIGURE 15. Double-time drum feel in 6/8.

---

33. I suppose there exists a third option for those readers that prefer the drum pattern to imply a normal-time feel, such that the song would begin in 6/8 and then switch to 3/4 at 1:12, with the eighth note in the 6/8 being equal to the quarter note in the 3/4. This approach mangles the form of the song, however, in my opinion.

at the extreme limit of perceptible beat rates.) If the pacing of the song were different, however, we might make a different choice.

As a final musical example, take the song "Lorelai" by the Fleet Foxes (2011). Based on the opening drum pattern, we might assess the song to be in 3/4 at a tempo of 145 BPM, which generates measure lengths of around 1.24 seconds. This metric interpretation, however, creates a serious misrepresentation of the song's form. Reading the song in 3/4, the first large vocal passage—spanning from about 0:34 to 1:14—would last thirty-two bars, and due to the melodic and harmonic structure of these bars, we would say that it is a thirty-two-bar AABA form. Yet this vocal passage includes none of the structural weight that we expect of a thirty-two-bar AABA; the final A is more of an afterthought than a return of a full-fledged section, and there is simply not enough musical content to warrant the thirty-two-bar AABA label. Instead, it seems more appropriate to consider this vocal passage as a sixteen-bar SRDC.[34] To do so, we must posit that "Lorelai" evinces a double-time 6/8 feel (with the eighth note equal to 145 BPM), with measure lengths twice as long as the normal-time 3/4. With this reading, the opening line (from "So guess I got old" to "sidewalk") constitutes a four-bar phrase, which seems like a more appropriate length for its melodic and lyric content.

CONCLUSION

The preceding paragraphs have moved through a number of musical examples, as well as a number of different metric organizations, and thus the reader might benefit from a top-down view of the entire scheme that I have described. In essence, my system classifies meter in pop/rock music using three basic categories, each of which has three standard options: (1) the time signature, which is usually 6/8, 3/4, or 4/4; (2) the drum feel, which can be normal-time, half-time, or double-time; and (3) the extent of swing, which can be none (straight), swing on the eighth notes, or swing on the sixteenths. Classifying the meter of a song requires choosing one (and only

---

34. SRDC is a term coined by Everett (2009, 140) that refers to a phrase structure of "Statement-Restatement-Departure-Conclusion," somewhat akin to the classical-era sentence. For a deeper discussion of AABA and SRDC forms, see my 2012 dissertation.

one) option from each of these three categories. A given song, for example, might be a normal-time 6/8 with swung sixteenths; another might be a half-time 3/4 with swung eighths. This classification system is relatively uncomplicated—only three categories, each of which has three standard options—but it allows us to describe the metric organization of a song in a relatively sophisticated way. Specifically, there are twenty-two viable combinations using this method.[35] This variety allows for a great degree of analytic flexibility, especially compared to the six standard time signatures used in traditional practice (i.e., 2/4, 3/4, 4/4, 6/8, 9/8, and 12/8).

The reader will probably have noticed that the system described above offers only three standard options for the time signature: 6/8, 3/4, and 4/4. I freely admit that some songs are best represented by other time signatures, such as 12/8 or 2/4. Similarly, I remind the reader that I have avoided any discussion of asymmetrical, complex, or odd meters, and I did not delve into changing meters or polymeters. My goal here has not been to provide an exhaustive discussion of all possible metric organizations found in pop/rock music; rather, I have intended to provide a blueprint for expanding the foundation of meter classification more generally. With this goal in mind, the time signatures of 6/8, 3/4, and 4/4 are able to account for the vast majority of songs in pop/rock music, because these three time signatures account for the most basic combinations of beats and divisions commonly found in pop/rock: two beats with two divisions (4/4), two beats with three divisions (6/8), and three beats with two divisions (3/4). For whatever reason, the remaining combination—three beats with three divisions (9/8)—is so rarely encountered in pop/rock music that I do not consider it to be a standard choice (although I do not deny that it is possible).[36]

Given the variety of possible metric organizations described previously, the reader might expect a long appendix of additional musical examples. Due to considerations of space, I have opted to post this appendix online at http://www.midside.com/skills/rhythm/_meter_id/. Having the

---

35. Three categories with three standard options give twenty-seven theoretical possibilities (3 × 3 × 3), but there are really only twenty-two possible combinations because 6/8 never has swung eighth notes and never seems to occur as a half-time feel.

36. Everett (2009, 305) confirms that compound triple meter is "virtually nonexistent" in pop/rock music.

appendix online allows me to provide audio files for each example as well as to continue adding examples as they are found. That said, I believe the reader should now be equipped to hear instances of these various metric organizations in their day-to-day listening of pop/rock music, and so I hope the reader begins to find new and interesting examples on their own.

In summary, I believe the approach I have described herein represents a new way of hearing and thinking about meter in pop/rock music. There are many ramifications of adopting this approach that remain open questions. For example, should we teach students how to perform rhythms with swing, both at the eighth-note and the sixteenth-note level? As rhythm reading is conventionally taught in an aural skills curriculum, rhythms are always performed "straight," with no swing. Similarly, should students—especially those in pop music or music industry curricula—be required to re-create different types of drum feels (akin to conducting) while performing rhythms? Ultimately, a large gap still remains between the skill sets that are developed in the traditional music classroom and those that might be relevant to musicians working with pop/rock materials. Hopefully, this chapter presents a useful conceptual framework to help bridge that gap.

▌ REFERENCES

Azevedo, Cláudia, Chris Fuller, Juliana Guerrero, Michael Kaler, and Brad Osborn. 2015. "An Ambiguous Murder: Questions of Intertextuality in PJ Harvey's 'The Words That Maketh Murder.'" In *Song Interpretation in 21st-Century Pop Music*, edited by Ralf von Appen, André Doehring, Dietrich Helms, and Allan F. Moore, 175–95. Burlington, VT: Ashgate.

Benadon, Fernando. 2006. "Slicing the Beat: Jazz Eighth-Notes as Expressive Microrhythm." *Ethnomusicology* 50 (1): 73–98.

Berry, Mick, and Jason Gianni. 2012. *The Drummer's Bible: How to Play Every Drum Style from Afro-Cuban to Zydeco.* 2nd ed. Tucson, AZ: See Sharp Press.

Biamonte, Nicole. 2014. "Formal Functions of Metric Dissonance in Rock Music." *Music Theory Online* 20 (2).

Burgoyne, John, Jonathan Wild, and Ichiro Fujinaga. 2011. "An Expert Ground-Truth Set for Audio Chord Recognition and Music Analysis." In *Proceedings of the 12th International Society for Music Information Retrieval Conference (ISMIR)*, October 24–28, edited by Anssi Klapuri and Colby Leider, 633–38. Miami: University of Miami.

Butler, Mark. 2001. "Turning the Beat Around: Reinterpretation, Metrical Dissonance, and Asymmetry in Electronic Dance Music." *Music Theory Online* 7 (6).

Butterfield, Matthew. 2011. "Why Do Jazz Musicians Swing Their Eighth Notes?" *Music Theory Spectrum* 33 (1): 3–26.

Covach, John. 2009. *What's That Sound? An Introduction to Rock and Its History.* 2nd ed. New York: W. W. Norton.

Danielsen, Anne. 2010. "Here, There and Everywhere: Three Accounts of Pulse in D'Angelo's 'Left and Right.'" In *Musical Rhythm in the Age of Digital Reproduction,* edited by Anne Danielsen, 19–35. Burlington, VT: Ashgate.

de Clercq, Trevor. 2012. "Sections and Successions in Successful Songs: A Prototype Approach to Form in Rock Music." PhD dissertation, University of Rochester.

———. 2016. "Measuring a Measure: Absolute Time as a Factor for Determining Bar Lengths and Meter in Pop/Rock Music." *Music Theory Online* 22 (3).

de Clercq, Trevor, and David Temperley. 2011. "A Corpus Analysis of Rock Harmony." *Popular Music* 30 (1): 47–70.

Everett, Walter. 2004. "Making Sense of Rock's Tonal Systems." *Music Theory Online* 10 (4).

———. 2009. *The Foundations of Rock: From "Blue Suede Shoes" to "Suite: Judy Blue Eyes."* Oxford: Oxford University Press.

Fraisse, Paul. 1982. "Rhythm and Tempo." In *The Psychology of Music,* edited by Diana Deutsch, 149–80. Waltham, MA: Academic Press.

Friberg, Anders, and Andreas Sundström. 2002. "Swing Ratios and Ensemble Timing in Jazz Performance: Evidence for a Common Rhythmic Pattern." *Music Perception* 19 (3): 333–49.

Fujita, Tetsuya, Yuji Hagino, Hajime Kubo, and Goro Sato. 1989. *The Beatles: Complete Scores.* Milwaukee, WI: Hal Leonard.

Hall, Anne. 2005. *Studying Rhythm.* 3rd ed. Upper Saddle River, NJ: Pearson Prentice Hall.

Iyer, Vijay. 2002. "Embodied Mind, Situated Cognition, and Expressive Microtiming in African-American Music." *Music Perception* 19 (3): 387–414.

Kostka, Stefan, Dorothy Payne, and Byron Almén. 2013. *Tonal Harmony with an Introduction to Twentieth-Century Music.* 7th ed. New York: McGraw-Hill.

Levy, Mark. 2011. "Improving Perceptual Tempo Estimation with Crowd-Sourced Annotations." In *Proceedings of the 12th International Society for Music Information Retrieval Conference (ISMIR),* October 24–28, edited by Anssi Klapuri and Colby Leider, 317–22. Miami: University of Miami.

London, Justin. 2012. *Hearing in Time: Psychological Aspects of Musical Meter.* 2nd ed. Oxford: Oxford University Press.

———. 2016. "Metre." *Grove Music Online.* Accessed May 12, 2016. http://www.oxfordmusiconline.com/subscriber/article/grove/music/18519.

Matthews, Neal, Jr. 1984. *The Nashville Numbering System: An Aid to Playing by Ear.* 2nd ed. Milwaukee, WI: Hal Leonard.

Mattingly, Rick. 2006. *All about Drums: A Fun and Simple Guide to Playing Drums.* Milwaukee, WI: Hal Leonard.

McCandless, Gregory. 2013. "Metal as a Gradual Process: Additive Rhythmic Features in the Music of Dream Theater." *Music Theory Online* 19 (2).

Moelants, Dirk. 2002. "Preferred Tempo Reconsidered." In *Proceedings of the 7th International Conference on Music Perception and Cognition (ICMPC)*, July 17–21, edited by Catherine Stevens, Denis Burnham, Gary Mcpherson, Emery Schubert, and James Renwick, 580–83. Sydney, Australia: University of New South Wales.

Moelants, Dirk, and Martin McKinney. 2004. "Tempo Perception and Musical Content: What Makes a Piece Fast, Slow, or Temporally Ambiguous?" *8th International Conference on Music Perception and Cognition*, 558–62.

Moore, Allan. 1992. "Patterns of Harmony." *Popular Music* 11 (1): 73–106.

———. 2001. *Rock: The Primary Text: Developing a Musicology of Rock*. 2nd ed. Burlington, VT: Ashgate.

Morgenstein, Rod, and Rick Mattingly. 1997. *The Drumset Musician*. Milwaukee, WI: Hal Leonard.

Osborn, Brad. 2010. "Beats That Commute: Algebraic and Kinesthetic Models for Math-Rock Grooves." *Gamut* 3 (1): 43–68.

———. 2014. "Kid Algebra: Radiohead's Euclidian and Maximally Even Rhythms." *Perspectives of New Music* 52: 1–25.

Parncutt, Richard. 1994. "A Perceptual Model of Pulse Salience and Metrical Accents in Musical Rhythms." *Music Perception* 11 (4): 409–464.

Pieslak, Jonathan. 2007. "Re-casting Metal: Rhythm and Meter in the Music of Meshuggah." *Music Theory Spectrum* 29 (2): 219–45.

Pollack, Alan. 1993–1999. "'Notes On' Series." Accessed May 16, 2017. http://www.recmusicbeatles.com/public/files/awp/awp.html.

Potter, Dee. 2001. *The Drummer's Guide to Shuffles*. Milwaukee, WI: Hal Leonard.

Randall, Robin, and Janice Peterson. 1997. *Lead Sheet Bible*. Milwaukee, WI: Hal Leonard.

Riley, Jim. 2010. *Song Charting Made Easy: A Play-Along Guide to the Nashville Number System*. Milwaukee, WI: Hal Leonard.

———. 2015. *Survival Guide for the Modern Drummer: A Crash Course in All Musical Styles for Drumset*. Van Nuys, CA: Alfred Music.

Rosenberg, Nancy. 2011. "Popular Music in the College Music Theory Class: Rhythm and Meter." In *Pop-Culture Pedagogy in the Music Classroom*, edited by Nicole Biamonte, 47–71. Lanham, MD: Scarecrow Press.

Semjen, Andras, Dirk Vorberg, and Hans-Henning Schulze. 1998. "Getting Synchronized with the Metronome: Comparisons between Phase and Period Correction." *Psychological Research* 61 (1): 44–55.

Stephenson, Ken. 2002. *What to Listen for in Rock: A Stylistic Analysis*. New Haven, CT: Yale University Press.

Temperley, David. 1999. "Syncopation in Rock: A Perceptual Perspective." *Popular Music* 18 (1): 19–40.

Temperley, David, and Trevor de Clercq. 2013. "Statistical Analysis of Harmony and Melody in Rock Music." *Journal of New Music Research* 42 (3): 187–204.

Williams, Chas. 2012. *The Nashville Number System*. Nashville, TN: Chas Williams.

Wyatt, Keith, Carl Schroeder, and Joe Elliott. 2005. *Ear Training for the Contemporary Musician*. Milwaukee, WI: Hal Leonard.

Zoro. 2007. *The Commandments of R&B Drumming: A Comprehensive Guide to Soul, Funk, and Hip-Hop.* Van Nuys, CA: Alfred Music.

———. 2013. *The Commandments of the Half-Time Shuffle: A Comprehensive Guide to the Most Beloved Yet Mystifying Grooves in Drum History.* Van Nuys, CA: Alfred Music.

CHAPTER 7

"Home I'll Never Be"

LOCATION, MEANING, PERSONA, AND REALISM IN THE
MUSIC OF TOM WAITS AND BRUCE SPRINGSTEEN

JACOB ARTHUR

UNIVERSITY OF MICHIGAN

D rawing on the field of music geography and traditional musical
analysis, this chapter examines the physical locations that Bruce
Springsteen and Tom Waits use in their lyrics and why they chose these
places. I also examine how they set these places musically to heighten
the realism and themes in their respective works. This is done by conducting close readings of the artists' lyrics and interviews, mapping the
lyric locations using Geographic Information System (GIS) software
to ensure greater accuracy, researching the historical and social significance of these locations, and performing music analytic techniques to
explore connections between the location and themes brought about
in the lyrics and the musical performance. In doing so, this chapter
reaches across several disciplinary lines to gain a better understanding
of the music.

The opening paragraph of Tim Cresswell's book *Place: An Introduction* states that "place" is a "concept that travels quite freely between
disciplines and the study of place benefits from an interdisciplinary approach."[1] Cresswell goes on to quote philosopher Jeff Malpas,
who argues that "place is perhaps the key term for interdisciplinary

---

1. Cresswell, 2015 p. 1.

research in the arts, humanities and social sciences in the twenty-first century."[2] This chapter exemplifies how place easily allows for an interdisciplinary approach, as it incorporates elements of geography, music theory, and musicology to gain insight into how place is used in music.

In the 2015 article "'Miami, New Orleans, London, Belfast, and Berlin': An Analysis of Geographic References in U2's Recordings," geographer Joel Deichmann examines and maps the lyrics of the band U2. From there, Deichmann categorizes the spatial and nonspatial elements of their work, allowing him to demonstrate how the band uses place to highlight certain themes. In doing so, he divides the spatial and nonspatial songs further by subcategorizing the nonspatial themes as "Romantic Love," "Brotherly Love," "Spiritual Love," and "Love of Mother."[3] The spatial elements are categorized as "US & UK Foreign Policy," "Conflict," "Biblical Events," "Perserverance," "Addiction," and "Discovery."[4] One area where Deichmann's study falls short, however, is in the connection to the lyrics and their context in a piece of music. In the sections that follow, I hope to build onto Deichmann's work, demonstrating the value of examining locations in lyrics while also providing examples of how places are illustrated musically through case studies of Tom Waits's "I Wish I Was in New Orleans (in the Ninth Ward)" and Bruce Springsteen's "Born in the U.S.A."[5] I also explore Springsteen's cover of Tom Waits's song "Jersey Girl" to examine how Springsteen alters a song to make it better fit his persona.

The notion of physical places carrying associated meaning has a long history in the stories and music of oral traditions. Philosopher David Abram's *Spell of Sensuous* (1996) outlines the importance of physical place in cultures ranging from the Australian aboriginals to the American Indians of the southwestern United States. In all these cultures, locations not only represent the physical realm but also host a myriad of spiritual, emotional, and moral connections. Recognizing these connections, American

---

2. Malpas, 2010.
3. Deichmann, 2015 p. 110.
4. Deichmann notes, however, that many of these categories overlap and these categories do not represent an exhaustive list.
5. While this current study does not explicitly categorize the places in the manner that Deichmann does in his study, political, social, and romantic themes do still emerge.

songwriter Lyle Lovett has stated that he does not "insert [locations] into a song as an academic exercise"; instead, he chooses to incorporate a place only when it "evokes the spirit of what it is that [he is] trying to say."[6] Perhaps in a similar vein, Tom Waits stated in a 1999 interview that "every song needs to be anatomically correct: you need weather, the name of a town, [and] something to eat."[7] These interviews indicate that places in songs are chosen deliberately and with care. These places are significant to the meaning of the song, the realism of the song, and how the artist is choosing to portray themselves. In addition to Waits, Springsteen, and U2, artists such as Randy Newman, Bob Dylan, Ray Charles, Louis Armstrong, and Neil Young have all incorporated specific locations into their music as a means of heightening realism or highlighting themes.[8] Despite the significance of location in music, there is very little music scholarship addressing the role that place has in shaping an artist's public persona or its role in adding elements of realism to songs.

Music geographer George Carney echoes David Abram's sentiment, writing that "place refers to a location, but specifically to the values and meanings associated with that location. A place is a location that demonstrates a particular identity."[9] In relation to the young field of music geography, scholar Blake Gumprecht states that the field "focuses on origins, diffusion, and distribution of musical styles" while advocating for Susan Smith's declaration that the field should instead examine "the extent to which sound generally, and music in particular, structures space and characterizes place."[10] Despite this assertion, much of music geography still focuses on "origins, diffusion, and distribution" with little explanation of *why* an artist chooses to set songs in certain locations or *how* these places are illustrated musically.[11]

---

6. Lovett, 2015.
7. Valania, 1999 (2011) p. 271.
8. Hayes (2009) examines many of these artists and includes an extensive discography of recordings that feature US cities and states from 1924 to 2006.
9. Carney, 1999 p. 10.
10. Gumprecht, 1998 p. 62; Susan Smith, 1994 p. 232.
11. As a result, many of these studies are regional, as they tend to focus on how a style is associated with a place purely because of the music's or the artist's origin. See Carney (1999) and Gumprecht (1998).

One of the most recent and comprehensive large-scale studies of popular music and geography is the 2003 book *Sound Tracks: Popular Music, Identity, and Place* by geographers John Connell and Chris Gibson. Over the course of the book, Connell and Gibson outline the relationship between location and musical style, starting with early American folk and bluegrass. One area where this book falls short, however, is in its study of song lyrics. The authors assert that "the sounds and rhymes of names, rather than the 'reality' of place, have often exerted a major role in the choice of location."[12] In other words, the locations in lyrics are dismissed as insignificant choices made purely for the sonic quality of the place names and not for the extramusical associations that these places might possess.[13]

I chose to examine Tom Waits and Bruce Springsteen for several reasons: they are contemporaries (both released their debut albums in 1973), they have genre crossover with "rock" and "folk rock," and they are celebrated as *American* songwriters. Thematically, both musicians' lyrical output focuses on some aspect of American life. Because they are hailed as songwriters, the lyrics of their music are primarily composed by the artists themselves.[14] Lastly, Waits and Springsteen have cultivated specific personas that exist in their music as well as their public appearance: Tom Waits has spent years cultivating his image as a drunken, bohemian, vagrant poet. Bruce Springsteen, on the other hand, has imagined himself as a patriot and a champion of working-class Middle America.[15] Given the importance Springsteen and Waits place on their lyrics, a close reading of these artists' use of location gives us a better understanding of how they choose to represent themselves and add realism to their narratives.

---

12. Connell and Gibson, 2003 p. 72.
13. As it turns out, several of the locations that Connell and Gibson state that artists would not write about are found in the catalogs of both songwriters used in this study.
14. While a case can be made that the lyricist's opinions should matter less than those of the interpreter, I chose to restrict this study to songs performed by the original lyricist, as I believe it allows for stronger connections to be made between the location and the musical setting.
15. Everett (1975), Cullen (1997), Harde (2013), and Carroll (2011) all address these personas.

COMBINED MAP

Before delving into each artist individually, examining a combined map of the two artists' lyrics reveals several similarities and differences among the locations that Tom Waits and Bruce Springsteen choose. The combined map (Figure 1) shows that the densest areas are found on the coasts, primarily New York City on the East Coast and Southern California on the West Coast. This map also shows that Waits's noncoastal locations tend to lie close to the Mississippi and Ohio Rivers, while Springsteen's tend to be either in the "Rust Belt" or west of the Mississippi in areas such as Texas, Colorado, and Utah.

There are several reasons for these trends. The first, and perhaps primary, explanation is that both artists originate from coastal urban or suburban areas; Waits is from Pomona, California, and Springsteen from Belmar, New Jersey. A second explanation is that these areas are among the most densely populated areas in the United States.[17] It stands to reason that these areas would be prevalent in either artist's mind, as these are large areas of commerce, culture, and tourism. Given the size of the cities in these areas, it is certain that both artists traveled through them

FIGURE 1. Combined Waits/Springsteen US map. Waits is red, Springsteen is blue.[16]

---

16. Nordström (2014) served as the jumping-off point for the Tom Waits map. It was thoroughly reviewed and inaccuracies were corrected.

17. See United States Census Bureau (2015) for visual representations of these population densities.

often, and audiences across the nation are likely to be more familiar with those places and some of the associative characteristics that go with them. Similarly, there might be commercial reasons for focusing on these areas. When discussing U2's use of location, geographer Joel Deichmann writes, "Given the strong representation of Europe and the United States in U2's recorded material, it is likely that the band deliberately invokes images of place to appeal to its fans and increase music sales."[18] Waits and Springsteen might be doing the same with their choices of location.

The differences in international location choices can best be explained by how the individual artists portray themselves in their music. As a politically charged and internationally conscious artist, Springsteen focuses on the areas of conflict that were present in the minds of Americans at the time that he was writing these songs; America was still feeling the reverberations of the conflict in Vietnam, with the Korean War not far behind it. It makes logical sense that, as an artist painting himself as a patriot and mouthpiece for working America, Springsteen chooses to focus his international songwriting efforts in these areas. It is for similar reasons that Springsteen also focuses more on Mexico, as he expresses his stance on immigration through his music. Waits, on the other hand, generally avoids politics in his music and persona in favor of an avant-garde bohemian identity, resulting in more locations in Europe.[19]

▎TOM WAITS

In Tom Waits's debut album, *Closing Time*, only two specific locations are named, appearing in a single line of "Midnight Lullaby" as places for the listener to dream of. While these places carry some meaning in the song (one of distant, far-off lands), it is not until his follow-up album that Waits makes use of location to put more meaning and character into his music.

The Heart of Saturday Night (1974) places Waits in his hometown region of San Diego. The setting is given early, as the second song is titled "San Diego Serenade," priming the listener to hear the rest of the album

18. Deichmann, 2015 p. 103.
19. Waits, 2004 pp. 349–53.

in this geographical context, including retroactively hearing the opening track of the album, "New Coat of Paint," as being about the Southern California area. Waits solidifies his and the album's placement in this region in the song "Diamonds on My Windshield," in which he mentions Oceanside, San Clemente, and Riverside, California, before closing the album with "The Ghosts of Saturday Night (after Hours at Napoleone's Pizza House)."[20]

When placing all these points on a map, it is easy to see that the majority of California locations mentioned in this album fall in close proximity to California Route 15 and Route 5 (Figure 2). This is especially intriguing when looking at "Diamonds on My Windshield," in which Waits describes driving between Oceanside and San Clemente (and briefly mentions Route 5). Mapping these points indicates that Waits has an intimate knowledge of the area and heightens the realism of the lyrical road trip.

After *The Heart of Saturday Night*, Waits slowly broadens the scope of his music beyond California, from *Small Change* (1976) onward until

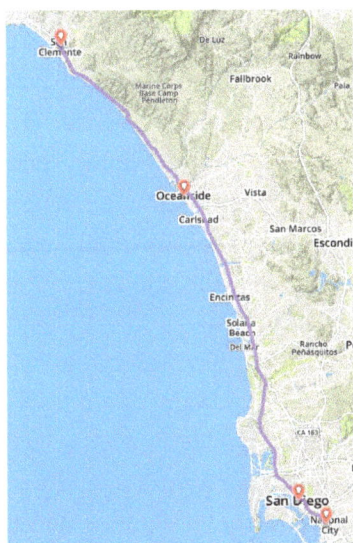

FIGURE 2. From top to bottom—San Clemente, Oceanside, San Diego, Napoleone's Pizza House. Route 15 traced in purple

---

20. Perhaps not incidentally, Napoleone's Pizza House is where Waits worked nights as a teenager (Wiseman, 1975).

Rain Dogs (1985), which focuses primarily on New York City. This is unsurprising because the majority of the album was written and recorded in Manhattan, where Waits was living at the time. Much like how he used specific locations to show off his knowledge of Southern California and prove himself as a real figure there, Waits strives to achieve a similar goal in his new home. Demonstrating intricate knowledge of the area, Waits is precise when denoting place in "Union Square." In the song, Waits describes patrons walking out of a Cinema 14 around the corner from Union Square. If one references a map of New York City, one will find that there is, in fact, a Cinema 14 movie theater there. This specificity confirms Waits as a believable character in the city and provides another layer of realism, transporting the listener to Union Square. The more specific Waits can be about a location, the more accurately he can portray it, thus creating a very real setting for his music.

Waits also places himself in New York City musically with the instrumental track "Midtown." Because there are no lyrics, the title is the only textual indication of where the song is placed. Over drums, an ostinato bass, and a big-band theme, horns sound in free-form solos in swooping dynamics and dissonant harmonies. With the title in mind, the cacophony of horns sound as re-creations of the Midtown traffic Waits was hearing in New York. In other words, Waits creates a musical and sonic portrait of New York traffic. This interpretation would not be possible without Waits's title placing the sounds. The title gives the song context and, by extension, extramusical value.

While Waits often provides a specific location in his songs, the themes of the songs themselves allow for Waits to still be perceived as an "everyman." This is an important factor in his success, as he would potentially only gain regional popularity and notoriety if he was established as a real character in only one area. Instead of limiting himself to a single region, Waits places himself in specific locations from coast to coast—from the busy streets of San Diego and New York to the empty stretch of highway between East St. Louis and Kansas City. At the same time, Waits portrays common themes regardless of where he is situated. The most common of these themes are longing and isolation. In a 1976 interview, Waits states, "There's a common loneliness that just sprawls from coast to coast . . . it's like a common disjointed identity crisis."[21] So while Waits is aiming to effectively place himself in a city as a real character, he is also portraying themes that listeners can relate to across the United States—or even the world.

Analogous to how he displays his knowledge of the Southern California coast on "Diamonds on My Windshield" from *The Heart of Saturday Night*, Waits shows similar knowledge of the Australian landscape in "Town with No Cheer" from 1983's *Swordfishtrombones*. Confirming the song's place, Waits includes Australian terminology, referring to both the "Overlander" and the "Vic Rail" in the song.[22] Waits also makes passing reference to the immigrant weed *Echium plantagineum* by its local colloquial name, "Paterson's curse."[23] As it turns out, this song was generated from a newspaper article. Waits states in an interview that this song is "about a miserable old town in Australia that made the news when they shut down the only watering hole. We found an article about it in a newspaper when we were over there and hung onto it for a year."[24] Given that the song is based on a newspaper article, it makes sense that Waits would try to preserve the realism of the location. However, the storyline of the song itself remains clear regardless of setting, allowing the central story and theme to be understood by anyone around the world. The realism of the song, provided by the location and local terminology, contributes to the relatability of the themes. If it were not for this realism, the story itself could be passed over as fantasy, and thus, the themes would be lost on the listener.

There are several recurring locations in Waits's catalog. Interestingly, many of these places are set or referenced in a similar fashion each time, implying that they have an assigned affect. One of the most prominent examples of this is the state of Illinois, as mention of both the state and the towns within it are given similar treatment.[25] All these "Illinois songs" either are treated as love ballads or feature Illinois as the object of one's

---

21. Carter and Greenberg, 1976 p. 60.
22. The Overlander is an Australian railway, and VicRail is the organization that operates trains in that region.
23. Parsons and Cuthbertson, 1992 pp. 325–30.
24. Waits, 1983 p. 132.
25. Exceptions to this are Chicago and East St. Louis, which both have different affects.

longing. These treatments appear in *Swordfishtrombones* in the song "Shore Leave" and later in "Johnsburg, Illinois" from the same album. Waits most likely uses Illinois as an object of affection and longing because his wife was born there before moving to the East Coast. He takes his personal treatment of Illinois further, however, in 2004's "Day after Tomorrow," where he describes a soldier longing for his home in Rockford, Illinois.[26] So as a result of his personal, familial connection to the state, Illinois comes to represent a home, a family, and a place to long for across his catalog—not just songs about his wife.

Another recurring location is the intersection of Vine Street and Hollywood Boulevard in Los Angeles. This first appears on *Blue Valentine* (1978) in "A Sweet Little Bullet from a Pretty Blue Gun." The intersection even serves as the title of 1980's *Heartattack and Vine*.[27] "Sweet Little Bullet" goes on to mention the Gilbert Hotel, which lies three blocks from the intersection. Again, when using this level of specificity, Waits demonstrates that his locations are not chosen arbitrarily and provide more depth to the setting and the musical work. Both songs set at this intersection describe a scene filled with drugs, prostitution, and violence. This imagery is consistent with how other Hollywood residents would characterize this area at the time the songs were released.[28] While the intersection once housed some of the largest movie production companies in the '20s, many moved away in the '60s, and the area quickly degenerated.[29] It is of little surprise that Waits would adopt this area as a setting in his music—especially earlier in his career, when he was making an effort to seem degenerate himself. Waits sets both songs in an eight-bar blues form in a minor key accompanied by his vocal growl. These songs could be categorized as aligning with the Chicago urban blues style, given their instrumentation.[30] The accompaniment in these songs is unsurprising, as they thematically fit with the expectations of Chicago blues. Waits's repeated thematic imagery, as well as his recurring musical

---

26. Establishing his familiarity with the area, Waits mentions Rockford's relative location to the Wisconsin border.
27. In the promotional materials for this album, Waits explains that he renamed Hollywood Boulevard as Heartattack Boulevard.
28. Poole, 2008.
29. Ibid.
30. Oliver, "Blues."

accompaniment associated with this Hollywood intersection, indicates that he attaches a specific affect to this location.

TOM WAITS: "I WISH I WAS IN NEW ORLEANS (IN THE NINTH WARD)"

This song from 1976's *Small Change* shows Waits dreaming of drunkenly stumbling through New Orleans's Burgundy Street in the Ninth Ward. Drawing on New Orleans's reputation as a hub for jazz, alcohol, and debauchery, Waits portrays his character as inebriated and, in doing so, illustrates the scene in New Orleans that he longs for.[31] This portrayal begins before the first note sounds; the recording begins with Waits counting in the band, but beats three and four are jumbled into unintelligible grunts rather than numbers (0:00–0:04). Mimicking physical stumbling, the vocal anacrusis in measure 8 seems to fall into the downbeat of the verse as it is juxtaposed against the equal quarter- and eighth-note rhythms of the introduction (Figure 3). This stumbling is portrayed throughout the song as the tempo slows at half cadences before "falling" back into the initial tempo with the arrival of the tonic.

Waits also vocally displays his character's inebriation throughout the song. He slurs many of his words together, particularly at cadence points, and he often slides upward into the melody, beginning in measure 10 (Figure 4). Adding color to his slurs, Waits often substitutes the sound *z*

FIGURE 3. Waits's vocal line breaks the straight rhythm of the introduction as it stumbles into the verse. Transcription from *Tom Waits: Anthology* (1988).

---

31. The book *Louisiana: A Guide to the State* claims that "New Orleans became noted both for its bawdiness as a river town and for its gaiety as cultural center" as early as the 1750s (American Guide Series, 1941 p. 320).

into words that end with *s*, such as "Orleans," "dreams," and "beans." He also uses improper grammar at points in the song, such as "What I wants is red beans and rice."

Illustrating Waits as a wandering, drunk narrator, the final phrase of the A section needs to be extended by a measure of 2/4 as it approaches the cadence, highlighting the wandering and rambling nature of the narrator (Figure 5). Waits invokes the New Orleans jazz tradition at the close of the first iteration of the B section as he imagines hearing "that tenor saxophone callin' [him] home," accompanied by a prominent saxophone melody in the band.

Besides portraying drunkenness as a way of highlighting the scene that Waits is imagining in New Orleans, he also uses a harmonic technique that invokes the style of fellow songwriter Randy Newman and, by extension, Newman's ties to New Orleans. Waits's chromatic descent over a descending fifths progression mirrors the harmonic paradigm that Peter Winkler identifies in the 1988 article "Randy Newman's Americana" (Figure 6a, b, c). While Winkler makes the connection between this harmonic paradigm and barbershop harmony, this progression can also be connected with the music of vaudeville (whose musical development happened concurrently with barbershop).[32]

New   Or - leans

FIGURE 4. Waits uses large, ascending vocal scoops hinting at his inebriation.

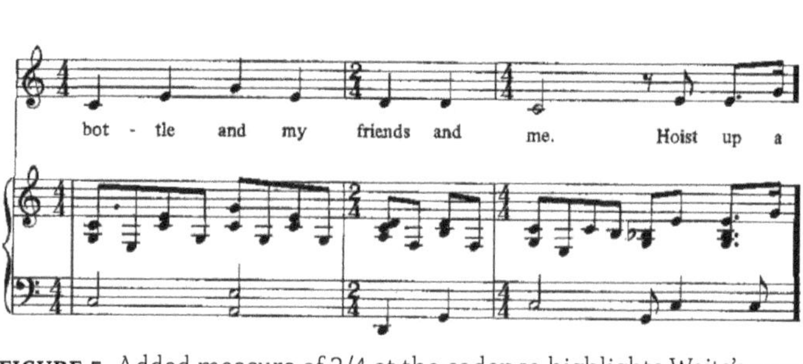

bot - tle   and   my   friends and   me.   Hoist up   a

FIGURE 5. Added measure of 2/4 at the cadence highlights Waits's wandering. Transcription from *Tom Waits: Anthology* (1988).

---

32. Winkler, 1988 p. 5.

Though often thought of a West Coast songwriter, Randy Newman spent many years of his childhood in New Orleans and has long celebrated the region and its music throughout his career.[33] In fact, his 1988 album *Land of Dreams* is composed of childhood vignettes from New Orleans.[34] It is perhaps not that much of a stretch to attribute this passing moment in "I Wish I Was in New Orleans" to Randy Newman's

FIGURE 6A. Waits's "Randy Newman Gesture." Transcription from *Tom Waits: Anthology* (1988).

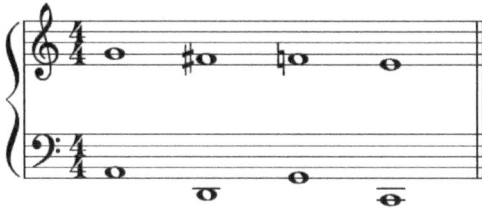

B. Reduction of the gesture.

c. Examples from Randy Newman borrowed from Winkler, 1988 (examples are transposed into C for easy comparison).

33. Ibid., p. 1.
34. Newman, 1988.

style. While this song was composed in 1975, Waits began citing Randy Newman as an influence as early as 1974, describing him as "a craftsman when it comes to putting a song together."[35] So while Waits draws on New Orleans's reputation to musically portray his seedy character as a part of the city, he also borrows a brief but potent harmonic technique used by another songwriter who often celebrates New Orleans.

BRUCE SPRINGSTEEN

Much like Tom Waits's early work, Bruce Springsteen's early writing places him in his hometown. The title alone of Springsteen's debut album, *Greetings from Asbury Park, N.J.* (1973), labels him as a proud native and representative of the New York and New Jersey region. Of the twelve locations given over the course of the album, nine of them are in New York and New Jersey (Figure 7). Furthermore, the locations named outside of this area are not the focal points of the songs that contain them. Harvard and Zanzibar are mentioned in passing as part of the inner-rhyme, stream-of-consciousness writing that marks many of Springsteen's earlier works, and Arkansas is used as a descriptor of the title character in "Mary Queen of Arkansas."

In ways similar to Waits, Springsteen demonstrates knowledge of his location to establish himself as a real character from the region. In *Greetings from Asbury Park*, Springsteen is sure to mention streets and boroughs throughout New York City as well as more precise locations, such as Bellevue Hospital and the Hotel Chelsea. Both historic landmarks, these specific places are recognizable to residents of the city as well as others who know its neighborhoods. Naming these places in his songs effectively establishes Bruce Springsteen as a real character in this region.

Springsteen's first five albums show him rarely leaving New York and New Jersey. In fact, his 1975 breakthrough album, *Born to Run*, never leaves this region. Instead, the album features the most instances of precise locations across his entire career. For example, "the Palace" that Springsteen mentions in the album's title track is a reference to Palace Amusements, found on the Asbury Park Boardwalk. Mentions of

---

35. Waits, 1974 p. 25.

precise places such as this put some frame of reference on more ambiguous locations included in the song; knowing that "the Palace" is on the boardwalk makes it easy to assume that "the beach" is along the Jersey Shore. While having knowledge of these locations might not have a significant effect on these songs' meanings, they do effectively place Springsteen as a New Jersey native as well as add a layer of realism to the music, giving the narrative and themes a greater sense of relatability because they reflect reality.

It is not until *Nebraska* (1982) that Springsteen shows significant diversity in locations. Despite this diversity, New York and New Jersey still receive the most attention. This album also features the highest frequency of discrete locations at this point in Springsteen's output. One reason for this increase might be the acoustic nature of the album, aligning it more closely to folk and country musical traditions, which are more likely to include place names than the rock tradition.[36] In other words, in order for Springsteen to convincingly write songs in the folk tradition, he needed to incorporate more discrete locations.

Even though the majority of locations that appear throughout *Nebraska* are found in the Northeast and the album itself was recorded in Springsteen's New Jersey apartment, the title combined with the acoustic nature of the album primes listeners to hear and interpret the work

FIGURE 7. *Greetings from Asbury Park* shows a heavy concentration in the New York/New Jersey region.

---

36. Connell and Gibson, 2003 p. 35.

through the lens of Middle America.[37] The emptiness of the lo-fi sonic landscape is brought out visually in the album cover, which shows the expanse of an open road presumably in Nebraska. Springsteen's interpretation of Nebraska reflects his developing trend of focusing his songwriting efforts toward Middle, working-class America. Placing himself closer to this region and socioeconomic class will prove to be an important part of Springsteen's music and persona throughout the rest of his career. *Nebraska* is also the last album in which Springsteen places his songs primarily in New York and New Jersey. After *Nebraska*, Springsteen instead focuses on the Rust Belt and the Southwest. This shift is easily seen when looking at the map of *The Ghost of Tom Joad*.

While *Nebraska*'s musical style and album art created the illusion of Middle America, *The Ghost of Tom Joad* signifies Springsteen's actual shift to the American heartland as he further steeps himself in the American folk tradition.[38] Highlighting this shift, Springsteen incorporates forty discrete locations into *The Ghost of Tom Joad*, while his previous work averaged fourteen locations per album (Figure 8). Even more noticeable is that the majority of these locations are in California, showing a leap from the East Coast to the West. Once again, an explanation for the significant increase in places could be that Springsteen recognizes some of the lyric and musical characteristics of the folk style. The jump from one coast to another parallels Tom Waits's move from the West Coast to the East, since both artists changed their location focus after moving across the country. More important, however, the primary theme that runs through the album is the plight of immigrants coming into the United States through Mexico. Highlighting this struggle, Springsteen looks toward border towns, such as those in Southern California. The second theme that runs through this album is that of America's shrinking industrial cities. Highlighting this theme and Springsteen's development as a working-class hero and a mouthpiece for factory workers, he frequently uses cities

---

37. Sufjan Stevens later achieved a similar effect with his abandoned Fifty States project, in which he set out to write an album for each state. After writing an album for Illinois and Michigan, Stevens abandoned the project and has since called it a promotional gimmick.
38. In fact, *Ghost of Tom Joad* won a Grammy Award in 1997 for Best Contemporary Folk Album.

whose commerce and jobs have suffered as a direct result of factories shutting down Youngstown, Ohio, and Pittsburgh, Pennsylvania.

The song "Youngstown," named for the historic Ohio steel-mill city, celebrates the history of factory towns and laments their decline. Singing a haunting minor-mode melody, Springsteen outlines the rise of the city and its importance in war efforts beginning with the Civil War through the conflict in Vietnam. Springsteen goes on to say that the Monongahela Valley, Mesabi iron range, and the coal mines of Appalachia have all suffered similar fates. The poignancy is highlighted by the realism found in the song, as the story is told from the viewpoint of a Youngstown, Ohio, native. Instead of broadly addressing the Rust Belt, Springsteen draws attention to the struggles of a single town in the first three verses of the song before applying these themes to factory towns as a whole in the last verse.[39] Choosing Youngstown as the setting for this song is appropriate because it was once the center of "Steel Valley" and was the founding site of Republic Steel, among other national steel organizations.[40] Since the '60s, however, Youngstown has gone through economic turmoil with the downturn of steel production. Currently, it is one of the

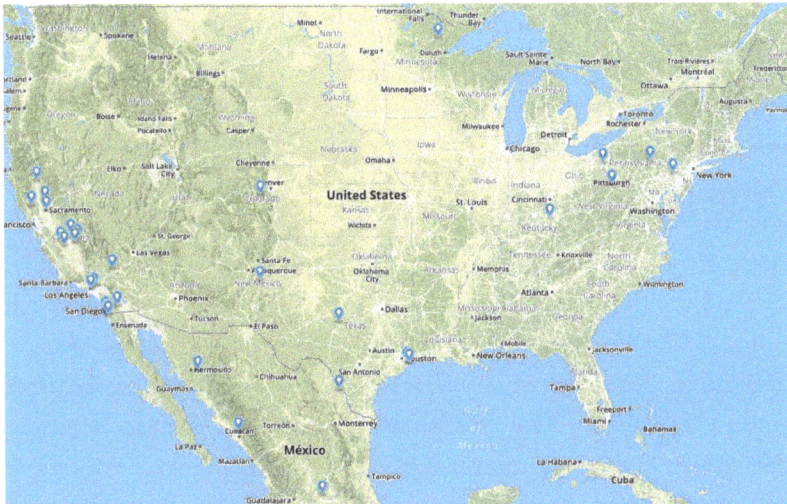

FIGURE 8. *Ghost of Tom Joad* locations.

---

39. This is perhaps comparable with Waits's notion of finding common themes across the country that can be brought out in any one location.
40. Posey, 2013.

fastest-shrinking cities in the United States.[41] Youngstown's drastic situation makes it an ideal setting for exposing the difficulties that these steel
towns and their residents now face.

Springsteen's primary international locations lie in Southeast Asia, specifically Vietnam. The first instance of this occurs on the album *Born in
the U.S.A.* (1984).[42] At the time of its release, much of American media
related to the conflict in Vietnam was centered on disturbed and potentially violent Vietnam veterans.[43] Instead of adhering to this stereotype,
Springsteen writes about the struggle those veterans faced adjusting to life
after serving in Vietnam on the album's title track. Making the experience
all the more potent, Springsteen's narrator describes a brother who fought in
Khe San, the site of a major battle in the conflict, and "had a woman
in Saigon." While Springsteen does not provide any further detail, his
naming of these specific regions rather than generalizing with a simple
country label brings a level of specificity and depth that gives the song
more meaning. In other words, it creates a more reliable narrator, thus
strengthening the song's message.

Springsteen continues to use Vietnam as focal point in several political songs in *The Ghost of Tom Joad*. Creating a deeper sense of realism,
Springsteen uses specific areas of Vietnam, such as Saigon, Quang Tri,
and Chu Lai. Instead of connecting with veterans using the United
States as common ground, Springsteen uses Vietnam. While these locations might not be widely known to the average American, they would
resonate with soldiers stationed in Vietnam and, if nothing else, give
Springsteen's songs more depth and confirm him as an advocate for
Vietnam veterans.

The Ghost of Tom Joad marks the point where Springsteen is invested
in immigration reform and the lives of migrant workers from Mexico.
Springsteen tries to place himself closer to the issues by creating narrators
whose "[families are] from Guanajuato" or who know that "men in from
Sinaloa were looking for some hands." By making use of specific locations

---

41. Ibid.
42. Interestingly, the only mention of any domestic location on this album is the "U.S.A."
in the title track.
43. Chapter 4 of Masciotra (2010) outlines movies, music, and literature from 1977 to
1989 that conform to this stereotype.

instead of simply stating "Mexico," Springsteen places himself closer to the people that he is addressing or trying to emulate in his characters. This specificity implies a level of knowledge and accuracy in relation to immigration issues, again heightening the realism of the work and giving way to the notion that Springsteen is an advocate for immigrants' rights. By depicting the struggles of both factory workers and immigrants, Springsteen confirms his persona as a workingman and advocate for the "American Dream."

The albums that follow *Tom Joad* show a significant decrease in specific and meaningful locations.[44] For example, the only four locations mentioned in *Magic* (2007) occur in succession in "Terry's Song" as Springsteen lists "wonders of the world." While these places are recognizable worldwide, no single location in the song carries deeper musical value. Similarly, Springsteen employs a succession of locations in the song "We Take Care of Our Own" from *Wrecking Ball* (2012) by using easily recognizable landmarks to emphasize that, as a country, "we take care of our own." This theme is made clearer with the repeated lyric "Wherever this flag is flown."[45] In other words, while Springsteen uses specific locations in this song, they do not carry weight in regards to the musical meaning of the song because the location could simply be "wherever this flag is flown." This recent downturn in locations is indicative of how Springsteen has chosen to represent himself and broaden his scope. He has moved from a hometown hero, to a working-class hero, to an advocate for immigrants, to a national icon.

▎ BRUCE SPRINGSTEEN: "BORN IN THE U.S.A."

Whereas Tom Waits gives similar musical treatment to specific locations, Bruce Springsteen tends to use particular treatments with different regions and themes. Songs from New Jersey or addressing the United States as a whole tend to be aligned in the rock and folk-rock tradition, often

---

44. The exception to this is 2005's *Devils and Dust*, which marks a return to the acoustic nature of both *Nebraska* and *Tom Joad* and, unsurprisingly, features the highest number of specific locations among the albums that followed *Tom Joad*. In fact, several of the songs found on this album are from the *Tom Joad* era (Springsteen, 2005).

45. Springsteen, 2012.

backed by the E Street Band. This trend is partly a result of the band's beginnings on the Jersey Shore, leading them to arrange songs from that region more in line with their musical associations there. At the same time, when addressing the nation, the large electric style is still preferred, given the anthemic sound produced from a larger band. These songs tend to treat America as a prized nation. Songs that take a more political or critical stance or relate a more personal story are more likely to be set acoustically. This music tends to be more personal and intimate, and the message or story tends to be more involved; thus a subdued arrangement is more suitable.

Springsteen is cognizant of these settings and their effectiveness as evidenced by his changing treatment of 1984's "Born in the U.S.A." When first released, the full band arrangement with the anthem-rock repetition of the chorus led to many misinterpretations. Springsteen's lyrics depict a shell-shocked veteran who feels abandoned by his country after returning home from Vietnam. *Washington Post* columnist George Will, however, believed that Springsteen was celebrating America because "closed factories and other problems always [seem] punctuated by a grand, cheerful affirmation: 'Born in the U.S.A.!'"[46] Perhaps even more memorable was Ronald Reagan's comments at a 1984 rally in New Jersey, where he stated that "[America's future] rests in the message of hope in the songs of a man so many young Americans admire—New Jersey's own Bruce Springsteen."[47] Had Reagan been familiar with the lyrics of "Born in the U.S.A." (or almost any of the songs from *Nebraska* onward), he would not have labeled Springsteen's songs as "messages of hope."

This misinterpretation of the lyrics is easy to come by, given the arrangement of the song as it appears on the album in 1984. Behind synthesizers, guitars, and booming drums, Springsteen shouts the lyrics behind the bombastic accompaniment. The only lyric that can be consistently heard clearly is the repeated lyric "Born in the U.S.A.," which is further highlighted by the synthesizer doubling the vocal line (Figure 9). Furthermore, this synthesizer line opens the piece and repeats incessantly throughout both the verses and the chorus, making the melody (and

46. Cowie and Boehm, 2006; Will, 1984.
47. Dolan, 2014.

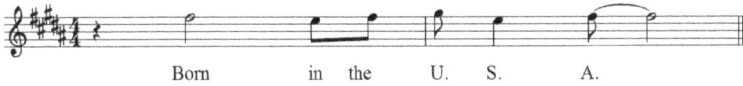

FIGURE 9. "Born in the U.S.A." chorus and synthesizer melody.

its accompanying lyric) the most salient characteristic of the song. This, combined with the inaudibility of the verse lyrics behind the band and Springsteen's characteristically poor enunciation, makes it difficult to put the focus of the song on anything but the declarations of being born in the U.S.A.

Moving away from the album recording and subsequently shifting the focus of the song away from the title lyric, Springsteen has played "Born in the U.S.A." acoustically with an almost blues-like slide guitar accompaniment since the midnineties.[48] This new arrangement features only Springsteen and the twelve-string acoustic guitar down-tuned to D-A-D-A-A-D. The result of this tuning combined with the additional strings doubling each pitch an octave higher is an open and initially modally ambiguous sonic field.[49] The accompaniment primarily consists of a whole-note harmonic rhythm with the chord struck once at the downbeat of each measure, creating a much sparser texture compared to the 1984 album recording. This texture points back to the folklike styling that Springsteen uses throughout *Nebraska*. In fact, Springsteen originally wrote the song to be included on that album before rearranging it for the 1984 album.[50] Springsteen's intentions to include "Born in the U.S.A." on *Nebraska* further indicate that the song's themes perhaps fit better with Springsteen's acoustic stylings over his band accompaniments.

While the verses of the album version are sung using the fifth as a reciting tone that only resolves down to tonic in the final measure, the newly arranged verses traverse down an octave, splitting the lines of the verse into being recited on tonic in the first half and on

---

48. Cullen, 1997 p. 75.
49. "Bruce Springsteen-Born In The USA (acoustic)," YouTube video, 3:05, from a performance televised on *Música Sí* on December 14, 1998, posted by "bruchee," December 14, 2006, https://www.youtube.com/watch?v=d8TwMqpBeL4.
50. Masciotra, 2010 p. 67.

subdominant in the second half. This variety and larger range combined with the sparse accompaniment gives the melodic line a clear direction and makes the lyrics both more coherent and poignant, as the larger descent mirrors the despair that the narrator feels as he returns from the Vietnam War (Figure 10a, b). This motion and clarity places an emphasis on the lyrics and, by extension, Vietnam that does not exist in the album recording.

While the first iteration of the choral lyric is based on the contour of the chorus on the album version, the second iteration is once again set with a descending line (Figure 11). Moreover, the second iteration of the lyric features Springsteen scooping up into b^3 with the phrase "U.S.A.," giving it an added minor-blues emphasis and, again, contradicting the notion that this song is celebrating the United States. Perhaps the strongest contrast between the two versions is that this chorus is sung a tenth lower than the album version—a far cry from the shouting that is displayed in the album. Springsteen also cuts down the declarations of the chorus from four times to two, shifting the focus of the song further away from the United States.

By arranging this song acoustically and aligning it more closely with the folk songs of *Nebraska*, Springsteen better conveys the meaning of the

Born down in a dead man's town   the first   kick I   took was when I   hit the ground

FIGURE 10A. Album verse.

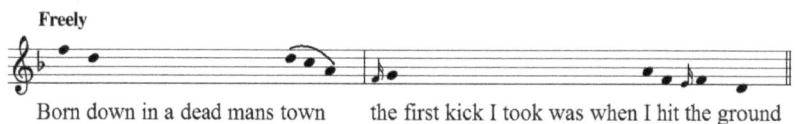

Born down in a dead mans town   the first kick I took was when I hit the ground

B. Live acoustic verse. (Note: because the rearrangement verses are performed without strict meter, the transcription only reflects changes of pitch.)

Born   in the U. S.   A.   Born   in the   U. S.   A.

FIGURE 11. Chorus in the acoustic rearrangement.

song. Springsteen achieves this by creating a sparser texture and a more directional melodic line that places heavier emphasis on the verses and by cutting repetitions of the chorus lyric. This emphasis on the verses highlights the protagonist's struggles in postwar America, contradicting the nationalistic interpretations of the 1984 album version.

"JERSEY GIRL": CROSSOVER BETWEEN WAITS AND SPRINGSTEEN

Tom Waits's 1980 song "Jersey Girl" and Bruce Springsteen's cover of it exemplifies how Waits and Springsteen use place to highlight aspects of their created personae. While Waits originally wrote and recorded the song, Bruce Springsteen has performed it more frequently and has even altered and added lyrics.[51] Whereas Waits opens the song stating that he has no interest in the "whores on Eighth Avenue," Springsteen states disinterest in the "girls on Eighth Avenue." Although a minor change, the implication is significant; Waits intentionally portrays himself as a lowlife in the city with knowledge of the sex industry in the song's setting, while Springsteen—someone who is known as a celebrant of the region—chooses to appear more innocent.

Bruce Springsteen also adds a new verse to the song. In it, he speaks to his tired lover and proposes an evening out along the Jersey Shore. This proposition shows a shift in the focus of the song. Unlike the previous verses that have focused on the woman, Springsteen's added verse focuses on New Jersey and describes it as a place for entertainment and love. In adding this Jersey-centric verse, Springsteen glorifies the region, confirming the persona that he created for himself in his first albums. In other words, Waits may have written the original song, but the sentiment of it combined with the added verse causes it to align more closely with the persona of Springsteen.

CONCLUSION

Both Tom Waits and Bruce Springsteen use locations to illustrate their persona and bring across themes in their music. In each of their earlier works,

---

51. Setlist.fm, 2015.

they use specificity to place themselves in a region and add realism to the songs. As they tour more extensively and write more music, more variety in their choice of location appears. Waits highlights themes that exist across the United States by depicting them in detail in a single location. At the same time, he chooses places that reflect the vagrant persona that he has chosen for himself. This persona and use of specific locations remains consistent through Waits's career. Springsteen takes a similar approach to Waits in his use of specificity to highlight particular themes, particularly in issues regarding factory workers and immigration. However, while Waits remains true to a single theme and persona, Springsteen's theme changes over the course of his career, and as a result, the locations that he chooses and how he uses them also change. As Springsteen moves from hometown hero to national icon, he shifts his focus from New Jersey to the Rust Belt to the West Coast and, finally, the nation at large. As a result, Springsteen uses fewer specific locations in this most recent phase, while Waits's use remains consistent. Springsteen's place at any time is more ambiguous and one that allows him to survey the country from any location, placing him as a resident on "Main St., USA."

In either case, both artists use location to build their identities as an "everyman." Recognizing that locations can carry meaning, both Springsteen and Waits choose their places carefully to best reflect the narrative of a particular song. Moreover, the inclusion of these places adds an element of realism to the music, giving the narratives and themes more power and immediate relevancy. More broadly, mapping and analyzing these songwriters' uses of location gives us a better understanding of how they choose to compose music. Certain places have particular affects (seen in Illinois and the intersection of Hollywood Boulevard and Vine Street), and some places are more appropriate for given themes (such as in the Southwest and old industrial towns). While it is not always a central issue, location is a crucial element in many popular songs and should be taken into greater consideration as we strive to gain a clearer understanding of popular music. I hope that future research in this area will incorporate my interdisciplinary approach, because drawing from the fields of both music theory and musicology allows for a more holistic view of music. For this reason, an interdisciplinary approach such as this could also prove useful in the growing field of popular music education.

REFERENCES

Abram, David. 1997. *The Spell of the Sensuous: Perception and Language in a More-than-Human World.* New York: Pantheon Books.

Alterman, Eric. 1999. *It Ain't No Sin to Be Glad You're Alive: The Promise of Bruce Springsteen.* Boston: Little, Brown.

American Guide Series. 1941. *Louisiana: A Guide to the State.* New York: Hastings House.

Brackett, David. 2000. *Interpreting Popular Music.* Berkeley: University of California Press.

Brackett, Donald. 2008. *Dark Mirror: The Pathology of the Singer-Songwriter.* Westport, CT: Praeger.

Carney, George. 1999. "Cowabunga! Surfer Rock and the Five Themes of Geography." *Popular Music and Society* 23 (4): 3–29.

Carroll, Cath. 2000. *Tom Waits.* New York: Thunder's Mouth Press.

Carter, Betsy, and Peter Greenberg. (1976) 2011. "Waits on Being the Voice of Everyman." Reprinted in *Tom Waits on Tom Waits: Interviews and Encounters,* edited by Paul Maher, 60. Chicago: Chicago Review Press.

Cavicchi, Daniel. 1998. *Tramps like Us: Music and Meaning among Springsteen Fans.* New York: Oxford University Press.

Coles, Robert. 2003. *Bruce Springsteen's America: The People Listening, a Poet Singing.* New York: Random House.

Connell, John, and Chris Gibson. 2003. *Sound Tracks: Popular Music, Identity, and Place.* New York: Routledge.

Cowie, Jefferson, and Lauren Boehm. 2006. "Dead Man's Town: 'Born in the U.S.S.,' Social History, and Working-Class Identity." *American Quarterly* 58 (2): 353–78.

Cresswell, Tim. 2015. Introduction to *Place: An Introduction.* Hoboken: Wiley-Blackwell.

Cullen, Jim. 1997. *Born in the U.S.A.: Bruce Springsteen and the American Tradition.* New York: Harper Collins.

Deichmann, Joel. 2015. "'Miami, New Orleans, London, Belfast, and Berlin': An Analysis of Geographic References in U2's Recordings." *Rock Music Studies* 2 (2): 103–24.

Dolan, Marc. 2012. *Bruce Springsteen and the Promise of Rock 'N' Roll.* New York: W. W. Norton.

———. 2014 "How Ronald Reagan Changed Bruce Springsteen's Politics." *Politico.* Accessed December 29, 2016. http://www.politico.com/magazine/story/2014/06/bruce-springsteen-ronald-reagan-107448.

Everett, Todd. 1975. "Tom Waits: In Close Touch with the Streets." *Los Angeles Free Press,* October 17–23. Also Printed in *New Musical Express,* November 29, 1975.

Everett, Walter. 2007. "Beyond the Palace: Casing the Promised Land." *Interdisciplinary Literary Studies* 9 (1): 81–94.

Griffiths, Dai. 2003. "From Lyrics to Anti-lyric: Analyzing the Words in Pop Song." In *Analyzing Popular Music,* edited by Allan F. Moore, 39–59. Cambridge: Cambridge University Press.

Gumprecht, Blake. 1998. "Lubbock on Everything: The Evocation of Place in Popular Music (a West Texas Example)." *Journal of Cultural Geography* 18: 61–81.

Guterman, Jimmy. 2005. *Runaway American Dream: Listening to Bruce Springsteen.* Cambridge, MA: Da Capo Press.

Harde, Roxanne. 2013. "'Living in Your American Skin': Bruce Springsteen and the Possibility of Politics." *Canadian Review of American Studies* 43 (1): 125–44.

Harde, Roxanne, and Irwin Streight. 2010. *Reading the Boss: Interdisciplinary Approaches to the Works of Bruce Springsteen*. Lanham, MD: Lexington Books.

Hayes, David. 2009. "'From New York to L.A.': US Geography in Popular Music." *Popular Music and Society* 32 (1): 87–106.

"Jersey Girl by Tom Waits Song Statistics." *Setlist.fm*. Accessed February 2015. http://www.setlist.fm/stats/songs/tom-waits-3bd6c0ac.html?song=Jersey+Girl.

Kirkpatrick, Rob. 2009. *Magic in the Night: The Words and Music of Bruce Springsteen*. New York: St. Martin's Griffin.

Larman, Howard. (1974) 2011. "Interview with Tom Waits." Reprinted in *Tom Waits on Tom Waits: Interviews and Encounters*, edited by Paul Maher, 20–26. Chicago: Chicago Review Press.

Lovett, Lyle. 2015. Interview by Jacob Arthur, October 17.

Malpas, Jeff. 2010. "Place Research Network." *Progressive Geographies*, November 4. Accessed June 7, 2015. https://progressivegeographies.com/2010/11/04/place-research-network/.

Marsh, Dave. 1996. *The Bruce Springsteen Story*. New York: Thunder's Mouth Press.

Masciotra, David. 2010. *Working on a Dream: The Progressive Political Vision of Bruce Springsteen*. New York: Continuum.

Montandon, Mac. 2005. *Innocent When You Dream: The Tom Waits Reader*. New York: Thunder Mouth's Press.

Moore, Allan F. 2012. *Song Means: Analysing and Interpreting Recorded Popular Song*. Burlington: Ashgate.

Nordström, Jonas. 2014. "Tom Waits Map." http://tomwaitsmap.com/.

Oliver, Paul. "Blues." *Oxford Music Online*. Accessed October 9, 2015. http://www.oxfordmusiconline.com.ezp1.lib.umn.edu/subscriber/article/grove/music/03311.

Parsons, W., and E. Cuthbertson. 1992. *Noxious Weeds of Australia*. Melbourne, Australia: Inkata Press.

Poole, Bob. 2008. "Turning the Corner at Hollywood and Vine." *LA Times*, May 4.

Posey, Sean. 2013. "America's Fastest Shrinking City." *The Hampton Institution*. Accessed May 28, 2015. http://www.hamptoninstitution.org/youngstown.html.

Smith, Larry. 2002. *Bob Dylan, Bruce Springsteen, and American Song*. Westport, CT: Praeger.

Smith, Susan J. 1994. "Soundscape." *Area* 26: 232–40.

United States Census Bureau. 2015. "Thematic Maps." Accessed February 2015. https://www.census.gov/geo/maps-data/maps/thematic.html.

Valania, Jonathan. (1999) 2011. "The Man Who Howled Wolf." Reprinted in *Tom Waits on Tom Waits: Interviews and Encounters*, edited by Paul Maher, 263–77. Chicago: Chicago Review Press.

Waits, Tom. 1988. *Anthology 1973–1982*. New York: Amsco.

———. 2007. *The Early Years: The Lyrics of Tom Waits (1971–1982)*. New York: Ecco.

———. (1983) 2011. "A Conversation with Tom Waits." Reprinted in *Tom Waits on Tom Waits: Interviews and Encounters*, edited by Paul Maher, 130–36. Chicago: Chicago Review Press.

Werner, Craig. 1998. *A Change Is Gonna Come: Music, Race & the Soul of America.* New York: Plume.

Will, George. 1984. "Bruce Springsteen, U.S.A." *Washington Post*, September 13, A19.

Winkler, Peter. 1988. "Randy Newman's Americana." *Popular Music* 7 (1): 1–26.

Wiseman, Rich. 1975. "Tom Waits, All-Night Rambler." *Rolling Stone*, January 30. http://www.rollingstone.com/music/news/tom-waits-all-night-rambler-19750130.

Albums

Springsteen, Bruce. 1973. *Greetings from Asbury Park, N.J.* Columbia Records. PC 31903, compact disc.

———. 1973. *The Wild, the Innocent & the E Street Shuffle.* Columbia Records. PC 32432, compact disc.

———. 1975. *Born to Run.* Columbia Records. PC 33795, compact disc.

———. 1978. *Darkness on the Edge of Town.* Columbia Records. OC 509876, compact disc.

———. 1980. *The River.* Columbia Records. PC 38654, compact disc.

———. 1982. *Nebraska.* Columbia Records. QC 38358, compact disc.

———. 1984. *Born in the U.S.A.* Columbia Records. QC 38653, compact disc.

———. 1987. *Tunnel of Love.* Columbia Records. OC 40999, compact disc.

———. 1992. *Human Touch.* Columbia Records. COL 657872 7, compact disc.

———. 1992. *Lucky Town.* Columbia Records. CK 53001, compact disc.

———. 1995. *The Ghost of Tom Joad.* Columbia Records. COL 481650 2, compact disc.

———. 2002. *The Rising.* Columbia Records. COL 504190, compact disc.

———. 2005. *Devils and Dust.* Columbia Records. CN 93900, compact disc.

———. 2007. *Magic.* Columbia Records. COL 88697 17060, compact disc.

———. 2009. *Working on a Dream.* Columbia Records. COL 741355, compact disc.

———. 2012. *Wrecking Ball.* Columbia Records. COL 88691942541, compact disc.

———. 2014. *High Hopes.* Columbia Records, compact disc.

Stevens, Sufjan. 2003. *Michigan.* Asthmatic Kitty Records. AKR 007, compact disc.

Waits, Tom. 1973. *Closing Time.* Asylum Records. AS 53 030, compact disc.

———. 1974. *The Heart of Saturday Night.* Asylum Records. AS 53 035, compact disc.

———. 1976. *Small Change.* Asylum Records. AS 53 050, compact disc.

———. 1977. *Foreign Affairs.* Asylum Records. AS 53 068, compact disc.

———. 1978. *Blue Valentine.* Asylum Records. AS 53 088, compact disc.

———. 1980. *Heartattack and Vine.* Asylum Records. AS 52 252, compact disc.

———. 1983. *Swordfishtrombones.* Island Records. IS 90095, compact disc.

———. 1985. *Rain Dogs.* Island Records. IS 90299, compact disc.

———. 1987. *Franks Wild Years.* Island Records. IS 90572, compact disc.

———. 1992. *Bone Machine.* Island Records. IS 512 580, compact disc.

———. 1999. *Mule Variations.* ANTI-Records. AN 86547, compact disc.

———. 2004. *Real Gone.* ANTI-Records. AN 86678, compact disc.

———. 2011. *Bad as Me.* ANTI-Records. AN 87151, compact disc.

PART III

Classroom Applications

CHAPTER 8

Learning and Teaching Popular Music

DISCOVERY OF THE DIVERSITY IN MUSIC LEARNING PROCESSES

LILY CHEN-HAFTECK AND FRANK HEUSER

UNIVERSITY OF CALIFORNIA, LOS ANGELES

Developing a music teacher education program that can adequately prepare new teachers for the needs of today's music-teaching careers has become increasingly challenging. Prospective teachers must acquire excellent musicianship skills, become polished performers, and be able to demonstrate creative abilities through composition and improvisation in addition to cultivating the pedagogical abilities and dispositions necessary to succeed in elementary and secondary schools. Because music is constantly evolving, the very specific skills that were once sufficient for teaching general music and large ensembles now must be supplemented with the knowledge necessary to teach world and popular music. Accomplishing this can be difficult for teacher educators whose own expertise leans toward the traditional rather than popular musical genres. This chapter reports on how university music education faculty members are exploring ways of preparing prospective teachers to meet the challenges of providing popular music instruction in elementary and secondary schools. The following discussion includes some of the reasons for offering professional preparation in popular music pedagogy, a review of pertinent research and philosophical literature, a description of how the inclusion of popular music in the school curriculum might lead to culturally responsive music pedagogies, and a report on how this is being accomplished in the UCLA music education program through the use of juxtapositional pedagogy both in the university classroom and during student teaching. Despite the challenges we and our students experience during the processes, we are highly encouraged by the positive responses from the students to continue in this journey of exploring diverse musical genres, including those that are not central to our musical and pedagogical expertise.

THE NEED FOR INCLUDING POPULAR MUSIC IN THE CURRICULUM

The need for including popular music instruction in school music programs has been a topic of significant discussion and research over the past several decades (Campbell 1995; Green 2003). Society is undergoing rapid sociocultural changes that are influencing and transforming music as well as the ways people experience and interact with the art (Allsup 2008; Kratus 2007; Williams 2011). Young people are drawn to the enormous varieties of popular music genres that have a broad audience, are intended and created for the enjoyment and enrichment of people in their everyday lives (Bowman 2004; Lamont and Maton 2010), and are instantly available through digital media downloads. Although school-age students enjoy music, a relatively small percentage of them participate in music instruction programs on their school campuses (Rabkin and Hedberg 2011). In an attempt to address this issue, a number of music educators are including popular music genres in their teaching, but these efforts are still relatively uncommon. The curricular offerings in school music education programs tend toward classical, folk, and jazz traditions that are not as appealing to young people as the popular forms of music they listen to daily (Kratus 2007; Williams 2007, 2011).

In his historical overview of popular music in American schools, Humphreys (2004) outlines multiple reasons for the narrow focus of school music curriculum, including the desire to improve musical tastes, a cultural bias against American art forms, and a fear of music that appeals to youth culture. However, he suggests that some forms of popular music have always been present in school and were employed for utilitarian reasons, such as supporting church singing, enhancing community relations, and providing a means of recruiting students to study "serious" music. Because most current music programs continue to rely on a narrow repertoire that appeals to a diminishing audience, Kratus (2007) believes that music education in American schools has reached a tipping point, where traditional large ensemble practices must change or become increasingly irrelevant. He calls for curricular changes that incorporate the music young people actually listen to and experience in their lives. This view is echoed by Griffin (2010), who contends that in order for music education programs to provide students with meaningful experiences, the music studied in schools needs to be connected to music that children encounter in their daily lives. Williams (2011) also states that the large ensemble model of music education no longer adequately meets the needs of a majority of students. He suggests creating different instructional models that expand the musical styles studied; employ smaller classes; promote student-centered learning, creative decision making, and aural development; and incorporate technology. These learning approaches are central to popular music and very much in line with the informal learning processes that Green (2001) describes.

Following their investigation of how the introduction of popular music has impacted music education in Australian schools, Dunbar-Hall and Wemyss (2000) conclude that its use is profoundly influencing instructional practices and is "reshaping thinking about music teaching and learning" in the country (30). First, in contrast with the score-reading and notation-focused approaches that are central to teaching art music, the learning processes in popular music include aural-based active music making and improvisation. When score reading is used in popular music, notation tends to be presented in the skeletal form of a lead sheet, which requires that learners master "numerous musical skills" and acquire a working "knowledge of music theory" for effective interpretation and meaningful performance (25). Second, the researchers found that using popular music in schools encourages individualized learning and adds dimensions of music technology, musical sound production, and music creation to the curriculum. Finally, the genre shares attributes with and has contributed to multicultural music education by providing openings for discussions linked to specific ethnicities, ideologies, religions, and sexual identities. Because popular music freely draws from and "exists as a network of styles," its use can promote many different aspects of music education and offers numerous curricular benefits for the field (26). Herbert and Campbell (2000) and Rodriguez (2004) also provide strong arguments in support of popular music in school. While matching student musical preferences and drawing a closer connection between music activities in and out of school, popular music education can also meet the traditional goals and standards of music education through informal learning approaches that demonstrate best practices in education. Therefore, all the previously mentioned studies indicate that it is beneficial to expand school music programs by including the study of popular music.

PEDAGOGY FOR TEACHING POPULAR MUSIC

Green (2006, 2008) argues that introducing popular music in school lessons requires more than just bringing the repertoire into the classroom. The informal learning processes that reflect the ways that popular music is learned must be employed to enrich the authenticity of such experiences. Her research found that informal music learning practices include (1) starting with music that learners know and like; (2) copying recordings of real music by ear; (3) learning alone and in groups with peers without adult guidance or supervision; (4) learning that is not progressive from simple to complex but instead holistic, idiosyncratic, and haphazard; and (5) integrating listening, performing, improvising, and composing throughout the learning process (2008, 178). When applying these principles in the classroom, Green (2006) found that informal pedagogy can be an effective approach for motivating music learning. Additionally, once established, the informal processes inherent in learning popular music can also be used to learn classical music through increasing students' interest, as reported in Green's findings (2006). The Musical Futures project that originated from Green's work on informal pedagogy continues to demonstrate success and has become a "music learning revolution" in the United Kingdom (http://www.musicalfutures.org), thereby benefitting the musical education of many students.

Green's approach of bringing informal popular music learning procedures into the classroom places responsibility on students to use their existing musical knowledge and experiences in the process of exploration and self-discovery to initiate music learning. Letting students choose the music they want to learn seems inherently self-motivational and results in a successful classroom environment in which students are active learners discovering how to make music in a rock band. Some educators, however, question the use of a purely informal learning paradigm, where teachers remain on the periphery and serve as facilitators who do not intervene with the learning process. Allsup (2008) suggests that this approach undermines the role of the music teacher who has expertise and experiences that can enrich students' music understanding. He worries that if educators fail to "provide formal spaces in which dialogue and critique can occur," they actually abandon the responsibilities involved in educating (6). This in turn implies that teacher educators must provide opportunities for future music teachers to explore both formal and informal learning processes and learn to discern the most effective ways to employ each in school settings.

Furthermore, it is overly simplistic to consider classical and popular music as binary opposites that are associated directly with formal (classical) and informal (popular) learning processes. Recent observational studies of exemplary music teachers have shown that these approaches instead function as a continuum, with both processes interacting with each other. Cain (2013) reported on how one music teacher provided effective learning experiences for her students by incorporating both informal and formal procedures in her classroom. McPhail's (2013) study of six teachers demonstrated that both classical and popular styles of music are supported by varying proportions of formal and informal learning processes and that these processes depend on how the knowledge available becomes recontextualized.

McPhail (2013) adopted a theoretical framework created by educational sociologist Basil Bernstein (2000) to interpret his research findings. In this framework, Bernstein (2000) describes differing ways of knowing as vertical and horizontal discourses, with vertical knowledge being what is required for academic learning and what is developed through systematic sequential instruction, while horizontal knowledge is learned through everyday experience. Bernstein's theory suggests that educators recontextualize and balance horizontal and vertical knowledge to meet the needs of students in their classrooms. McPhail discovered that although the teachers participating in the study recognized and affirmed students' musical interests and learning needs, they as educators also felt the need to provide students with access to knowledge that is culturally significant to both the teachers and society. Findings indicate that teachers recontextualize the horizontal discourses of their students' lived musical experiences into the vertical structures of formal schooling. McPhail concludes that learning in school should not be "simply a reflection of real-world musical practices" but provide "a place where students come into contact with a structured form of knowledge acquisition under the guidance of an expert teacher" (2013, 15). Music learning at school should expand students' knowledge base and not be limited to simply facilitating their performance practices. In addition to affirming and validating students' interests and experiences by employing informal learning processes, teachers need to balance this with formally provided knowledge that they think is epistemologically important. The music classroom needs to be "a site for both affirmation and dissonance" (18). Some dissonance is required to inspire learning, while consonance is also required for students to recognize themselves and their value in school. This results in fluctuating boundaries between formal and informal learning processes as teachers recontextualize both musical and pedagogical understandings to meet the interests of students being served in their particular classrooms. It also implies the significance of knowing both how and when to nurture the two instructional modes as well as how to blend these seemingly contradictory learning approaches.

When examining popular music pedagogy, we should not be too focused on whether the instructional approach is formal or informal. Students in music classes should not just aim to learn about music but, more important, learn to become better musicians and develop their lifelong interest in music. As Allsup (2008) has pointed out, rather than adopting "formalist or informalist ideologies" (7), the focus of instruction within the context of a democratic classroom should be on the interactions among teachers and students who freely share ideas with the purpose of maximizing musical learning.

▌IMPLICATIONS FOR MUSIC TEACHER EDUCATION

Wright (2008) correctly points out that when we bring popular music and informal pedagogy into schools, we need to reconsider the types of people who might be suited to become music teachers as well as the kind of music education and teacher education that is required to make such instruction work: "This will require a new type of teacher possessed of the empathy to 'kick' their dominant habitus where necessary and enter the musical worlds of their pupils" (400). This "new type of teacher" will not be intent on reproducing the kinds of ensemble programs that have dominated past practices regardless of the social backgrounds and musical interests of students. Instead, an empathetic teacher will examine the cultural milieu within which they become an active participant in designing a music program that will benefit learners and lead to students' happiness in their musical activities. In this regard, Allsup (2008) feels that the older models of music teacher preparation, which focused primarily on mechanical skills like conducting technique and woodwind fingerings without reference to the context of schools and neighborhoods, are no longer adequate. Modern music teachers will work in schools that might vary greatly in terms of their sociocultural context and status. He questions whether the knowledge and skills that have traditionally been considered as essential to highly qualified music teachers can help them face such new challenges in music education. Therefore, he suggests that preparation programs must equip teachers to comfortably interact in informal learning classrooms, community settings, and diverse populations.

Davis and Blair (2011) echo these concerns regarding music teacher education: "If teachers are to be effective in the world in which we live, we must change the way in which higher education in America approaches music methods classes" (136). They report a threefold process that can help music education students develop teaching skills in popular music. First, there is disequilibrium that is the result of future teachers' dependence on notation due to their uncomfortable feelings when first encountering the informal learning process central to music learning. Next, students start breaking down existing barriers and discover a new perspective of music teaching and learning. Finally, transformation of students occurs, and they are ready to teach a broader range of musical and learning styles. Therefore, in order to be prepared for the current needs of music education, music teacher candidates with backgrounds in Western classical music need to experience teaching unfamiliar genres in settings that might make them uncomfortable. Because future music educators tend to come from traditional school music backgrounds and often presume that they will spend their careers in similar settings, this task is challenging. Preparing future teachers to work in diverse venues and become open to change requires flexibility and commitment from both the teacher educators and the teacher candidates.

TEACHING POPULAR MUSIC AS CULTURALLY RESPONSIVE PEDAGOGY

Culturally responsive teaching attempts to provide all children with equitable learning experiences (Lind and McCoy 2016, 20) and suggests that teachers must learn to "recognize, honor and incorporate the personal abilities of students" into their instructional strategies (Gay 2010, 1). These ideas are particularly important as the United States becomes increasingly diverse. Statistics from the US Census Bureau (2010) suggest that states such as California (57.6 percent white, 37.6 percent Hispanic or Latino, 13.0 percent Asian, 6.2 percent black or African American, 1.0 percent American Indian, 0.4 percent Native Hawaiian and Pacific Islander) represent a diverse and multicultural population that is increasingly typical in many parts of the country. Because this change in demographics is reflected in many school districts that are located in urban areas throughout the country, it is essential that future music educators are prepared to teach students from diverse cultural backgrounds.

Although public schools are becoming increasingly diverse, the reality is that most educators are white and grew up in middle-class communities (Gay, Dingus, and Jackson 2003). This is particularly true for music teachers whose admission to a university music education program often required a high level of proficiency in musical performance skills (Elpus 2015). The technical skills necessary to participate in tertiary-level music programs are usually acquired through many years of private music instruction, which is affordable mostly to affluent families. Because a majority of music education majors come from relatively privileged backgrounds, they are not prepared to work in environments with diverse students. It is essential that music education programs prepare future teachers to employ the principles of culturally responsive pedagogy in order to be effective when working in increasingly diverse schools (Ladson-Billings 2004; Vavrus 2002).

Culturally responsive pedagogy (Gay 2010) was originally developed to improve the low levels of academic achievement observed in many students of color who attend schools in areas with economic challenges. Gay contends that conventional educational reform efforts have failed because they have a deficit orientation that focuses on what ethnically, racially, and culturally diverse students do not have and cannot do rather than building on what the students can bring to the learning environment. Culturally responsive pedagogy acknowledges the legitimacy of the cultural heritages of different ethnic groups that affect students' dispositions, attitudes, and approaches to learning. It teaches students to know and praise their own as well as others' cultural heritages.

Teaching popular music can contribute to culturally responsive pedagogical practices in music. This is particularly the case if we include popular music such as hip hop and R&B as well as different styles of Latino pop that are favored by African American and Hispanic students, respectively. This means that elementary and secondary school students who might have much less experience with classical music than many of their Caucasian and Asian American counterparts will not be disadvantaged. Therefore, in order to teach in a culturally responsive manner, it is important that future music educators, who might be more familiar with classical than popular traditions, acquire the knowledge and skills needed to include popular music in their curriculum.

▌ JUXTAPOSITIONAL PEDAGOGY AT UCLA

The music education program at UCLA has provided future music teachers with traditional preparation for several decades. Recently, the curriculum was redesigned to address the demographic changes seen in schools as well as the evolving musical interests of modern K–12 students. The curricular revisions are based on the concept of juxtapositional pedagogy (Heuser 2014), which is a curricular approach that places contrasting pairs of musical learning experiences that would usually be taught in separate method courses together in a single instructional setting (specific examples of juxtapositions are provided later in this chapter). The purpose of these couplings is to create spaces where the nature of musical thinking and learning can be critically examined and understood from multiple perspectives. Such juxtapositions allow traditional and innovative methodologies to be creatively combined for the express purpose of reconceptualizing and revitalizing music teacher preparation. This approach allows the faculty to provide future music educators with the skills necessary to teach the traditional offerings of large ensembles and general music in schools while simultaneously preparing them to function in the areas of popular music and multicultural music education.

In this juxtapositional approach, popular music pedagogy is not studied as a discrete course but instead infused into all music education method courses. This reinforces our belief in the value of studying diverse musical styles from a variety of perspectives and cultures. The approach also supports our contention that experiencing different and sometimes contradictory learning experiences allows one to grow as a teacher. Since it is impossible to provide in-depth knowledge of all the musical styles teachers will need in their careers, this methodology aims to facilitate the development of dispositions needed for future music teachers to become advocates for diversity in music education. The approach also nurtures the flexibility required to adapt to constantly fluctuating classroom environments and student learning needs. Our goal is to cultivate future teachers who can function in diverse school settings and understand that teaching in a musical or cultural tradition other than their own is possible. To achieve this, novice teachers need to be willing to take risks, move beyond a single "methodology," and construct unique pedagogical approaches by applying excellent formally and informally acquired aural musicianship skills. Helping future educators acquire the skills and dispositions to approach teaching in these ways occurs throughout our undergraduate program and continues as the novices begin their professional preparation.

LAYING THE FOUNDATIONS FOR DIVERSE LEARNING APPROACHES IN MUSIC EDUCATION

The foundations for achieving our music education program's instructional goals are established in the freshman year through the course titled "Learning Approaches in Music Education," in which students explore the philosophical, psychological, sociological, and historical foundations of music education. Additionally, they also learn both clarinet and guitar aurally with a formal modeling methodology employing solfeggio used for the clarinet and an informal "listen-copy-play" approach employed for the guitar. By engaging in aural learning on both the clarinet and guitar, students develop the confidence in nontraditional learning processes. The final course assignment requires forming small ensembles with peers of their own choosing, selecting a popular cover song, and performing it for the class without using notation. To further push the students beyond their comfort zones, they cannot use their major instruments and must create the arrangements by working together, thus avoiding having one of the ensemble members predetermine how the arrangement will progress. This process requires the integration of informal skills, or what Bernstein (2000) would term horizontal discourses with already held formal or vertical knowledge. Furthermore, the assignment provides the foundation for other creative activities, such as making music videos and composing through technology, that the students will be required to do throughout the program to nurture their creative teaching skills.

Interestingly, it is through this process that we as faculty frequently discover our students' musical identities, which we might not be aware of through observations in formal teaching environments. Working on and presenting popular music seems to encourage a more lively and engaging performance style than what we see when students engage with and teach classical music. All too often, our music education majors seem to conceptualize teaching as a very formal and fairly rigid process, which initially prevents them from actually engaging the students. Discovering that many seem to have a more animated and playful personality when they work in popular genres might allow us to help them be comfortable in their teaching settings. Such findings echo the arguments of Rodriguez (2012), who advocates thinking more broadly about musicality among future music educators. In order to develop the skills and dispositions needed to teach popular music, one needs to examine the conceptions of musicality, which can change over time; develop a broader view of popular music in students' lives; and overcome the challenges of the changing roles of teachers and students.

We are still in the process of discovering how we can help our students apply their newly emerging musical identities and conceptions of musicality from the engagement in popular music to the formal teaching context. For instance, we encountered challenges in working with a particular student who seemed to have a quiet and reserved personality. He was extremely uncomfortable working with his classmates and unable to interact successfully in a formal classroom setting. However, in a popular music video project that he presented with his peer group, we were surprised to see that this student came alive and had a lot of fun. This suggests that providing music education students with diverse musical opportunities where they learn to express themselves in different ways is important for discovering latent musical skills, developing a teaching identity, and nurturing the confidence necessary to eventually teach in a lively manner that engages and motivates student learning. This also provides different ways for professors to learn more about students and design instructional experiences to best suit their specific educational needs.

By experiencing the power of informal and aural learning while working with popular music, our music education students begin to discover that they can teach in different ways than they were taught. By juxtaposing seemingly incompatible instructional approaches within the same course, students are challenged to think in new ways as they come to understand that pedagogies need not be rigid and that classical and popular music are not incompatible in educational settings. For example, student reflections indicate that they began to understand the power of aural learning. One student reported that such an approach "involves me generating the music internally before translating it into the act of playing, which to me requires more effort than simply reading sheet music to generate a song." They also discovered the power of aural learning by finding out how singing melodies with solfeggio reinforces learning. One student wrote about learning the clarinet: "One thing I was not expecting to find out was just how effective solfeggio really was in the learning process. The benefits are limitless, from students developing an ear for pitch relations, to internalizing a pulse. One realization I just came upon however is that by having students sing a phrase before playing it, you have effectively disguised an extra repetition of your material without anyone realizing it. You more or less fool them into practicing something twice."

Although students are initially skeptical of learning guitar informally with the "listen-copy-play" approach, once they experienced success, most echoed the feelings of this student: "My initial reaction to learning guitar using the informal approach was very negative because I had no idea how to learn the guitar without formal instructions of a teacher. I've been so used having all the information that is needed to learn anything. I actually had to take the initiative to learn. After a lot of work I've realized that it's easier for me to retain all the information. I think the informal approach to learning guitar, so far, has been successful and I've been enjoying learning it this way."

The final assignment requires students to move beyond their usual range of musical activities by cooperatively creating and performing arrangements of cover songs. Most of them enjoy this process. The reflection of this student typifies the overall reaction to this "final exam": "I really enjoyed this activity! It taught me a few things about teamwork, but best of all, it was a chance to escape from the 'UCLA Classical Music School' and play something enjoyable and contemporary. . . . Overall, I'd say this is a great ending project for us to do, because it lets us have fun playing a song we all want to play, and it forces us to use different means of figuring the song out."

Although our foundation course in music education is not a course in popular music, infusing aural learning and creating assignments that use popular music pedagogies are central to this course and can serve the purpose of preparing our students to teach popular music when needed in their future careers. Instead of focusing on popular music, the course requires our teacher candidates to think critically about becoming a teacher and nurture the dispositions necessary to generate innovative instructional approaches as they progress in their careers.

REINFORCING POPULAR MUSIC TEACHING PRACTICE THROUGH STUDENT-TEACHING EXPERIENCE

The UCLA music education program provides future music educators with the skills needed to function in traditional classes by having students teach beginning violin. The novices each assume responsibility for a single fourth-grade class, and all the children participate and present a demonstration of what they learned after fourteen lessons. This experience nurtures the skills necessary to manage large groups of students, to analyze and respond to teaching problems in real time, and to sequence instruction in a meaningful manner. Since the new curriculum was introduced in 2014, we now provide a juxtapositional student-teaching experience that incorporates traditional violin and popular guitar instruction in two elementary schools, respectively. Each class consisting of thirty to forty fourth- and fifth-grade students participates in the program over the course of ten weeks.

The violin curriculum that the novices use is carefully sequenced with clearly defined instructional objectives. The structure helps student teachers focus their students' attention on basic playing skills and classroom management. In contrast, novices teaching popular guitar in the first year of the program were given freedom to construct a creative curriculum using teaching materials of an established popular music program, Little Kids Rock (Wish et al. 2002). Although hoping to teach in an informal manner, the large size (up to forty students) of these classes, the limited physical space available for teaching, and the behavioral expectations of the classroom teacher required the student teachers to adopt a structured approach to instruction. Basic playing techniques through direct instruction and fundamental drills following the type of protocols in the violin class were employed because the relatively freer learning environment of the guitar class often resulted in noise and management issues. In Year Two, learning from the experience of Year One, we decided that a balance of formal and informal pedagogy was necessary, as illustrated by Cain (2013) and McPhail (2013). Therefore, student teachers received additional support through a sequential guitar instructional guide that provided curricular structure. Through this formal pedagogy, the new teachers were able to enhance the beginning students in developing playing techniques through a progressive approach. At the same time, due to the nature of popular music, informal pedagogy of learning by ear instead of reading notation was implemented.

Once the guitar teaching was on track, some attempts were made to transfer aspects of popular music pedagogies (e.g., aural learning, rhythmic movement, improvisation) to violin teaching. It was interesting to observe that at the final concert of the violin class, a student teacher experimented with bringing in elements of their popular music concert, which involved the audience (parents in attendance) as active participants. This student teacher invited the audience to participate by singing the songs that the violin students played. That caught us, the supervisors, by surprise. Yet it was a pleasant surprise because it livened up the concert and received nice responses from the parents. For the student teachers who moved beyond the comfort zone of their classically focused training, these "cross-fertilization" field experiences provided important insights that transform both novices and teacher educators alike into more flexible music educators. However, because such processes happened during the early stage of learning how to teach and due to the limited amount of classroom time available to the novice teachers, the results of such "cross-fertilization" seemed somewhat limited. Additional efforts will be required for faculty to learn how we can benefit from such mutually valuable interactions between popular and classical music learning experiences.

Feedback collected from the student teachers provides insights into their thoughts and feelings of such juxtapositional field experiences. The three-fold process of developing popular music pedagogy (Davis and Blair 2011) has been illustrated particularly well in this reflection: "I learned how to be a bit more loose with the students and open up with them. In the beginning I was very hesitant about moving and making myself look a little silly in front of the class; however, once I was able to break this barrier it really did become fun to be able to work with the students."

Moreover, it is clear that the student teachers believe in the value of popular music education: "Popular music in the form of guitar lessons is a great way to get students interested in music. Students love to be able to play their favorite songs and with instruments like guitars, which is very easily possible." This echoes the argument of Griffin (2010), who stresses the significance of connecting school music to the music of students' daily lives.

Student teachers were able to draw connections between teaching popular and classical music and found the commonality between teaching music of two different styles. This is a strong support for the advantages of juxtapositional pedagogy (Heuser 2014) as discussed previously:

"Teaching popular music yields an overall positive response from students because they can easily identify with the genre. That being said, it is the planning and how you engage students in learning that creates the interest, not solely the music itself. For this reason, I think teaching Western Classical Music, for example, would have been just as effective, but the course would need to be much longer to accommodate the technical demands."

They also felt the significance of their work, which has made a difference in children's lives. It is very rewarding for new teachers when they witness the positive impact that music education can have on students and discover how meaningful the teaching profession can be: "I learned by the end that I had more of a positive influence on my students than I thought, and I hope to continue to discover this in the future of my music-teaching career. I was happy to learn that I made a child feel special in his achievement with music and that I created a special place and experience for them in this guitar class that they may not have otherwise gotten the opportunity to have during the school year."

It became evident that beginning teachers will require more in-depth preparation to effectively teach popular music in schools. They need to question their understanding of what music teaching and learning are and put aside preconceived ideas of how a teacher should function in front of a class based on their own music education experiences. Classical and popular music are not just distinct musical styles but also different musical experiences requiring musicianship of a different nature. Classical music training stresses accuracy and prescribed techniques that are usually taught through formal pedagogy. Popular music allows more freedom in expression and creativity in performance and promotes aural skills, which are usually developed through informal learning. Experiencing music, particularly rhythm, through the ear and body—expressing musical understanding through the freedom to move and improvise—is the essence of the popular music experience. Although Green (2006) promotes informal learning practices in the music classroom, it appears that adding some formalized procedures is essential for beginning teachers in classrooms with large numbers of students, even when teaching popular music. This is especially important for new teachers who still need to acquire a wide range of instructional and management skills. Helping

novice educators learn how to balance popular methodologies and traditional classroom protocols in popular music teaching and understand
how to transition between these different approaches are essential parts
of a music teacher education program.

REFLECTIONS ON THE ROLE OF POPULAR
MUSIC IN MUSIC TEACHER EDUCATION

Preparing future music educators to teach in twenty-first-century schools
is a particularly daunting task. University mentors must provide an undergraduate environment that helps future music teachers prepare for the
current job market and provides experiences that will enable educators
to creatively redesign curricula as music programs evolve in response to
societal changes. The juxtapositional approach used at UCLA was created specifically to meet this challenge by pairing formal with informal
learning, notation-based instruction with aural music learning, and classical traditions with popular genres. By infusing popular music pedagogy
within the courses in this curriculum, music education majors develop
the knowledge, skills, and dispositions needed to explore ways to include
those genres in K–12 classrooms. The focus is on approaches rather than
exact methodologies so that educators develop the capacity to analyze the
music learning needs of school communities and use their broad musical
knowledge to design curricula that are responsive to the students in their
classrooms.

In most university settings, both music teacher educators and future
music teachers tend to have backgrounds based on classical rather than
popular music practices. Additionally, the school settings in which
preservice teaching experiences take place are most likely to offer traditional general music and large ensemble classes, where informal- and
constructivist-based instructional practices cannot be employed. Under-
standably, the master teachers who provide initial professional induction
are reluctant to introduce alternative instructional approaches that might
result in classroom management problems. Because the majority of school
music instruction takes place in such traditional settings, future educators need to develop the skills required to manage student behavior in
conventional classrooms. This in turn suggests that although informal

learning practices are central to popular music, newly emerging educators might need to modify those practices as they begin working in traditional classrooms. Mentors and novices will need to be flexible as they adapt popular music pedagogies for use in schools. The important issue will be developing ways to include popular music in the teacher education process so that novices begin to understand that using popular music can be a powerful means of motivating students and reaching young people who might not otherwise participate in music classes.

Emerging music teachers can be hesitant to try teaching in ways that differ from the practices through which they were taught. Children, however, are often very accepting of different musics and different approaches to instruction. For example, while planning an elementary general music lesson on Japanese culture, one of our students was asked why she did not include some significant traditional musical culture of Japan, such as Noh theater. Her response was that she was afraid that the children would find it too slow and too boring. After careful discussion, she designed an activity in which the children listened to the music of Noh theater and an upbeat Japanese pop song alternatively, and their task was to dance according to the music they heard. A paper mask that looked like one used by Noh theater performers was made for each child in the class, and he or she had to use it while dancing to the Noh theater music. The children enjoyed both genres and had no problem identifying and switching between the two very different styles of music. It seems that the beauty of slow music and movement of Noh theater can be highlighted when it is contrasted with exciting and rhythmic feeling of fast music and movement of the Japanese pop song. Thus we observe that traditional and popular music become increasingly engaging to students when presented in this fashion.

Furthermore, popular music can be used in the teacher preparation process to help faculty discover aspects of their student teachers' personalities that might be suppressed. As these new teachers establish their own teaching identities, many of them attempt to adopt the behaviors of their former teachers rather than meet the learning needs of their current students. Because the model of the very serious ensemble director has been so firmly imprinted into the consciousnesses of most music education majors, learning to bring amusement and joy into the teaching process in order to motivate students can be quite difficult. Providing future educators with opportunities to move away from classical music by creating cover songs with peers of their choosing offers a nonthreatening way for music education majors to explore and discover aspects of their own personalities that they might not be aware of. In our program, we have discovered that when asked to create a music video during a music technology class, students will often surprise us and reveal aspects of their personalities that are anything but the reserved presences they portray when trying to teach as music directors from the podium. Using the mediums of popular music and video, we are better able to understand our music education majors and encourage them to include aspects of their "popular musician identities" in their teaching personas.

Black is not black without white, and white is not white without black. Moreover, what makes black and white more interesting is combining the two in ways that become different shades of gray. Although both classical and popular music share many commonalities, the instructional practices central to each genre are often thought of and treated as opposites that must not be combined. Our work at UCLA suggests otherwise. When thoughtfully paired, both styles offer music teacher educators ways to understand the novice teachers who are studying to enter the profession and provide future music educators with ways to adapt to changing curricular needs in schools and motivate their own students.

▌CONCLUSION

The field of music education experiences constant calls for reform. In the mid-twentieth century, Mursell (1956) suggested that by focusing on large performing ensembles, school programs were ignoring the basic tenets of music education, and House (1958) encouraged deep examinations of the ways curricula might be constructed. The Tanglewood Declaration (Choate 1968) paved the way for jazz, world music, and popular genres to be taught in schools and encouraged attempts to develop comprehensive instructional approaches such as the Manhattanville Music Curriculum Project (Thomas 1970; Walker 1984) and other efforts to help music educators develop meaningful lessons for use in large ensembles (O'Toole 2003; Sindberg 2012). However, as both Kratus (2007) and Williams (2011) insist, learning in large ensembles might no longer appeal to modern students because of the ubiquitous presence of popular music throughout the culture. As the research cited in this chapter suggests, popular music is both a legitimate and an effective means for providing music instruction in academic settings. When it is thoughtfully employed, popular music can motivate students to participate in school programs and learn different styles of music.

Preparing future music educators to employ popular music in schools presents many challenges for university programs where the curriculum is usually based on twentieth-century instructional practices. This means that music teacher educators must develop ways to include popular music making experiences throughout undergraduate coursework and create avenues for student teachers to engage in teaching popular music during their preservice practice. Providing novice teachers with experience in popular music instruction will also challenge university faculty members who might not be fluent in popular music pedagogy. By working with novice educators, curricular change can be nurtured and encouraged throughout the entire teacher induction process, providing opportunities for growth to both new teachers and teacher educators alike.

▌ BIBLIOGRAPHY

Allsup, Randall E. "Creating an educational framework for popular music in public schools: Anticipating the second-wave." *Visions of Research in Music Education, 12* (2008): 1–12.

Cain, Tim. "'Passing it on': Beyond formal or informal pedagogies." *Music Education Research, 15* (2013): 74–91.

Campbell, Patricia S. "Musical meaning in children's cultures." In *International handbook of research in arts education,* edited by Liora Bresler, 881–97. Dordrecht, Netherlands: Springer, 2007.

———. "Of garage bands and song-getting: The musical development of young rock musicians." *Research Studies in Music Education, 4* (1995): 12–20.

Choate, Robert A. *Documentary report of the Tanglewood symposium.* Washington, DC: Music Educators National Conference, 1968.

Davis, Sharon G., and Deborah V. Blair. "Popular music in American teacher education: A glimpse into a secondary methods course." *International Journal of Music Education, 29* (2011): 124–40.

Dunbar-Hall, Peter, and Kathryn Wemyss. "The effects of the study of popular music on music education." *International Journal of Music Education, 36* (2000): 23–34.

Elpus, Kenneth. "Is it the music or is it selection bias? A nationwide analysis of music and non-music students' SAT scores." *Journal of Research in Music Education*, 63 (2013): 314–35.

Emerson, Greg. "The most diverse states in America." *Main Street*, February 11, 2011. Accessed July 1, 2016. https://www.mainstreet.com/slideshow/most-diverse-states -america.

Gay, Geneva. *Culturally responsive teaching: Theory, research, and practice*. New York: Teachers College Press, 2010.

Gay, Geneva, Jeannine E. Dingus, and Carolyn W. Jackson. "The presence and performance of teachers of color in the profession." Unpublished report prepared for the National Collaborative on Diversity in the Teaching Force, Washington, DC, 2003.

Green, Lucy. "Group cooperation, inclusion and disaffected pupils: Some responses to informal learning in the music classroom." Paper presented at the RIME Conference, Exeter, UK, 2007. *Music Education Research*, 10 (2008): 177–92.

———. *How popular musicians learn: A way ahead for music education*. Aldershot, UK: Ashgate, 2001.

———. "Music education, cultural capital, and social group identity." In *The cultural study of music: A critical introduction*, edited by Martin Clayton, Trevor Herbert, and Richard Middleton, 263–73. London: Routledge, 2003.

———. "Popular music education in and for itself, and for 'other' music: Current research in the classroom." *International Journal of Music Education*, 24 (2006): 101–18.

Griffin, Shelly M. "Inquiring into children's music experiences: Groundings in literature." *Update: Applications of Research in Music Education*, 28 (2010): 42–49.

Hebert, David G., and Patricia Shehan Campbell. "Rock music in American schools: Positions and practices since the 1960s." *International Journal of Music Education*, 1 (2000): 14–22.

Heuser, Frank. "Juxtapositional pedagogy as an organizing principle in university music education programs." In *Promising practices in 21st century music teacher education*, edited by Michelle Kaschub and Janice Smith, 107–24. New York: Oxford University Press, 2014.

House, Robert. "Curriculum construction in music education." In *Basic concepts in music education*, edited by Nelson B. Henry, 236. Chicago: University of Chicago Press, 1958.

Humphreys, Jere T. "Popular music in American schools: What history tells us about the present and the future." In *Bridging the gap: Popular music and music education*, edited by Carlos X. Rodriguez, 91–106. Reston, VA: MENC, the National Association for Music Education, 2004.

Kratus, John. "Centennial series: Music education at the tipping point." *Music Educators Journal*, 94 (2007): 42–48.

Ladson-Billings, Gloria. "New directions in multicultural education: Complexities, boundaries, and critical race theory." In *Handbook of research on multicultural education*, edited by James A. Banks and Cherry A. McGee Banks, 145–66. New York: MacMillan, 2004.

Lamont, Alexandra, and Karl Maton. "Unpopular music: Beliefs and behaviours towards music in education." In *Sociology and music education (SEMPRE studies in the psychology of music)*, edited by Ruth Wright, 63–80. Basingstoke: Ashgate, 2010.

Lind, Vicki, and Constance McKoy. *Culturally responsive teaching in music education: From understanding to application*. New York: Routledge, 2016.

McPhail, Graham. "The canon or the kids: Teachers and the recontextualisation of classical and popular music in the secondary school curriculum." *Research Studies in Music Education, 35* (2013): 7–20.

———. "Informal and formal knowledge: The curriculum conception of two rock graduates." *British Journal of Music Education, 30* (2013): 43–57.

Mursell, James. *Music education: Principles and programs*. New York: Silver Burdett, 1956.

O'Toole, Patricia. *Shaping sound musicians*. Chicago: GIA, 2003.

Rabkin, Nick, and Eric Christopher Hedberg. "Arts education in America: What the declines mean for arts participation. Based on the 2008 survey of public participation in the arts. Research report #52." *National Endowment for the Arts* (2011). http://files.eric.ed.gov/fulltext/ED516878.pdf.

Rodriguez, Carlos X. "Bringing it all back home: The case for popular music in the schools." *Bridging the Gap: Popular Music and Music Education. Reston, VA, MENC* (2004): 3–9.

———. "Popular music in a 21st century education." *Yearbook of the National Society for the Study of Education, 111*, no. 1 (2012): 133–45.

Sindberg, Laura. *Just good teaching: Comprehensive musicianship through performance in theory and practice*. Lanham, MD: Rowman & Littlefield, 2012.

Thomas, Ronald B. *MMCP synthesis: A structure for music education*. Bardonia, NY: Media Materials, 1970.

US Census Bureau. "Profile of general population and housing characteristics: 2010, Table DP-1." Accessed July 1, 2016. http://factfinder.census.gov/faces/tableservices/jsf/pages/productview.xhtml?src=bkmk.

Vavrus, Michael. *Transforming the multicultural education of teachers: Theory, research and practice*. New York: Teachers College Press, 2002.

Walker, Robert. "Innovation in the music classroom: II The Manhattanville Music Curriculum Project." *Psychology of Music, 12* (1984): 25–33.

Williams, David A. The elephant in the room. *Music Educators Journal, 98*, no. 1 (2011): 51–57.

———. "What are music educators doing and how well are they doing it?" *Music Educators Journal, 94*, no. 1 (2007): 18–23.

Wish, David, Chuck Speicher, Ryan Zellner, and Keith Hejna. *Music as a second language & the modern band movement*. Verona, NJ: Little Kids Rock, 2002.

Wright, Ruth. Kicking the habitus: Power, culture and pedagogy in the secondary school music curriculum. *Music Education Research, 10* (2008): 389–402.

CHAPTER 9

Opening the "Hermeneutic Window" in Popular Music Education

REBECCA RINSEMA

NORTHERN ARIZONA UNIVERSITY

I n recent decades, the acceptance of popular music (broadly conceived) as music worthy to be taught in formal music education
settings in the United States has increased. This is evidenced by the
variety of ways that students can engage with popular music in formal
settings at the elementary, middle, and high school levels that were
not available to students in the past. Such engagements include guitar
classes, rock bands, a cappella groups, show choirs, and hip hop groups,
among others.[1] Despite these advancements in popular music education,
many music educators and scholars argue that opportunities to engage
with popular music in formal settings are not yet accessible to enough
students. The large ensemble tradition, which includes band, choir, and
orchestra and stems from European music traditions, still largely dominates the music education landscape in the United States. A limited
number of schools in each state provide students the opportunity to be

---

1. Carlos Xavier Rodriguez, "Popular Music Ensembles," in *Oxford Handbook of Popular
Music*, vol. 1, ed. Gary E. McPherson and Graham F. Welch (Oxford: Oxford University Press, 2012), 878–89.

part of what has historically been the most recognized popular music ensemble: the rock band.

Recent advocates for popular music in schools have focused primarily on increasing opportunities for students to make or create popular music that are consistent with popular music making in the "real world," whether that is by way of composing, improvising, or performing. In this chapter, I introduce another way students can engage with popular music "on its own terms" within the classroom.[2] It is a way that focuses on what all students seem to already be doing with popular music—that is, listening to it.

I begin with a brief history of how popular music made its way into public schools in the United States in the middle of the twentieth century, highlighting possible reasons for the emphasis on popular music performance and production. Next, I provide an introduction and demonstration of an approach to teaching popular music that focuses on music listening experiences and music meaning, an approach that I have come to call hermeneutic exploration. Finally, I provide an argument for why hermeneutic exploration seems especially relevant for today's students and lay out some advantages and challenges this approach has for incorporation into the classroom.

BRIEF HISTORY

Since the 1960s and before, music educators have discussed broadening the types of music that students engage with in formal music education settings. Such discussions are motivated by the heavy emphasis on Western classical music and other traditional school musics stemming from the European tradition that music teachers and students witnessed and continue to witness in all levels of music education throughout the twentieth century and today.

The Tanglewood Symposium held in the Massachusetts Berkshires in 1967 is often cited as the first time this issue was addressed in a coordinated

---

2. By "on its own terms," I'm referring to popular music engagements that reflect "real world" practices and do not manipulate popular music to fit into the dominant large ensemble models.

way. The symposium brought together a wide swath of scholars and professionals in the areas of music, education, and business and resulted in the Tanglewood Declaration. The second statement of the declaration is most important for our purposes here, as it incites music educators to broaden music curricula to include popular music as well as avant-garde music, folk music, and music of other cultures: "*Tanglewood Declaration Statement #2*: Music of all periods, styles, forms, and cultures belongs in the curriculum. The musical repertory should be expanded to involve music of our time in its rich variety, including currently popular teenage music and avant-garde music, American folk music, and the music of other cultures."

While some aspects of the Tanglewood Declaration had profound and identifiable effects on the music education in the United States—for example, establishing music as a core part of the curriculum—the actions necessary to fulfill this statement have been slower to take effect, especially at the middle school and high school levels. This is partly due to a general suspicion in the music education profession of popular music's value and sophistication compared to Western classical music.

Even as late as 2004, articles addressing the implementation of more opportunities for students to engage with popular music in the schools were necessarily prefaced with arguments for the value of popular music. We see this in the edited volume *Bridging the Gap: Popular Music and Music Education* (the title alone evidencing the state of affairs in the early aughts), where scholars repeatedly respond to arguments against the incorporation of popular music and its practices in the schools.[3]

As music educators and researchers in the United States debated the value of popular music in schools during the first decade of the twenty-first century, music educators and researchers outside the United States developed popular music pedagogies for teaching and learning musicianship skills in popular music. For example, we have the Musical Futures project, inspired by Lucy Green's research, which established popular music education programs across the United Kingdom that simulate the

---

3. Wayne Bowman, "'Pop' Goes . . . ? Taking Popular Music Seriously," in *Bridging the Gap: Popular Music and Music Education*, ed. Carlos Xavier Rodriguez (Reston: Music Educators National Conference, 2004), 29–50.

learning processes of popular musicians outside formal settings. Another example includes the state-funded cultural centers in Sweden that have provided all students access to instruction in the performance of popular music for the past two decades.[4] Similar programs also exist in Finland. The systematic implementation of popular music and its practices within school music programs and/or within music schools that are freely accessible to the public has yet to be realized in the United States.

And yet, it is not as though popular music does not exist in the schools in the United States on a large scale. The existence of popular music is widespread in modified forms to accommodate its performance within large ensembles—for example, marching bands playing tunes from the Top 40, annual pops concerts, choirs performing raps, and so on.[5] This has been true for decades. However, those who advocate for popular music in schools are advocating, more specifically, for its *performance and production practices* to be taught within the schools, whether they be the forming of garage/rock bands, mixing and editing recordings, writing songs in the singer-songwriter tradition, writing rap or freestyling, and/or digitally composing and producing music.[6]

One of the main barriers to making popular music performance and production practices a widespread reality are the music teacher education programs themselves. Housed within college and university systems, they train preservice music teachers in skills associated with directing bands, choirs, and orchestras—very often to the exclusion of training them in skills associated with facilitating almost all other types of musical practices. As it currently stands, if music teachers want to incorporate popular music practices into their classrooms, by and large, they must seek the training to do so outside music teacher education programs.

4. Marja Heimonen, "Music and Arts Schools: Extra Curricular Music Education in Sweden: A Comparative Study," *Action, Criticism, and Theory for Music Education* 3, no. 2 (2004): 2–35.
5. A capella groups are the rare exception where a school music ensemble actually has become a phenomenon in the "real world" of popular music. School a capella groups now reflect performance and production practices of the "real world" of popular music.
6. Heidi Westerlund, "Garage Rock Bands: A Future Model for Developing Musical Expertise?," *International Journal of Music Education* 24, no. 2 (2006): 119–25; Robert H. Woody, "Popular Music in School: Remixing the Issues," *Music Educators Journal* 93, no. 4 (2007): 32–37, http://www.jstor.org/stable/4127131.

Recently, advocates for popular music practices in public schools have begun establishing programs that remedy the problem of the stalwart music teacher education and certification system in the United States. Such programs can be found both in and outside university/college degree programs. However, as of yet, they are few and far between.[7]

▌ THE PERFORMANCE AND PRODUCTION EMPHASIS

As I explained in the previous section, advocates for popular music have emphasized providing opportunities for students to perform and produce popular music in the schools, exerting considerably less effort on providing students opportunities to engage with popular music as listeners. I think it is worth exploring possible reasons for this emphasis. I do so in order to provide a fuller picture of how hermeneutic exploration, described in the next section, might be a novel contribution to the conversation about popular music education in the schools.

Since the 1930s, when the wind band and wind band competitions became a primary focus of music education in the public schools, the performance of music from the European tradition and the skills associated with it (e.g., reading music from a score) has dominated music education curricula in the United States. The wind band movement came just after a relatively brief period straddling the fin de siècle in which listening skills and singing skills were a dual focus. The focus on singing skills dates back to Lowell Mason's work on establishing music education in US public schools. The focus on listening skills stemmed from a much later coordinated effort on the part of music industry professionals, music educators, music critics, and music scholars to elevate the American public's taste and geopolitical status through the appreciation of Western classical music (which was really mostly German classical music).

---

7. To my knowledge, the following institutions have begun to adapt their preservice music educator programs to address this problem: University of South Florida, UCLA, Michigan State University, University of Michigan, California State University (Long Beach), and Ithaca College. Little Kids Rock is a nonprofit organization that introduces music teachers to the core instrumentation and genres of the "rock band" using a curriculum called Modern Band. The organization is primarily geared toward teachers in underserved school districts in the United States.

In the middle of the twentieth century, the coordinated effort to promote music appreciation began to die out, along with its influence on the music education curricula. However, a related philosophy also rooted in the German tradition began to dominate the field of music education. Based on the work of first-generation German American philosopher Suzanne Langer, Bennett Reimer posited the first comprehensive philosophy of music education in 1970: aesthetic music education focused on aesthetic experience as a means to educate the emotions.[8] For several decades, Reimer's was the one and only philosophy of music education taught in preservice music teacher education programs. This was the case despite its emphasis on procuring aesthetic experiences through listening to "good" music, which seemed to run counter to the music education curriculum of the time, a curriculum that was almost exclusively centered on performance skills. For decades (1978–97), Bennett Reimer was chair of the music education department at Northwestern University just north of Chicago and founded the Center for the Study of Education and Musical Experience, exerting significant influence on music education research and philosophy.

The 1990s saw a paradigm shift in the philosophy of music education when, in 1995, David Elliott introduced his praxialist philosophy of music education. Elliott described praxialism as a philosophy in opposition to Reimer's aestheticism in that it focused on music making instead of music listening. Elliott posited that music making was the best way to focus student cognition in a way that promoted or led to musical understanding, while music listening had limited potential, if any at all, for promoting or leading to musical understanding.[9] Reimer's philosophy, even though it also dealt with performance, was characterized as listening-centric. With praxialism's focus on music making, or "musicking"—that is, music as an embodied musical activity through which embodied cognition occurs— Elliott affirmed much of what was already happening in public schools: music performance. Reimer's response to Elliott's philosophy came in his 2003 edition of *A Philosophy of Music Education*, in which Reimer

---

8. Bennett Reimer, *A Philosophy of Music Education* (Englewood Cliffs: Prentice Hall, 1970).
9. David Elliott, *Music Matters: A New Philosophy of Music Education* (New York: Oxford University Press, 1995).

identified a number of areas of convergence between his aestheticism and Elliott's praxialism.[10]

Starting in the early 2000s, Thomas Regelski developed his own praxial philosophy of music education. He characterized the praxial/aesthetic divide in this way: "Praxial theory redresses the imbalance the aesthetic orthodoxy has promulgated on behalf of listening, and reasserts the importance of musical agency through various kinds of amateur performance."[11] Thus Regelski took a similar position to Elliott with respect to listening. Regelski further characterized Reimer's philosophy as a form of music education that is guided by music appreciation as aesthetic connoisseurship (MAAC), thereby linking Reimer's aestheticism to the music appreciation movement that was listening focused and had a short-lived influence on school music of the early twentieth century.

So in the late '90s and this first part of the twenty-first century, music educators and preservice music educators encountered a context in which both music education in practice and music education in theory/philosophy aligned to promote music performance over and against music listening.

It has been in this context that concerns pertaining to the relevance of formal music education and the gulf between formal music education and music in everyday life, with respect to both form and content, have surfaced in music education research.[12] Empirical studies resulting from such concerns have illuminated the stark contrast between the types of music that students engage with in school and the types of music that students engage with in everyday life (which are primarily variations on the theme of popular music). And naturally, in this particular performance-focused context, the way toward bridging the gap between formal music education and music in everyday life has been to promote the performance and

10. Bennett Reimer, *A Philosophy of Music Education: Advancing the Vision* (Upper Saddle River: Prentice Hall, 2003).
11. Thomas Regelski, "Praxial vs. Aesthetic Philosophies," in *Praxial Music Education: Reflections and Dialogues*, ed. David Elliott (Oxford: Oxford University Press, 2009), 234.
12. John Sloboda, "Emotion, Functionality and the Everyday Experience of Music: Where Does Music Education Fit?," *Music Education Research* 3, no. 2 (2001): 243–53; Kari Batt-Rawden and Tia DeNora, "Music and Informal Learning in Everyday Life," *Music Education Research* 7, no. 3 (2005): 289–304.

production of popular music.[13] After all, advocating for popular music performance in schools has proven to be a formidable enough task, let alone advocating for *listening* to popular music in schools in what seems to be a culture of music educators that value the performance and production of music over listening to music.

Before I go further, it is important to note that in pointing out this emphasis on the performance and production of music, I am not arguing that advocates for popular music in schools should abandon their efforts. Instead, I am arguing that we should at least consider how other ways of engaging with popular music in schools, particularly those related to listening, might be beneficial for students of today.

It is also worth learning from the practitioners and researchers from those countries that have established programs in the performance and production of popular music (United Kingdom, Sweden, Finland). In fact, some music researchers from those countries are beginning to question the heavy emphasis their programs place on performance, specifically that of rock band–type ensembles. For example, Eva Georgii-Hemming and Victor Kvarnhall have questioned the predominance of rock band ensembles in Sweden's public cultural centers and have explored the role music listening lessons could possibly play in deconstructing the problems of inequality (gender, racial, etc.) that are reproduced when popular music performance and production practices are enacted within the context of a music classroom.[14]

For these reasons, I am motivated to present an approach to popular music education that focuses on music listening experiences—not defined in terms of Reimer's aesthetic experiences or other modernist approaches to music as an object or "musical work." It is an approach that focuses on music listening while also sustaining the notion of music as a human activity. It thereby moves beyond the bounds of music appreciation of the nineteenth and twentieth centuries. It is an approach that works

---

13. Other ways to bridge this gap have been suggested beyond the performance and production of popular music. But here I am focusing on the response of advocates of popular music in the schools to the problem of incoherence between formal music education and music in everyday life.

14. Eva Georgii-Hemming and Victor Kvarnhall, "Music Listening and Matters of Equality in Music Education," *Svensk tidskrift för musikforskning/Swedish Journal of Music Research (STM–SJM)* 97 (2015): 27–44.

independently of the dominant performance and production approach to popular music education or one that could work alongside the dominant approach. In my mind, this is not an either/or scenario (or doesn't have to be); rather, it is both/and.

▌INTRODUCTION TO HERMENEUTIC EXPLORATION IN MUSIC

Traditionally, hermeneutics is defined as the branch of knowledge dealing with interpretations and meanings, specifically of Biblical and literary texts. Through the work of such phenomenologists as Dilthy, Heidegger, and Gadamer, among others, it has become widely accepted that hermeneutic texts come in a variety of forms; contemporary scholars interpret nonverbal communications, multimedia, and even social interactions as hermeneutic texts. Thus hermeneutics has been applied to a whole range of areas beyond theology and literary criticism. Such disciplines include sociology, psychology, media studies, international relations, and most importantly for our purposes, music studies.

Lawrence Kramer was one of the pioneers in applying hermeneutics to music. By his own account, he has devoted his career to music and meaning.[15] Four principles have guided his projects from early on and can be found in his book *Music as Cultural Practice* (1990). These principles can be summarized as follows: (1) works of music have discursive meanings, (2) music's discursive meanings are "definite enough to support critical interpretations,"[16] (3) music's discursive meanings should not be considered "extramusical"[17] but rather are integrally bound with the form and style of the music, and (4) music's discursive meanings are part of "the continuous production and reproduction of culture."[18] Music is thus an expressive act with meanings that can be interpreted through reflection.

In recognizing and reflecting on an expressive act, we empower the interpretive process; we open what Kramer calls "a hermeneutic window through which our interpretation can pass." Kramer's three hermeneutic

---

15. Lawrence Kramer, *Interpreting Music* (Berkeley: University of California Press, 2011).
16. Lawrence Kramer, *Music as Cultural Practice* (Berkeley: University of California Press, 1990), 1.
17. Ibid.
18. Ibid.

windows are as follows: (1) textual inclusions, (2) citational inclusions, and (3) structural tropes, which seem to be even more implicit citational inclusions.

When we engage in musical hermeneutics, we explore what music means in and through its contexts.

GUIDE TO HERMENEUTIC EXPLORATIONS
IN THE MUSIC CLASSROOM

Teacher Preparation

In order to get such explorations off the ground for teachers, I have adapted Kramer's three hermeneutic windows for teachers to use to guide their own preliminary hermeneutic explorations.

HERMENEUTIC WINDOW 1: MEDIA INTEGRATIONS. Media integrations are explicit links between music and other types of media—for example, when music and video are explicitly linked in a music video. Text is also considered a form of media here. Song lyrics, as well as something as simple as a song title, provide us a hermeneutic window through media integration. An album cover, which typically includes text and visual art, is another example of media integration.

This window invites us to explore how the music and the other media forms relate with one another explicitly. For example, in a music video, how do the structural moments of the music and the video relate? Do the narratives and themes expressed through the sounds of the music, the text (lyrics or other associated texts), and the visuals of a music video seem congruent or conflicting?

HERMENEUTIC WINDOW 2: ALLUSIONS. Allusions are more implicit than media integrations. The general definition of an allusion is helpful here. Allusions are expressions designed to call things to mind without mentioning them explicitly; they are an indirect or passing reference. This window "includes titles that link a work of music with a literary work, visual image, place, or historical moment; musical allusions to other compositions; allusions to texts through the quotation of associated music; allusions to the styles of other composers or of earlier periods; and the inclusion (or parody) of other characteristic styles not predominant in the work at hand."[19]

For an example of allusion, consider Jimi Hendrix's performance of the "Star-Spangled Banner," the US national anthem, at Woodstock in 1969. In the middle of the performance, Hendrix plays intervals and rhythms recognizable as "Taps," a simple melody often played at American military funerals. Through his allusion to "Taps," Hendrix links patriotism (or lack thereof?) to death and warfare.[20]

HERMENEUTIC WINDOW 3: ACTIONS. This last hermeneutic window concerns itself with the human activities and actions that are associated with the music. Using this window, we ask the following questions: When, where, and how do listeners engage with the music? Who are the listeners? When, where, and how is the music created? Who are the creators?

This window invites us to explore how the music might have different meanings when it is associated with different kinds of human activities and actions. For example, do the meanings differ when a person listens to a film soundtrack while studying as opposed to while watching the film, and if so, how do they change? Do musical meanings change when audiences have an influence on the sounds/creation of the music through social media or other technological means?

This third hermeneutic window is not included in Kramer's original discussion of the hermeneutic windows but seems consistent with his other work. He writes, "In its modern form, the problem of meaning arose with the development of European music as something to be listened to 'for itself' as art or entertainment rather than as something mixed in with social occasion . . . or ritual."[21]

Outside this modern context, music *is* mixed up with all kinds of activities, like social occasions and rituals, among a panoply of other individual activities. I don't see any reason for Kramer to disagree with this.

19. Ibid.
20. Hendrix's Woodstock performance of the "Star-Spangled Banner" is a rich site for hermeneutic exploration. Here I use it to simply convey the concept of allusion in music without going into the full complexities of the possible meanings of the use of "Taps" or the other allusions within this performance.
21. Lawrence Kramer, *Musical Meaning: Toward a Critical History* (Berkeley: University of California Press, 2002), 1.

It also seems that just like the interaction among music and other media can serve as a hermeneutic window, so the interaction between music and activity can serve as a hermeneutic window.

Teaching Demonstration

I will now demonstrate a hermeneutic exploration that I engage in with my students in a course titled "Cultural Study of Popular Music: 1970s to Present." I guide the students through an exploration of M.I.A.'s (Mathangi "Maya" Arulpragasam) song and music video "Paper Planes" (2009).[22] During the class session, I have the students first listen to the song without the video and then watch the music video with the music. I do this so that the class can first engage in a discussion about the sounds of the music and then discuss the music and the video in conjunction with each other.[23]

I divide the hermeneutic exploration of "Paper Planes" into four stages for the students: sounds, lyrics, contexts, and a fourth stage where we "bring it all into focus." This division has proven to be intuitive for the students, even though by the standards of the hermeneutic windows mentioned previously, contexts are technically explored during every stage of the exploration. I begin with sounds and move through each of the stages.

SOUNDS. After listening, the class engages in a discussion, during which I affirm the students when they recognize the characteristics of the song listed below. I fill in some of the details when the students are on to something good but seem to need a little extra guidance.

1. A female vocalist who sings with a somewhat arrogant swagger.
2. Children's voices for the chorus (or hook).

---

22. I have adapted this lesson plan from Andrew Berish's lecture notes for his course titled "Introduction to the Cultural Study of Popular Music," taught at the University of South Florida.
23. This is an introductory lesson intended for a group of roughly ninety undergraduate university students. For a smaller group of students, I would likely develop different types of activities for this same exploration. It is also important to note that in successive lessons, students choose their own music to interpret and participate in self- and/ or group-guided explorations.

3. Sounds recognizable as a cash register opening and a gun shooting. The pressing of the cash register button sounds the same as cocking a gun. Violence and money and/or capitalism are thus linked through sound effects.
4. Short, repeated (looped) accompaniment to the vocals and the downward melodic motive in the accompaniment on the scale degrees 1, 5, and 4.
5. Beats divided into fours, a strong emphasis on the first beat with a bass drum thud and then emphases on the backbeats (2 and 4) through a variety of "brighter" sounds, one being the *ding* of the cash register.
6. Repeated chord progression I, IV, V, I.
7. Simple melody sung by the vocalists primarily on the scale degrees 1, 3, 5, and 7. The melody hovers around the tonic (home) and the leading tone (strong inclination back to home). In this way, the melody is reminiscent of many children's songs. The simplistic nature of the melody and the use of the children's voices call to mind the idea of innocence.

Also during this stage of the exploration, I bring to the students' attention a musical allusion in the song. (Sometimes I ask the students if they have heard the accompaniment before in another song to see if they can recognize the allusion on their own.) I play for the students the beginning of a song by the '70s band the Clash called "Straight to Hell." Many of them immediately recognize it as the same looped accompaniment that they heard in "Paper Planes." The musical allusion leads us right into the second stage of the exploration, a discussion of the lyrics of the songs.

LYRICS. First, I have the students look at the lyrics of "Paper Planes." I have the students read the lyrics and talk in pairs about what they think is going on in them. When we come back together, the themes of "drugs and violence" are usually mentioned right away. I ask the students what lyrics tipped them off to these themes, and they commonly point to the lyric "get high like planes" or "some I murder, some I let go" and other references to guns. The perceptive students will recognize these themes as being linked through a unifying theme of illegal immigration, indicated by the second line, "If you catch me at the border, I got visas in my name."

At this point in the exploration, I return to the musical allusion to "Straight to Hell" and describe how this allusion further solidifies the theme of illegal immigration. "Straight to Hell" itself is a song about the treatment of immigrants in the United Kingdom in the '70s and '80s. Like many of the Clash's other songs, it is a protest song that calls out what the band members identify as social injustice. The link between the two songs, through musical allusion, not only solidifies the main theme of "Paper Planes" as immigration but also situates "Paper Planes" within a history of British protest music.

There are two other allusions that I draw the students' attention to in the lyrics stage of the exploration. The first lyrical allusion is in the lyrics of the hook, "All I wanna do is (bang, bang, bang, bang)," which, for some, recalls the '90s song "Rump Shaker" by Wreckx-n-Effect. The lyrics of the hook in "Rump Shaker" are "All I wanna do is zooma zoom zoom and a boom boom"—it is all about the male gaze. The music video of the song shows male rappers zooming in on female body parts with a VHS camcorder. One of the differences in how Wreckx-n-Effect deliver the lines of the hook and how they are delivered in "Paper Planes" is that there is an upward trajectory implied by the melody and rhythm in "Rump Shaker," whereas in "Paper Planes," there is a downward trajectory implied by the melody and rhythm. I address the possible importance of this a bit later in the last stage of the exploration.

A little more than halfway through the song, there is an important structural moment: much of the accompaniment drops out, and M.I.A. speaks instead of sings. She says, "Third-world democracy / Yeah, I got more records than the K.G.B. / So, uh, no funny business." Here lies another allusion. The lyrics "third-world democracy" reference a book about Sri Lanka, M.I.A.'s home country, published in 1979. I tell the students to hang on to that allusion while we (finally) watch the music video.

CONTEXTS. Before watching the video, I tell the students to watch out for ways in which the images seem congruent or in conflict with what we have said about the song so far. I also tell them to watch so that they can talk to their peers about what they see. After watching the video,

I have the students talk to each other in pairs about the images. When the class comes together to talk about the video, students typically make the following observation: rather than killing people, M.I.A. is selling sandwiches out of a food truck, buying ordinary items at a convenience store, and walking/dancing down an urban street with a group of other women. The students also notice the flying paper planes through the streets, which at the very end of the video appear to be descending on New York City. Finally, they notice the ominous-looking truck, which on the inside contains only the usual trappings of a food truck.

In this stage, I also ask the students to do a little of their own research on M.I.A.'s personal story. At this point, they already know that she is from Sri Lanka because of the reference to the book about her home country, but I tell them that there is more to her story that seems to be relevant here. After some quick Google searches, the students usually discover that her father fought with the Tamil Freedom Fighters, a terrorist group by the US government's assessment. In her success as a hip hop artist in the United States, her residency in the United Kingdom, and her father's link to the civil war in Sri Lanka, she is a bridge between the first world of the United States and the United Kingdom and the third world of Sri Lanka.

BRINGING IT INTO FOCUS. In this final stage, I ask the students to again consider how the lyrics, the music, and the video seem congruent or in conflict with each other. We discuss how one might expect to see drugs, guns, violence, and stealing in the video, but those are nowhere to be found. Instead, M.I.A. is selling sandwiches and buying things at a convenience store. We also discuss how the words and the music seem to be in conflict with each other. The simplistic nature of the melody and the children's voices seem to be in conflict with the weighty adult themes expressed in the lyrics. I tell them it is at the site of conflict where we can begin to understand one of the major meanings of the song and the video.

The song is about perceptions and realities of illegal immigrants. The perception is that they are violent, stealing addicts who lack any interest in contributing to society; these perceptions are conveyed through the lyrics. But according to the video, the reality is that the vast majority of illegal immigrants spend time doing things like selling sandwiches to "get by" and are ordinary consumers just like the majority of legal citizens. The paper planes and the children's voices can thus be read as symbolizing the fragility and innocence of illegal immigrants. Because illegal immigrants must negotiate society's negative perceptions of them and the reality that they have limited resources as "illegitimate" members of democratic societies, they live in an in between bridge space—a third-world democracy.

To further help the students bring all this into focus, I ask them in what sense M.I.A.'s arrogant swagger might also be have a bit of a mocking tone to it—that is, I ask them whom she might be mocking. At this point, I see many students' eyes light up. The references to drugs, murder, and stealing provide a caricature of the illegal immigrant from the perspective of legal citizens, who consider the illegal immigrant a "lethal poison to the system." She is mocking the irrational, petty fears of the members of the "ruling class" who are preoccupied with people stealing their money and threatening their "way of life."

The mockery seems to be intended to take back power and, at least momentarily, invert the power structure. I tell students that this aspect of "Paper Planes" places it squarely within the genre and history of hip hop music, the details of which we get to later in the course. If there is time left in the session, I help the students see another possible way the song engages with power structures. As a female rapper, M.I.A. places herself in a subjective role rather in the objective role, where women typically find themselves in hip hop culture. Thus the reference to "Rump Shaker" and the inversion of the melodic trajectory of the "all I wanna do . . ." hook could be read as an inversion of the traditional male/female power structure in hip hop culture. M.I.A. momentarily takes back power for women just as she momentarily takes back power for the illegal immigrant.

IN M.I.A.'S WORDS. In the case of "Paper Planes," we also have the artist's commentary on the circumstances under which she wrote the song. I conclude the exploration with her words:

[The sample of the gun reloading and then the cash register ringing] was a joke. I was having this stupid visa problem, and I didn't know what it was, aside from them thinking that I might fly a plane into the Trade Center—which is the only reason that they would put me through this. I actually recorded that in Brooklyn, in Bed-Stuy. I was thinking about living there, waking up every morning—it's such an African neighborhood. I was going to get patties at my local and just thinking that really the worst thing that anyone can say [to someone these days] is some shit like: "What I wanna do is come and get your money." People don't really feel like immigrants or refugees contribute to culture in any way. That they're just leeches that suck from whatever. So in the song I say all I wanna do is [sound of gun shooting and reloading, cash register opening] and take your money. I did it in sound effects. It's up to you how you want to interpret. America is so obsessed with money, I'm sure they'll get it.[24]

In general, the students seem to appreciate that our discussion concludes with a quote from M.I.A. that lays plain some aspects of the themes that came out through our exploration. However, I remind the students that as a cultural activity, music and its possible meanings always extend beyond what performers and composers say about them.

THE BOTH/AND PROPOSITION

A natural extension of a series of hermeneutic explorations, as described previously, would be for students to create their own music in the styles and genres that had been explored. The courses that I teach do not contain this particular extension; rather, I extend these explorations by developing students' English writing skills—I am required to do so in my particular context. But I see a great potential for students to move from (1) hermeneutic explorations of a few songs within a genre, to (2) compositional explorations of those same songs, to (3) a process where students compose, produce, or improvise their own songs within that same genre.

---

24. "Video+Interview: M.I.A., 'Jimmy,'" *Fader*, August 7, 2007, http://www.thefader .com/2007/08/07/video-interview-mia-jimmy.

An advantage of this three-step approach is related to the high degree that popular music, and especially hip hop, incorporates musical reference, context, and allusion. Hermeneutic exploration provides students the opportunity to identify those features as "tools" to be utilized in their compositional, production, and/or improvisational processes. That being said, I view hermeneutic explorations as having music educative value on their own terms, independent of the two subsequent steps. I mention this because the second and third steps have a more tangible product and thus a potential, at least in the area of music education, to be elevated as more worthwhile. Related to this, I think the challenge for the teacher would be changing hats from interpreter (and facilitator of interpretation) to composer (and facilitator of composition), a requirement for moving from the first to the second step of the approach. This challenge, however, is one that certainly could be overcome.

HERMENEUTIC EXPLORATION, TWENTY-FIRST-CENTURY STUDENTS, AND MUSIC LITERACY

Hermeneutic exploration seems particularly relevant for twenty-first-century students. Students today regularly encounter music in recorded (most often digital) forms. To demonstrate just how ubiquitous recorded music is, over and against live music, I'll share a teaching experience: Each semester, I assign a short essay where students must write about a time when they experienced live music. Each semester, I have one or more students come to me distraught because they cannot recall a time when they heard music live. I remind them that they are welcome to write about *any* live music, not just a formal concert where live music was performed, including, for example, a street busker. As I try to jog the students' memories with possible circumstances in which they might have heard live music, many of them begin to recall a time when they experienced such a thing.

What I aim to communicate with this teaching experience is the degree to which music is now inseparable from both media and technology. Digital recordings, the Internet, and iPhones are now more closely linked to students' conceptions of *what music is* than live performances. Media technologies afford student engagement with music in tandem with other activities and art forms such as visual media, video games, movies, commercials, and so on. And let us not forget how music is integrated into students' daily activities—like getting ready for the day, commuting to school, or playing some basketball. For many students, music accompanies virtually everything they do and experience, and those experiences are necessarily mediated.

Music and media are thus more entangled than they ever have been. Music education curricula that are relevant to today's students should take into account this entanglement. It should also take into account the media-saturated and information-saturated nature of students' lived experiences more generally. Students need the skills to navigate these experiences. In other words, students need skills that help them interpret the meanings of these experiences so that they can make choices about how to respond to them.

Hermeneutic exploration, with its focus on the ways music, activities, and media integrate to create meaning, is one way music educators can begin developing these kinds of skills within students. Hermeneutic exploration can be conceived of as a form of media education, the result of which is media literacy and, in this particular case, a new type of music literacy.

Traditionally, musical literacy has been associated with students' abilities to read music from a score and demonstrating those abilities by playing or singing the notes on the page. The type of musical literacy that I am proposing here would instead focus on students' abilities to read/interpret music and sound and as it relates to and is mediated through various technological, visual, and social contexts. Notation system(s) might sometimes play a part in building such abilities, but not always. There would also be a focus on students' abilities to *create* meaningful music and sound as it relates to and is mediated through various technological, visual, and social contexts. As such, this is a type of music literacy that bears similarities to and falls under the umbrella of media literacy, which at present concerns itself with students' abilities to analyze, evaluate, interpret, and create and participate in audio, visual, and print media forms. Furthermore, with this type of music literacy, the interpreting of music and the creation of music would go hand in hand, just as reading (interpreting) and writing (creating) go hand in hand in English language and literature classes.

ADVANTAGES AND CHALLENGES FOR HERMENEUTIC EXPLORATION

There are several advantages for incorporating hermeneutic explorations in the music classroom. I highlight three in the following sections.

Advantage 1

Hermeneutic exploration brings popular music into the classroom on its own terms rather than in terms of another tradition. It does so by recognizing popular music's performance and production practices as part of popular music's constellation of meanings. In this way, hermeneutic exploration and advocates of performance and production of popular music in the schools are in alignment. Both work to limit student encounters with popular music in terms of the large ensemble, European classical music–inspired tradition. I have already provided examples of this; however, I will remind the reader again: this is when members of a choir rap together and learn the rap from sheet music. Groups of people do not, or very rarely, rap simultaneously within the hip hop tradition.

Advantage 2

Hermeneutic exploration validates student engagements with music in their everyday lives as listeners. And since virtually all students already engage with music as listeners, this approach has the potential to reach a large number of students. A smaller number of students engage with music as producers or performers in their everyday lives. It is reasonable to think that those students who do not engage with music as producers or per-formers might more readily entertain exploring music in the classroom if at least some of the focus were on listening than if the focus were exclu-sively on production and performance.

Advantage 3

Teachers can facilitate hermeneutic explorations in settings where resources are limited. No expensive instruments, computer applications, or mixers must be purchased. Instead, a single computer, simple amplification system, and projection equipment are all that are necessary. Such technologies are available in most classrooms.

The advantages I have highlighted all relate to inclusion and validation of a wide variety of musical genres and experiences that exist outside of the classroom. Because of this, there is an ethical argument to be made for the incorporation of hermeneutic explorations into the music classroom—I will make that argument elsewhere. Of course, there are also challenges associated with incorporating something that seems to be new to the curriculum, especially in K–12 settings. I identify the two main challenges for incorporating musical hermeneutics into K–12 music classrooms and respond to them in the following sections.

Challenge 1

As it stands, preservice music educators are not taught to explore musical meanings or how to facilitate them in the ways outlined previously. A similar problem faces those who advocate for the performance and production of popular music in schools. But solving this problem for hermeneutic exploration seems a bit more manageable than solving it for the performance of popular music because many music departments already have the resources to begin tackling this problem. A number of musicologists and music theorists, and some performers, have developed hermeneutic skills in music in their graduate programs. Their expertise is a resource that could be tapped for developing within next generation of music educators skills associated with facilitating hermeneutic exploration.

Challenge 2

The content of the music and visual images in popular culture is sometimes questionable and/or offensive. This is a problem that has faced advocates for popular music in schools since the 1960s. Roger Scruton, Heidi Westerlund, and Randall Allsup explain the problem this way: popular music can be "violent, misogynistic, homophobic, and miseducative."[25] For some, these attributes render the music of youth culture unsuitable for the classroom. Westerlund and Allsup think otherwise, viewing criticality and agency as important features in the response to this problem: "Perhaps agency, the manner in which young people adapt, feel ownership, and

---

25. Roger Scruton, *Culture Counts: Faith and Feeling in a World Beseiged*, quoted by Allsup, Westerlund, and Sheih (2012), 462.

transform the cultural knowledge they construct and create both in and out of school, may provide a way of negotiating the tensions around youth culture."[26] Hermeneutic exploration, as I have described it, capitalizes on student agency and criticality in precisely this way.

CONCLUSION

Throughout this chapter, I have explored hermeneutic exploration as a way music educators can include popular music in curricula, thereby fulfilling one of the statements of the Tanglewood Declaration. I described how recent popular music advocates have focused primarily on providing students more opportunities to compose and perform popular music. To situate this focus, I provided a brief history of how the philosophy of music education began with an emphasis on music listening and music as an object and moved toward an emphasis on the creation of music and music as an activity. The hermeneutic exploration described subsequently is an example of how teachers can focus on music listening in the classroom while also upholding the praxialist definition of music as an activity. As such, hermeneutic explorations restore a degree of importance to music listening, bringing pedagogy in line with "real-world" practices of students who regularly listen to popular music several hours per day.

Without mention, I have also been exploring a way to fulfill a second statement of that declaration. This statement gets much less conversational traffic but, in my mind, is no less important. The first portion of the statement reads as follows: "Programs of teacher education must be expanded and improved to provide music teachers who are specially equipped to teach high school courses in the history and literature of music, courses in the humanities and related arts." Hermeneutic exploration is well suited to incorporation into the secondary education and encompasses history, literature, the humanities, and related arts. It does so in a way that takes into account the media-saturated lived experiences of the twenty-first-century

26. Randall Allsup, Heidi Westerlund, and Eric Shieh, "Youth Culture and Secondary Education," in *The Oxford Handbook of Music Education*, vol. 1, ed. Gary McPherson and Graham Welch (Oxford: Oxford University Press, 2012), 537.

student. Hermeneutic exploration, thus, has the potential to fulfill not one but two statements of the Tanglewood Declaration.

BIBLIOGRAPHY

Allsup, Randall, Heidi Westerlund, and Eric Shieh. "Youth Culture and Secondary Education." In *The Oxford Handbook of Music Education*, vol. 1, edited by Gary McPherson and Graham Welch, 460–75. Oxford: Oxford University, Press, 2012.

Batt-Rawden, Kari, and Tia DeNora. "Music and Informal Learning in Everyday Life." *Music Education Research* 7, no. 3 (2005): 289–304.

Bowman, Wayne. "'Pop' Goes . . . ? Taking Popular Music Seriously." In *Bridging the Gap: Popular Music and Music Education*, edited by Carlos Xavier Rodriguez, 29–50. Reston, VA: Music Educators National Conference, 2004.

Elliott, David. *Music Matters: A New Philosophy of Music Education*. New York: Oxford University Press, 1995.

Georgii-Hemming, Eva, and Victor Kvarnhall. "Music Listening and Matters of Equality in Music Education." *Svensk tidskrift för musikforskning/Swedish Journal of Music Research (STM–SJM)* 97 (2015): 27–44.

Heimonen, Marja. "Music and Arts Schools: Extra Curricular Music Education in Sweden: A Comparative Study." *Action, Criticism, and Theory for Music Education* 3, no. 2 (2004): 2–35.

Kramer, Lawrence. *Interpreting Music*. Berkeley: University of California Press, 2011.

———. *Musical Meaning: Toward a Critical History*. Berkeley: University of California Press, 2002.

M.I.A. Interview by Alex Wagner. *Fader*, August 7, 2007. http://www.thefader.com/2007/08/07/video-interview-mia-jimmy.

Regelski, Thomas. "Praxial vs. Aesthetic Philosophies." In *Praxial Music Education: Reflections and Dialogues*, edited by David Elliott, 219–47. Oxford: Oxford University Press, 2009.

Reimer, Bennett. *A Philosophy of Music Education*. Englewood Cliffs, NJ: Prentice Hall, 1970.

———. *A Philosophy of Music Education: Advancing the Vision*. Upper Saddle River, NJ: Prentice Hall, 2003.

Rodriguez, Carlos Xavier. "Popular Music Ensembles." In *Oxford Handbook of Popular Music*, vol. 1, edited by Gary E. McPherson and Graham F. Welch, 878–89. Oxford: Oxford University Press, 2012.

Scruton, Roger. *Culture Counts: Faith and Reason in a World Besieged*. New York: Encounter Books, 2007.

Sloboda, John. "Emotion, Functionality and the Everyday Experience of Music: Where Does Music Education Fit?" *Music Education Research* 3, no. 2 (2001): 243–53.

Westerlund, Heidi. "Garage Rock Bands: A Future Model for Developing Musical Expertise?" *International Journal of Music Education* 24, no. 2 (2006): 119–25.

Woody, Robert H. "Popular Music in School: Remixing the Issues." *Music Educators Journal* 93, no. 4 (2007): 32–37.

CHAPTER 10

Popular Music Pedagogy

A LOOK INTO CURRICULAR POSSIBILITIES

DEBORAH VANDERLINDE WITH VIVIAN ELLSWORTH, HALLA
HILBORN, ALLISON VERNON, AND ALEXANDER WALKER

OAKLAND UNIVERSITY

T he aim of this chapter is to share pedagogical possibilities for popular music curriculum in middle and high school music classrooms. To this end, I will share my own ideas and those of my students drawn from an undergraduate course at Oakland University—"Teaching Music in the Twenty-First Century II"—that focuses on digitally based projects and popular music. This class comes at the end of the methods coursework that includes elementary, choral, and instrumental methods as well as music for learners with exceptionalities.

CONTEXT OF THE CLASSROOM

All the methods courses in our program (as well as classes in educational psychology and music education philosophy) share a constructivist approach.[1] This student-centered approach that values musical problem solving, learner agency and autonomy, and hands-on mindful collaborative experiences is central to the ways we interact with students and how we prepare preservice teachers to interact with their future students. This

---

1. Citations in this chapter are intentionally drawn from readings used in our methods courses.

section does not aim to be an exhaustive description of constructivism; however, it will provide a brief overview of constructivism, highlighting characteristics that will inform the examples provided in the following sections.

Constructivism

Constructivism, a vision of how people learn, values the notion that people must construct their own understanding of their world and their role in it. Not a method but rather a theoretical frame for human learning and interaction (Fosnot, 2005), constructivists posit that learning must be experiential with meaning making as a synergistic interplay of thinking, doing, and social interaction in holistic contexts: "The theory describes knowledge not as truths to be transmitted or discovered, but as emergent, developmental, nonobjective, viable constructed explanations by humans engaged in meaning-making in cultural and social communities of discourse . . . A constructivist view of learning suggests an approach to teaching that gives learners the opportunity for concrete, contextually meaningful experience through which they can search for patterns; raise questions; and model, interpret, and defend strategies and ideas" (p. ix).

A Vygotskian scholar, Smidt (2009) suggests that "we are all the sum total of our experiences and our interactions with the people and the ideas and the cultural tools we encounter throughout our lives" (p. 10) and that "for Vygotsky, all learning was social" (p. 14): "He meant social in the sense that ideas and concepts are often mediated by more experienced learners; that learning takes place in a context which may well be social in origin; that learning builds on previous learning; and that learning takes place primarily through cultural and psychological tools" (p. 15).

Bruner (1966; Wood, Bruner, & Ross, 1976) is credited with coining the term "scaffolding"—that is, the many ways learners are supported in their learning by more experienced others.

Agency

Learners of all ages and in every capacity must have a sense of agency—that is, the "ability to make things happen in [their] immediate environment" (Smidt, 2009, p. 2). Fostering agency in the classroom might occur when a learner senses that her active engagement and "musical say" (Davis, 2011) will inform her own—and contribute to her peers'—process and outcomes. Wiggins (2015, 2016) writes extensively regarding musical agency, or the ways that learner agency plays out in music classrooms or communities: "Learning requires initiative and intent on the part of the learner. To be willing and able to enter a learning situation, *learners must have a sense of personal agency*—that is, a belief in themselves, a sense that they have the capacity to engage, initiate and intentionally influence their life circumstances (Bandura, 2006) . . . They must believe their ideas will be valued" (Wiggins, 2015, p. 22).

It is a process to learn to support students' agency. Most of us have experienced more directed and less collaborative styles of teaching and learning in our own schooling. For this course, an explicit study of student-centered practices in our projects included the unpacking of constructivist ideas so that we can better reflect, design, and assess our own progress as constructivist preservice teachers and teacher educators. We affirm this goal: "When the classroom environment in which students spend so much of their day is organized so that student-to-student interaction is encouraged, cooperation is valued, assignments and materials are interdisciplinary, and students' freedom to chase their own ideas is abundant, students are more likely to take risks and approach assignments with a willingness to accept challenges to their current understandings. Such teacher role models and environmental conditions *honor students as emerging thinkers*" (Brooks & Brooks, 1993/1999, p. 10; emphasis added).

Application of Theory to Practice

For the purposes of this chapter, I will focus on key characteristics of constructivism that were salient in this course and that are demonstrated in the examples that follow.

Opportunities for choice that support learners' interests will enable students to connect to and creatively invest in a new learning experience. Agency is fostered when students can choose their topic and their means of musical expression within a framework of curricular goals. Student-centered schooling takes "its cues from young people's interests, concerns, and questions" (Zemelman, Daniels, & Hyde, 2005, p. 12). The nature of this dual approach—developing a rigorous curriculum while creating a space for choice and expression—was often discussed throughout the university course and supported by Brooks (2002) and Zemelman, Daniels, and Hyde (2005). They challenged us to find essential questions that could support developing physical skills, conceptual understanding, and the taking of risks and promote collaborative and creative thinking: "Knowledge depends on questions, and the process of coming to 'really know' something entails revisiting the essential concept in new settings, under new conditions, and with the parameters often enough to challenge one's own thinking" (Brooks, 2002, p. 20). In considering the design of lesson plans or units, we revisit musical dimensions through new parameters of digital projects and popular musics (here, for their expression in a school setting) that challenge learners to stretch musical boundaries or skillsets in new ways—to "help students connect their current ideas with new ones" (p. xi). Opportunities for choice in these contexts allow learners to take the lead as the "more knowledgeable other" and to find ways to make "acute discriminations and broad connections" in a new context (Reimer, 2003).

Students will enter and make meaning socially through their shared experiences and individually through the lens of their unique prior experiences and worldviews: "Our prior life experiences frames our view of the world and, in many ways, determines how we will choose to act and react in new experiences. This provides the basis for multiple perspective—that each of us understands the world a bit differently because we interpret new experience through the frame of our prior experience" (Wiggins, 2015, p. 8). As teachers honor students' prior experiences and create opportunities for students to expand and develop musical interests and ideas, a sense of agency and musical independence can thrive.

A constructivist vision of learning honors the notion that "all knowledge is socially constructed. Social interaction is an essential ingredient of the learning process," with scaffolding at the core of peer and/or teacher interaction (Wiggins, 2015, p. 14). Collaborative projects allow students to better understand the contributions of others and might enhance the sense of musical community in the classroom, much like the ensemble experience: "In a genuinely democratic classroom, children learn to negotiate conflicts so they work together more effectively and appreciate one another's differences. They learn that they are part of a larger community, that they can gain from it, and that they must also sometimes give to it" (Zemelman, Daniels, & Hyde, 2005, p. 20).

Because learning is socially and individually constructed, students must have opportunities to construct their own understanding. Characteristics of these experiences include the following:

- People are best able to construct understanding when new information is presented in a holistic context—one that enables them to understand how parts connect to the whole.
- Learners need to understand the goals of the experience and have sufficient grounding in the processes and understandings necessary to achieve the goals.
- The ideal learning/teaching experience enables learners to engage in the solution of authentic problems, rooted in authentic contexts. Good problems are structured in ways that enable learners to find and seek solutions to new problems. Problems for learning should be designed in ways that will provide multiple points of entry and invite multiple solutions—and the various solutions should be considered and valued for their uniqueness, creativity, and originality. (Wiggins, 2015, p. 25)

The notion of musical problem solving is at the core of our pedagogical approach in this course and across the coursework in our teacher education program. Preservice teachers experience musical problem solving in their university methods courses and are expected to design musical problems for their future students. Rather than interacting with a teacher for what to do or how to be musical, learners themselves engage with musical ideas and processes that will develop their own musicianship (Blair, 2009).

CURRICULAR POSSIBILITIES

The ideas noted previously are central to the course "Teaching Music in the Twenty-First Century II." Together, the students and I focus on innovative practice for middle and high school musicians within digital and popular music contexts. The preservice teachers are challenged to create a space where their future music students can discover ideas and stretch boundaries with a freedom to pursue musical projects with a wide range of choices yet still provide the groundwork and scaffolding that will enable student success. Preservice teachers are encouraged to explore big ideas and essential questions while getting to the details needed to support specific musical problems and contexts. We reconsider musical experiences in contexts that are meaningful and relevant with pedagogical goals that foster a collaborative social environment.

Brooks's (2002) *Schooling for Life: Reclaiming the Essence of Learning* urges students to question the nature of learner choice/agency within a curricular frame, with goals that include immediate skills and understandings but that might reach beyond to more essential questions. Brooks suggests, "A good education . . . is a system of opportunities for students through which they build the foundational skills of an intellectual, ethical, aesthetic, and physically fit life that they can both use in the present day . . . and transfer to their future" (p. 13).

As with most methods classes, exemplary models are presented with full classroom engagement followed by discussion to unpack the pedagogical strategies demonstrated explicitly and implicitly. Instruction is proposed as a bridge that connects previous experiences with new experiences, allowing students to function successfully within their "Zones of Proximal Development" (Vygotsky, 1978), where students perform—with support—on the outer boundaries of felt zones of competence and confidence. Dewey (1916) offers insight to this delicate instructional balance: "A large part of the art of instruction lies in making the difficulty of new problems large enough to challenge thought, and small enough so that, in addition to the confusion naturally attending the novel elements, there shall be luminous familiar spots from which helpful suggestions may spring" (p. 157).

As noted previously, this course aims to explore ways to study popular music for its own value and to pursue a pedagogy that values a fluid blend of formal and informal ways of learning and expressing musical ideas. To support these ideas and to explore models, the preservice teachers consider the work of Allsup (2011), Davis (2005), Green (2005), Ruthmann (2007), and Williams (2014) to broaden their pedagogical landscape.

Students have also had the opportunity to attend a Little Kids Rock[2] workshop as part of another course.

Thus the preservice teachers are required to design extended general music units for middle or high school students that include the musical processes of listening, performing, and creating while learning themselves how to balance learner choice with musical outcomes. The course provides a series of projects that inherently foster a continuum of choice within a curricular frame. Class projects include creating

- a "musical journey" in any digital format to share their musical histories;
- a group iPad cover of a popular song;
- a GarageBand recording and composition project;
- a lesson to scaffold any part of producing a cover or GarageBand project;
- a flipped lesson[3] to support any of the lessons already created;[4]
- a popular music unit that can draw on a wide range of musical ideas and skills (for example, riffs and hooks, sampling, mash-ups, style, covers, dance genres, harmony/chords, genre crossing/blending, multimedia, YouTube artists [Postmodern Jukebox, Boyce Avenue, Pomplamoose], and so on); and[5]
- an interdisciplinary unit that includes another arts discipline (students read Barrett, 2001; Wiggins, 2001; Wiggins, 2015).

The following curricular examples demonstrate some of these ideas. The characteristics of constructivism noted earlier are evident here in the

---

2. See http://www.littlekidsrock.org/.
3. For more information on flipped classrooms, see https://www.knewton.com/infographics/flipped-classroom/, http://www.thedailyriff.com/articles/how-the-flipped-classroom-is-radically-transforming-learning-536.php, and http://www.edutopia.org/blog/flipped-classroom-best-practices-andrew-miller.
4. In a flipped lesson, the teacher-provided information takes place at home (e.g., via video presentation or narrated PowerPoint), and the activity that would traditionally be considered homework is practiced or completed collaboratively in class.
5. Another interesting approach is to explore artists that have longevity in popular music with questions about cultural, historical, and musical trends that have shaped their musical journeys. Simon and Garfunkel's own versions of *Hazy Shade of Winter* from 1967 and 2003 provide a starting point for this discussion, while Paul Simon's *Wristband* (2016) offers a more current example.

musical problem solving, opportunities for choice and learner autonomy within a scaffolded pedagogical environment, collaborative and
creative thinking, and experiential learning within a space that honors
multiple perspectives and entry points. We hope these examples will
offer ideas for curricular possibilities for the unique students in your
own classrooms.

"Mas que Nada": Listening, Performing, and
Creating in a Popular Music Context
I created this set of lessons as a workshop for International Society for
Music Education (ISME; VanderLinde, 2014) using "Mas que Nada"
by Jorge Ben Jor (http://jorgebenjor.com.br/novo/) and popularized by
Sergio Mendes (https://www.youtube.com/watch?v=qK631u3d_n8). We
begin with the Mendes version because it is closer to the sound world of
popular music and provides a closer schema connection for young learners
(Dewey's "luminous familiar spot," 1916). The lessons begin with melodic
contour in order to scaffold students as they figure out the differences
between the singable verse and chorus, followed by a form chart that
organizes the verses, choruses, intro, bridge, and coda. A "what else do you
hear?" chart (Wiggins, 2015, pp. 173–181) extends the musical problem
so that students can learn to listen and collaboratively describe (in their
own words, providing for multiple entry points) what they hear and how
it informs the form (see Figure 1).

   Students then continue listening to other examples of this piece:
the original by Jorge Ben Jor (http://jorgebenjor.com.br/novo/), followed by covers by Al Jarreau (https://www.youtube.com/watch?v=5
-gyskWUty4) and Dizzy Gillespie (https://www.youtube.com/watch
?v=zeOt8WzGEAU), all of whom bring their own musical strengths
to their renditions and adjust the form slightly—which, of course,
students are asked to "figure out," along with the requisite "what
else do you hear?" The final listening example is performed again by
Sergio Mendes some forty years later, this time joined by the Black
Eyed Peas (https://www.youtube.com/watch?v=Tfa6fRjPlUE). The
form is doubled, and students are asked to figure out the expanded
form and describe what the Black Eyed Peas contribute to this version
(see Figure 2).

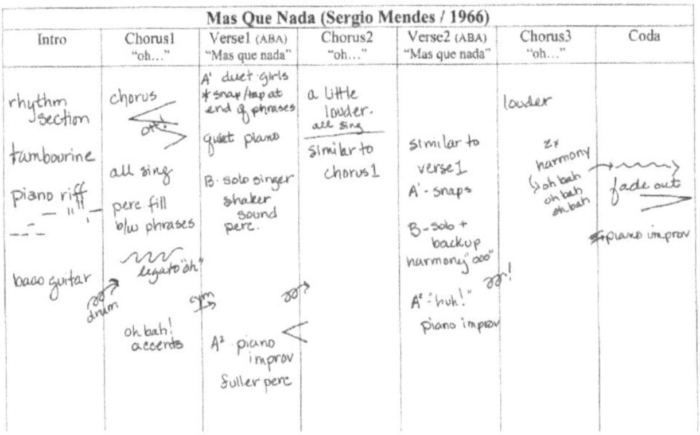

FIGURE 1. Form chart for "Mas que Nada," performed by Sergio Mendes.
Completed chart demonstrates typical student comments.

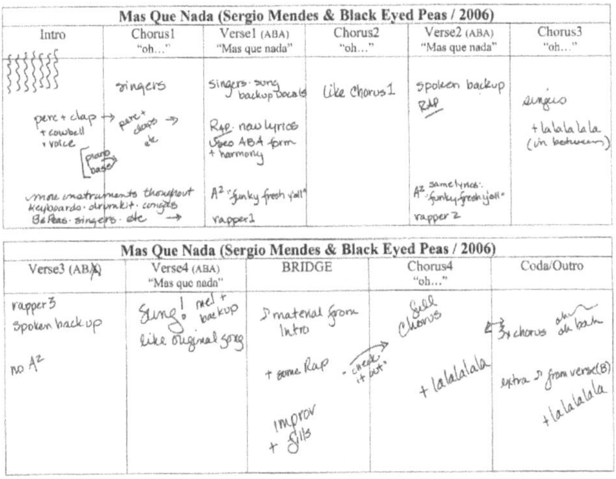

FIGURE 2. Form chart for "Mas que Nada," performed by Sergio Mendes and the Black Eyed Peas.

By now, the students have moved from an initial inquiry of melody and form to include a wide array of musical dimensions (see Figure 3). Finally,[6] students are invited to use the ideas of these composers, arrangers, and performers—and to draw on their own musical strengths—to work collaboratively to create a cover of "Mas que Nada."[7] An alternative assignment could offer students the opportunity to create

---

6. These musical dimension diagrams are used with the permission of Wiggins (2015).
7. See example online at https://youtu.be/CypybdclX4k.

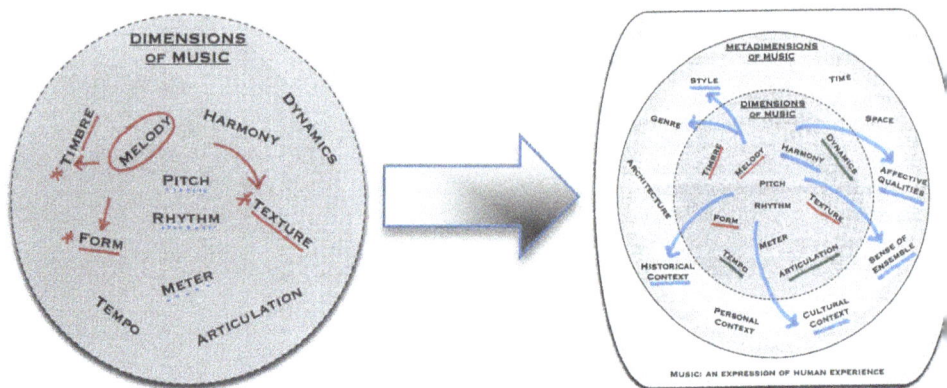

FIGURE 3. Musical dimensions from the initial inquiry to multiple music ideas.

a digital cover in GarageBand or to use a riff from one of the versions as a sampling project.[8]

Allison Vernon: Scaffolding a Cover Project

Making covers is a popular project in many music courses, but I (Allison) wondered how we could scaffold that experience for students who have little or no knowledge of the musical concepts behind a song. Starting with the goal in mind (Wiggins & McTighe, 2005), I knew I wanted students to be at a level of competence with the technology and the musical concepts that would enable them to create their own covers or even record an original composition. The final project at the end of this unit would give the students ample opportunities to make creative decisions for themselves and to choose what medium they would want to use.

In an ideal classroom, each student would have access to her or his own iPad or keyboard. After sufficient experience with melody and an introduction to the concept of chords, the students would listen to a piece of music that has limited chords but with changes that are easy to hear. Sam Smith's song "Stay with Me" (https://www.youtube.com/watch?v=pB-5XG-DbAA) meets these qualifications and is a popular song that most students would know.

In the first lesson, the students' goal is to create their own lead sheet. They would work in pairs with a copy of the lyrics and notate where they

---

8. See example online at https://youtu.be/4nhhVIuX7rs.

hear chord changes. Then, using the smart keyboard function in GarageBand, they will figure out which chords fit into each spot. The smart keyboard function is ideal because the chords are easy to hear under the keyboard setting and there are limited options, so the students still must do some listening work to figure out which chord fits where, but there are not so many options that they will feel overwhelmed.

After completing the lead sheets, the students will have an opportunity to create their own cover of "Stay with Me," which would have been used previously to discuss melody; it has an easily singable range and only uses notes in the diatonic scale. For this part of the unit, their choices are limited to specific musical apps on the iPad. GarageBand is highly recommended for ease of use, but other apps[9] such as WI Orchestra, Progression, Chordica, and so on can be used to create the harmony section. Students should also employ percussion apps and their voices to add the percussion and melody.[10]

The final aspect of the unit comes with many more opportunities for choice, supporting learner agency as students develop skills and become more confident in their abilities. The goal of the final project is to allow students some creative license with a musical composition (either a cover or their own composition) and then record their piece into GarageBand.

To efficiently scaffold their experience with recording into Garage-Band, I will use a flipped lesson. Students will watch a short presentation on how to edit the chords in smart instruments and then record a chord progression as homework and upload it to the class SoundCloud page (http://soundcloud.com).

Once the students have some actual experience recording in Garage-Band, they are prepared to create their own recording. I like this project because students who have experience singing or playing an instrument can use those skills, but students who have little or no experience with either of those mediums can use the iPads to create a composition that is equally meaningful and relevant.[11] This unit allows students to express

---

9. WI Orchestra, https://itunes.apple.com/us/app/wi-orchestra/id434371426?mt=8. Progression, https://itunes.apple.com/us/app/progression/id424281020?mt=8. Chordica, https://itunes.apple.com/us/app/chordica/id302869050?mt=8.
10. This is an example of what that could look like: https://youtu.be/Qcr5j94PlLM.
11. This is a recording that I created as an example: https://youtu.be/pDHi8tDbysI.

their own musical voice within guided parameters with a final goal that is achievable with the appropriate scaffolding by the educator.

Alexander Walker: Popular Music That Explores Social Justice
In this unit, students will explore several examples of popular music that reflect a particular social justice stance. The students uncover and discuss uniquely *musical* features of the music and examine the historical/cultural situation in which the music arose. Ultimately, they will determine how the two are connected. The unit starts out using the iconic American musical artifact "We Shall Overcome." It begins with the class listening several times to the original Pete Seeger recording (https://www.youtube.com/watch?v=RJUkOLGLgwg), discussing initial reactions, and constructing a form diagram (verse, chorus, etc.).

Next, the students will read a brief Library of Congress article (see Appendix A) about the song and its unique place in American history, specifically during the civil rights movement. Students will also watch a video of Joan Baez singing the song at the 1963 march on Washington (https://www.youtube.com/watch?v=V3VhgJC2M1Y). Discussion should address the musical, lyrical, and other features of the song that made it so popular, viewed through the lens of its cultural context.

To engage interactive meaning making, the students will then perform an in-class cover of the song. Students can use iPads, voices, or any instruments available, including drums or body percussion. The objective is to give students the choice—with our resources, what can/should we use?

Finally, the group watches or listens to the Diana Ross performance of the piece (https://www.youtube.com/watch?v=2yx89KLkiIQ); students can listen while filling out a Venn diagram with similarities and differences. Class discussion can address essential questions: What is different here? What are the gains and the losses in this version? Does it change the attitude or message? How do the musical choices affect that?

In the next lesson, students will discover how contemporary popular music can reflect social issues and present them in a compelling way. This lesson utilizes the song "Americano" from Lady Gaga's 2011

Grammy-nominated album *Born This Way* (https://www.youtube.com/watch?v=fHGKG9dyTKI).

After listening once as a class to garner initial reactions, the students use a "workalong" sheet and continue through the rest of the lesson individually using iPods, computers, or phones/headphones to listen to the music as they complete the worksheet (see Appendix A). Students are guided to identify and describe their initial reaction to the song, construct a basic form diagram, and analyze the song's lyrics (including translations), paying attention to social issues presented. It also includes contemporary musicological research; for example, they will read a portion of an interview with the song's producer to learn that the song was written in the days after Proposition 8 was repealed in California, which brings deeper meaning to (and explains the genesis of) many of the song's lyrics (https://play.google.com).

Students need time for class discussion to discover each other's opinions on the song and, more important, how everyone thinks the music and the social message work together—that is, what was the song's purpose and does it achieve it? The teacher can mention some critical reception of the song: good beat/production, bold house/mariachi fusion, bad Spanish accent, and mediocre lyrics.

The final lesson of the unit is where the real opportunities for choice occur. The previous lessons explored musics that reflected a social stance, and students examined *how* exactly the music achieved that end. The logical assessment here, then, is to have students now employ those tools via a composition project. In small groups, students will compose a song in a popular style that clearly articulates a social position.

I envision this beginning by having the whole class brainstorm ideas. Students must first compose the song with lyrics, melody, and chords. The teacher provides scaffolding by reviewing the musical product thus far with the students, and then students can extend their musical ideas by producing the song in GarageBand. The song must be sung, but students can use autotune or vocal effects (especially if they are making a statement of some sort).

If the students hits a compositional "roadblock," there are myriad examples of popular music that articulate a social position: "Blowin' in the Wind" by Bob Dylan; "Ohio" by Crosby, Stills, Nash, and Young;

"A Change Is Gonna Come" by Sam Cooke; "Strange Fruit" sung by Billie Holiday; "The Fear" by Lily Allen (explicit); "Primadonna Girl" by Marina & the Diamonds; "Royals" by Lorde; "Concrete Jungle" by Bob Marley; and "War" by Edwin Starr.

The teacher can offer some of these pieces, asking, "What is their message? What musical ideas do the artists use to achieve their message? Is it the style? Production? Lyrical constructs (simile, metaphor, etc.)?" Studying an exceptional musical construction in one or more of these songs could also be an intermediary lesson, revealing a compositional technique to the students.

A sharing of songs in class, on a school YouTube channel, or school radio station (with student permission) would be an appropriate culminating event.

Halla Hilborn: Music in Advertising

I (Halla) would begin the discussion of this topic by asking students to consider why music is so prevalent in advertising and to think about the different ways it is used (see Appendix B for advertising principles and commercial resources).[12] After some brainstorming and looking at examples, we would move to these categories and note the definitions for each one:

1. Entertainment—engage the attention of audience (in a good or bad way)
   Example: Mountain Dew, "PuppyMonkeyBaby," https://www.you tube.com/watch?v=ql7uY36-LwA
2. Structure/continuity—ties together images or narrative to provide continuity
   Example (images): Apple, "Save Time," https://www.youtube .com/watch?v=3SHMbzEvxIo
   Example (narrative): Android, "Rock, Paper, Scissors," https:// www.youtube.com/watch?v=UYxpX3N20qU
3. Memorability—help audiences remember the product thereby increasing their probability to purchase

---

12. Halla notes that these ideas were drawn from Huron (1989, pp. 557–574).

Example: Kit Kat, "Give Me a Break," https://www.youtube.com/watch?v=0nkcVz1mad0

4. Lyrical language—conveys a verbal message in a nonverbal way through use of poetic appeal

    Example: ASPCA, "In the Arms of an Angel," https://www.youtube.com/watch?v=tjZ5dld2qHs

5. Targeting—use of a musical style that is well liked and relatable to the product's demographic

    Example: Chevy, "Like a Rock," https://www.youtube.com/watch?v=iMs4X2GOZkw

6. Authority establishment—expert testimony or endorsements; use of celebrities to appeal to audience

    Example: M&Ms, "Zedd and Blacc Singing in the Studio," https://www.youtube.com/watch?v=ZELmYM0oM1E

With the scaffolding of this whole group discussion, students will now work in small groups to explore additional examples, determining the category for each. These include the following:

- Microsoft, "Women Made," https://www.youtube.com/watch?v=48m24w5MIkQ (structure/continuity)
- Kia, "The Truth," https://www.youtube.com/watch?v=MjnFWcr6s3A (targeting—luxury as opera and authority establishment)
- Coca Cola, "I'd Like to Teach the World to Sing," https://www.youtube.com/watch?v=ib-Qiyklq-Q (memorability)
- Honda, "New Truck to Love," https://www.youtube.com/watch?v=ogXjiFMtVyI (entertainment)
- Volkswagen, "Darth Vader," https://www.youtube.com/watch?v=eGZNocni6zE (entertainment and continuity)
- Chrysler, "Imported from Detroit," https://www.youtube.com/watch?v=SKL254Y_jtc (authority establishment)

In the next lesson, we will explore the elements of advertising that are needed in a commercial. Students are asked for ideas about the kinds of things advertisers need to consider before making a television commercial. Explain that for every product, the commercial should

- have developed and organized a clear concept,
- know the target audience, and
- make an impression.

Every ad should also follow the attention, interest, desire, and action (AIDA) model (see Appendix B). Students will reassemble into their small groups from the previous lesson and watch some of the videos. As they are watching, ask the students to think and discuss how the commercial uses the advertising principles described previously, answering questions such as "What is the concept?" "Who is the target audience?" "How does this make an impression?" and "What purpose did the music serve in the commercial?" After each video, students will share their ideas with the class.

Next, students will watch the videos again and describe the songs used in the commercials with musical terms—for example, how the elements of texture, mode, melody, dynamics, tempo, mood, and style play a role in the overall message the commercial is trying to convey. As the discussion progresses, state that studies show consumers associate the major mode with pleasant and happy feelings and that faster tempos make consumers feel positive.

Here are some additional videos to use:

- Oreo, "WonderFilled," https://www.youtube.com/watch?v=XFsZ 6BO4LU0
- Hyundai, "First Date," https://www.youtube.com/watch?v=-R_483 zeVF8
- Pepsi, "Monks," https://www.youtube.com/watch?v=Br0panO RnWU

In the next lesson, students will work again in small groups, with each student having a classroom iPad with GarageBand on it. Explain that students will compose the music to accompany the Coca Cola "Catch" commercial (https://www.youtube.com/watch?v=S2nBBMbjS8w). Remind them to consider both the roles of advertising and the ways that musical dimensions will play a role in expressing their ideas. Have the video playing continuously (silently) in the classroom while the students are working.

Once students are finished, each group will share their composition for the commercial. Allow the class to discuss how the group's composition utilized music and advertising concepts. Finally, after all groups have finished presenting, play the commercial with the original music and have students discuss the musical concepts that the original utilized.

After this activity, students can take on the project of creating their own commercial, either individually or in small groups. The students will need to create a product and idea for the commercial. They can do this using iMovie and still images or by filming their own commercial. Next, they would have to either compose music to accompany the commercial or use a preexisting song and edit it to match the flow of the commercial. Students would then need to answer what purpose the music serves in the commercial, how they utilized advertising principles, and how the metadimensions of the music enhanced the commercial.

Vivian Ellsworth: How We Experience, Understand, and Express Conflict; the Story of Romeo and Juliet in Music, Literature, Theatre, and Dance
To begin this set of lessons, note that students should have experience with form, texture charts, icons (graphic representations of music), mapping, Noteflight (http://www.noteflight.com), and GarageBand and be able to create schema maps and/or lists of musical dimensions. It will be necessary to ask a lot of questions to involve and support students in making the connections across the arts for intentionally scaffolded meaning making.

Students will be assessed in three main areas during this unit:

1. Discussion participation. Students will ask questions and/or make comments verbally or in writing. As part of our discussion, we will be making a list (or schema map) of ways that writers, musicians, and choreographers create music to express conflict (through words, text, rhythm, timbre, instrumentation, motives, lighting, dynamics, repetition, etc.).

2. Understanding of musical examples. Students will demonstrate this by completing the following:
   a. Create a map of Prokofiev's "Montagues and Capulets."

      b. Create an iconic representation of a repeated rhythmic or melodic motive from Bernstein's "Mambo."

      c. Create a texture chart for a movement from Nino Rota's *Romeo and Juliet* soundtrack.

      d. Create a form chart for Michael Jackson's "Beat It."

  3. Creation of a soundtrack. With a partner, using Noteflight or GarageBand, students will make a one-minute segment of one of the following:

      a. fight scene in Zefferelli's *Romeo and Juliet*

      b. *Dance of the Montagues and Capulets* (Prokofiev—ballet)

      c. rumble or dance from *West Side Story*

      d. Michael Jackson's "Beat It"

The goal and objective of the first lesson is to get the students thinking about and listening for the ways authors, composers, and artists show conflict. Before we listen to or discuss any of the music, we look at specific lines from Shakespeare's *Romeo and Juliet* and talk about Shakespeare himself. Examples can include act one, scene one to think about the foreshadowing that occurs there and act three, scene one for the rising tension of the fight. We will then do the following:

- Watch the ballet clip of a dance where the feuding families, the Montagues and the Capulets, are gathered. *Do you feel conflict in this music? Do you see conflict or tension? How are the dancers moving? Can you tell from the dance how they feel about the other people in the room? What specifically does Prokofiev do in the music to show conflict?*[13]
- Watch the following clip[14] of an orchestra playing the music from "Montagues and Capulets." *As you watch the orchestra playing, what do you feel? Have you ever seen an orchestra perform in person? Would it be different than watching a ballet and hearing the same music? What are you feeling as you listen to this music? What is Prokofiev doing to make you feel that way?*

---

13. See Prokofiev, "Montagues and Capulets," from *Romeo and Juliet* suite, Ballet Corella, http://www.youtube.com/watch?v=bI9akyHz_wc&feature=related.

14. See Prokofiev, suite no. 2, *Romeo and Juliet*, "Montagues and Capulets," https://www.youtube.com/watch?v=p1_JUTAO0SA&list=RDp1_JUTAO0SA#t=37.

- Listen to an orchestral version several times to add further musical ideas to the incomplete musical map (with partners). The map shows the main violin line, yet there are many layers that students can explore (see Figure 4).

FIGURE 4. Incomplete texture map.

The next lesson focuses on the Zefferelli fight scenes. Play a fencing scene with and without music. Working independently, students will analyze the "background music" during the fight scene with a texture chart by drawing in other musical layers. The follow-up discussion will be scaffolded by the work on the texture charts. The teacher might ask how the music adds to the tension of the fight scene or instruct students to describe the texture. Students can also investigate which instruments are used to create the mood of conflict.[15]

Other musical problem solving activities include creating an iconic representation of a melodic or rhythmic motive that students hear in one of the movements and/or form and texture charts for other movements. The teacher can ask the following questions: Do you hear anything repeated in this music? Does seeing the graphic map help you to identify where it repeats? Do the same instruments always play the motive you chose?

Select movements with clear themes, as this is a time-intensive project that requires critical and creative thinking. The mambo (dance at the gym) from *West Side Story* would also provide context for discussing improvisation and the inherently competitive tension.[16]

In a final lesson, we explore Michael Jackson's music video[17] for "Beat It" (http://www.youtube.com/watch?v=Ym0hZG-zNOk) to analyze the

---

15. See act three, scene one, https://www.youtube.com/watch?v=ADvHO-lGjOs.
16. See https://www.youtube.com/watch?v=kokbJvSEMUY.
17. See also https://www.youtube.com/watch?v=H6Q8Lec1Wjg.

form of this song and complete the "What Do You Hear?" section of the form chart (see Figure 5). Additional questions might include the following: What is the role of the electric guitar in this piece? Where do you hear it? Is it the same each time you hear it? The guitar in the introduction is foreshadowing the fight, like Shakespeare does in his play.

Teachers might ask students to consider these questions: What will help you create music in your scene? What have other composers done that you can do? Will you use a rhythmic or melodic motive? Will you repeat segments of your music? Which beat patterns will you use? Which instruments will you use? Will you use acoustic or electronic instruments? A sharing of compositions will take place, with students describing their musical choices.

This unit provides a wide array of opportunities for musical thinking and doing across the arts that focus on essential questions (Brooks, 2002) and foster musical meaning making and personal expression.

▋ CLOSING THOUGHTS

The aim of this chapter was to provide curricular examples that can offer teachers and teacher educators suggestions using popular music, media,

Form Chart for Michael Jackson's *Beat It*

1	2	3	4	5	6	7	8
Intro	Intro 2	A Verse 1	A Verse 2	B Chorus	A Verse 3	A Verse 4	B Chorus
What Do You Hear?							

9	10	11	12	13	14	15	16
B Chorus	Bridge	C	B Chorus	B Chorus	B Chorus	B Chorus	Chorus, fades
What Do You Hear?			3:25	3:53	4:06	4:20	4:35

FIGURE 5. Form chart for Michael Jackson's "Beat It."

and digitally based projects in their classrooms. This chapter provides an overview of a course that I teach with these goals in mind and includes examples designed by preservice music teachers that give a window into their vision of what might be possible for their future students.

With an intentionally constructivist approach to learning and teaching, these examples include aspects of learner choice, problem solving and posing, multiple perspective and multiple entry points, and connections across the arts. There is a focus on big ideas and essential questions with opportunities for creative and collaborative thinking and doing. As noted earlier, constructivism is not a method or a set of sequential steps to follow; these examples are provided as a framework that can be adjusted for one's own students and classroom. Constructivist pedagogy requires a shift of attention from *what* to *whom*: "To understand constructivism, educators must focus attention on the learner . . . In order to realize the possibilities for learning that a constructivist pedagogy offers, schools need to take a closer, more respectful look at their learners" (Brooks & Brooks, 1993/1999, p. 22). Brooks and Brooks also state that

> educational settings that encourage active construction of meaning have several characteristics:

> • They free students from the dreariness of fact-driven curriculums and allow them to focus on large ideas.
> • They place in students' hands the exhilarating power to follow trails of interest, to make connections, to reformulate ideas, and to reach unique conclusions.
> • They share with the students the important message that the world is a complex place in which multiple perspectives exist and truth is often a matter of interpretation. (pp. 21–22)

A big-picture outcome for educators is that designing student-centered musical experiences can cultivate learner agency. Bruner (1996) defined agency as "taking more control of your own mental activity" (p. 87) and noted that "the agentive view takes mind to be proactive, problem-oriented, attentionally focused, selective, constructional, directed to ends" (p. 93). The ability and opportunity to make musical decisions, use creative strategies in collaborative settings, and create frames (here, digitally and in popular music contexts) that foster understanding are key components of an agentive approach. But beyond the recognition of experiential activity, "what characterizes human selfhood is the construction of a conceptual system that organizes . . . as 'record' of agentive encounters with the world, a record that is related to the past . . . but that is also extrapolated into the future-self with history and with possibility" (p. 36). Teachers and learners will continue to interact in communities of learning—with a sense of history in the study of exemplars and with possibility as they envision and enact new forms of musical expression.

▌REFERENCES

Allsup, R. E. (2011). Popular music and classical musicians: Strategies and perspectives. *Music Educators Journal, 97*(3), 30–34.

Barrett, J. R. (2001). Interdisciplinary work and musical integrity. *Music Educators Journal, 87*(5), 27–31.

Blair, D. (March 2009). Stepping aside: Teaching in a student-centered music classroom. *Music Educators Journal, 95*(3), 42–45.

Brooks, J. G. (2002). *Schooling for life: Reclaiming the essence of learning.* Alexandria, VA: Association for Supervision and Curriculum Development (ASCD).

Brooks, J. G., & Brooks, M. G. (1993/1999). *In search of understanding: The case for constructivist classrooms.* Alexandria, VA: ASCD.

Bruner, J. (1966). *Toward a theory of instruction.* Cambridge, MA: Harvard University Press.

Bruner, J. (1996). *The culture of education.* Cambridge, MA: Harvard University Press.

Davis, S. G. (2005). "That thing you do!" Compositional processes of a rock band. *International Journal of Education & the Arts, 6*(16). http://ijea/asu.edu/v6n16/.

Davis, S. G. (2011). Fostering a "musical say": Identity, expression and decision-making in a US school ensemble. In L. Green (Ed.), *Learning, teaching and musical identity: Voices from across cultures* (267–280). Bloomington: Indiana University Press.

Dewey, J. (1916). *Democracy and Education.* New York: McMillan.

Fosnot, C. T. (Ed.). (2005). *Theory, perspectives, and practice.* New York: Teachers College Press.

Green, L. (2005). The music curriculum as lived experience: Children's "natural" music-learning processes. *Music Educators Journal, 91*(4), 27–32.

Huron, D. (1989). Music in advertising: An analytic paradigm. *Musical Quarterly, 73*(4), 557–574.

Reimer, B. (2003). *A philosophy of music education: Advancing the vision* (3rd ed.). Upper Saddle River, NJ: Prentice-Hall.

Ruthmann, A. (2007, March). The composers' workshop: An approach to composing in the classroom. *Music Educators Journal, 93*(4), 38–43.

Smidt, S. (2009). *Introducing Vygotsky: A guide for practitioners and students in early years education.* New York: Routledge.

VanderLinde, D. (2014). "Mas que Nada": Fostering musical understanding through listening, performing, and creating in popular music contexts (Workshop). ISME World Conference, Porto Alegre, Brazil, July 20–25.

Vygotsky, L. S. (1978). *Mind in society: The development of higher psychological processes.* Cambridge, MA: Harvard University Press.

Wiggins, G., & McTighe, J. (1998). *Understanding by design* (2nd ed.). Alexandria, VA: ASCD.

Wiggins, J. (2015). *Teaching for musical understanding* (3rd ed.). New York: Oxford University Press.

Wiggins, J. (2016). Musical agency. In G. McPherson (Ed.), *The child as musician: A handbook of musical development* (2nd ed., 102–121). New York: Oxford University Press.

Wiggins, R. (2001, March). Interdisciplinary curriculum: Music educator concerns. *Music Educators Journal, 87*(5), 40–44.

Williams, D. A. (2014). Another perspective: The iPad is a REAL musical instrument. *Music Educators Journal, 101*(1), 93–98.

Wood, D. J., Bruner, J. S., & Ross, G. (1976). The role of tutoring in problem solving. *Journal of Child Psychiatry and Psychology, 17*(2), 89–100.

Zemelman, S., Daniels, H., & Hyde, A. (2005). *Best practice: Today's standards for teaching and learning in America's schools* (3rd ed.). Portsmouth, NH: Heinemann.

| APPENDIX A: MATERIALS FOR ALEXANDER WALKER LESSONS

"We Shall Overcome"
Historical Period: Postwar United States, 1945–68

It was the most powerful song of the twentieth century. It started out in church pews and picket lines, inspired one of the greatest freedom movements in US history, and went on to topple governments and bring about reform all over the world. Word for word, the short, simple lyrics of "We Shall Overcome" might be some of the most influential words in the English language.

"We Shall Overcome" has its roots in African American hymns from the early twentieth century and was first used as a protest song in 1945, when striking tobacco workers in Charleston, South Carolina, sang it on their picket line. By the 1950s, the song had been discovered by the young activists of the civil rights movement, and it quickly became the movement's unofficial anthem. Its verses were sung on protest marches and in sit-ins, through clouds of tear gas and under rows of police batons, and it brought courage and comfort to bruised, frightened activists as they waited in jail cells, wondering if they would survive the night. When the long years of struggle ended and President Lyndon B. Johnson vowed to fight for voting rights for all Americans, he included a final promise: "We shall overcome."

In the decades since, the song has circled the globe and has been embraced by civil rights and prodemocracy movements in dozens of nations. From Northern Ireland to Eastern Europe, from Berlin to Beijing, and from South Africa to South America, its message of solidarity and hope has been sung in dozens of languages, in presidential palaces and in dark prisons, and it continues to lend its strength to all people struggling to be free.

As you listen to "We Shall Overcome," think about the reasons it has brought strength and support to so many people for so many years. And remember that someone, somewhere, is singing it right now.

Citation
"We Shall Overcome." *Library of Congress for Teachers*. Library of Congress, n.d., June 2015. http://www.loc.gov/teachers/lyrical/songs/overcome.html.

"Americano" by Lady Gaga: Workalong

- Listen to the song one time through and jot down five or six of the most salient *musical features* you hear. These can be instruments/timbres, lyrics, formal/structural elements, and so on.
- On the back of this page, construct a *form diagram* for this song. On the top of each section of the form, give the section a name. Underneath each section of the form, write as many unique musical or lyrical characteristics as you hear.
- Go pick up a copy of the *lyrics* and listen to the song again while reading along.
  - Are there words or phrases you don't understand? Look them up or translate them, and write the translation on the lyrics. (Staple the lyrics to this page and turn it in to me.)
  - This song came out in 2011. What do you think the main social theme of this song is? Below, reference at least two supporting examples from the lyrics (you can use line numbers).
- Go to Wikipedia and type in "Americano (song)." Read the section titled "Background."

○ Did this illuminate yet another social issue explored in the song? What is it, and *how* was it weaved into this composition? (Hint: Think choices about musical instruments, or look at the "Credits & Personnel" section of the Wiki page.)

Pay close attention to producer Fernando Garibay's remarks about *when* the song was written. Can you find a reference to this in the lyrics?

APPENDIX B: RESOURCES FOR H. HILBORN "MUSIC IN ADVERTISING" UNIT

http://www.marketingcharts.com/television/the-average-american-is
-exposed-to-more-than-1-hour-of-tv-ads-every-day-42660/
http://www.businessinsider.com/ace-metrix-most-well-liked-ads-of-2016
-2016-4/#2-mms-zedd-and-blacc-likeability-score-756-attention
-score-760-9
http://www.businessinsider.com/ace-metrix-most-well-liked-ads-of-2016
-2016-4/#2-mms-zedd-and-blacc-likeability-score-756-attention-score
-760-9
http://superbowlcommercials.tv/33442.html
http://www.superbowlcommercials2016.org/best-commercials/best-2016
-super-bowl-commercials/
http://people.howstuffworks.com/culture-traditions/tv-and-culture/10
-catchiest-commercial-jingles1.htm
http://www.creativebloq.com/3d/top-tv-commercials-12121024/2

Advertising Principles Research

Http://www.nielsen.com/us/en/insights/news/2014/effective-advertising
-more-than-a-creative-black-box.html
http://www.brandingstrategyinsider.com/2010/10/10-principles-of
-advertising-bill-bernbach.html#.V8dKumViBsM

AIDA Model

http://thewire.cableone.net/basic-principles-advertising

PART IV

Reconceptualizing the Education of Musicians

.

CHAPTER 11

The Twenty-First-Century Music Conservatory

CHALLENGES AND CHANGES

CARLOS XAVIER RODRIGUEZ

UNIVERSITY OF MICHIGAN

INTRODUCTION

Music conservatories provide a valuable function to society and culture—helping musicians develop the knowledge and skills for professional careers in music. In the United States, the formal education of musicians has historically focused primarily on classical music,[1] favoring and appealing to students who have strong backgrounds in instruments and voice and desire to play in professional ensembles or become directors of bands, choirs, and orchestras. Of those who pursue music careers, only a small percentage actually support themselves through professional performance. Despite the intended outcome of a traditional music conservatory degree, most graduates combine music performance with teaching privately or in schools. Thus it is little wonder that bands, choirs, and orchestras have prevailed for so long as the most visible representations of public school music education.

Much of this is now changing. As the world endures the inexorable nature of social, cultural, and technological change, conservatory faculty

---

1. For purposes of brevity, in this chapter I refer to Western European common practice as "classical" music.

members are under pressure to adapt to the more extensive and diversified needs for musical understanding in the communities they serve.
This pressure has been largely "bottom-up"—beginning from public
demand, filtering upward through elementary and secondary
public schools—and now challenges American music conservatories to
reevaluate what they do and how they do it. The pressure derives from
shifting emphases toward personal creativity, technology, world music,
popular music and culture, diversity, and inclusiveness. Having advocated for the increased prominence of these elements in music degree
programs for many years, I begin with an assumption: further advocacy
is not as quite as crucial as assessing the new musical landscape of higher
education. What follows is my understanding of the principal forces
that have stimulated music conservatories to modify their missions,
which I believe include the effects of postmodernism culture on traditional aesthetic philosophy, broadening conceptions of musicality, and
the materialization of a popular music vernacular.

CULTURE OF POSTMODERNISM

Is classical music "better" than popular music and thus more worthy of
study? Does either possess characteristics that render it more or less susceptible to intensive examination? These questions have been entertained
by philosophers, theorists, historians, and educators for generations. The
long-standing preference for the Western canon over popular music by
traditional instruction carries the belief that classical music is high art and
popular music is low art and that schools and educators must concern
themselves with only the highest quality examples of the discipline. This
preference has become more problematic through emerging scholarship
arguing against this distinction. Fisher (2005) provided a helpful summary of this scholarship, claiming that typical distinctions between high/
low, good/bad, and art/nonart become more problematic upon careful
scrutiny, thus presenting a challenge to the future of aesthetics.[2] Indeed,

---

2. J. A. Fisher, "High Art versus Low Art," in The Routledge Companion to Aesthetics, 2nd *ed., ed. Berys Nigel Gaut and Dominic* Lopes (London: Routledge), 527–40.
Fisher's summary provides commentary on whether a single distinction between high

the notion that classical music permits a higher form of aesthetic experience than popular music has gradually diminished in the second half of the twentieth century due to increasingly conflicting aesthetic perspectives. Shelly (2015) stated, "For the most part, aesthetic theories have divided over questions particular to one or another of these designations: whether artworks are necessarily aesthetic objects; how to square the allegedly perceptual basis of aesthetic judgments with the fact that we give reasons in support of them; how best to capture the elusive contrast between an aesthetic attitude and a practical one; whether to define aesthetic experience according to its phenomenological or representational content; how best to understand the relation between aesthetic value and aesthetic experience."[3]

What does it mean for an object to be aesthetic or for someone to have an aesthetic attitude or experience? In his book *Art as Experience* (1934), John Dewey offered an explanation of aesthetic experience through his analysis of expressiveness,[4] claiming that opportunity and practice improved sensitivity to above-ordinary experiences. Prall (1929) explained a similar viewpoint: "It is objects as of specific discriminated character, and in their variety of detail, that most fully satisfy us. And the discriminating of such absolutely specific natures and of such internal character, as distinguished from noticing that an object is of some general kind, conveniently named, or the following out of relations to other objects or to interests and purposes, is the very heart of aesthetic activity. Without such specific discrimination, continuous and more and more refined, aesthetic experience remains mere day-dreams, mere relaxation or truancy, a rest perhaps, but not a refreshment and delight in perception."[5]

The traditionalist presumption that certain standards, forms, or characteristics of things were intrinsically superior to others, and the application of this presumption to classical music, is now historical. Postmodernist

---

and low art can be formulated, whether it represents aesthetic differences, whether it is theoretically coherent, and how it relates to the concept of art.

3. J. Shelley, "The Concept of the Aesthetic," in *The Stanford Encyclopedia of Philosophy*, ed. Edward N. Zalta (Winter 2015), https://plato.stanford.edu/archives/win2015/entries/aesthetic-concept/.

4. John Dewey, *Art as Experience* (New York: Perigee, 1934). See chapter 4, "The Act of Expression," and chapter 5, "The Expressive Object."

5. D. W. Prall, *Aesthetic Judgement* (New York: Thomas Y. Crowell, 1929), 35.

thinking rejects the idea of "beauty" as an objective quality, meaning that aesthetic perception and experience cannot and should not be described, or assumed to exist, in any normative sense. The postmodern perspective allows that no one can say for anyone but oneself what music is, or what it means, or what's important in or about music. Postmodernist thinking was sufficiently dominant by the end of the twentieth century that leading music education philosophers began writing from decidedly postaesthetic lenses,[6] signaling forthcoming changes in the way music should be taught and learned.

Returning to the question of whether classical music is "better" than popular music, it remains a matter of philosophical perspective, yet the perspective leading to an affirmative answer no longer dominates contemporary society. While it is certainly accurate that classical music is typically the *best* of the genres and styles it represents, this is obviously not true of popular music. However, as time progresses, it becomes easier to note those artists and performances that rise to the top—in the power of their message, in the extent of their innovation, in the scope of their influence—and doing so characterizes intelligent consumers of musical culture. Creating, performing, and listening to popular music are considered naïve activities only by those who have limited knowledge, interest, or experience in them or who hold a categorical belief that popular music is simply "amateur" music. Classical music is no more worthwhile than popular music for the reasons humans attend to music in the first place. As Gracyk (2004) explained, "The argument in favor of exclusive structural 'listening' . . . rests on the principle that an activity requiring specialized or refined knowledge is superior to one that employs only basic knowledge. But this principle is without basis in fact. Specialized knowledge is required to read the *Journal of Abnormal Psychology*, but it hardly follows that I will gain greater insight into human nature by reading that journal in place of the novels of Charles Dickens and Henry James."[7]

---

6. See David Elliott (1995), Estelle Jorgensen (1997), and Bennett Reimer (2003) as examples of transitional, postaesthetic philosophical writing in music education during this time.
7. Theodore Gracyk, "Popular Music: The Very Idea of Listening to It," in *Bridging the Gap: Popular Music and Music Education,* ed. Carlos Xavier Rodriguez (Reston: MENC—the National Association for Music Education, 2004), 60. Gracyk also

In his examination of the contrasting worlds of classical and rock music, Baugh (1993) concluded that when someone says the latter suffers from overly simplistic form, it reveals a bias toward the aforementioned specialized knowledge—the belief that good music should be more structurally complex or refined—and also misses the point of rock music.[8] Such dismissive attitudes are subsiding as newer generations of musicians and scholars, having been educated in more inclusive curricula, respond to increasing pressure to temper their attitudes about their specialties in relation to the specialties of others and realize the mutual benefits of doing so. As Bowman (2004) stated, "Taking popular music seriously will make the classics—the greatest musical achievements of the past—all the more momentous. They become far more vital concerns to the extent that they are appropriately seen as part of a continuous, dynamic musical field rather than constituting the whole of it. Rather than museum pieces that demand reverent appreciation, they become part of a broader, living culture—culturally vital, vibrant, and rich in their power to enrich here-and-now experience in the real world."[9]

These views represent changing sensibilities and suggest an increasingly comprehensive strategy for educating professional musicians in which any particular music tradition provides neither the organizing principles nor the specific subject matter for learning. In pursuit of significant change in the academy, educators are becoming more mindful of musicianship "categories" where some genres are considered "better" or "more advanced" than others and thus more worthy of study—first, because they are arbitrary[10] and second, because they are increasingly irrelevant based on the

cites limitations of traditional aestheticians in addressing musical experience in an era dominated by recorded music.
8. Bruce Baugh, "Prolegomena to Any Aesthetics of Rock Music," *Journal of Aesthetics and Art Criticism* 51, no. 1 (1993): 25. In this article, Baugh makes the distinction that classical music tends to support perception and appreciation of formal qualities, while "rock music" appeals to bodily rhythmic impulses.
9. Wayne Bowman, "'Pop' Goes . . . ? Taking Popular Music Seriously," in *Bridging the Gap: Popular Music and Music Education*, ed. Carlos Xavier Rodriguez (Reston, VA: MENC—the National Association for Music Education, 2004), 44.
10. Steven Pinker, *How the Mind Works* (New York: W. W. Norton, 1997), 308. Pinker presents a compelling view of how categories are "arbitrary conventions" of language while noting "deconstructionism, poststructuralism, and postmodernism in the humanities take this view to an extreme."

consumption habits of communities served by higher education. Without the guidelines and conditions of a dominant musical tradition, music conservatories will witness a shift in focus from the institution to the individual, a trend evident in music education at the global level. Georgii-Hemming and Westvall (2012) presented new priorities for Swedish music educators that are comparable to those in other Scandinavian countries: "Music as a phenomenon is not a focus, and music is certainly not seen as an autonomous object. However, the meaning of music is perceived as a unique source for personal and social development. Therefore every student must be respected, learn to cooperate, be given opportunities to find their identity and become a fulfilled human being with self-confidence. They must also be made aware of—and take responsibility for—what he or she [sic] learns, and discover their own abilities and the potential value of aesthetic knowledge."[11]

These new challenges warrant a reevaluation of *musicality* because it is a direct way to study the humans these academies exist to educate. What does it mean to call someone musical? In the following section, I address this question in hopes of revealing what musicians of different backgrounds and interests share in terms of personality characteristics, working habits, competencies, and challenges, which minimize the distinctions between them often used to determine who might benefit best from advanced instruction.

| BROADENING CONCEPTIONS OF MUSICALITY

The term *musicality* can describe a characteristic of humans or a quality of sound. I prefer using it to describe humans: it encompasses skills and knowledge of varying styles and traditions and attendant sensitivity to the subjective aspects of musical experiences. This sensitivity is easy

---

11. Eva Georgii-Hemming and Maria Westvall, "Music Education: A Personal Matter? Examining the Current Discourses of Music Education in Sweden," in *Future Prospects for Music Education: Corroborating Informal Learning Pedagogy*, ed. Sidsel Karlsen and Lauri Väkevä (London: Cambridge Scholars, 2012), 100. See also Marja Heimonen, "'Bildung' and Music Education: A Finnish Perspective," *Philosophy of Music Education Review* 22, no. 2 (2014): 188–208. Heimonen explains how Frede Nielsen and others have interpreted the German concept of *Bildung*, which emphasizes personal responsibility in one's education.

to overlook in instruction, but there is evidence that encouraging students to attend to and conceptualize their affective responses leads to more relevant *listening* to music.[12] Another reason for using musicality in terms of humans rather than sound is the decided reemphasis of philosophical and psychological research from the musical object to the musical person near the beginning of the twenty-first century. Christopher Small introduced the term *musicking*, which exemplifies this marked shift in the concept of music from products to processes.[13] Meanwhile, music psychology transformed into the social psychology of music as the digital music world evolved. Adrian North and David Hargreaves (2008) wrote:

> The hierarchy of 100 years ago placed at the top the composer who handed down completed pieces of music to a passive audience who listened in clearly defined environments (e.g. concert halls). In the modern era, the composer is now effectively in a process of continual negotiation with an active audience who can freely choose between and alter the works in question whenever and wherever they like. In short, it is increasingly easy and prevalent for both music listening and performing to be carried out in a wide range of different circumstances. This increasing contextualization of musical behavior has led to a corresponding interest among researchers in the social psychology of music.[14]

The relevance of these new directions for the concept of musicality is a basis for understanding all musical behavior, regardless of background or specialization. This is not to endorse musical "universals"—that is, to argue that all musical behavior is normative—rather, it suggests that previously accepted hierarchies of musical competence that separate experts

---

12. The development of evaluative responses to visual art is addressed in Michael J. Parsons, *How We Understand Art: A Cognitive Developmental Account of Aesthetic Experience* (Cambridge: Cambridge University Press, 1989).

13. Christopher Small, *Musicking: The Meanings of Performing and Listening* (Hanover: Wesleyan University Press, 1998).

14. Adrian North and David Hargreaves, *The Social and Applied Psychology of Music* (Oxford: Oxford University Press, 2008), 2. In the opening chapter, North and Hargreaves invoke Thomas Kuhn's concept of paradigms from his book *The Structure of Scientific Revolutions* (1962) to explain how music psychology, focused previously on cognitive questions and experimentation, left many unanswered questions that could only be addressed through a shift to social psychology.

from amateurs don't help us understand, nor do they represent well, the richness and diversity of human musical activity.

Classical and popular musicians share similar skills and knowledge, personality types, learning styles, and professional challenges. Davies (1999) concluded that music listening invokes the perceptual tendency to seek patterns to distinguish it from noise,[15] a parsing strategy employed regardless of training and experience. Music listening simultaneously involves "looking backward" to recognize and process musical sounds and "looking forward" to formulate expectations.[16] Musicians are adept at reasoning across multiple temporal spaces, even while engaged in generative musical skills—performing, composing, and improvising. Memorization is another mental skill on which musicians rely. As the culmination of a professional music degree, it is standard to expect the senior recital to include extended pieces, or even an entire program, performed from memory, just as rock band members must perform an entire album's worth of music (or more) from memory during a live concert. It is not possible to function as expected in a bluegrass jam unless one has committed to memory at least dozens—and perhaps even hundreds—of songs that can be sung, accompanied, and improvised to.

Musicians, like all artists, exert extraordinary influence over others through sympathetic induction of desired emotional states. A dependable sign of an accomplished musician is the ability to perform without demonstrating the intended emotion themselves. A famous example of this skill was Elton John's controlled performance of *Candle in the Wind* at Princess Diana's funeral, which reinforces the belief that accomplished musicians *understand* emotion enough to hold sway over it. Musical ability is associated with pathemia,[17] a personality dimension characterized by pronounced subjective awareness and a potential source of attraction between humans—it enables musicians to influence the feelings of

---

15. Stephen Davies, "Rock versus Classical Music," *Journal of Aesthetics and Art Criticism* 57, no. 2 (1999): 193–204.

16. John Booth Davies, *The Psychology of Music* (Stanford: Stanford University Press, 1978), 73–74.

17. Raymond Bernard Cattell, *Personality and Mood by Questionnaire: A Handbook of Interpretive Theory, Psychometrics, and Practical Procedures* (San Francisco: Jossey-Bass, 1973). Cattell derived three factors of pathemia in adults—outgoingness, sensitivity, and imagination.

others in socially beneficial ways. Anthony Kemp (1996), interpreting the research of Cattell, described pathemia in this way: "On the surface, pathemia may be associated with a relaxed and even indulgent life of feeling, the individual appearing warm, sentimental, and prone to daydreaming and living through sensitive emotions. At the contrasting pole, cortertia, the individual operates in an alert and realistic fashion; feelings are cool and well under control."[18]

Musicians, regardless of training, generally approach tasks and situations intuitively and are prone to preferring sensory qualities of musical experiences rather than theoretical knowledge. This is not to imply that musicians do not want or readily benefit from systematic instruction— merely that they often choose to explore possibilities rather than recognize and conform to practicalities, thus suggesting the importance of creative reasoning and self-expression. One exercise I plan for the first day of methods class is to listen to the introduction of the opening song "Playground" from the album *Wasp Star: Apple Venus Volume 2* by the rock group XTC.[19] It features two bars of a guitar riff alone, followed by guitar riff and added staggered drum hits for the next four bars, composing an exciting anacrusis that I believe is one of the best album introductions ever. We discuss as a class and then I inform the students that there is a drumming strategy being employed—each iteration is one stroke longer than the previous one, creating a compelling syncopated pattern when laid over the four bars. We listen again with this added analytic information and then discuss again. We listen a third time, and I ask them to try to listen as they did the first time, when their responses noted the raw energy and excitement. It is not possible once you "understand" the strategy.[20] This exercise illustrates the point that musicians have a

18. Anthony Kemp, *The Musical Temperament: Psychology and Personality of Musicians* (Oxford: Oxford University Press, 1996), 69. Chapter 4, "Sensitivity," is dedicated to the interpretation of various personality test data, most prominently Cattell's construct of pathemia. Cattell provided a thoughtful foreword for Kemp's book.
19. XTC, *Wasp Star (Apple Venus Volume 2)*, released May 23, 2000, Cooking Vinyl/Idea Records.
20. Chuck Sabo claimed, "That fill was completely spontaneous. It just came out of me, after hearing the count-in to the song." Chuck Sabo, personal communication, March 28, 2017.

certain nature in which they are united: differences arise with the amount and type of education they are given or pursue.

When certain areas of formal music instruction prevail, other areas might remain undeveloped. When I completed training in the Orff approach during the 1980s, several of the in-service music teachers dis-enrolled because they were unwilling to complete the substantial creative movement–based segment of the training. These were elementary general music educators who ostensibly help children use their bodies to understand and react to music. I have never met an accomplished music student who didn't bemoan a lack of improvisation and composition skills, yet most of my upper-level undergraduate methods students have simply never been asked to improvise or compose prior to my class. It is ironic to note that much of what makes popular music attractive is its connection with movement, or dance, and the self-granted creative latitude used by artists and groups to extend their personalities through their music.[21] One might legitimately argue that musically creative activity is the most distinguishing characteristic of the musical personality—a natural expectation for and of accomplished musicians, which becomes more apparent as we consider the diverse ways music makers function beyond the academy.

Music is gratifying to the nervous system, using the same reward pathways as food, drugs, and sexual pleasure.[22] This observation likely accounts for contemporary digital technology development that supports increasingly accessible, sustained, and sophisticated musical behavior. One of the more tangible features of such behavior is *mediation*, in which participants become vulnerable to social and identity exploration and growth through a process of communication with like-minded individuals.[23] The mediation involves sharing ideas; permitting others to critique,

---

21. With respect to guitar chords, there are finite ways to finger a chord; fewer than that are typically used. What brings infinite variety to them is the manner in which the guitarist activates the strings—astute listeners can tell if it is Adrian Belew or Eric Clapton playing.

22. Adiel Mallik, Mona Lisa Chanda, and Daniel J. Levitin, "Anhedonia to Music and Mu-Opioids: Evidence from the Administration of Naltrexone," *Scientific Reports* 7:41952 (2017), doi: 10.1038.

23. Lauri Väkevä, "Digital Musicianship in the Late Modern Culture of Mediation: Theorizing a New Praxis for Music," *Signum Temporis: Journal of Pedagogy and Psychology* (2013), doi: 10.2478.

change, and reperform them; critiquing and changing them oneself and then reperforming; and so forth. Since the building blocks for this sharing are already available in the form of preexisting music and other media, the process of creation involves combining and reframing these blocks to produce new meanings—ones that invoke the sensibilities and cultural milieu of the original sources. Electronic dance music (EDM) relies heavily on this hybrid creativity, and it is currently the most popular music genre in the world. Today's music and nonmusic majors are already exposed to these practices both in their coursework[24] and in the "real world." In its most recent version, GarageBand now has an EDM music creation interface, and it is accessible to millions of iPhone owners.

The practices of digital musicianship bear out Small's concept of musicking and North and Hargreaves' portrayal of the changing social dynamics of music performance and consumption and are consistent with broadening conceptions of musicality based on humans rather than music traditions. Classical music training alone has proven to be more limited—in its purposes, performance protocols, and future employment potential—to the ways popular music thrives across the world. It is an exception of the grandest sense to the ways that humans have utilized music since ancient times.[25] Still, one might wonder whether popular music has a historical legacy and integrity comparable to classical music— whether it can prevail with a historical tradition all its own. Thanks to the growing number of music theorists, musicologists, and music educators oriented toward popular music, that legacy is alive, well, and prospering.

| MATERIALIZATION OF A POPULAR MUSIC VERNACULAR

History is the central component of a popular music vernacular. I use the term *vernacular* in the sense that learning about it helps one "speak" its language. For several decades toward the end of the twentieth century,

---

24. I recently taught a class entitled "Aesthetics of Rock," which surveyed musical practice in the contemporary world and focused on how individual students situate themselves in relation to music performance and consumption. Students largely determined the artists and genres we surveyed.
25. Steven Brown, "Biomusicology, and Three Biological Paradoxes about Music," *Bulletin of Psychology and the Arts* 4 (2003): 15–17.

I heard from many popular music enthusiasts that pop music history "begins with Elvis," yet this belief has waned in favor of a more serious approach to the study of popular music in the United States—namely, the role of American roots music. What used to be called "folk music" by scholars near the start of the twentieth century began as the music of European Americans in the rural South but soon encompassed the songs of African Americans, Mexican Americans, Cajuns, American Indians, and other small ethnic groups. These traditions represented the cultural beliefs and values of ordinary people. Popular styles emerged from this base, evolving into blues, jazz, rhythm and blues, and rock and roll. During the 1960s, the folk music revival brought national attention to these original music traditions, and they have collectively become known as examples of American roots music. American roots music reveals how songs function as important cultural forms through which people assert themselves, preserve their own histories in the face of changing social conditions, and even encourage collective action. The history of American popular music is well documented now.[26] It is significantly the history of African American music in the United States. One might take a geographic perspective of this history: it emanated from the South, up the Mississippi River, to the large cities near the river, then eastward and westward, following the Great Migration of African Americans in the twentieth century.

A second component of a popular music vernacular is its signature instruments, including acoustic and electric guitar, bass, drums, piano and electronic keyboard, banjo, fiddle, accordion, mandolin, harmonica, and others. This instrumentation is clearly part of the materiality of popular music. In contemporary music classrooms, these instruments, combined with microphones and laptop computers, carry the name "Modern Band" to distinguish them from previous "band" ensembles and to enhance their integrity as a learning medium. Understanding the idiomatic constraints and advantages of these instruments, and acquiring the highest levels of performance skill, is every bit as challenging and time-intensive as it is for instruments of the symphony orchestra.

---

26. For example, see Larry Starr and Christopher Waterman, *American Popular Music: From Minstrelsy to MP3*, 4th ed. (Oxford: Oxford University Press, 2013).

A third component of a popular music vernacular is technological development. When radio broadcasts began in the 1920s, it was possible for all Americans to experience the same music, regardless of their location. The widespread distribution of the phonograph allowed users to hear music without making it themselves or seeing it performed live. This technology legacy continues on through cassettes, CDs, and MP3s, leading some to contend that popular music is a recorded medium.[27] With this legacy comes analysis of its constituent parts—principally, studio-recorded tracks, as Kania (2006) argued—which provide effective comparison points with the longer-established classical music tradition.[28]

The interpretive potential of popular music might also be considered part of its vernacular. As socially driven and transforming practice, popular music ventures far beyond the sensory and intellectual pleasures of good performances and recordings—it provides a means for performers and listeners to explore the space between the music and their identities. This is also central to the materiality of popular music. Adventuresome practitioners in some genres (e.g., punk) take this aspect to the extreme, accepting larger risks for achieving greater cultural disruption.[29] Because it is everywhere, and with so many possibilities for self-definition and understanding, popular music is rightfully scrutinized for all the nuances of its consumption. As Valentine (1995) wrote:

> [This] paper makes a distinction between three different processes of consuming music. First, it focuses on the consumption of live music at public venues. Here, the act of consumption is intentional and all the senses are engaged, not just hearing. Secondly, it examines the way that music forms a backdrop to our everyday activities—the soundscape—and is therefore often heard or "overheard" (in that the act of consumption is not deliberate) in "public" places. Thirdly, it considers the process of consciously listening to music. This is an act that typically takes place in "private"

---

27. Theodore Gracyk, *Rhythm and Noise: An Aesthetics of Rock* (Durham, NC: Duke University Press, 1996).
28. Andrew Kania, "Making Tracks: The Ontology of Rock Music," *Journal of Aesthetics and Art Criticism* 64, no. 4 (2006): 401–14.
29. Jesse Prinz, "The Aesthetics of Punk Rock," *Philosophy Compass* 9, no. 9 (2014): 583–93.

space and often involves using music as a vehicle to transport the listener to an imaginary or fantasy world.[30]

Conceptualizing the artifact of music listening as a "space" is useful for capturing the intricacies of individual affective responses interconnected with the varied circumstances of listening experience.[31]

| CODA

The ideas presented in the foregoing sections highlight the pervasive philosophical, artistic, psychological, and historical changes faced by music conservatories. Consequently, many schools are indeed changing—some by instituting new degree programs, some through merging, and some through the addition of new popular music courses. Overall, progress toward the acceptance of popular music in higher education is palpable, notably since the publication of *Bridging the Gap: Popular Music and Music Education* in 2004.[32] Yet there is still much progress to make. Specifically, popular music scholarship and performance practice has yet to be integrated equitably with existing curricula. This lack of integration is evident in many areas: major ensembles, applied instruction, theory, musicology, and pedagogy. It is not sufficient to merely add courses to degree programs; subject matter from multiple music traditions will need to be fused in a comprehensive approach to educating professional musicians. In practical terms, this means we will have to "make room" for popular music education to a more significant degree and in a more meaningful way.

The topic of music notation skills continues to be problematic. Would any school of music admit a student who cannot read music? It depends on the school's mission. If the school's primary mission were to pursue note-reading excellence on par with the finest players in the world in

---

30. Gill Valentine, "Creating Transgressive Space: The Music of kd lang," *Transactions of the Institute of British Geographers* 20, no. 4 (1995): 474–85.
31. Carlos Xavier Rodriguez, "Music Listening Spaces," in *The Musical Experience: Rethinking Music Teaching and Learning,* ed. Janet R. Barrett and Peter Webster (Oxford: Oxford University Press, 2014), 88–102.
32. Carlos Xavier Rodriguez, ed., *Bridging the Gap: Popular Music and Music Education* (Music Educators National Conference, 2004).

preparation for a life of professional ensemble performance, the answer would have to be no. If the school's mission were to help musically talented individuals of diverse backgrounds and skills pursue a career in music, the answer would have to be yes, of course, in accordance with the evaluation of other qualifications unique to the degree program. Just like everyone else, music students learn far less from transmission, or conscious showing and telling, than they do from accretion, or unconscious learning. The educational worth and potential of an institution is thus in the quality of its students, not its faculty. We should be mindful of our collective responsibility to meet the needs for musical understanding in our communities as they constantly change, even if it means leaving some of our expertise behind, because it presents educators with the same challenge facing students—becoming something you have yet to achieve—and demonstrates the value that what you know is not nearly as useful as knowing how to learn.

BIBLIOGRAPHY

Baugh, B. "Prolegomena to Any Aesthetics of Rock Music." *Journal of Aesthetics and Art Criticism* 51, no. 1 (1993): 23–29.

Bowman, W. D. "'Pop' Goes . . . ? Taking Popular Music Seriously." In *Bridging the Gap: Popular Music and Music Education*, edited by Carlos Xavier Rodriguez, 29–49. Reston, VA: National Association for Music Education, 2004.

Brown, S. "Biomusicology, and Three Biological Paradoxes about Music." *Bulletin of Psychology and the Arts* 4 (2003): 15–17.

Davies, J. B. *The Psychology of Music*. Stanford, CA: Stanford University Press, 1978.

Davies, S. "Rock versus Classical Music." *Journal of Aesthetics and Art Criticism* 57, no. 2 (1999): 193–204.

Dewey, J. *Art as Experience*. New York: Perigee, 1934.

Elliott, D. J. *Music Matters: A New Philosophy of Music Education*. Oxford: Oxford University Press, 1995.

Fisher, J. A. "High Art versus Low Art." In *The Routledge Companion to Aesthetics*, 2nd ed., edited by Berys Nigel Gaut and Dominic Lopes, 527–40. London: Routledge, 2005.

Georgii-Hemming, E., and M. Westvall. "Music Education: A Personal Matter? Examining the Current Discourses of Music Education in Sweden." In *Future Prospects for Music Education: Corroborating Informal Learning Pedagogy*, edited by Sidsel Karlsen and Lauri Väkevä, 97–114. London: Cambridge Scholars Publishing, 2012.

Gracyk, T. "Popular Music: The Very Idea of Listening to It." In *Bridging the Gap: Popular Music and Music Education*, edited by Carlos Xavier Rodriguez, 51–70. Reston, VA: National Association for Music Education, 2004.

Heimonen, M. "'Bildung' and Music Education: A Finnish Perspective." *Philosophy of Music Education Review* 22, no. 2 (2014): 188–208.

Jorgensen, E. R. *In Search of Music Education.* Urbana: University of Illinois Press, 1997.

Kania, A. "Making Tracks: The Ontology of Rock Music." *Journal of Aesthetics and Art Criticism* 64, no. 4 (2006): 401–14.

Mallik, A., M. L. Chanda, and D. J. Levitin. "Anhedonia to Music and Mu-Opioids: Evidence from the Administration of Naltrexone." *Scientific Reports* 7, no. 41952 (2017). doi: 10.1038.

North, A., and D. Hargreaves. *The Social and Applied Psychology of Music.* Oxford: Oxford University Press, 2008.

Parsons, M. J. *How We Understand Art: A Cognitive Developmental Account of Aesthetic Experience.* Cambridge: Cambridge University Press, 1989.

Pinker, S. *How the Mind Works.* New York: W. W. Norton, 1997.

Prinz, J. "The Aesthetics of Punk Rock." *Philosophy Compass* 9, no. 9 (2014): 583–93.

Reimer, B. *A Philosophy of Music Education: Advancing the Vision.* Upper Saddle River, NJ: Prentice Hall, 2003.

Rodriguez, C. X., ed. *Bridging the Gap: Popular Music and Music Education.* Music Educators National Conference, 2004.

Rodriguez, C. X. "Music Listening Spaces." In *The Musical Experience: Rethinking Music Teaching and Learning,* edited by Janet R. Barrett and Peter Webster, 88–102. Oxford: Oxford University Press, 2014.

Shelley, J. "The Concept of the Aesthetic." In *The Stanford Encyclopedia of Philosophy,* edited by Edward N. Zalta (Winter 2015). https://plato.stanford.edu/archives/win2015/entries/aesthetic-concept/.

Small, C. *Musicking: The Meanings of Performing and Listening.* Hanover, CT: Wesleyan University Press, 1998.

Starr, L., and C. Waterman. *American Popular Music: From Minstrelsy to MP3.* 4th ed. Oxford: Oxford University Press, 2013.

Väkevä, L. "Digital Musicianship in the Late Modern Culture of Mediation: Theorizing a New Praxis for Music," *Signum Temporis: Journal of Pedagogy and Psychology* 6, no. 1 (2013). doi: 10.2478.

Valentine, G. "Creating Transgressive Space: The Music of kd lang." *Transactions of the Institute of British Geographers* 20, no. 4 (1995): 474–85.

CHAPTER 12

Teaching Popular Music in the Music Theory Core

FOCUS ON HARMONY AND MUSICAL FORM

JANE PIPER CLENDINNING

FLORIDA STATE UNIVERSITY

▌INTRODUCTION

Where, when, and how to incorporate popular music in the undergraduate music theory curriculum has been the subject of intense discussion in recent years, especially as research regarding popular music theory and analysis has become increasingly prolific and prominent in the music theory profession. Though there have been recent calls from outside music theory circles to completely revise the undergraduate music theory curriculum foregrounding popular and world music,[1] the most likely place for popular music analysis to find a foothold in the near future is as a part of the current music theory core.

This chapter identifies ways that popular music is currently incorporated in some music theory textbooks for the music theory core curriculum and considers two case studies that illustrate how teaching harmony and musical form as employed in popular music is at odds with the overall content of a standard music theory undergraduate curriculum, especially if the popular music is viewed as a part of an extended Common Practice.[2] The chapter concludes with consideration of why it is essential to include popular music in the undergraduate core, preparation of teachers to engage this material, and where to go from here.

CURRENT TREATMENT OF POPULAR MUSIC IN THE CONTEXT OF TRADITIONAL CORE THEORY COURSES

For at least the last half century, the traditional objective of core music theory courses for undergraduate music majors has been to prepare students to analyze music from established eighteenth- through early twentieth-century canonic Western concert music repertoires: recognizing typical and atypical harmonic, melodic, and formal practices; labeling and interpreting rhythmic and metrical features; and identifying style and genre. Common Practice harmony (as currently taught) balances harmonic progression and functional aspects with voice-leading—smooth, conjunct, parsimonious connections in each voice or part between chords. In this scenario, harmonic progressions and successions can be explained either with reference to functional categories (such as root progressions, or tonic, predominant, and dominant in the T-PD-D-T phrase model) or as "linear progressions" (such as sequences, functional area expansions, and voice-leading chords), where the smooth connection through voice-leading obviates the necessity for strong root motion.[3] There is an assumption that all parts of the texture coordinate with the harmonic progression (with the exception of pedal points and other well-understood contexts), that embellishing tones outside the harmony can be identified and labeled, and that all parts of the texture are in the same key or mode until a key change.

When basic theory curricula include repertoire composed after 1900, the most common repertoires studied are early twentieth-century non-tonal music (Bartók, Stravinsky, Schoenberg, Webern, and their contemporaries), perhaps with some works by Debussy, Ravel, and other composers. The repertoire selected for both Common Practice and post-1900 music focus on male European composers and works within concert music traditions, with a smattering of American composers such as John Cage and minimalists in the twentieth-century materials, though several recent prominent post-1900 textbooks have actively engaged some works by non-Europeans and women.[4] With few exceptions, popular music repertoire was completely excluded from these courses until around the turn of the twenty-first century, and even now, many traditional university core music theory textbooks and courses do not include popular music examples.

When popular music has been incorporated in textbooks and course teaching materials for the music theory core, the most common approach is to find musical examples that seem to be "doing the same thing" as examples from the Common Practice repertoire and to sprinkle them in among the Common Practice examples. For music fundamentals topics, such as reading pitches; identifying intervals, chords, and scales; and understanding rhythmic and metrical elements, popular music examples can easily be included if they are chosen carefully to legitimately fit the criteria of the topic they are being used to illustrate and if they are employed as "positive" examples (what to do, instead of what not to do), like other music literature engaged in such a course. It does not take much effort to include popular music terminology and concepts where they fit into the study of fundamentals, such as introducing popular music chord symbols alongside the Roman numerals when triads and seventh chords are introduced. Indeed, excerpts can be included later in the curriculum as well, particularly from older popular music, such as Broadway show tunes and jazz standards, where the harmonic practices conform to Common Practice progressions and voice-leading for the most part, with only additions of chord extensions and harmonic elements—like the added sixth—that can be easily illustrated and explained.

Integrating popular music theory and analysis into topics in the music theory undergraduate core beyond the fundamentals presents notable challenges, especially if the teacher would like to present a popular music example along with each core content topic. Popular music examples are readily available for some topics, such as harmonic sequences, but for others—such as Neapolitan sixth chords or augmented sixth chords, which are not typical of popular music—convincing examples are difficult to find. Though the viewpoint persists among music theorists that popular music is a continuation of the tonal Common Practice, problems arise if one attempts to treat all post-1950 popular music with the same approaches as older tonal music, because many of these late twentieth- and early twenty-first-century pieces simply do not conform to eighteenth- and nineteenth-century standards. This is particularly obvious in the area of harmony, as the two case studies that follow will illustrate. Music theorists have taken two approaches to this issue: adapting older analytical methods for the new repertoire—which works well enough for some repertoire and not as well for others—and exploring new means of describing and theorizing the new harmonic patterns of popular music. This process of theorizing new approaches to harmony in popular music is an ongoing pursuit in the field of popular music theory and analysis—one where students and teachers can be a part of the exploration.

FIRST CASE STUDY: KATY PERRY, "ROAR"

To consider a few ways that popular music harmonies diverge from the Common Practice, start by listening to a recent example that I hope will be familiar to you—and certainly will be to almost all your students: Katy Perry's "Roar."[5] Please find a recording of this piece online and listen as you read about each of the examples. While there are a number of interesting aspects of this song, for now, focus on the melody, bass line, and chord progression throughout, and also listen for the keyboard part, which enters first in the introduction. You might also want to read the text, which is significant in shaping of the song's form. Listen first to the entire track while following along on the form chart in Example 1 to become oriented to the song (especially if it is unfamiliar); the measure counts were determined by conducting along in 4/4 meter.[6]

The first minute and a half of the track spans the first large A section (verses 1 and 2, prechorus, chorus, and postchorus) of a composite quaternary form (A A' B A") through the beginning of the third verse, which audibly marks the end of this large section. This excerpt is followed by a second A' section (with only one verse), a relatively short bridge, or B section, and a final A" that only includes the chorus and postchorus, which completes the song. As is typical of recent songs in this genre, the larger sections (e.g., A, A') consist of multiple smaller sections. Repeated text plays a role in identifying the smaller sections: both the prechorus and the postchorus have the same text each time they return, which differentiates them from the verse; the verse has a different text each time it returns, revealing the protagonist's changing thoughts about her situation. The

INTRO (2 MEASURES; 4 MEASURES IN VIDEO VERSION)

A	Verse 1:	"I used to bite my tongue . . ."	(4 measures)
	Verse 2:	"I guess that I forgot . . ."	(4 measures)
	Prechorus:	"You held me down . . ."	(4 + 4, for 8 measures*)
	Chorus:	"I got the eye . . . [refrain]"	(8 measures*)
	Postchorus:	"Oh oh oh . . . [refrain]"	(5 measures*)
A'	Verse 3:	"Now I'm floating . . ."	(4 measures)
	Prechorus:	"You held me down . . ."	(4 + 4, for 8 measures*)
	Chorus:	"I got the eye . . . [refrain]"	(8 measures*)
	Postchorus:	"Oh oh oh . . . [refrain]"	(5 measures*)
B	Bridge:	(instrumental, then) "Roar-oar . . ."	(3 + 4, for 7 measures)
A"	Chorus:	"I got the eye . . . [refrain]"	(8 measures)
	Postchorus:	"Oh oh oh . . . [refrain]"	(9 measures; extension!)

* elision or ambiguous phrase boundary

EXAMPLE 1. Overview of form of Katy Perry's "Roar."

prechorus text reflects the protagonist's gradually increasing sense of self-advocacy and command of her situation, brought out through increasing intensity and energy in her voice and culminating in the dramatic anacrusis ("I've got the eye . . .") into the high-energy chorus. After the chorus, the repeated "Oh oh oh" text of the postchorus distinguishes it from the chorus, while the decrease in energy level from its height in the chorus prepares for the return of the relatively low-intensity verse.

The chord progression throughout the entirety of each of the large A sections includes four chords (B♭, Cm, Gm, E♭), with the rhythm shown in Example 2. In popular music contexts, this type of repeated harmonic progression is called a harmonic loop.[7] The progression, which is repeated throughout the entirety of the song except the bridge, is harmonically ambiguous if considered in isolation, though it is certainly possible to identify a tonic and provide Roman numerals for the chords as I, ii, vi, and IV in the context of the other layers in this song. This progression notably lacks the dominant harmony in the key of B♭ (F). It has an added feature of including two nested plagal progressions—subdominant harmony to tonic (IV-I), if the Cm-Gm is considered iv-i in G minor—and in any case, those chords give a minor presence in the middle of this loop. When the full harmonies are most audible in the chorus (as opposed to primarily hearing the bass line under the verses), the chords are all root position triads connected by parallel motion.

We now return to the keyboard part. It is a two-measure-long loop that features parsimonious voice-leading, though it is essentially a B♭ chord "pedal," F5-B♭5-D6, repeated twelve times in eighth notes, with B♭5 replaced by an upper neighbor tone (C6) for the last four eighth notes to finish out the two-measure-long unit. Like the four-measure-long bass and chord pattern, this two-measure unit is looped throughout the song, with the exception of the bridge, forming an ostinato. The keyboard part's insistence on the B♭ triad prevents the Cm and Gm chords from presenting G minor as a contender for tonic.

The song's melody also influences how the harmonies are perceived: in this song, the entire melody is based on a B♭ major pentatonic scale (B♭, C, D, F, and G), except for the bridge. The melodic line is structured around arpeggiations of the B♭ major triad (B♭3-D4-F4), with C4 primarily as a passing tone between D4 and B♭3, and G4 as an upper neighbor to F4, until the vocal range expands upward in the chorus. There the melody moves from F4 to G4 to B♭4 and on up to B♭4-C5-D5 in the upper register, bringing out the "gapped" nature of the pentatonic. The melodic line itself is quite repetitive, with one measure or shorter melodic segments separated by rests, except in the chorus, where the short melodic segments are connected together and sung more continuously. The metrical placement of the melodic segments provides insight into the character's progress from "zero" to "my own hero": in the verse, the text reveals her uncertainty, represented rhythmically by entries of the melodic segments after the downbeat of the measure; as she gains confidence in the prechorus, some of the segments have an anacrusis to the downbeat of the measure, making the rhythmic placement somewhat more assertive; and in the triumphant chorus, the melodic segments either anticipate the downbeat of the measure or have an anacrusis to the downbeat, beginning with the long anacrusis that elides with the end of the

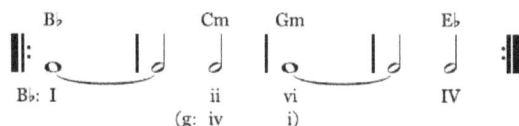

EXAMPLE 2. Harmonic progression of Katy Perry's "Roar."

prechorus (shown by the asterisk in Example 1), expanding the chorus to nine measures if the elided anacrusis measure is included. The postchorus reestablishes the placement of melodic entries after the downbeat, preparing for the next verse. As many of the melodic ideas are contained within a measure, the vocal line adds a one-measure layer to the two-measure keyboard ostinato and the four-measure harmonic loop. At this point, I encourage you listen again to "Roar" from the beginning to hear the elements described in previous paragraphs and to listen specifically for the change in the harmonies and melody in the bridge, to which we turn next.

The bridge section features the only arrival of F major (dominant) harmony in the song, and the melody here (repeating the hook lyric, "roar") moves G4 to F4, then G4 to A4, and finally B♭4 to C5, emphasizing the chord members of the F major harmony, which leads into the final return of the chorus and postchorus. From the viewpoint of harmony through the lens of harmonic function and prolongation, the song's harmonies express T (for a very long time!)-D-T.

Considering this song from the perspective of Common Practice harmony, there are not a lot of similarities other than that it is diatonic overall (based on a B♭ major pentatonic collection—a diatonic subset), it has triadic harmonies in one of the layers, and it is possible to identify a tonic. The T-PD-D-T (tonic-predominant-dominant-tonic) phrase design is completely absent, as are any standard harmonic cadences. It exemplifies instead many features that, individually and collectively, are typical of a variety of popular music styles and that are *not* typical of Common Practice repertoire, including nonfunctional harmonic loops, parallel voice leading (or planing of chords), and semiautonomous layers (coordinated, but each working according to its own principles) in the voice, keyboard part, and the bass/harmonic loop (and drum parts). The chord succession features harmonies in a plagal relationship instead of a tonic/dominant axis. In addition, there is no final cadence in the Common Practice sense—the harmonic loop simply loops to the end, landing on a B♭ harmony.

In Common Practice repertoire, the melody and harmonies are constructed such that the melody coordinates in both pitch and rhythm with the harmonies. On the contrary, in many recent popular styles, there is no presumption of coordination: the melody does not have to fit the chords, and even if the melody and chords end up at the same harmony, they do not have to do so at the same time. This is the result of the construction of songs in layers, where any part of the texture could have been the starting point: a harmonic progression, an instrumental riff, lyrics, a groove, the melody, or something else altogether. The construction of songs based on harmonic loops (repeated 3–4 chord sequences), shuttles (alternation between two chords), and other repeated progressions as a part of a groove reflect a different role for harmony in the texture and in creating musical form than does the T-PD-D-T basic phrase. Often these loops by themselves are harmonically ambiguous; the melodic line might identify tonic unambiguously as here, or it might not resolve the question.

Another way that this song does not conform to the Common Practice norms is in regard to voice-leading. In teaching tonal music, we tend to emphasize parsimonious (stepwise) voice-leading, with conjunct and contrary motion as the contrapuntal ideals. The contrapuntal guidelines were drawn from sixteenth- and eighteenth-century music written for choirs with the goal of making smooth, easily singable vocal lines or for seventeenth- or eighteenth-century keyboards following the guidelines of counterpoint and with the goal of moving the hand the least distance. Working with the physical inclinations of the instruments of the "rock quartet"—two guitars, bass, and drums—and other post-1950 popular music ensembles did not lend itself to the traditional tonal voice-leading patterns. Parallel voice-leading is normative for performance on guitars, where commonly employed chords are easily connected using a shift of the hand position up or down the fingerboard. Its meaning in a context is style-dependent: it could represent a "doubling" of a given line with a triad, as is the case in planing, or it could be more timbral in origin, depending on the application of distortion and other performance-related features. Guitar-based voice-leading has become ubiquitous in popular music, including keyboard and synthesized parts where it would be quite easy to employ contrary-motion-based parsimonious voice-leading instead of parallel motion, as performers often follow the lead of the fretted string instruments to connect chords in a consistent way across the ensemble.

SECOND CASE STUDY: FREDDIE MERCURY, "CRAZY LITTLE THING CALLED LOVE"

There are many indications in the scholarship on popular music that pla-gal harmonic motion might be much more common overall in popular music of the past half century than the dominant-tonic of the Common Practice. Recent corpus studies have documented the prevalence of sub-dominant progressions over dominant-based ones in specific repertoires.[8] This tendency to have motion involving the subdominant rather than dominant subverts the "dominant paradigm" of Common Practice tonal music.

To examine others of the typical popular music plagal progressions, we will consider another example—this time a much earlier one, from 1979: "Crazy Little Thing Called Love" by the rock band Queen.[9] Find a recording of this song online, and if you are unfamiliar with it, listen through the entire song following the form chart in Example 3. Though this song clearly has blues influences, including the length of the verse and chorus (each of which is twelve bars long consisting of three four-measure-long units) and a statement-elaborated restatement-conclusion organization for the lyrics, it does not follow a standard twelve-bar blues harmonic progression. Listen again, focusing on the four-measure-long chord progression shown in Example 4, which is repeated to accompany the first eight measures of each verse. After a measure of tonic harmony (D), the progression shown in Example 5 completes the verse, accompa-nying the refrain line "crazy little thing called love."

Some common popular music progressions, such as the so-called dou-ble plagal ♭VII-IV-I (all major triads), on which this song's repeated pro-gression is based, defy pigeonholing into functional categories. The name "double plagal" comes from the IV-I plagal motion being preceded by the plagal motion IV-I in the key of IV—sort of like a V/V-V-I descending fifths root progression, except that the descending root motion in this case is by perfect fourths. The "Aeolian cadence" ♭VI-♭VII-I is employed here as well, providing closure on the refrain line "crazy little thing called love."

Both of these progressions feature harmonies that in Common Prac-tice parlance would be considered "mode mixture" or "borrowed" chords, but ♭VI and ♭VII do not appear in the same progressions in popular

INTRO (4 MEASURES)

Verse 1:	"This thing called love . . ."	(12 measures, 4+4+4)
Verse 2:	"This thing called love . . ."	(12 measures, 4+4+4)
Chorus:	"There goes my baby . . ."	(12 measures, 4+4+4)
Verse 3:	"I gotta be cool . . ."	(12 measures, 4+4+4)
Chorus:	"There goes my baby . . ."	(12 measures, 4+4+4)
Verse 3:	"I gotta be cool . . ."	(12 measures, 4+4+4)
Verse 1:	"This thing called love . . ."	(12 measures, 4+4+4)

Outro (Repeat Refrain and Fade)

EXAMPLE 3. Overview of form of Freddie Mercury's "Crazy Little Thing Called Love."

$$
\begin{array}{ccccc}
\text{D} & |\ \text{D} & |\ \text{G} & |\ \text{C} & \text{G} \quad| \\
\text{D:}\ \ \text{I} & \text{I} & \text{IV} & \flat\text{VII} & \text{IV}
\end{array}
$$

EXAMPLE 4. Verse harmonic loop of Freddie Mercury's "Crazy Little Thing Called Love."

$$
\begin{array}{ccc}
\text{B}\flat & |\ \text{C} & |\ \text{D} \quad| \\
\text{D:}\ \flat\text{VI} & \flat\text{VII} & \text{I}
\end{array}
$$

EXAMPLE 5. Refrain line of Freddie Mercury's "Crazy Little Thing Called Love."

music as in Romantic-era contexts. The subtonic $\flat$VII is infrequent in Common Practice music except when employed in conjunction with the mediant $\flat$III—either in a dominant-tonic relationship in the relative major in a minor context within a Baroque- or Classical-style composition or in a mode mixture situation tonicizing a chromatic mediant during the Romantic era. Furthermore, and their inclusion does not necessarily carry the same implications for musical meaning as these chords would in a nineteenth-century art song, where the presence of mixture chords is often linked to text painting, or in instrumental music, where mixture may invoking Romantic-era images through tone painting.

Popular music scholar Allan Moore was early to point out the special use of the subtonic ($\flat$VII), listing many songs including it in quite varied contexts.[10] Over subsequent years, this chord has engendered much discussion among scholars specializing in popular music regarding its role and function. The harmony ♭VII is quite commonly used as a dominant substitute in minor-key contexts in folk music,[11] yet it appears very typically in post-1950 popular songs in a major mode context. Mark Spicer indicated that the ♭VII-IV-I can substitute for the V-IV-I at the end of the archetypal blues progression.[12] Christopher Doll labels the use of ♭VII as a "rogue dominant"[13] capable of creating dominant function at a cadence. Drew Nobile controversially goes even further, labeling any harmony leading to tonic as a "dominant," including IV (which leads back to I in the double plagal progression).[14] Nicole Biamonte theorizes that the progression ♭VII-IV-I should be considered within the context of modal and pentatonic patterns.[15] She takes issue with Walter Everett's view of ♭VII in the double plagal progression as a neighbor chord of a neighbor chord. Everett would consider the G chord (IV) in "Crazy Little Thing Called Love" as prolonging D (I) as a kind of I-IV-I "neighbor progression"—following the treatment of IV as prolonging tonic as employed in contextual analysis of Common Practice tonal music—and the C chord (♭VII in D but IV of G) as prolonging G in a I-IV-I "neighbor progression" as well, making nested plagal neighbor progressions.[16] While the progressions including ♭VII employed by Queen are only two of many progressions featuring this chord that are commonplace in rock and other popular genres, the range of divergence in viewpoints of these progressions highlight the disagreement in the music theory scholarly community about how to interpret and theorize popular music harmonic progressions that do not have strong associations with Common Practice music. These differences might stem in part from the repertoire each music theorist is examining but also from their position as to the degree to which popular music is a continuation of the Common Practice (with some changes) or something new and different altogether—a new practice—requiring its own theories of harmonic progression and chord connection.

One of the reasons popular music harmony does not consistently follow Common Practice norms is that the harmonic practice in post-1950 popular music draws strongly from at least three musical streams: (1) Common Practice harmony as employed and expanded in Tin Pan Alley and Broadway show tunes—especially those songs performed as jazz standards; (2) the blues, which was an especially strong influence on the Beatles, the Rolling Stones, Led Zeppelin, Cream, and other prominent groups of the 1960s and 1970s; and (3) folk music, including both the types of traditional folk repertoire future musicians learn while children through community and school music programs and the songs that were "rediscovered" or newly composed during the folk music revivals of the 1940s through the 1960s. Many of the frequently encountered progressions from popular music that are not typical of older tonal music are based on harmonies from the blues or modal folk music traditions. Combining these styles has resulted in harmonic progressions that, on cursory inspection, appear to be tonal—in part because they are triadic and it is possible to identify a tonic—but actually incorporate chords in a modal or pentatonic context that might behave quite differently than the "standard" major or minor progressions.[17]

Divergence between the modality or tonality of the melody and of the harmonic progressions is another possibility brought into popular music practice from this combination of influences. For example, in blues and blues-based rock, the melody in blues might be minor-inflected, and in blues-based rock, it might be minor, Aeolian, or Dorian (minor-sounding modes), while the harmonic progression is firmly in a major key. Other combinations of modal and tonal pairings are possible as well. The presence of a melody and harmony that express two different keys or different modes is sometimes called a "melodic-harmonic divorce."[18] This practice is in contrast to Common Practice repertoire, where even if mode mixture is employed, it is not typical for the melody and harmonies to express different modes.

The Queen song "Crazy Little Thing Called Love" provides an example of the ways major and minor elements can be combined in a blues-based rock song. Though the harmony in the introduction is D major, firmly establishing the primary key and mode of the song, Freddie Mercury's melody is primarily D Aeolian with a prominent F♮, a minor inflection (e.g., on the syllable *han* of "handle it," the word *round* of "round to it," and most importantly, on *crazy little* of the refrain line "crazy little thing called love"). The Aeolian modal identification is confirmed not only by the F♮ (flat scale degree 3) but also by the avoidance in the melody of C♯, the leading tone in D major. The only C in the piece is a C♮ (on the word *cool* of "cool, cool sweat"), which is immediately answered in the bass part by a C♯. The melody does occasionally include an F♯ (e.g., at the words *ready* and *like* in the ninth measure of the verses), in each case accompanied by a strong tonic (D major) chord and text expressing a positive view of his predicament.

Interestingly, the subject matter and treatment of melodic and harmonic elements in the Queen song shares some commonalities with the way mode mixture as employed for text painting in Common Practice repertoire. In this song, the harmonic choices and the melodic inflections are coordinated: the F♮s appear as an accented dissonance above the C major (♭VII) chord in the verse harmonic loop and above the B♭ major (♭VI) of the Aeolian cadence; the C natural is above an F major harmony (♭III) at the end of the chorus. All these would be traditionally considered "mixture chords" in the context of the song's D major tonality.

While connections between the harmonies and musical meaning expressed in the text cannot be assumed to always be present in popular music contexts employing mixture chords such as ♭III, ♭VI, and ♭VII as would be typical in nineteenth-century art songs, there are certainly songs where that is the case, and text-musical links are worth investigating. For example, "Crazy Little Thing Called Love" is about how crazy and confusing it is to be in love, with emotional states alternating among not being ready to handle it, shaking like a jellyfish, feeling hot and cold, and knowing he must relax, get ready, and take it on. An apt comparison might be made to Mozart's "Voi, che sapete" from the opera *The Marriage of Figaro*, where the character Cherubino expresses similarly confusing and contradictory sentiments regarding love, also expressed musically through harmonic and melodic mode mixture.

The I-ii-vi-IV harmonic loop of "Roar" and the progressions including ♭VII in "Crazy Little Thing Called Love" are both nonnormative for Common Practice music and fairly typical in recent popular music. For students who are in the process of being inculcated with traditional employment of tonal harmonic progressions, many popular music harmonic practices present challenges to the traditional harmonic guidelines that they have only recently learned and might seem to be "breaking the rules" because they fall outside of these constraints.

SOME GUIDELINES FOR TEACHING POPULAR MUSIC EXAMPLES

In teaching a popular music example, it is essential to encourage students to evaluate harmony in the song on its own terms by asking questions such as the following:

- What key(s) are expressed in this song?
- What chords are used? What is their relationship to the key or mode?
- What is the relationship of the harmonies to the melody of the song?
- How are the harmonies connected?
- What progressions are present?
- Are there harmonic loops?

It is also essential to consider the relationship between scale, melody, and chords when considering progressions, including questions such as these:

- Is the song tonal or is it modal?
- Are the melody and harmonies expressing the same key or mode?
- What chords are used at the closes of phrases or sections?

Closes of phrases and sections might not be reflected in a harmonic resting point if a harmonic loop or shuttle is employed, and students should be warned to not be surprised if there are progressions treated as "cadential" that are not typical at all of older tonal repertoire.

INTERACTIONS BETWEEN HARMONY AND FORM

The differences between the conventions of Common Practice music as taught in the music theory undergraduate core and typical practices in recent popular music are not limited to harmony. For example, consideration of musical form can also be problematic, in part because of the ambiguities swirling around interpretation of harmonic progression in recent popular music and because aspects that are considered "secondary parameters" in discussion of elements contributing to traditional tonal musical forms, such as texture, timbre, melodic shape, and rhythm and meter, become paramount features determining formal boundaries in some recent popular music pieces.

Musical form as taught in the undergraduate core curriculum focuses on the identification of cadences to locate and confirm the ends of phrases. Students are taught that there are a limited number of acceptable harmonic cadence types that create and shape musical form at both the phrase and the section level, all involving dominant harmony (V) and either tonic harmony (I, or vi as a tonic substitute) or an avoidance of it (in the half cadence). The "plagal cadence," or IV-I, once taught as an additional category of tonal cadence along with the perfect authentic, imperfect authentic, deceptive, and half cadences, is discussed in recent textbooks as an expansion of tonic employing subdominant after a conclusive close employing V-I, rather than a means to end a phrase or formal section. Though the consideration of harmonic aspects is the primary determinant of form, the relationships between melodic design and harmonic progressions are also considered in determining whether phrases form period structures, phrase groups, or other phrase forms and in the labeling of formal sections from phrase level to large sections.

In considering musical form in recent popular music, the various means of creating cadences, forming phrases, shaping sections, and combining sections in the piece as a whole often do not conform to terminology and analytical frameworks borrowed from earlier eras and other styles. While the repetition or change in musical materials and in the song's text continue to be essential considerations in identifying formal units within a popular song, change or continuity in timbre, texture, instrumentation, melodic range, musical layers, and other dimensions that are not the primary determinants in traditional tonal analysis must be considered when harmonic features that were so essential to section identification— such as harmonic cadences and phrase forms they delineate—are replaced by harmonic loops or other harmonic progressions that might continue unchanged from one section to another and do not lead to a cadence.

While the standard cadence types that students will have learned for Common Practice music do appear in some popular songs, particularly those of the 1950s and 1960s (and later songs making reference to those styles), they are not as common as one might expect in many styles of post-1970 popular music. When seemingly familiar cadential progressions do appear, their meaning in context might be different. For example, ending a phrase on V (dominant) occurs quite frequently, including V at the end of a harmonic loop, yet the term "half cadence" might not make sense, as there are many songs where there is no harmonic arrival of a later cadence on I (tonic), nor any assumption that a tonic arrival will happen. Plagal cadences, perhaps stemming from blues progressions, are much more ubiquitous in popular music than in Common Practice repertoire and typically take the place of an authentic (V-I) cadence instead of following one as a tonic expansion. Other types of progressions that would not be considered cadential at all in Common Practice repertoire—such as the Aeolian cadence ♭VI-♭VII-I, or simply ♭VII-I—frequently end musical units that sound and act like phrases, though no V harmony is present.

An additional element of complexity arises in that terminology for components of musical form in popular music is employed in tonal music analysis with a different meaning. Terms such as *refrain, chorus,* and *verse* have been used for hundreds of years in reference to many types of music, with nuanced differences in what they refer to depending on the context and time period. For example, I previously referred to the text "crazy little thing called love" as a refrain line, which in popular music contexts of the 1950s through the 1980s is a repeated short lyric, always set to the same harmonic progression and melody, that appears as a sort of "catchphrase" at the beginning or end of the verse or chorus. As in the Queen song, this type of refrain is not an independent section but rather a short (but memorable) component of one. The same term, *refrain,* is also employed for the returning A section in a Classical- or Romantic-era rondo form (such as five-part rondo A B A′ C A″) or a part of a hymn or song that is repeated after each verse with the same words and music (also known as a chorus).

There have also been significant shifts in meaning within popular music's own terminology. *Refrain, chorus,* and *bridge* are all examples of terms whose meaning changed significantly between the popular music of Tin Pan Alley and Broadway show tunes and the popular songs of the

1960s and 1970s. In early twentieth-century popular song in verse-refrain form, the *refrain* is the second large section of the song (not a short, repeated melodic fragment like "crazy little thing called love"), repeated with the same works and music, which is typically the most memorable part of the song. A familiar example of verse-refrain form is George and Ira Gershwin's "I Got Rhythm," in which the forgettable verse ("Days can be sunny . . .") is followed by the refrain (which begins with the lyric "I got rhythm" but is an entire section, including several musical phrases). In that style, *chorus* referred to the repeated "a" phrases within the refrain's quaternary song form (a a′ b a″), while the *bridge* is the "b." Each of these phrases in the quaternary song form is typically eight measures long, making thirty-two-bar song form. This early twentieth-century terminology for *verse, refrain, chorus,* and *bridge* was in use by the Beatles and other musicians in the 1960s who knew and performed older popular songs, but the newer use of the term *bridge*—an independent contrasting section that appears after several repetitions of the verse and chorus to prepare for their return—came into use not long after that, as did the new meanings of *chorus* and *refrain*. In postmillennial songs, such as "Roar," the quaternary formal plan (a a′ b a″) is applied to larger sections that contain at least a verse and chorus pair, possibly also a prechorus and postchorus for a composite A A′ B A″ form, as shown in Example 1.

For undergraduates only beginning to learn about musical form in their core music theory courses, it is clear how these terms and concepts can be confusing if not taught in regard to specific repertoires with the differences in terminology clearly acknowledged and explained. Even something so simple as considering potential connections between musical elements and text setting can be fraught with problems, as the text could have been the last part of the song that was completed, rather than a starting point. Considering the differences between what students will need to understand about popular music and the other topics they are being taught in their "tonal harmony" classes, it is not surprising that some teachers of undergraduate music theory courses choose not to engage these topics. If it is so problematic, why do it?

▌WHY SHOULD STUDENTS STUDY POPULAR MUSIC ANALYSIS?

Popular music is a significant repertoire of the twentieth and twenty-first centuries and is enjoyed by listeners worldwide as a part of their everyday lives. This repertoire is not "new"—though additional pieces are being composed every day—as this has been an active style since the 1950s. It is a significant oversight for undergraduate core courses that are intended to prepare students for lifelong careers in music to omit from consideration the very music that many of them spend the most time listening to and that surrounds them in their world every day.

As the percentage of music listeners who "consume" concert music shrinks and the number of those who enjoy various types of popular music worldwide grows, there is work available for those who are knowledgeable in this area—not only as performers but also as composers/songwriters, producers, and other roles. Even Classical music performers are often called on to perform popular music works, and some professional chamber ensembles have focused on inclusion of popular music examples to build audiences. To meet these professional requirements, all students—even and especially including those hoping for careers as orchestra members, choir directors, and chamber musicians—need to be exposed to terminology and concepts associated with popular music repertoires, at least to the extent they are introduced to counterpoint, form, twentieth-century techniques, and other core topics.

Incorporating popular music has distinct benefits for the multitude of students in undergraduate programs training as music educators and music therapists, as well as for those preparing for work in music-related professions such as arts administration, music business, and music-related legal services. State standards for music teachers require that they teach popular repertoire as a part of a balanced music program—those who are responsible for educating future educators should not put teachers we train in a position to have to teach materials they have never studied. Students who wish to work as music therapists will be primarily employing popular music in clinical settings, as they select music for therapeutic applications that is preferred by their clients. Our students who put their bachelor of arts in music degree to work in music-related professions will most likely need to be knowledgeable regarding popular music.

Though I have consistently used the term "Common Practice" as a shorthand to designate traditional tonal music of the years 1600–1900, the idea that there is one true "Common Practice" is as much a myth as the assumption that all popular music works the same way—there are vast differences in practice and style between earlier music from the Baroque and late Romantic practices; among choral, keyboard, large instrumental ensemble, and chamber music; and in musics from different cities, countries, and cultural centers. Study of popular music has an added benefit in that it enriches students' understanding of older repertoire by highlighting the great diversity of musical practices—which should be done as well with Common Practice styles. Finally, studying very recent music builds analytical skills potentially useful for music of the future.

In order for all music majors to benefit, the place to include popular music instruction is in the core music theory courses—even with restrictions on the time and scope of what can be covered. Every music student should have the opportunity to engage these materials. Ideally, a specialized popular music analysis semester-long class would be available for undergraduates seeking more in-depth exposure, and graduate students who aspire to teach music theory should be expected to have training in popular music analysis at a comparable level to their other analytical training.

TEACHER (RE)TRAINING AS A NECESSITY

As popular music examples have begun to enter core music courses on music analysis, one of the great obstacles to inclusion of popular music repertoire in undergraduate theory classes is that teachers trained in traditional conservatory or university colleges, schools, or departments of music might not actually know that much popular music. I have spoken with many excellent music teachers who specialized their whole life in European concert music yet think popular music consists of Broadway show tunes that are now more than fifty years old and folk songs, or maybe the Beatles and some Disney songs that they learned by watching movies with their kids. When mentioning to colleagues (especially those who teach vocal, keyboard, or instrumental performance) that I am teaching popular music, a surprisingly common reaction is to inquire why one would do that—"Isn't it all based on the same three chords?" This lack of knowledge is not limited to age; some of the graduate student teachers I supervise admit they know little popular music, in part because it was not included in their own undergraduate experience. Even those who frequently listen to popular music likely do not have the tools to analyze it with the same level of depth and specificity as other repertoire we teach if they have not been taught this content. If it is a goal to "main-stream" popular music into undergraduate theory classes, this is a serious problem. If university programs wish to incorporate popular music into the undergraduate curriculum, teachers must be knowledgeable about popular music and methods of analyzing it, be able to choose appropriate examples, and understand how to use them in a positive, accurate, and musical-context-sensitive fashion. The best way to make this happen is to teach future teachers how to analyze popular music.

▎CONCLUSIONS

As we have seen through these two brief case studies, incorporating popu-lar music examples into teaching concepts and practices of harmony can be problematic for several reasons. First, the stylistic norms of the Com-mon Practice era—especially as presented in a condensed fashion in most core music theory courses—and the harmonic practices of much post-1950 popular music are divergent, with significant differences in the types of chord progressions, voice-leading, treatment of tonality, and the role of harmony as a part of the texture. The divergence in treatment of harmony also requires a reconsideration of musical form, as the traditional tonic-dominant cadence is no longer present in much recent music. Second, as popular music is a relatively new area of interest for music theorists, there are also fundamental disagreements about how to interpret and analyze common types of harmonic progressions in popular music con-texts. The quick pace of basic theory instruction does not allow much (if any) time for unpacking of these conflicts of viewpoint. Third, the chord progressions explored in the rock era (post-1950) are rich and varied. To study them in the same detail as we have the progressions of Baroque, Classical, and Romantic music would require more time than could be allotted without sacrificing other curricular elements or would require a rebalancing of content in the undergraduate core—which likely will happen gradually. For now, we can teach the popular music examples we choose to engage in a nuanced and detailed way. Fourth, teachers need to be trained to teach popular music. We cannot assume they can work with their knowledge of Common Practice music and make the transfer from there. Teaching harmonic practices specific to a broad range of popular music honestly and on its own terms means it cannot be easily subsumed under the Common Practice umbrella, as has been illustrated through examples considered in this chapter.

Acknowledging up front that there is a difference between the use of harmonic materials in post-1950 popular repertoires and their use in typical Common Practice contexts is an essential start; the next step is addressing the differences and encouraging students to listen and analyze recent popular music with an open mind—without expecting the progressions to necessarily follow earlier norms. Fortunately, students with a basic level of music literacy will not have substantial difficulties engaging in analytical investigations of pieces such as those we have heard if they are introduced to repertoire-specific terminology and expectations, use both their aural skills and available scores to engage the music, and are shown how to get started on an analysis.

If we feel that popular music analysis should be taught, the first step is for those who are knowledgeable about the repertoire and who care about this music to begin teaching it. We are more likely to raise a new generation of skilled teachers and researchers if they are trained in what we know already about analyzing popular music—even with our awareness that we don't know enough about specific topics. To quote Chinese philosopher Lao Tzu (c. 604–531 BC), "A journey of a thousand miles begins with a single step," which is also sometimes translated as "The longest journey begins from where you stand." Change in the undergraduate music major curriculum will only come as those of us who teach music theory are willing to take the first step. The research under way toward understanding and analyzing specific repertoires is a starting point, and conferences where information is gathered and disseminated are steps in the right direction. It is incumbent on teachers to be aware of the pitfalls in incorporating popular music into the music theory core curriculum and to have a plan to avoid them. They should choose teaching

310 Jane Piper Clendinning

examples carefully, treat the music fairly, and delve as deeply into this music as any other repertoire they teach. Popular music deserves to be taught on its own terms, as a significant content area of the core music theory courses. Paradigm shifts take time and effort, and repertoire that is new to a teacher takes time to master—but this problem will ease as rising generations routinely study recent popular music as a part of their degree coursework. We have to start somewhere, and it is time to do it!

NOTES

1. The call for radical revision has come most notably from a task force organized in 2014 by ethnomusicologist and College Music Society (CMS) president Patricia Shehan Campbell. The task force report, "Transforming Music Study from Its Foundations: A Manifesto for Progressive Change in the Undergraduate Preparation of Music Majors," was originally issued November 2014 and generated substantial discussion at the Society for Music Theory, American Musicological Society, and Society for Ethnomusicology Fall 2015 conferences, as well as at the College Music Society conference. A copyedited version dated January 2016 is available for viewing or download on the College Music Society website, http://symposium.music.org/index.php ?option=com_k2&view=item&id=11118:transforming-music-study-from -its-foundations-a-manifesto-for-progressive-change-in-the-undergraduate -preparation-of-music-majors&Itemid=126, accessed September 10, 2016. Despite the CMS task force's claims to the contrary, this is a "zero-sum" game—the number of class hours allotted to music theory instruction in the undergraduate core are limited, and we cannot put something in without removing or minimizing topics that are already included. We can gain a little by efficiencies—such as textbooks or lesson plans that use the time available for student learning as efficiently as possible by excellent organization of content and inclusion of all needed scores, recordings, worksheets, instructional videos, and other materials to maximize instructional time on task—but not enough to add new content without removing topics that were previously included.

2. Though I will use the term "Common Practice" throughout this chapter to represent the traditional core repertoire encompassing music composed with tonal music practices written between about 1600 and 1900, please do not assume that I consider this repertoire to employ tonal practices in a consistent and uniform manner. There are vast differences in harmonic practices between early and later repertoires, among various genres of pieces, and in the particular uses of composers in specific locations and time periods. These are reflected quite clearly in my teaching, as represented in my textbooks.

It is simply much easier to say Common Practice than to repeatedly state "Baroque, Classical, and Romantic music" or other terminology.

3. For more information regarding any of these aspects of commonly taught concepts of the basic music theory core curriculum and to gain a sense of the scope of an up-to-date university basic theory sequence, see widely used textbooks such as my own—Jane Piper Clendinning and Elizabeth Marvin, *The Musician's Guide to Theory and Analysis*, 3rd ed. (New York: W. W. Norton, 2016)— or Steven Laitz, *The Complete Musician*, 4th ed. (London: Oxford University Press, 2015). The Clendinning/Marvin textbook incorporates popular music examples as described in this chapter, as do some other textbooks; it is also the only widely used core music theory book that includes a complete chapter on popular music. The Laitz textbook is more typical in that it focuses on Common Practice repertoire.

4. In addition to the coverage of music after 1900 in the Laitz and Clendinning/Marvin textbooks cited above, representative current textbooks engaging music post-1900 used in undergraduate core courses for music majors include Miguel Roig-Francoli, *Understanding Post-tonal Music* (New York: McGraw-Hill, 2007), and Joseph Straus, *Introduction to Post-tonal Theory*, 4th ed. (New York: W. W. Norton, 2016). All these books engage a more diverse selection of music than the serialism and sets of earlier textbooks on twentieth-century music and also include some works by American composers and by women.

5. Composition credits include Katy Perry, Lukasz Gottwald, Max Martin, Bonnie McKee, and Henry Walter for "Roar," which is performed by Katy Perry on her studio album *Prism* (2013).

6. This example and others provided in this chapter regarding this song appear in chapter 29 of the third edition of *The Musician's Guide to Theory and Analysis* (New York: W. W. Norton, 2016), 610–11, 615; they were developed by this author in conjunction with this chapter prior to inclusion in the textbook.

7. Philip Tagg, *Everyday Tonality II* (New York: The Mass Media Music Scholars' Press, 2014), e-book; chord loops and shuttles are introduced and discussed on pp. 371–450.

8. Trevor De Clercq and David Temperley, "A Corpus Analysis of Rock Harmony," *Popular Music* 30, no. 1 (2011): 47–70; Christopher White and Ian Quinn, "Harmonic Function in Popular Music" (paper presented at the Society for Music Theory National Conference in St. Louis, MO, October 30, 2015).

9. "Crazy Little Thing Called Love" was composed by Freddie Mercury in 1979 and performed by the rock band Queen on their album *The Game* (1980); it also appears on their *Greatest Hits* compilation album (first released in 1981).

10. Allan Moore, "The So-Called 'Flattened Seventh' in Rock," *Popular Music* 14 (1995): 185–201; see also Allan Moore, "Patterns of Harmony," *Popular Music* 11 (1992): 73–106.

11. I am personally familiar with its employment in accompaniments for Cape Breton–style minor-mode (Aeolian or Dorian) fiddle tunes from performing and studying repertoire in this style.

12. Mark Spicer, "Large-Scale Strategy and Compositional Design in the Early Music of Genesis," *Expressions in Pop-Rock Music: A Collection of Critical and Analytical Essays*, ed. Walter Everett (New York: Garland, 2000), 106n19.

13. Christopher Doll, "Listening to Rock Harmony," PhD diss., Columbia University, 2007. This topic is introduced on pp. 68–76 and engaged throughout the remainder of this dissertation.

14. Drew Nobile, "A Structural Approach to the Analysis of Rock Music," PhD diss., City University of New York, 2014. He introduces this topic on p. 5 and discusses it in detail on pp. 35–88 passim. See also his article "Harmonic Function in Rock Music: A Syntactical Approach," in the *Journal of Music Theory* 60, no. 2 (Fall 2016).

15. Nicole Biamonte, "Triadic Modal and Pentatonic Patterns in Rock Music," *Music Theory Spectrum* 32, no. 2 (2010): 95–110, reprinted in *Rock Music (Ashgate Library of Essays on Popular Music)*, ed. Mark Spicer (New York: Routledge, 2011).

16. Walter Everett, "Pitch down the Middle," in *Expression in Pop-Rock Music: Critical and Analytical Essays*, 2nd ed., ed. Walter Everett (New York: Routledge, 2008). See pp. 154–55 for Everett's discussion of this point and p. 95 of Biamonte (2010) for her discussion of Everett's viewpoint.

17. See, for example, Nicole Biamonte, "Triadic Modal and Pentatonic Patterns in Rock Music," *Music Theory Spectrum* 32, no. 2 (2010).

18. David Temperley, "The Melodic-Harmonic 'Divorce' in Rock," *Popular Music* 26, no. 2 (2007): 323–42.

CHAPTER 13

"High Brow, Low Brow, Knot Now, Know How"

MUSIC CURRICULA IN A FLAT WORLD

JOHN COVACH

UNIVERSITY OF ROCHESTER AND
EASTMAN SCHOOL OF MUSIC

THE DEATH OF CLASSICAL MUSIC?

Writing more than ten years ago, music historian Joseph Horowitz summarized the state of classical music in America as he saw it:

Taken as a whole, American classical music describes a simple trajectory, rising to a height at the close of the nineteenth century and receding after World War I. In the decades of ascendency, the quest for an American canon was its defining virtue, whether or not the reigning German model proffered true hope for an indigenous American style. The decades of decline were at first highly interesting: a new culture of performance was crowned by amazing feats of virtuosity and probity, and textured, as well, by an exciting if subsidiary pursuit of the American symphony. After 1950, the absence of a native canon was a defect no longer disguised or minimized by spectacular borrowed goods. By century's end, intellectuals had deserted classical music: compared to theatre, cinema, or dance, it was the performing art most divorced from contemporary creativity, most susceptible to midcult decadence.[1]

For Horowitz, American classical music culture in the twentieth century would have done better to focus on American composers rather than on performers—orchestras and ensembles who mostly played the music of European composers. The spectacular rise of celebrity conductors like Arturo Toscanini in the first half of the twentieth century brought with it a kind of neglect of American composers that ultimately led, in Horowitz's view, to classical music's lack of relevance to contemporary intellectual life in the United States. Summoning the name of perhaps the last great celebrity advocate for classical music in American culture, Horowitz writes, "Americans of the 1930s, 60 percent of whom said they liked to listen to classical music, knew who Toscanini was; for most people today, Leonard Bernstein is not even a memory."[2]

It is worth noting that laments over the "death of classical music" have continued to sound in recent years. Gigi Douban (2015), for instance, refers us to sales figures: "Classical music sales have been struggling for years now. They make up just 1.4 percent of music consumption, compared to 29 percent for rock, according to a Nielsen survey last year. Symphonies from Nashville to Canada's Prince Edward Island are dealing with mountains of debt. And audiences of classical music haven't changed much, which makes it tough for artists who aren't Andrea Bocelli to make it in the industry."[3]

Such figures will not surprise many who have been engaged in the creation, performance, promotion, or teaching of classical music over the last twenty-five years. In fact, a Nielsen report (2017) for the year 2016 places classical music at 1 percent of total music sales in the United States.[4]

---

1. Horowitz (2005), 516. Horowitz's use of the term "midcult" here is influenced by McDonald (1960).

2. Horowitz (2005), 508. See also Horowitz (1987). Bernstein, of course, advocated not solely for classical music but also for musical theater and pop.

3. Douban (2015). Mark Vanhoenacker (2014) addresses the issue more boldly and succinctly: "When it comes to classical music and American culture, the fat lady hasn't just sung. Brünnhilde has packed her bags and moved to Boca Raton." Farber (2014) is more optimistic. For more on the kinds of issues facing symphony orchestras, see Flanagan (2012).

4. A chart on p. 10 of Nielsen (2017) also reports that jazz represents just 1 percent of overall music sales in the United States. At the top of this list is rock at 29 percent, followed by R&B/hip-hop at 22 percent, pop at 13 percent, and country at 10 percent.

Classical music today is simply not as popular among the general music-consuming public as other styles are. And taking into account Horowitz's observations about classical music's status in the intellectual community, it is also not considered the only type of music worthy of sophisticated listening and discussion. As musicologist Robert Fink writes: "It is no longer even news, as it seemed to be in the mid-1990s, that 'popular' styles like indie rock and hip-hop have more artistic credibility for the average reader of, say *The New Yorker*, than the sound of the downtown avant-garde. Vernacular music is, by now, so interwoven with remnants of the Western canons of art music and jazz that today's hard-working and adaptable composers don't even expect special credit for knowing and loving it all."[5]

This chapter will focus especially on how this change in the cultural standing of classical music might impact the ways we teach music at universities, which traditionally have been primarily focused on classical music. But before engaging in that discussion, it will be useful to explore some of the factors that have played a role in this music-cultural transformation. If classical music is no longer regarded as the only music worthy of serious consideration among listeners, performers, critics, and scholars, how did this shift in cultural standing happen?

HIGHBROW/LOWBROW AND MUSIC IN A FLAT WORLD

The terms "highbrow" and "lowbrow" were used in academic discussions of culture for many years before Lawrence Levine's 1988 book *Highbrow/Lowbrow: The Emergence of Cultural Hierarchy in America* prompted a

---

5. Fink (2014). In an essay first published in 2007, Richard Taruskin (2009) wrote: "Since the 'British invasion,' nearly half a century ago, it has been socially acceptable, even fashionable, for intellectuals to pay attention primarily to commercial music, and they often seem oblivious to the existence of other genres. Of no other art medium is this true. Intellectuals in America distinguish between commercial and 'literary' fiction, between commercial and 'fine' art, between mass-market and 'art' cinema. But distinction in music is no longer drawn, except by professionals. Nowadays most educated persons maintain a lifelong fealty to the popular music groups they embraced as adolescents, and generation gaps between parents and children manifest themselves musically in contests between rock styles" (335).

fresh discussion of the topic within academia.[6] Levine chronicles how a sense of sophistication came to be associated with various aspects of American culture. He devotes his most sustained attention to the plays of Shakespeare, positing that in the nineteenth century, these plays were enjoyed by both simple and sophisticated audiences. By the end of the nineteenth century, however, Shakespeare's plays became strong and distinct markers of highbrow culture, and Levine examines how this transformation took place. Levine also explores other areas of culture, including fiction, park design, museum curation, and—central to the concerns of this chapter—the rise of classical music. One of his fundamental claims is that the highbrow/lowbrow distinction in cultural status is constructed within society, and as such, it is subject to change over time. He writes, "One of the central arguments of this book is that because the primary categories of culture have been the products of ideologies which were always subject to modifications and transformations, the perimeters of our cultural divisions have been permeable and shifting rather than fixed and immutable. To accept this thesis is to accept a picture of the American cultural past and present that departs considerably from the images most of us have learned to accept, which is never an easy thing to do."[7]

French sociologist Pierre Bourdieu makes a stronger claim for such cultural stratification, arguing that distinctions between highbrow and lowbrow provide a mechanism for the upper classes to retain a hold on political power. He employs the term "cultural capital" to explore how some aspects of culture can benefit one element of society over another. For Bourdieu, these distinctions can allow individuals to maintain status within society, to ascend within that society, and to even prevent (or strongly impede) ascent in social, political, and economic standing.[8] It

6. Important and vigorous discussions of the highbrow/lowbrow divide occurred, for instance, in the mid-twentieth century with regard to the rise of middlebrow culture, as well as in discussions of mass culture. See Rubin (1992), McDonald (1960), and Rosenberg and White (1957). For the origin of the terms "highbrow" and "lowbrow" in the late nineteenth century and their derivation from phrenology, see Levine (1988), 221–22.

7. Levine (1988), 8. For a fuller discussion of Levine's work, see Rubin (1992), Rubin (2014), and Covach (2016). Much of the material in this and the following several paragraphs summarizes a more detailed discussion in Covach (2016).

8. While several of Bourdieu's works pursue some aspect of this general argument, his 1979 book *Distinction: A Social Critique of the Judgement of Taste* (published in English

is important to note that Bourdieu's work—and particularly the data on which he bases his analysis—focuses on French culture in the 1960s. As a consequence, it might not be directly applicable or strongly analogous to American culture in the twenty-first century.[9] The possibility that high-brow/lowbrow distinctions might reinforce social inequities in today's American musical culture, however, is worth bearing in mind, especially as we consider how such distinctions might affect the ways we design our music curricula.

Horowitz (1987, 2005) provides an in-depth chronicle of the origins of the highbrow/lowbrow distinction in American culture and the rise of classical music as a marker of highbrow status. Beginning with the origins of the Boston Symphony Orchestra and the Metropolitan Opera in the late nineteenth century, Horowitz follows the growth of classical music in America into the age of radio and those halcyon days in which, as noted previously, classical music enjoyed a certain popularity among the general listening public. The rise of great conductors like Toscanini and Leopold Stokowski, and the celebrity that went with it, was made possible by many of the same entertainment-business vehicles (radio and movies) that also made stars of Fred Astaire, Judy Garland, and Bing Crosby. The difference was that classical music—although it was thoroughly commercial—projected an image of art for art's sake: to many, it was music that rose above the everyday concerns of commerce, elevating the soul and ennobling the spirit. It is this sense of artistic authenticity that was (and remains) crucial to classical music's appeal.[10] The idea that classical music is culturally superior to other styles, according to Horowitz, goes back to John Sullivan Dwight, a nineteenth-century

---

translation in 1984) is probably his best known. Discussing *Distinction*, Hans Joas and Wolfgang Knöbl (2011) write, "Bourdieu wishes to show that what aesthetic theory acclaims as great music, great paintings, and great literature is, in reality, nothing other than a form of perception derived from specific economic realities" (27). For additional discussion of Bourdieu's work, see Jenkins (1992), 128–51, and Robbins (1991), 117–31.

9. Jenkins (1992) writes, "I am less convinced than Bourdieu . . . that the use of French data does not undermine the general relevance of the argument. It may be that there is, for example, something highly specific about the relationship of the French metropolitan elite to Culture. America or Britain may be very different" (148).

10. See Covach (2016) for a more detailed discussion of the common features regarding marketing in classical and pop music in the twentieth century.

Boston writer who played a key role in establishing this distinction. Horowitz reports that Dwight "particularly esteemed Beethoven's symphonies as the embodiment of ethical striving, and considered music as entertainment invalid and corrupt. He inveighed against whatever seemed frivolous, bacchanalian, or exhibitionist. He espoused 'classical music.'"[11] For Dwight, there was classical music and then there was everything else.

For most of the twentieth century, classical music's highbrow status was widely recognized and relatively unchallenged. Other styles might be thought of as approaching highbrow status—third-stream jazz and some forms of ambitious pop and rock, for instance—but classical music's highbrow standing has never been significantly diminished.[12] Classical might have become less popular in recent decades, but it has retained its clear association with high art and culture. While Fink argues that intellectuals and artists might also regard other musical styles as interesting and worthy of critical appreciation and study—perhaps even preferring these other styles to classical—this does not mean that classical music is no longer considered sophisticated. Classical music has not lost prestige as much as it is now forced to share it. This new sharing of cultural status is an indicator of a levelling of the historical distinction between highbrow and lowbrow in American musical culture.

In his 2005 international bestseller *The World Is Flat*, Thomas L. Friedman coins the term "flat world" to describe an increasingly global economic and technological environment that he believes is fueling a crucial transformation in civilization. The idea at the center of the book is that the rise of digital technology has made the world a smaller place and provided dramatically increased access to resources to a greater number of

---

11. Horowitz (2005), 27. Levine (1988) refers to this elevation of classical music as "sacralization," writing that "the urge to deprecate popular musical genres was an important element in the process of sacralization . . . If symphonic music was . . . divine, then it followed that the other genres must occupy a lesser region . . ." (136). With regard to Beethoven, it is perhaps worth noting that there is only one composer's name above the stage of Boston's Symphony Hall.

12. For a discussion of classical music and third-stream jazz, see Joyner (2000); for an examination of rock music and its relationship to classical-music ideals and values, see Covach (2007). The special issue of *Contemporary Music Review* in which the Joyner article appears contains several other contributions that explore the relationships of popular music to classical music in the twentieth century. See especially Caswell and Smith (2000).

people worldwide. The world is flat, at least in part, because the hierarchical structures that had previously restricted access to resources have been bypassed.[13] And as the popularity of classical music has declined in recent decades, the distinctions between highbrow and lowbrow have become less pronounced: in many ways, we are living in a flat world of musical styles—a world in which almost any style can be given serious intellectual consideration. As more styles of music have access to the elevated cultural standing once held only by classical music, the highbrow/lowbrow distinction collapses—or is at least dramatically reconfigured. In the flat world of music, highbrow and lowbrow seem increasingly useful only as historical terms—as categories that help us understand how people made such distinctions in the past.

The technological changes that are such a crucial part of Friedman's argument have also had a significant impact on the world of music. The rise of the Internet has made more music available to more people than at any other time in history. The often controversial practice of file sharing has both created a serious threat to record labels (since many listeners want to download music for free) and made a vast range of music readily and easily available to any listener with a playback device and an Internet connection.[14] The rise of digital technology has made it possible to inexpensively record music, while specialized websites have provided ways for musicians to get their music to fans worldwide. If a flat world means that more people have access to markets, ways of creating a product, and abilities to promote it, then music has certainly become a much flatter world than it has ever been.[15] And in this new flat world of music, more

---

13. Friedman (2007) writes, "Whenever civilization has gone through a major technological revolution, the world has changed in profound and unsettling ways. But there is something about the flattening of the world that is going to be qualitatively different from the great changes of previous eras: the speed and breadth with which it is taking hold" (49).

14. On the problems facing the music industry, see Knopper (2009). On the impact of Napster on the practice of file sharing, see Menn (2003). For a historical account of the rise of the Internet, see Isaacson (2014) and Ryan (2010). Sterne (2012) provides a detailed account of the rise of the mp3 audio format.

15. Digital technology has brought with it certain problems as well. For instance, having the ability to make recordings easily and inexpensively does not necessarily correlate with making good recordings. And being able to make one's music readily available on the Internet does not solve the problem of how listeners will find the music there.

classical music is available to more people free of charge than ever before. The fact that the music is plentiful and easily accessed, however, has not done much to reverse classical's reduced popularity among listeners.

We are living in a flat musical world in which classical music is no longer seen as the only music worthy of being considered art.[16] As we turn our attention back to music school curricula, it is important to note that many of our students have backgrounds outside of classical music—and sometimes very rich backgrounds. Given the present status of classical music in our culture, should we insist that the musical education of these students be dominated by classical music?

▍MUSIC CURRICULA IN A FLAT WORLD

In his recent memoire reflecting on a life spent as an administrator in the performing arts—including a lengthy term as director of the Eastman School of Music—Robert Freeman acknowledges the changes that music schools need to grapple with:

> It is a central part of the message of this book that in a world of very rapid change, music teaching, still the predominant way musicians make a living, has been very slow to change, as have the curricula of our major music schools and the pedagogical goals towards which those curricula have been directed. The assumptions that basic study in fundamental musicianship may be put off till college, that the symphony orchestra should remain the backbone of a music school's enrollment plans, that instrumental and vocal students learn optimally from weekly lessons from well-known specialists, and that the road to musical heaven lies straight

---

Technology may have flattened the music world, but it has also made it seem much more crowded.

16. This chapter argues that a decline in classical music's popularity has occurred, but it does not directly engage *why* this happened. The reasons for the waning interest in classical music over the past few decades would make an interesting study, and at least one of these reasons would likely include the loss of classical music's exclusive highbrow standing. As Rubin (1992) and Horowitz (1987, 2005) have pointed out, a significant part of classical music's appeal during the height of its popularity had to do with the listeners' view that understanding this music offered a path to cultural self-improvement. As it stopped being viewed as the only path, it also became far less traveled.

through the practice room remain unexplored axioms inherited from the nineteenth century.[17]

Freeman clearly suggests here that the old ways might no longer be the best ways when it comes to music school curricula. Elsewhere, he suggests that today's students need greater educational exposure to popular music.[18] Considering the status of classical music in a flat world and its limited appeal within the culture at large, an outsider observing current university-level music training and education might wonder why classical music is still so central to the curriculum. She might also wonder what the situation has been in music schools historically that would make it necessary to even have to propose including study of other music to the curriculum—the music that most people outside the music school actually listen to far more often.

In a 1995 book entitled *Heartland Excursions*, ethnomusicologist Bruno Nettl provides a fair-minded examination of what we might call "school-of-music culture" (he calls it the "Music Building").[19] Nettl observes that most programs focus on what he calls a "central repertory," which is roughly analogous to what we have been calling "classical music" here. Nettl writes, "The center is classical Western music (almost exclusively European music) composed roughly between 1720 and 1930. There is no single accepted term that represents this sector of art music, but the music community often uses *common-practice music* or *standard music*.

---

17. Freeman (2014a), 10. Freeman was director at Eastman for twenty-four years, from 1972 to 1996.
18. Freeman (2014a) discusses European and American repertories, roughly equating them to classical music and pop. He writes, "While 638 NASM schools focus on the first of the two repertories, only Boston's Berklee School of Music concentrates on the second. It is a principal thesis of this book that musicianship of the twenty-first century will necessarily include both bodies of music, now assimilating, in addition, new influences from Asia, Eastern Europe, the Caribbean, Latin America, and Africa" (66–67). There are other schools besides Berklee that focus on pop, but Freeman's point here is clear. See Covach (2015a), Randles (2016), and Freeman (2014b).
19. For another insider's view of music study, see Kingsbury (1988). Nettl writes about a Midwestern music school, while Kingsbury recounts life at a northeastern conservatory. While there may be differences between the two, the focus on classical music is not one of them.

322 • John Covach

I would suggest the term *central repertory*. It is what the music school considers music par excellence."[20]

Nettl claims that pop music—he mostly means rock and country music—is actively suppressed in the Music Building, writing that "rock and country music groups appear 'once in a blue moon'" and that "music school teachers prefer that their students avoid contact with these musics lest they become irrevocably polluted." Such musical styles are not banned completely, however: "Musics outside the central repertory may enter the hallowed space by way of a servants' entrance: classes in musicology. They may be accepted (performed) so long as they behave like the central repertory (performed in concerts with traditional structure) but remain separate."[21]

Following the highbrow/lowbrow distinction discussed by Levine and Horowitz, the word *music* in "Music Building" is mostly synonymous with "classical music," and the principal focus on classical is an unmistakable consequence of the highbrow status of this style in the culture during the mid-twentieth century, when music curricula began to standardize.[22] To be fair, many schools have offered significant jazz programs for decades, and a far smaller number now offer programs in pop music (or commercial music). But at the core of many music schools' curriculum is still—more than twenty years after Nettl wrote about it and now well into the twenty-first century—the central repertory.[23]

---

20. Nettl (1995), 84.
21. Ibid., 96. Similarly to Bourdieu, Nettl also picks up on the political angle: "It is difficult to avoid the comparison with the colonialist who expects the colonized native to behave like himself (adopt Christianity and give up having two wives) but at the same time to keep his distance (avoid intermarrying with the colonialist population)."
22. The wind band tradition also plays an important role in many schools, especially those with large athletic departments that support the marching band. But even though the roots of the wind bands are different from those of classical music in the United States, wind ensembles in the Music School mostly aspire to the status of the symphony orchestra, performing often aesthetically demanding concert-hall works, frequently by contemporary composers. See Battisti (2002) for a comprehensive history of the wind band and wind ensemble in American music. For a more general view that takes the broad history of American music into account, see Crawford (2001). For an interesting account of Frederick Fennel and the founding of the pivotal Eastman Wind Ensemble in 1952, see Lenti (2009), 96–99.
23. In the remarks quoted above, Nettl mentions classes in musicology. In contrast to the adherence to the central repertory in performance programs in the Music School,

The centrality of the central repertory should probably cause us to pause for at least a moment; it is as if the Music School existed in a time warp, cut off from the world around it but nonetheless producing students who will necessarily enter it after their training is complete. Even the most generous figures in music sales would only award 5 percent of the market to classical and jazz combined.[24] This would seem to indicate that—in most but not all cases—music schools ignore or place a markedly secondary emphasis on 95 percent of the music the rest of the world seems to want to hear.[25] Such a narrow focus cannot possibly serve most music students well. For those who will play in professional orchestras, or even those who will teach in music schools and conservatories, such a limited specialization might not prove problematic. But often enough, the most narrowly focused classical musician will emerge from music school into a world that will require that graduate to build a career, often freelancing and teaching without the security of a full-time position in classical music. In such an environment, a broader range of musical skills and experience are a significant asset.

It is thus clear how the focus on classical music in college and university music curricula arose—it paralleled the rise of classical music in America during the twentieth century. The highbrow status of classical music made it a good fit for college and universities, placing music

---

graduate programs in music theory and musicology have mostly embraced the study of popular music. Twenty years ago, a student took a significant professional risk by writing a dissertation on a popular music topic, both in terms of landing her first job and later in terms of earning tenure. Today, a specialty in popular music is often considered an advantage, both on the job market and in terms of publication opportunities. This makes the contrast with the traditional performance programs all the more pronounced. See Covach (2015b).

24. As mentioned above, Nielsen (2017) reports classical music sales at 1 percent of the total market; with jazz also at 1 percent, this makes for a total of 2 percent combined. Expecting that some readers may find this figure inaccurate or variable from year to year, I use 5 percent for the purposes of this argument.

25. Certainly music sales are not the only way to gauge popularity. Advocates of classical music might argue that such figures do not capture the attendance at community orchestra and school concerts or even classical music as it is performed in church services. But it is also true, viewed from the popular music side, that these figures do not capture the many bands and artists performing nightly in bars, clubs, and concert halls across the country nor the enormous amount of free pop music produced by independent artists that floods the Internet.

comfortably beside literature, philosophy, and other disciplines in the arts and humanities. But in a flat world, one in which the highbrow/lowbrow distinction has been strongly attenuated and in which classical can no longer claim an exclusive place as the sole musical style in the pantheon of serious art forms, how must music curricula change to reflect the new musical environment?

▍ THE INTEGRATED CURRICULUM

Consider the following hypothetical case: A flagship state university offers a top-ranked music program. Somewhere in that same state, there is an enormously talented and dedicated guitarist who is eager to study music. This student is very accomplished at playing rock music but has not yet been challenged to broaden her skills. She auditions for a program in guitar performance but has not mastered either jazz or classical—the only two choices available at this school. Members of the music school faculty and admissions staff recognize the talent in this student but do not have a program of study that does not force this student to either abandon her focus on performance (perhaps focusing on music business or technology) or change styles to one of the available options. The school remains dedicated primarily to the central repertory, largely owing to the influence of the faculty, who hold that no style of music other than classical or jazz is worthy of study at their school. In a state in which this student's parents pay taxes, and at a school that is a direct beneficiary of state support, this student is forced to study somewhere else—or worse, not at all. This student cannot attend the best school in the state because she plays the wrong kind of music—she does not play the 5 percent of music this school cares about.[26]

I have argued elsewhere for what I call the "integrated curriculum."[27] At the center of this proposal to reorganize our music programs is the idea that musicians of all types should study together in an environment that challenges all but privileges none. It is not beneficial to create a separate

---

26. I posit this here as a hypothetical case, but I have personally seen this scenario unfold many times during the past four decades.
27. See Covach (2015b).

education for pop musicians, as a handful of schools have done; students who specialize in a wide range of musical styles should study together in an environment that privileges no repertory over any other, at least early in the curriculum.[28] All students benefit from being pushed beyond their musical comfort zones into an experience of music and musical practices they might not otherwise have sought out.[29] The integrated curriculum is an approach that interprets the meaning of *music* to be broader and more inclusive than that of the Music School. This breadth does not mean that students cannot specialize and develop an extremely high degree of mastery, even in traditional classical performance; rather, it means that music schools would open their programs to a broader range of young musicians than they typically do now—a wide variety of students focusing on a wide variety of styles.[30]

Figure 1 provides a summary of the integrated curriculum. It is intended to serve as an outline for bachelor of arts in music (BA) and bachelor of music (BMus) degrees that more effectively blend training

---

28. Providing instruction devoted exclusively to pop can result in a kind of pedagogical pandering by which students are assured they will study only the music they already like without having to confront or engage other styles and practices. It is worth noting, however, that there is certainly tuition revenue to be generated by offering such programs. Pop programs began to appear in the 1970s, with Berklee and the Guitar Institute of Technology (GIT, now the Musicians Institute) being the best-known schools for providing instruction centering on jazz and rock. Initially these programs were dismissed by many in the Music School as "trade schools." Over the years, Berklee has become one of the most recognized music schools in the United States and recently merged with the Boston Conservatory. The trade school criticism was misguided, however, since in many ways the traditional conservatory degree is not much different from what Berklee and GIT offered. The problem with the programs developed by Berklee and GIT decades ago, as well as with some of the programs developed in the first jazz departments, is that they suffered from the same stylistic narrowness that afflicts the Music School programs.
29. "Students studying rock, for instance, need significant exposure to classical music and musicians. Classical musicians need to know about jazz and recording technology. Jazz musicians need to know more about musical theater and world music. All students need to understand the business of music and to develop entrepreneurial skills. Keeping those aspects of music-making and creative activity in separate boxes and segregating students by program hurts them both artistically and practically" (Covach 2015b).
30. For other solutions and discussions of music curriculum revision, see the "CMS Manifesto" (Sheehan Campbell 2014), which has sparked lively debate, as well as Weston (2017) and Baumer (2015), which explore new approaches to teaching music history.

in a broad range of musical styles. Each school, department, or program could customize this outline to serve its own particular profile and needs and emphasize its own strengths and distinctive character. The crucial elements of this curriculum are (1) stylistic diversity (providing meaningful training for a wide range of musicians) and (2) integration of students of differing specialization (encouraging versatility) as opposed to segregation of students by specialization. Let us examine each component of this curriculum in more detail.

THEORY (4 SEMESTERS)

- semesters 1 and 2 integrated, includes harmony, melody, some voice-leading, rhythm and meter, and form (could be done in a large-class format)
- semesters 3 and 4 specialize (smaller classes), including options in advanced harmony/voice-leading/counterpoint, form and analysis, pop and jazz harmony and practice, posttonal analysis, songwriting and arranging, analysis of world music

AURAL SKILLS (3 SEMESTERS BA; 4 SEMESTERS BMUS)

- traditional emphasis on sight-singing, melodic and harmonic dictation
- additional emphasis on form, timbre, and production
- blends wide range of styles

HISTORY/LITERATURE (4 SEMESTERS)

- semesters 1 and 2 integrated, featuring short units on a contrasting variety of styles, blending classical, with pop, jazz, and world music
- semesters 3 and 4 specialize (smaller classes) with more detailed studies of individual styles and eras (such as classical, baroque, jazz, rock, world music)

ENSEMBLE (4 SEMESTERS BA, 8 SEMESTERS BMUS), AS SPECIFIED BY EMPHASIS

- traditional band, orchestra, and choir
- jazz band and rock combo
- world music ensemble

LESSONS (4 SEMESTERS BA, 8 SEMESTERS BMUS)
• students study principal instrument in style of emphasis

MUSIC ELECTIVES, REQUIREMENTS SPECIFIED
BY SPECIALTY DISCOURAGED
• traditional electives in theory and history/literature, with the additional of upper-level electives in jazz, pop, and world music
• music business, technology, and entrepreneurship
• all students encouraged to take at least one semester of ensemble outside of their specialty

FIGURE 1. Integrated curriculum for the BMus and BA in music.

MUSIC THEORY. As it is currently taught, music theory gives strong priority to common-practice harmony and voice-leading. These courses should be recalibrated to create greater parity among repertoires and reserve the most detailed study of voice-leading for second-year courses and electives. To a certain extent, many instructors are already incorporating popular music and jazz into their first-year courses. If the first-year sequence becomes more diverse, it creates an instructional environment in which students focusing on different styles come together with no style considered more fundamental than any other. From a technical point of view, emphasis is put on the features of musical understanding that cross stylistic boundaries such as form, rhythm and meter, texture, and to some extent, harmony and melody. Students should emerge from the first-year sequence able to identify and follow the form in a variety of pieces, focusing primarily on cadence points. They should be able to recognize and notate rhythms in a variety of styles as well as understand the fundamental elements of tonal harmony, including chromaticism and modulation—in many cases without extensive part-writing experience. There would be no emphasis on chorale-style writing.[31]

---

31. While there has been a greater integration of popular music into theory textbooks over the past few years, the tendency has been to add pop to a framework that remains driven almost exclusively by the concerns of common-practice music. Snodgrass (2015) is probably the most centered on pop, followed closely by Holm-Hudson (2017), though the latter remains strongly committed to the values of classical music (i.e., partwriting, figured bass, and counterpoint). An integrated theory text would

Second-year course offerings would build on the first year, revisiting materials with an eye toward greater detail. Emphasis on part-writing, counterpoint, the finer points of rhythm and meter, and more complicated examples of form are appropriate here. These courses would be style specific, so a course emphasizing classical music need not consider other styles. Likewise, courses in pop, jazz, or world music need not base any element of the instruction on models established to study classical music (though they may well choose to do so). While all students would study together in the first year, in the second year, students would specialize according to emphasis. These second-year courses could also serve as electives for students outside of the emphasis, and such diversity should be encouraged. Courses such as the ones suggested in the outline currently exist in many programs but often only as electives.

AURAL SKILLS. Like theory, aural skills would privilege no particular repertoire, and in many cases, this is already the norm. In the early semesters, detailed work on sight singing would be partly replaced by emphasis on longer-range hearing: identifying the location of phrase beginnings and endings, as well as the cadences and harmonic/melodic/contrapuntal schemes that accompany them (sonata form, fugue, twelve-bar blues, AABA form, etc.); texture (number of parts present, roles of the instruments in an ensemble, stereo placement, effects, etc.); improvisation; and instrumentation. Harmonic dictation (not involving SATB transcription) would be placed early in the sequence, and detailed sight singing would appear later in the sequence. The organization of theory and aural skills proposed here advocates a progression from general to specific as the sequence unfolds, allowing students to perceive and conceptualize more of the big picture earlier and refine the details of that picture later.[32]

---

place elements of theory that a variety of styles commonly share at the center of the framework, at least in the first year, in order that no repertory is considered even tacitly superior to any other.

32. Integrating pop music into aural skills training can occur quite organically. Dictation and sight singing of pop melodies can be done easily from sheet music, and collections of pop songs are plentiful, readily available, and inexpensive. Assignments that require students to transcribe from recordings or simply figure out the chords can be integrated into other more traditional kinds of assignments.

MUSIC HISTORY/LITERATURE. The first-year sequence abandons the chronological survey of Western classical music. The first two semesters instead blend together a variety of units presenting often dissimilar styles with an emphasis on variety and no claim to comprehensiveness. A three-week unit on early polyphony, say, could be followed by successive units on the Beatles and the '60s, the symphonies of Mozart and Haydn, and finally the music of Schoenberg and Stravinsky. None of these units would have any less depth than they would have in a chronological sequence; they would simply occur in isolation and juxtaposition. The emphasis would be on how we study and understand the music, not on making sure we cover everything.[33] While some might claim that abandoning chronology in itself creates a lack of depth, the current manner of progressing through music history from plainchant to the new complexity is far too specialized for most degree emphases and—by virtue of its exclusion of other styles— has an inherent lack of depth with regard to other important styles. Many programs have already developed a more general approach to music history in the first semester of the first year, and one can imagine other ways of achieving a meaningful organization of first-year materials in keeping with the principles advocated in the outline. The key to the approach proposed here is that all students are together in the first year. In the second year, students might separate out according to emphasis (as with theory), with courses outside the emphasis acting as electives. Courses devoted to surveys of specific eras in Western music history could be offered in the second year, though students would not need to cover the entire chronology with such courses. In addition, courses in jazz and pop history could be offered in the second year, as well as courses focusing on world music.

ENSEMBLE. Traditional ensemble experiences in band, orchestra, choir, and jazz band would remain, though now augmented by ensembles in popular and world music. Lab bands in songwriting and arranging, as well as in music production, could also be developed to meet the degree

---

33. Effective implementation of this approach would depend heavily on the areas of expertise among the faculty and might require team teaching or shared teaching. But since no attempt is made to cover all styles, this approach also allows great flexibility in course planning. See Baumer (2015) and Lowe (2015).

requirement within certain emphases. Some programs have already developed excellent models for these pop ensembles.[34]

LESSONS. Students would receive private instruction in their principal instrument, though the types of lessons would now be extended to accommodate students with emphases in pop and world music.

MUSIC ELECTIVES. Many current BM degree programs allow very little room for students to take elective courses (the situation with the BA is often much more flexible). This proposal encourages programs to require students to take at least two electives outside of their emphasis.

Some traditional schools might choose to continue in the current mode of very high specialization, continuing to embrace the central repertory and rejecting the integrated curriculum—or any significant curricular change—completely. Others might adopt only some of ideas presented here, while some might develop the fullest curricular integration. Such a result would ultimately provide students with a rich variety of educational options between programs at various schools. Of course, programs providing professional accreditation, such as music education, must continue to follow state guidelines in their curricular design.[35]

This chapter has argued that most music curricula must change. Viewing the twentieth century from a historical perspective allows us to understand how music schools came to focus on the central repertory. But the decline of interest in classical music in American culture, combined with a flattening of the highbrow/lowbrow distinction, is forcing music school faculty to reconsider how to best educate, train, and prepare their students for a rich, rewarding, and successful life in music. We must protect the

---

34. Most pop and rock ensembles play almost entirely by ear, and thus in most cases there is no score for the director to work from in rehearsal. This practice can strongly reinforce aural skills training for students, as well as offer practical applications for theory concepts, as students work out their own parts and organize the form of the song at hand according to models learned in class.

35. This chapter addresses only curricular reform in college and university music teaching. There has been a burgeoning literature developing on the integration of nonclassical musics into K–12 teaching in the last few years, as indicated by the recent launch of the *Journal of Popular Music Education*.

great tradition of classical music, to be sure, and work to maintain the high standards we have established over the years. Music sales cannot dictate music curricula. But we also cannot bury our heads in the sand when it comes to music in the flat world. This seems obvious to almost everybody but us; within the music school community, we are just now—and especially in the last few years—having debates and discussions that might result in significant changes. The flat world of music brings with it many opportunities and possibilities. We need to embrace these changes and use them to our advantage. Critics might claim that this broader approach to musical education at the college level will ruin the great tradition—that classical music will suffer. But indeed, classical music is already suffering mightily. The only chance of saving it within our programs is to place it within a broader context that is in keeping with the real world of music outside of music school.

| REFERENCES

Battisti, Frank L. 2002. *The Winds of Change: The Evolution of the Contemporary American Wind Band/Ensemble and Its Conductor*. Galesville, MD: Meredith Music Publications.

Baumer, Matthew. 2015. "A Snapshot of Music History Teaching to Undergraduate Music Majors, 2011–12: Curricula, Methods, Assessments, and Objectives." *Journal of Music History Pedagogy* 5 (2): 23–47. http://www.ams-net.org/ojs/index.php/jmhp/article/view/165.

Bourdieu, Pierre. (1979) 1984. *Distinction: A Social Critique of the Judgement of Taste*. Translated by Richard Nice. Cambridge: Harvard University Press.

Caswell, Austin B., and Christopher Smith. 2000. "Into the Ivory Tower: Vernacular Music and the American Academy." In *Traditions, Institutions, and American Popular Music*, edited by John Covach and Walter Everett, 89–111. A special issue of *Contemporary Music Review* 19 (1).

Covach, John. 2007. "The Hippie Aesthetic: Cultural Positioning and Musical Ambition in Early Progressive Rock." Reprinted in *The Ashgate Library of Essays on Popular Music: Rock*, edited by Mark Spicer, 65–75. Farnham and Burlington, VT: Ashgate, 2012.

———. 2015a. Review of *The Crisis of Classical Music: Lessons from a Life in the Education of Musicians*, by Robert Freeman. *Music Theory Online* 21 (2). http://www.mtosmt.org/issues/mto.15.21.2/mto.15.21.2.covach.html.

———. 2015b. "Rock Me, Maestro." *Chronicle of Higher Education*, February 6, B14–15. http://chronicle.com/article/Rock-Me-Maestro/151423/.

———. 2016. "The Way We Were: Rethinking the Popular in a Flat World." *Analitica/ Rivista di Analisi e Teoria Musicale* 1 (2).

Crawford, Richard. 2001. *America's Musical Life: A History*. New York: W. W. Norton.

Douban, Gigi. 2015. "Classical Music Sales Enter 'Survival Mode.'" *Marketplace*, May 14. http://www.marketplace.org/topics/business/classical-music-sales-enter-survival-mode.

Farber, Jim. 2014. "Classical Music Explodes, Both in Sales and Expanding Boundaries." *New York Daily News*, February 21. http://www.nydailynews.com/entertainment/music-arts/classical-music-blowing-article-1.1618623.

Fink, Robert. 2014. "It Ain't Us Babe." *New Music Box*, September 15. http://www.newmusicbox.org/articles/it-aint-us-babe/.

Flanagan, Robert J. 2012. *The Perilous Life of Symphony Orchestras: Artistic Triumphs and Economic Challenges*. New Haven, CT: Yale University Press.

Freeman, Robert J. 2014a. *The Crisis in Classical Music: Lessons from a Life in the Education of Musicians*. Lanham, MD: Rowman & Littlefield.

———. 2014b. "Needed: A Revolution in Musical Training." *Chronicle of Higher Education*, August 29. http://chronicle.com/blogs/conversation/2014/08/29/needed-a-revolution-in-musical-training/.

Friedman, Thomas L. (2005) 2007. *The World Is Flat: A Brief History of the Twentieth Century*. 3rd ed. New York: Picador.

Holm-Hudson, Kevin. 2017. *Music Theory Remixed: A Blended Approach for the Practicing Musician*. New York: Oxford University Press.

Horowitz, Joseph. 1987. *Understanding Toscanini: A Social History of American Concert Life* Berkeley: University of California Press.

———. 2005. *Classical Music in America: A History of Its Rise and Fall*. New York: W. W. Norton.

Isaacson, Walter. 2014. *The Innovators: How a Group of Hackers, Geniuses, and Geeks Created the Digital Revolution*. New York: Simon & Schuster.

Jenkins, Richard. 1992. *Pierre Bourdieu*. London: Routledge.

Joas, Hans, and Wolfgang Knöbl. 2011. "Between Structuralism and Theory of Practice: The Cultural Sociology of Pierre Bourdieu." In *The Legacy of Pierre Bourdieu: Critical Essays*, edited by Simon Susen and Bryan S. Turner, 1–32. London: Anthem Press.

Joyner, David. 2000. "Analyzing Third Stream." In *Traditions, Institutions, and American Popular Music*, edited by John Covach and Walter Everett, 63–87. A special issue of *Contemporary Music Review* 19 (1).

Kingsbury, Henry. 1988. *Music, Talent, and Performance: A Conservatory Cultural System*. Philadelphia: Temple University Press.

Knopper, Steve. 2009. *Appetite for Self-Destruction: The Spectacular Crash of the Record Industry in the Digital Age*. New York: Free Press.

Lenti, Vincent A. 2009. *Serving a Great and Noble Art: Howard Hanson and the Eastman School of Music*. Rochester, NY: Meliora Press.

Levine, Lawrence. 1988. *Highbrow/Lowbrow: The Emergence of Cultural Hierarchy in America*. Cambridge: Harvard University Press.

Lowe, Melanie. 2015. "Rethinking the Undergraduate Music History Sequence in the Information Age." *Journal of Music History Pedagogy* 5 (2): 65–71.

McDonald, Dwight. (1960) 2011. "Masscult and Midcult." Reprinted in *Masscult and Midcult: Essays against the American Grain*, edited by John Summers, 3–71. New York: New York Review of Books.

Menn, Joseph. 2003. *All the Rave: The Rise and Fall of Shawn Fanning's Napster*. New York: Crown Business.

Nettl, Bruno. 1995. *Heartland Excursions: Ethnomusicological Reflections on Schools of Music*. Urbana: University of Illinois Press.

Nielsen Music. 2017. "Year-End Report, US 2016." The Nielsen Company.

Randles, Clint. 2016. "Why Music Lessons Need to Keep Up with the Times." *Huffington Post*, June 5. http://www.huffingtonpost.com/the-conversation-us/why-music-lessons -need-to_b_10314552.html.

Robbins, Derek. 1991. *The Work of Pierre Bourdieu*. Boulder, CO: Westview Press.

Rosenberg, Bernard, and David Manning White, eds. 1957. *Mass Culture: The Popular Arts in America*. Glencoe, IL: Free Press.

Rubin, Joan Shelly. 1992. *The Making of Middlebrow Culture*. Chapel Hill: University of North Carolina Press.

———. 2014. "Rethinking the Creation of Cultural Hierarchy in America." *Reception* 6: 4–18.

Ryan, Johnny. 2010. *A History of the Internet and the Digital Future*. London: Reaktion Books.

Sheehan Campbell, Patricia, David Myers, and Ed Sarath. 2014. *Transforming Music Study from Its Foundations: A Manifesto for Progressive Change in the Undergraduate Preparation of Music Majors*. Report of the Task Force on the Undergraduate Music Major, College Music Society, November. http://www.mtosmt.org/issues/mto.16.22 .1/manifesto.pdf.

Snodgrass, Jennifer Sterling. 2015. *Contemporary Musicianship: Analysis and the Artist*. Oxford: Oxford University Press.

Sterne, Jonathan. 2012. *MP3: The Meaning of a Format*. Durham, NC: Duke University Press.

Taruskin, Richard. (2007) 2009. "The Music Mystique: Defending Classical Music against Its Devotees." In *The Danger of Music and Other Anti-Utopian Essays*, 330–53. Berkeley: University of California Press.

Vanhoenacker, Mark. 2014. "Requiem: Classical Music in America Is Dead." *Slate*, January 21. http://www.slate.com/articles/arts/culturebox/2014/01/classical_music_sales _decline_is_classical_on_death_s_door.html.

Weston, Donna. 2017. "The Place of Practice in Tertiary Popular Music Studies: An Epistemology." *Journal of Popular Music Education* 1 (1): 101–16.

Witt, Stephen. 2015. *How Music Got Free: The End of an Industry, the Turn of the Century, and the Patient Zero of Piracy*. New York: Viking.

Index

and cultural policy, 60
curriculum, 245–46,
  249–52
and educational policy,
  53–54, 56–60, 67–68,
  74–75
effectiveness, 218
guidelines, 302
history, 222–29, 290
impact, 201–2
as institution, 67
integration, 291,
  327–28nn31–32
and justice, 38
justification, 13–14, 66, 223
legitimation, 13
methodology, 202, 292
and politics, 60
resistance, 66
segregation, 57
and social change, 31, 39,
  46–50, 49
and social justice, 37, 59–60,
  256–58
suppression, 322
value, 213, 216
programs, 72
music genres
blues, 178, 297, 300
classical, 49, 56, 58, 64, 139,
  203, 206, 214, 221–23,
  225, 231, 240, 273–77,
  283, 290, 306
decline, 313–14, 319–21
as high art, 274–76
rise, 316–18

as superior, 317–18, 323–24
country, 183
digital, 238
disco, 130–31, 133
electronic dance music
  (EDM), 283
folk, 183, 184, 284, 300
gospel, 117, 118n14
hip hop, 57, 207, 236, 238
jazz, 119–20, 127, 180, 322–24
pop, 57–58, 203
R&B, 207
rock, 13–14, 57, 139–64, 145,
  157–58, 162–64, 247–51
  blues-based, 300–301
  glam, 122–24
Musicians Institute, 325n28
musicking, 279, 283
musicology, 322
music teacher education, 55, 199–
  200, 205–6, 207–8, 224–25,
  226, 249–51, 277–78, 282,
  286, 306
  classical music, 215
  methodology, 209–13
  popular music, 215
music videos, 81–83, 230, 263

NafME. See National Association
  for Music Education (NafME)
narrative, 82, 88–89, 90–91
narrative artifacts, 86
narrative theory, 81–83, 83f, 86–87,
  88
National Association for Music
  Education (NafME), 56

www.ingramcontent.com/pod-product-compliance
Lightning Source LLC
Chambersburg PA
CBHW040412110426
42812CB00033B/3360/J

9 7 8 1 6 0 7 8 5 3 8 3 1